HARD LESSONS

Feminist Perspectives

Series Editor: Michelle Stanworth

Published

Veronica Beechey and Tessa Perkins, *A Matter of Hours*
Seyla Benhabib and Drucilla Cornell (eds.), *Feminism as Critique*
Harriet Bradley, *Men's Work, Women's Work*
Susanne Kappeler, *The Pornography of Representation*
Liz Kelly, *Surviving Sexual Violence*
Henrietta Moore, *Feminism and Anthropology*
June Purvis, *Hard Lessons*
Barbara Sichtermann, *Femininity*
Michelle Stanworth (ed.), *Reproductive Technologies*
Julia Swindells, *Victorian Writing and Working Women*
Sylvia Walby, *Patriarchy at Work*

Forthcoming

Jackie Bratton, *Women in the Victorian Music Hall*
Katherine Clarricoates, *Gender and Power in Primary Schools*
Judy Lown, *Women and Industrialization*
Michelle Stanworth, *Feminism and Sociology*
Gill Thomas, *Women in the First World War*

HARD LESSONS

*The Lives and Education of Working-class
Women in Nineteenth-century England*

June Purvis

University of Minnesota Press, Minneapolis

Copyright © 1989 by June Purvis
All rights reserved. No part of this publication may be reproduced,
stored in a retrieval system, or transmitted, in any form or by any
means, electronic, mechanical, photocopying, recording, or
otherwise, without the prior written permission of the publisher.

Published by the University of Minnesota Press
2037 University Avenue Southeast, Minneapolis MN 55414.

Printed in Great Britain

ISBN 0-8166-1822-4
ISBN 0-8166-1827-5 (pbk)

Library of Congress Catalog Card Number 89-051301

The University of Minnesota
is an equal-opportunity
educator and employer.

CONTENTS

PART IV   Conclusion

For my beloved daughter, Catherine Malvina

ACKNOWLEDGEMENTS

I would like to thank the staff of a large number of libraries and archives for the help they have given me when carrying out this research, and especially those at the British Library, London, and at the Inter-Library Loan Desk at the Open University, Milton Keynes. Librarians in a number of places, e.g. Manchester, Bradford, Devonport, Huddersfield and Portsmouth, provided me with useful information and offered good advice. The staff at Huddersfield Polytechnic Library (which houses the archives of the Huddersfield Female Educational Institute) and at Vaughan College, Leicester (which has its origins in the Leicester Working Men's College), made me most welcome on my visits.

This book originated from a doctoral thesis of the Open University. My supervisor, Madeleine Arnot, was a source of inspiration: her constructive criticisms of my work taught me much and my intellectual debt to her is gratefully acknowledged. During the years that my research was being undertaken, the Social Science Research Council (as it was then called) and the Open University provided grants; without such funding, it would have been impossible to engage full-time in research activity and I gratefully wish to thank them. Throughout these years, Michael and Catherine were continually supportive.

The publishers of *History of Education*, Taylor and Francis Ltd, kindly gave me permission to re-use material which first appeared in two articles entitled 'Working-class women and adult education in nineteenth-century Britain', published in 1980 (vol. 9, no. 3) and '"Women's life is essentially domestic, public life being confined to men" (Comte): separate spheres and inequality in the education of working-class women, 1854–1900', published in 1981 (vol. 10, no. 4). Len Barton, Stephen Walker, Ivor Goodson and Stephen Ball granted permission to use material from my articles in their edited collections – 'The double burden of class and gender in the schooling of working-class girls in nineteenth-century England, 1800–1870', in *Schools, Teachers and Teaching*, ed. L. Barton and S. Walker (Lewes, Falmer Press, 1981) and 'The experience of schooling for working-class boys and girls in nineteenth-century England', in *Defining the Curriculum: histories and ethnographies*, ed. I. F. Goodson and S. J. Ball (Lewes, Falmer Press, 1984). I also owe a debt to all those women who have cheerfully discussed various issues with me at conferences and day schools; for someone such as myself, who is still caught up in the intellectual excitement of women's history, such exchanges have been exhilarating.

Finally, I would like to thank Pauline Dowie and Elaine Cook for their efficient typing of this manuscript and Polity Press for its support; in particular, Caroline Richmond, my editor with Polity, was extremely helpful.

INTRODUCTION

Historians of women's education in nineteenth-century England have tended to concentrate overwhelmingly upon the experiences of middle-class girls and women and, in particular, upon the struggle by a minority of middle-class women to enter higher education.[1] In contrast, there are no major texts on the education of working-class women;[2] indeed, it is fair to say that the education of working-class women in nineteenth-century England is largely 'invisible', even in feminist histories of education, such as those by Delamont and Dyhouse.[3]

In addition, most of the research on the two major adult education movements in the nineteenth-century intended for the working classes, the mechanics' institute movement and the working men's college movement, has focused upon the experiences of working-class men. Tylecote, for example, in a pioneering study of the mechanics' institutes of Lancashire and Yorkshire before 1851, devotes about five pages out of 293 to women's education, and concludes that 'numerous men', successful in business and public life, acknowledged 'their debt of gratitude to the mechanics' institute for enabling them to win industrial and commercial honours'.[4] Harrison, while claiming that the mechanics' institutes were 'the most impressive – both in numbers and educational achievement' of all the institutions for adult education before 1870, refers to women in the institutes in a footnote.[5] Similarly, Harrison's history of the London Working Men's College, regarded as a key text for an understanding of the working men's college movement, offers a limited discussion of women's education, covering about six pages out of 191, even at a generous estimate.[6] Other histories of individual working men's colleges also give little attention to women.[7] It is unclear therefore just what part working-class women played in these movements. On the one hand, they may have entered the mechanics' institutes and working men's colleges in large numbers, only to be neglected by historians; alternatively, their participation in such institutions may have been minimal.

In this book, I shall show that working-class women were students in these educational institutions in not insignificant numbers, though this involvement was often treated in the nineteenth century as marginal or secondary to the main concerns of the institutes and colleges. I shall discuss how the founders of the mechanics' institutes and working men's colleges assumed the main clientele to be working-class men, especially skilled manual workers, and how the concepts of education offered in each movement were framed in terms of men's motivations and needs. Thus the differing ideals of these movements, the diffusion of scientific knowledge within the mechanics' institutes and, in contrast, the teaching of a liberal, humane curriculum within the colleges, were shaped by particular assumptions concerning the needs of working-class men. I shall also show how gender[8] differentiation shaped the education offered at the institutes and colleges and how, within this demarcation between men and women, women's education took a particular form that, in turn, was determined by nineteenth-century ideals of femininity. These ideals were class based and were related to the patriarchal and family ideologies of the middle classes.

Given such patterns, it is not surprising that twentieth-century historians have 'forgotten' this history of working-class women's education and lives. Further, their concentration upon men and male education relates to a concern among educational analysts with economic developments, and especially the process of industrialization; men were seen as the main initiators of such changes and as the main source of waged labour on which economic development was based. In contrast, the image of the Victorian woman tended to be either that of the leisured, middle-class housewife, tied to the home, or that of the single working-class domestic servant or factory worker, earning her own living. Neither of these images, however, even that of the factory worker, appeared to be important in terms of economic development. The full-time middle-class housewife was assumed to be 'removed' from the economy; working women were seen only as 'temporary' workers who would eventually retreat into domesticity, as wives and mothers. Since women were not viewed as 'productive' members of society in the same sense as men, it is not surprising that little attention has been given to their education.

In the first chapter I shall review some of the male-centred histories of nineteenth-century society and also the educational histories of that period, since such an exercise reveals the marginal place that has been given to working-class women's experiences. I shall also discuss the challenges posed by 'feminist' historians,[9] who point out the male biases of such accounts, seek to make women visible and also offer new categories, concepts, questions and issues that yield a different interpretative model for understanding the nature of women's lives. In particular, I emphasize that a feminist perspective is the most fruitful approach for researching and interpreting working-class women's lives in the nineteenth century.

Clearly, given the lack of analyses of working-class women's educational experiences in the nineteenth-century, this research has a feminist concern with making women visible. When engaging in such a task, we shall see that for some working-class women the most relevant educational experiences were not in elementary schooling, as is commonly assumed, but in adult education. The research therefore helps to provide a more accurate, 'rounded' picture of educational provision for the working classes in the nineteenth century than has been presented in histories up to now.

Feminist historical research is clearly also relevant to this study of the nineteenth-century patterns of working-class female education in that it provides not only sources of useful primary data, but, more importantly, a range of ideas for the interpretation of events. In particular, feminist insights into women's lives indicate what else might be relevant for any analysis of working-class women's participation in education other than their social class background – for example, women's involvement within the overlapping spheres of family life and paid work, ideologies about the family and gender, women's previous educational experiences when girls. Feminist research helps to identify the areas to be investigated and the paths to follow when tracing the 'lost' history of working-class women in the mechanics' institutes and working men's colleges in this period.

It became evident that working-class women's education could not be understood without reference to the patterns of their everyday lives – the theme of Part II. Thus in Chapter 2, working-class women's involvement in family life and in paid work is investigated, since this determined, to some extent, their possible participation in adult education, the experience of education and the kinds of curricula that might be studied. The various ideologies about woman's place in nineteenth-century society were also important aspects of women's lives, since such debates impinged upon and influenced educational provision. These themes are discussed in Chapter 3. Another aspect of the context of working-class women's lives that helped to determine the kinds of courses they might seek in mechanics' institutes and working men's colleges was the nature and extent of their previous schooling as girls. In Chapter 5, I investigate a range of forms of elementary schooling available to the working class in the nineteenth century.

Part III focuses specifically upon the two major adult education movements being researched. Chapters 5 and 6 examine the access of women to the mechanics' institutes, the terms of their membership, and the curriculum offered. Similar themes are discussed in Chapters 7 and 8 in regard to the working men's colleges. Throughout these four chapters, the nature of educational provision offered to working-class women is compared to that offered to middle-class women and to working-class men. Thus social class *and* gender differentiation are key themes of this research.

Finally, in Part IV, the concluding chapter brings together a number of themes that have been explored throughout this book and considers the impact that adult education may have had upon the lives of working-class female students.

Part I

FEMINIST HISTORY

1

HIDDEN FROM HISTORY

Introduction

Histories of the nineteenth century tend to offer somewhat complex and contradictory interpretations, depending on the perspective of the writer. Although it is not easy to categorize these histories, since, as Johnson notes,[1] historians are reluctant to 'map' the main tendencies of historical writing, a number of broad approaches have been identified, especially those of the political left.[2] Thus, while acknowledging the diversity of views within each approach, reference is often made to 'liberal', 'socialist' and 'Marxist' traditions.[3] We can see such differences clearly if we focus, in particular, upon liberal and Marxist histories, especially in so far as they describe women's experiences.

Male-centred histories

Liberal histories[4] of the nineteenth century have concentrated predominantly on the activities of 'great' individuals in political, economic, intellectual, literary and artistic circles. However, as Matthews points out, this emphasis upon individualism has been restricted to great men and powerful male elites.[5] Indeed, some assert that the 'dirty linen' of great men attracts more attention than the great deeds of unfamous women.[6] When women are mentioned in general histories of the period, it is mainly in relation to the struggle for suffrage; even then, the focus is usually upon one middle-class woman, Emmeline Pankhurst, and upon the organization she founded, the militant Women's Social and Political Union. Thomson, for example, in a popular history of nineteenth-century England first published in 1950 and reprinted up to 1969, limits his discussions to the following observations:

The demand for extension of the vote to women was nineteenth-century in origin. John Stuart Mill had come to favour it. In 1903 the Women's Social and Political Union was founded at Manchester by Mrs Pankhurst with strong affiliations with the Independent Labour Party.[7]

Working-class women's part in such activities has been largely ignored.

Liberal histories also tend to adopt a 'Whiggish' approach, i.e. they tend to study the past with reference to the present and to classify 'historical personages ... into the men who furthered progress and the men who tried to hinder it.[8] Such a division between Whig reformers 'fighting the good fight'[9] against Tory defenders of the status quo provides a rule of thumb by which the historian tends to select and reject evidence according to implicit or explicit assumptions about notions of 'progress' and 'advance'. As we shall see later in this chapter, feminist historians are critical about the concept of 'progress', especially when applied to women's lives.

The interpretative framework of liberal history has been consistently challenged by Marxist historians who offer, in contrast, a materialist analysis in which political and cultural events are related to the economic mode of production and its historical development. Such an approach derives mainly from the work of two nineteenth-century writers, Frederick Engels and Karl Marx.[10] Social class relations and, in particular, class conflict and class consciousness are central features of such historical analyses. For example, E. P. Thompson, in his epic study *The Making of the English Working Class*, covering the period 1780–1832, defines social class as a relationship that happens 'when men, as a result of common experiences ... feel and articulate the identity of their interests as between themselves, and as against other men whose interests are different from (and usually opposed to) theirs'.[11]

From a Marxist perspective, the contradictions that may arise within the economic mode of production and the compromises made between class interests are also key concerns. Thus the Centre for Contemporary Cultural Studies Education Group, utilizing a Gramscian perspective, identifies various compromises and settlements in education which are interpreted as a result of confrontations between different social classes and various power struggles. Such settlements are, however, unstable and contradictory arrangements which may easily develop into political crises. For the CCCS group, one way of understanding the history of educational policy is in terms of 'the succession of crises and settlements'.[12]

Where Marxist history differs from liberal history is, on the one hand, in its relative lack of emphasis on constitutional matters and on the activities of elites and, on the other hand, in its commitment to revealing the economic and social life of different social classes. There is an emphasis upon providing a 'history from below' or 'history from the bottom up'[13] as it is often called, concentrating especially on the lives of the working classes in nineteenth-century England – for example, the development of community life, trade unionism, education and work. Unfortunately, however, these studies are limited in their usefulness in discovering the experiences of working-class women. Even the most illustrious of Marxist historians seem to take the lead in the 'omission' of women from their accounts. For E. P Thompson the main focus is upon the way working-class men were active in creating a social class identity.[14] Hobsbawm, in his book specifically entitled *Labouring Men*, includes a range of topics relevant to the working classes, especially to working-class men in the nineteenth century. In a later piece of research, Hobsbawm admits that 'male historians in the past, including Marxists, have grossly neglected the female half of the human race'[15] and attempts to remedy this by examining images of men and women in painting and emblems associated with revolutionary and socialist movements of the nineteenth and early twentieth centuries. His account, however, attracted much criticism. Alexander, Davin and Hostettler, for example, point out that Hobsbawm assumes that the sexual division of labour within the working class is straightforward, since he states that 'typically' only men went out to work while 'conventionally' women stayed at home; Hobsbawm remains firmly within the tradition of labour history, say these critics, in that he ignores the paid and unpaid work that working-class women engaged in within the home.[16]

More recently, in *The Age of Empire 1875–1914*, Hobsbawm devotes a whole chapter to women, especially the so-called emancipated 'new women' of the 1880s onwards, who entered the masculine preserve of the professions, took part in competitive public sports (such as competition tennis) and fought for women's rights. The main focus, however, is upon the lives of *middle-class* women. Some limited attention is given to working-class women but it is assumed that a working-class wife and mother stayed at home, since industrialization brought about a 'separation' between homeplace and workplace that made it difficult for her to earn money in the 'publicly recognized economy': once again, Hobsbawm assumes that 'habitually' women went to work until they married and 'did not usually do so when married'.[17] Although one paragraph is devoted to the poorly paid work that many married working-class women undertook within their own homes, no mention is made of their unpaid work in looking after the men who would form the healthy soldiers and sailors necessary for the maintenance of an empire.[18] Rule's study of the labouring classes in early industrial England from 1750 to 1850 appears exceptional among Marxist histories in that about 6 per cent of the total text is devoted to discussing working-class women's lives in relation to such themes as the family, paid work, sexual exploitation, sexual freedom and prostitution:[19] furthermore, Rule hopes that 'soon a history of the working people will be able to fully incorporate working women'.[20]

This concentration on male experiences is found also, with a few notable exceptions,[21] in contemporary histories of education in the nineteenth century. The education of women, especially working-class women, where visible, is all too often represented as peripheral to the mainstream educational concerns of this period. The majority of histories of nineteenth century education, mainly written within a progressive, Whiggish framework, have tended to focus upon the administration of education and upon those educational institutions that boys and men were likely to attend, such as state-aided schools, secondary schools, public schools, technical institutions and universities.[22]

Sheldon Rothblatt's history of Cambridge university academics is a typical example of such research. Concentrating solely on male academics, he fails to refer either to the women who fought to enter this male stronghold or to the small number of female lecturers in the various colleges in Cambridge. Although he titled his book *The Revolution of the Dons: Cambridge and Society in Victorian England*, the 'revolution' being waged between the sexes at Cambridge is ignored.[23] Similarly, a 1977 collection of readings edited by Reeder, *Urban Education in the 19th Century*, assumes that working-class boys are the reference point; indeed, in one of the papers, the sparse references to working-class girls are sometimes made in parenthesis, e.g. 'the problem of boy (and girl) labour', 'the discovery of the boy (and girl) labour problem'.[24]

Some histories of nineteenth-century education for working-class children have offered limited discussion of the education of working-class girls, but often this represents a small part of the total work. Hurt, for example, in his study of state-aided elementary schooling and the working classes from 1860 to 1918, devotes at a generous estimate only 12 pages to this topic, and even then it is mainly in relation to the teaching of domestic subjects such as needlework, sewing and cookery. Furthermore, Hurt's language helps perpetuate the idea that most pupils in the educational system are male:

for the greater part of historical time children have received their education outside the classroom. Schooling has been the experience of the minority of *mankind* before the present century. Such phrases as 'got *his* book-learning' or 'got *his* schooling' vividly demonstrate the way in which the distinction between formal and informal education lives on in the minds of the elderly.[25]

The use of such language tends to hide or marginalize the presence of girls in educational institutions. In contrast, the work of Stephens and of Horn[26] appears exceptional in the attention given to the schooling of working-class boys *and* girls.

Marxist historians of working-class education in the nineteenth century, such as Silver, Johnson and Simon,[27] equally pay little attention to the education of females. One of the aims of Silver's *The Concept of Popular Education* is to explore the role of education in establishing 'a popular or working-class consciousness', while Simon attempts to relate the ideas of reformers and educational provision to 'social and political conflicts' of the period.[28] Although both writers broaden the concept of 'education' to include adult education and various self-help educational ventures, references to working-class women in these activities are conspicuous by their absence.

One might expect general histories of adult education to pay at least some attention to the experiences of working-class women in the nineteenth century, if only because at that time adult education was clearly associated with men and women in the 'lower' orders. Yet if Roderick and

Stephen's comparative account of the development of post-school education in England and America in the nineteenth century is an example, it is disappointing that coverage of the activities of working-class men is made with no reference to those of their womenfolk.[29] The same pattern can be found in Harrison's account of adult education in Yorkshire from 1790 to 1960.[30] Kelly's history of adult education in Great Britain does include some mention of working-class women as students in the nineteenth century but the amount of space given to the theme is minimal, e.g. a paragraph on women in an adult Sunday school, a paragraph on women in the working men's college movement.[31] My research will challenge these interpretations offered by male-centred educational historians; it will also develop and extend feminist historical work, since I am investigating an area that so far feminists have not explored.

Feminist challenges

Male-centred histories of the nineteenth century are now being scrutinized by feminist historians, who question the assumptions made, the boundaries within which such knowledge is produced and the lens through which such events are interpreted. Some account of the development of this critique is necessary before we define what is meant by 'feminist' history and consider its relevance for this study.

Some writers, such as Norris, Lewis and Purvis,[32] trace the development of recent interest in feminist history to the so-called second wave of the organized women's movement in Britain, Western Europe and the USA from the late 1960s. In England such an interest was fuelled by the presence within the women's movement of several socialist/Marxist feminists who, like many on the left, had an enthusiasm for investigating historical patterns; disillusioned with the male bias of socialist/Marxist history and with the way they were treated by the male left,[33] many of these women became immersed in feminist debates, theorizing and research.

An influential figure in England at this time was Sheila Rowbotham, whose book *Hidden from History: 300 years of women's oppression and the fight against it*, published in 1973, is usually regarded as the catalyst for the growth in the history of women, and especially of nineteenth-century women.[34] Other texts published since then, with words such as 'liberating', 'making visible', 'exploring' or 'rewriting' women's history in their titles,[35] capture the spirit of Rowbotham's book. It was a path that was forged overwhelmingly by women, though it was specifically feminists who set the pace.[36] Feminist history therefore developed as separate from mainstream history, and still has only an indirect relationship with it today.[37] In particular, some historians in the academic world will not accept the 'academic status' of feminist history; Professor Sir Geoffrey Elton, for example, refers to women's history and the history of minorities as 'non-existent'.[38]

As feminist historians developed their perspective in the 1970s, the approach became more complex. For some, studying women was not sufficient a justification for being a 'feminist' historian. And the debate about the concept of 'feminist' history continues today, linked, as it was in the 1970s, into theoretical divisions within the women's movement and different definitions of 'feminism'.

Various interpretations of 'feminism' are available. Radcliffe Richards, for example, argues that the essence of feminism is the belief that women suffer from systematic social injustice because of their sex. Oakley suggests that feminism is about putting women first, about judging their interests to be important and insufficiently represented and accommodated within mainstream politics and the academic world. Spender claims that a feminist is a woman who does not accept man's socially sanctioned view of himself and that feminism refers to the alternative meanings put forward by feminists. Stanley and Wise emphasize that the central core of feminism is the belief that women are oppressed by the sexual political system and by men. Smith stresses that feminism is the political theory and practice that struggles to free all women: women of colour, working-class women, poor women, disabled women, lesbians, old women – as well as white, economically privileged, heterosexual women. For Jaggar feminism refers to all those people seeking to end women's subordination.[39]

What unites such definitions, despite their differing emphases, is the view of feminism as being not only about women and for women but also about sexual, class and racial oppression. It is also clear that feminism cannot easily be defined purely as a set of beliefs or a particular perspective – it is a political movement involving political actions. And like many political movements it is complex, with a number of internal divisions that do not easily separate. These divisions have roots which may be traced back, claims Banks, to three intellectual traditions that had their origins in the eighteenth century – evangelical Christianity, Enlightenment philosophy and communitarian socialism.[40] The divisions between feminists today are hard to classify, given the variety of perspectives *within* each division as well as the overlap between divisions.[41] However, the following six groupings are commonly identified: radical feminism, Marxist feminism, socialist feminism, liberal feminism, black feminism and cultural feminism.[42] As we shall see, such differentiation, especially between the two main groupings – radical feminism and socialist feminism – has profound implications for the way history is interpreted.

It is important to note that whatever the definition of feminism and its divisions, not all female historians studying women wish their work to be placed under the umbrella of 'feminist' history.[43] There are also a number of male historians studying women's experiences who have no connection to feminist debates and feminist circles. Women's history is not therefore necessarily feminist history; neither does feminist history just concentrate upon women. Feminist history is not defined by its subject matter but by the ideas and theories that inform a feminist analysis.[44]

Clearly feminist history has involved questioning the form and content of historical knowledge since the majority of historical works are written by men and, as discussed earlier, generally *about* men. As Davin notes, men's activities – in war, courts, politics, diplomacy, administration and business – were the stuff of the drama. Women's activities were unrecorded at the time, and later were excluded as an area for study by the male-orientated definition of history.[45] Similarly, Lerner observes that men have defined their experiences as '*history*' and left women out.[46] Obviously, a problem exists if 'Men's histories' have been portrayed as 'universally human'.[47] Feminists, therefore, often call this perspective *man-made* or *male-stream* history – an historical view within which women have been ignored or hidden.

Various strategies are available to those wishing to make women visible in history. One strategy is to identify women who were particularly active or exceptional in a range of occupations, such as paid work, family life and politics. This involves discovering and investigating, for example, the lives of female writers now lost from history. Spender uses such a strategy in *Women of Ideas and What Men Have Done to Them*, identifying those women in the past who questioned male power in ways similar to those used by feminists today. Such women, she contends, have been erased from history through male control of knowledge: thus the knowledge that women produce can be used against women in the same way that the knowledge of our 'foremothers was used against them, and is denied to us'.[48] Similarly, in *Mothers of the Novel*, Spender challenges the received wisdom of the male literary establishment that Jane Austen was the first woman novelist; before Austen, according to Spender, there were one hundred 'good' female writers whose contribution to the history of the novel has been ignored.[49]

Making women visible in a 'compensatory' way,[50] however, has not been sufficient for some feminist historians. They also challenge the traditional ways in which women have been represented stereotypically as wives and mothers who are supportive towards, and supported by, their menfolk (especially their husbands and fathers). Degler, for example, describes their stereotypical approach to women in the following way:

women have been depicted in history as mothers, wives, daughters, and mistresses. Occasionally they have been well recognised and even celebrated as rulers in their own right, and sometimes, though more rarely, as military figures .... Somewhat more often they appear in written history as writers, artists, and reformers. But when women are depicted in these roles they have usually been viewed as appendages to men – as wives and daughters, for example – and therefore necessary, but really peripheral to history. When they appear as monarchs, or generals, or writers they are seen almost as men and are measured against a male standard. For as Simone de Beauvoir pointed out years ago, throughout most of written history at least, the standard of humanity has been the male. Women who act in the world have been seen as men manques – males with something missing. And in case anyone wondered what was missing, Sigmund Freud told us.[51]

Both liberal and Marxist historians, in the scant attention they have given to women have tended to trivialise these female contributions to history. As one feminist has noted, if the Marxist historian Harold Laski could describe Harriet Taylor as a 'really soft cushion' for John Stuart Mill, then arguably any misreading of women in history is possible![52]

Support for the feminist critique can also be found in Perkin's account of the origins of modern English society from 1780 to 1880, where little attention is given to the social and economic position of women and where working-class women, when discussed, are located in those sections dealing with the family. In examining nineteenth-century controversies about the effect of the factory system upon working-class life, Perkin appears uncritical of conventional myths that factory wives had no time to cook for and generally look after their families, and therefore drove their husbands to seek comfort in the public house and gin shop.[53] In other historical accounts of the nineteenth century, economically active working-class women are also represented as objects of 'enlightened' paternalist legislation which 'rescued' them from physically demanding work in pits and restricted their long hours of toil in factories;[54] what is significant in these accounts is the omission of any reference to the long hours women spent in unpaid and paid work in what was seen as typically female jobs, e.g. unpaid work in kitchens, paid work in laundries.

In contrast to these views, feminist history offers new representations of women as independent of, rather than dependent on, their menfolk. Women might still be studied in that context in which their relationship to men has been traditionally conceived – the family and the home – since feminists see this 'private' sphere as deserving equal attention to the 'public' sphere outside the home, the focus of conventional histories. However, when women are portrayed as housewives and mothers by feminist historians, they are more likely to be represented as actors in the making of history in their own right, not simply as passive beings whose lives are determined. Ross's study of poor working-class women in London from 1870 to 1914 is representative of such analyses. The contribution women made to working-class culture and the forms of self-help they developed through neighbourhood networks are described as follows:

Women had a pivotal place in working-class life ... not only in organising sheer group survival, but in structuring culture itself, particularly at domestic and neighbourhood levels. Wives' skills and tastes could do as much as husbands' wages to determine how comfortably their families lived, and the types of relationships their households formed with neighbours, shopkeepers, or charity case-workers. Wives' dress, their sexual, drinking, and socialising habits, their housekeeping and supervision of children – all contributed to the establishment of their family's (and often their street's) reputation on the continuum between 'rough' and 'respectable'.[55]

Increasingly, however, women's lives are being researched in a range of activities outside the 'traditional' sphere of home and family life e.g. paid work, philanthropic work, work as elected representatives, trade union activity and political activity. The investigation of women's paid and philanthropic work, in particular, offers fascinating insights into the nature of nineteenth-century society. Thus we have studies about women in such diverse fields as philanthropic home visiting, coal-mining, silk factory work, service on the London School Board, service in local government, religious sisterhoods, residential houses, women's colleges, boarding schools, schools, hospitals, social work settlements, tailoring, textile factory work, the hosiery industry, book-binding and printing trades, domestic service, clerical work and tin- and copper-mining.[56] The history of working-class women's political activity is also being rediscovered. Working-class women have been shown to have been active in the Chartist and Owenite movements in the early nineteenth century and in the campaigns for the vote in Lancashire cotton towns in the late nineteenth and early twentieth centuries.[57]

When involved in such research, feminists continually question and rework the concepts and analyses that are used in mainstream history. For example, when Carr suggests,[58] in a highly influential text, that history in its essence is 'change, movement, or – if you do not cavil at the old-fashioned word – progress', the question feminists ask is – to whom does the word 'progress' apply? What constitutes progress for men will not necessarily apply to women. As Kelly-Gadol asks – did women have a Renaissance? Some, such as Lewis, take the view that there has been no steady line of uninterrupted, unequivocal progress for women. Similarly, Dyhouse argues that even if the history of girls' education is narrowly conceived as a history of widening 'educational opportunities' for middle-class girls, there is no simple tale of steady progress towards sexual equality. Prentice points out that, despite the so-called revolution in middle-class women's education in nineteenth-century England, a feminist assessment of the situation might be that 'the women and their allies cannot be said to have won the war'.[59]

The categorization of 'social class' as used in most histories, especially Marxist histories, is another concept subject to feminist scrutiny. In particular, feminists question whether women can be incorporated into a class analysis, since definitions of social class, from the nineteenth century to the present day, are based mainly on occupational differences between men.[60] This poses a critical problem therefore, in defining what is meant by a *working-class woman* in the nineteenth century.

Among nineteenth-century writers it was especially the philosopher and economist Karl Marx who gave a specific meaning to the term 'social class', which influenced subsequent definitions of the term. In *The Communist Manifesto*, for example, Marx identifies two main classes in capitalist society – the bourgeoisie who own and control the means of production, and the proletariat who own nothing but their own labour which they sell to the bourgeoisie in the form of wages. However, the bourgeoisie and the proletariat are defined mainly in terms of the male sex: when women are mentioned, it is usually in family or sexual roles, as wives or mistresses.[61] Other nineteenth-century definitions of the 'working-class' are usually couched in terms of the specific occupations held by men. For example, for Ludlow and Jones, the terms 'working class' and 'working men' are synonymous, meaning those who work 'chiefly with their muscles, for wages, and maintain themselves thereby'.[62] In nineteenth-century debates, woman's position tended to be described through and by the social class position of her menfolk – usually a husband or father.

Most present-day historians use the concept of social class in a similar fashion. The Marxist historian Steadman Jones, for example, discusses in *Outcast London* the relationship between social classes in Victorian society with few references to the activities of women, especially working-class women. As Alexander notes, most historians define the working class *de facto* as working men, as if social production were an exclusively male prerogative.[63] Such a practice holds important implications for the women who are the subject of this research. Like women in the middle classes,[64] women in the working class were not generally found in the occupations in which their menfolk were engaged. We can distinguish especially between the wives and daughters of men who were the elite of the working class, the 'aristocracy of labour' and wives and daughters of men who formed the broad mass of waged workers, the unskilled and semi-skilled.

Women in the former category often merged into the less wealthy groups of the bourgeoisie or the lower-middle classes. Wives of artisans frequently helped their husbands in their work and did various home-based jobs such as taking in washing or running small shops. This was so even by the mid-nineteenth century, when ideas about 'respectability' and 'keeping a wife at home' were pervasive.[65] Wives of men in the artisan stratum might be placed in that grouping because of their husband's employment, but as paid workers themselves they might undertake tasks that were considered less respectable. Unmarried daughters might seek to enter employment that consolidated or raised the artisan status conferred on them by their father's occupation. Elementary school-teaching, for example, appeared to attract a high number of daughters from artisan families, especially before the 1890s.[66] Although such a job might have appeared to offer individual mobility into the middle class, this was not so. The elementary schoolmistress was viewed with prejudice among the comfortably off middle classes (who perhaps feared the rise of a new 'meritocracy')[67] and her employment was set apart from manual occupations within the working classes. Since she taught mainly working-class children in state-aided schools, she was associated much more easily with this stratum of society although, once again, she does not fit 'neatly' into a working-class classification.

When we look at the wives and daughters of men in the unskilled and semi-skilled labouring groups, further anomalies emerge. Most of these women were forced, out of economic necessity, to undertake some form of paid work, but it was employment that was usually regarded as 'less skilled' than that of their menfolk. It was also likely to be lower paid and to involve less exercise of authority. As we shall see in the following chapter, women with young children were often tied to the home and undertook casual, poorly paid work – simply because there was little choice. Even in jobs that could be undertaken outside the home, especially by those women with no young dependents, a sexual division was evident in the labour market.

The concept of 'social class', therefore, poses a number of problems for the feminist researcher trying to identify women's social class position in the nineteenth century. The diversity of women's lives, income and opportunities is such as to make one cautious of applying social class labels. One way forward is to use the conventional terminology, while recognizing its problems. Thus, when using the terms 'working-class women' and 'middle-class women' in this book, I am generally referring to women (i.e. those females over 14 years old)[68] whose menfolk were classified as working class and middle class, respectively, on the basis of their employment. When the term 'working women' is used, it refers to women in any social class grouping, and especially the working class, who were engaged in paid employment as a means of earning a living.

The idea of a 'separation' between the private sphere of family life and the public sphere of waged work, often found in conventional histories, is also being challenged by feminist historians, who suggest that women's lives do not fit neatly into such analytical pigeon holes.[69] Kelly extends this critique and suggests that the idea of a separation between the two spheres is one based on bourgeois family life and male experiences:

Mothering determines where and at what hours women work, and thus the jobs for which they are available. Conversely, the inferior pay and benefits of women's work in a sex-segregated labour market perpetuate women's economic dependence upon men. They pressure women to form sexual and/or familial attachments to men; and in the family ensure that the man's position will determine the place of residence and the unbalanced allotment of responsibility for domestic work and childcare to women.

Experiences such as these increasingly make us aware that *women's place is not a separate sphere or domain of existence but a position within social existence generally.*[70]

This intertwining of the two spheres of family and paid work is vividly illustrated in Copelman's study of married women teachers in London from 1870 to 1914. One such teacher, Lavinia Church, lived close to her workplace and did her shopping on her way home from school, made the beds at lunch time and often scrubbed the kitchen floor after the midday meal before going to the afternoon session at school. A female neighbour looked after her two sons until they were of school age.[71]

In sharp contrast to liberal and Marxist historians, feminist historians also take the sexual division of labour, the power relations between the sexes and the way these affect the lives of both men and women as focal points of analysis. For example, Alexander's study of women's paid work in London over the years 1820–50 discusses the sexual division of labour within the London labour market, whereby women, in comparison with men, were to be found mainly in poorly paid, casual and intermittent jobs, such as domestic service, washing, sewing, the distribution of food. Such jobs originated in, and paralleled, the sexual division of labour within the family. Similarly, Burstyn links her study of the opposition to the higher education of middle-class women in the nineteenth century to prevailing ideologies about sexual divisions within the middle classes. While middle-

class men were assumed to be the natural inhabitants of the public sphere
of economic activity, using education as a means of upward occupational
mobility, their womenfolk were identified with the private sphere of
home, acquiring their status through their relationship to a man – as a
father or husband.[72] The sexual division of labour within the family is also
a central aspect of Dyhouse's analysis of girls growing up in late Victorian
and Edwardian England:

Women were expected to occupy themselves in providing an environment – a
context in which *men* could live and work. ... Closely related to this emphasis ...
was the ideal of feminity as representing self-sacrifice. Women of all social groups
were encouraged from childhood to consider it selfish to become wrapped up in
their own interests, for the ideal was the serve others, and always consider the
interests of their menfolk first.[73]

An assumption common to feminist research is that women are
oppressed by men in a variety of ways. Thus 'patriarchy', that process by
which men dominate and exercise control over women,[74] is a frequently
used concept in feminist history. Taylor reveals how the tensions between
socialism and feminism in the first half of the nineteenth century may be
related to the power relations between men and women, and makes
extensive use of the concept of patriarchy: she notes, for example, that as
long as women remained subject to men within the patriarchal family, a
major source of social disunity was perpetuated. Showalter, in a study of
women, madness and English culture from 1830 to 1980, suggests that
madness is a clinical condition diagnosed in women by a male-dominated
profession. Within a patriarchal culture, women, lacking a language of
their own, have accepted such male terminology and classifications.[75]

The feminist historian using the concept of patriarchy is aware,
however, that it is often a 'catch-all' phrase which contains any number of
theoretical perspectives.[76] Critiques of the concept point to the problems
of assuming that male domination is universal and historical;[77] male domination, arguably, is not a 'fixed monolithic system' but changes in form and
intensity in response to various social and economic transformations and in
response to women's resistance.[78] Others caution that while men have much
to answer for, they cannot carry all the determinations of history.[79]

Debates around patriarchy and sexual divisions polarize historians,
particularly those using socialist-feminist and radical-feminist perspectives.[80] Often what distinguishes these two views is the degree of
emphasis given to sexual divisions, and especially to the concept of
patriarchy. Socialist feminists, on the one hand, emphasize the need for
materialist analyses and focus particularly upon the way in which women
in the past have been affected by the development of a capitalist mode of
production. Thus they tend to analyse historical date in terms of social
class divisions, such as the divisions between capital and labour and
between the bourgeoisie and the proletariat (or working classes). Class
domination and patriarchal relations are often brought together in the
analysis – encouraging considerable debate about what constitutes the
relationship between the two.

Such an orientation encourages socialist-feminist historians to investigate a range of questions. For example – what has women's position been within capitalism at various stages of its development? How can we understand women's position as waged workers in a changing labour force? What has the relationship of the family been to capitalism and what importance has the housewife for capital? In what ways do men in the different social classes oppress women? What role could women play? The debates surrounding what is called the 'unhappy marriage'[81] of Marxism and feminism have not been conclusive.

In contrast, radical feminists are concerned mainly with the social divisions between men and women in history, and especially the patriarchal control of men over women. The central questions radical feminists raise pertain to the range of relationships between the sexes in different locations and women's collective or common experiences. For example, research focuses around areas such as men's control over women's bodies and over fertility, male violence towards women, cultural representations of men and women, personal relationships between men and women in courtship, in marriage and in parenthood, women's friendships and sexuality. The emphasis in radical feminism focuses on the position of women *vis-à-vis* men, especially in the private world of personal relations, rather than with the macro-level analyses of the relationship between women and the wider society.

On the whole, feminist historians in the United States have tended to be radical feminists[82] giving far less emphasis to social class than their British counterparts. In contrast, socialist feminism appears to be the major influence upon feminist history in Britain (see, for example, the writings of Rowbotham, Alexander, Davin, Taylor, Liddington and Norris),[83] with far fewer cases of radical-feminist approaches being evident. However, the writings of Sarah and Jeffreys are two instances of the latter approach, clearly emphasizing that it is patriarchy, not capitalism, which is defined as the source of women's oppression.

Sarah stresses that the domination of men 'precedes and underlies' all other forms of oppression and social hierarchy, such as social class and race.[84] Furthermore, she criticizes socialist-feminist historians for working within what she sees as a male frame of reference:

In so far as a socialist feminist historical perspective selects 'women' as its subjects, it is feminist. But this is a minimal definition and, what is more, socialist feminist history has made women visible 'on male terms'. Socialist analysis denies the *communality* of female experience in the subordination of all women to men, by decreeing that since class oppression is fundamental, women must be *divided* by their class allegiances. Certainly, women occupy different class positions and command different resources (and middle-class women are relatively privileged in this respect). However, both capitalism and socialism are *male systems of power* (that is, created by men for their purposes); women do not have any stake in either system.[85]

The choice of perspective clearly has implications for interpretation. Socialist-feminist accounts of Christabel Pankhurst and the militant suffragette movement are not supported by Sarah. Such accounts, she argues, are permeated with the idea that feminism has significance as a radical social movement only through its alliance with socialist theory and practice. Yet Christabel Pankhurst and the Women's Social and Political Union treated all men, including socialists, as the enemies of women as long as they took no action actively to promote the interests of the female sex; it was this 'disregard' for the significance of class conflict, Sarah argues, which is unacceptable to socialist feminists, who 'damn' Christabel as 'middle-class and reactionary'.[86] Jeffreys is another British historian whose work is close to the radical-feminist approach, though she calls herself a revolutionary feminist.[87] She claims that feminist campaigns of the late nineteenth and early twentieth centuries to assert women's rights to control her own body were undermined by male sex theorists who promoted a sexual ideology that was hostile to women's independence.

The concern with women's lives in feminist research has led, not surprisingly, to importance being attached to women's experiences. One key premise of the present-day women's movement is that 'the personal is political'. As Gordon, Buhle and Dye note, 'feminist historians are asking what it was like to be a woman at various times in history and are exploring women's subjective responses to their environment'.[88] Capturing the personal experience of women is felt to be an important strategy capable of challenging the male-centred paradigms that govern contemporary research – paradigms that have emphasized the importance of objective and public forms of knowledge, of structures, patterns and institutions over individual experiences and consciousness. Such paradigms tend to ignore the subjective realm of an individual's response to a situation or an individual's capacity to instigate social reform and change. Clearly such a perspective, particularly when applied to women, is unacceptable to activists within the present-day women's movement.

Feminists researching the past, conscious of such issues, are particularly concerned with finding out how individual women came to terms with their subordinate position and what they experienced as women. The ways in which certain institutions and structures shaped women's experiences, and the meanings women gave to their lives are also central concerns. If researching the not too distant past, oral history is one means of collecting such information. Widdowson, for example, illustrates her study of women and elementary teacher training from 1840 to 1914 with taped recordings of interviews with retired schoolmistresses. Liddington and Norris, in a skilful blend of oral history and documentary evidence, narrate the experiences of female working-class suffragists – sometimes through the reminisences of their children.[89]

However, when researching the 'subjective' experience of women in the more distant past, as in the case of this research, the issue is more problematic. One has to rely upon various documents, and especially diaries, letters and autobiographies, that have survived with the passing of time. As we shall see in Chapter 2, the voices of working-class women in nineteenth-century England are hard to find in the available records – though some have been found.

Conclusion

The main themes of feminist research discussed here – making women visible, presenting women as actors in their own right, questioning concepts and analyses of mainstream research, exploring the sexual division of labour and the power relationships between the sexes, and capturing women's experiences – are useful when researching and interpreting working-class women's lives in the past, since they present a considerable challenge and an alternative paradigm to conventional history. As Kelly-Gadol has noted,[90] the task of restoring women to history and history to women has shaken the conceptual foundations of historical writing. Above all else, feminist historians reveal that one cannot simply put women *into* 'male-stream' history: some even suggest that one should use the term 'herstory' to describe the new women's history.[91] Part of the new herstory of working-class women in nineteenth-century England is the recognition that their experiences in education cannot be understood without reference to the wider context of their lives – in paid work and within the home, in regard to various ideologies about women's place in society, and in regard to their previous schooling as girls. These themes are now explored in Part II.

Part II

CONTEXT OF WORKING-CLASS
WOMEN'S LIVES

2

THE DOUBLE SHIFT OF WORK AND HOME

Introduction

It is important that we understand some of the material conditions that affected working-class women and the obstacles they had to overcome if they were to become students within mechanics' institutes and working men's colleges. An individual's level of income and the ability to afford to pay for education were clearly factors that influenced the take-up of adult classes. But other aspects of life could be equally important in this respect, e.g. the degree of control over one's income, the amount of spare time, interest, motivation and energy, the standard of prior education, and the level of control over one's life. What we shall see in later chapters is that those who founded and managed mechanics' institutes and working men's colleges made assumptions about the ideal woman student and her lifestyle which may not have matched the reality of living in nineteenth-century England.

In this chapter we shall consider working-class women's participation in paid work and also their involvement in the family. As feminist historians have argued,[1] the sharp distinction traditionally made between the worlds of paid work and family life are inaccurate for any analysis of women's existence. As we shall see, as far as working-class women in nineteenth-century England were concerned, the distinction between the two spheres was frequently blurred: family duties often merged with paid work and vice versa. This double shift of work and home, this integration of family responsibilities and employment, was not, of course, similar for all working-class women. In particular, there were differences between the experiences of single and married women, between urban and rural women, between women of different ages and different stages of the life cycle. Unfortunately, it is impossible in the space of this book to explore all these divisions, though reference will be made to single and married women.

Industrialization, paid work and family life

At the beginning of the nineteenth century, the onset of industrialization brought a movement of labour and resources away from primary production, as in agriculture, towards manufacturing, commercial and service activities. Factories were established for producing goods and the scale of production generally increased. Although the process of industrialization affected different occupations and groups of people in different ways, gradually an industrial mode of production began to replace the domestic mode of production. The number of peasants and craftsmen with a holding or workshop began to decline, and the number of propertyless persons working for wages increased.[2]

Assessing women's economic activity in the nineteenth century is not easy. The census data reveal certain patterns, but probably underestimate the extent of women's employment. As Higgs notes, the figures in the census tables are not 'hard facts' or 'raw data' but constructs created by men who held certain assumptions about women's position in society, especially their role as dependents. We know that the paid work of any woman was often subsumed within that of a male relative and thus recorded as 'his' work; also, both single and married women undertook a variety of casual and seasonal work which was often left unrecorded.[3]

It is, therefore, highly problematic trying to chart the changing patterns in women's employment by comparing census date in the nineteenth century. Even the classification according to age groupings is not consistent. The 1851 figures for occupied females, for example, include girls under ten years old, whereas the 1891 figures refer to females ten years old and upwards. In addition, the names and descriptions of the various occupations can change from one census to another, as in the cases given here.[4] Despite these difficulties, as table 2.1 shows, we can see at least a pattern in the kind of occupations in which women were found in the nineteenth century. Domestic service, millinery, cotton manufacture, washing and laundry work, and teaching were the most commonly recorded forms of employment for occupied females. In particular, women were found in the greatest numbers in domestic service, especially by 1891. Such statistics conceal, however, the range of activities within any one broad occupational grouping. In the 1851 census, for example, the number of recorded female domestic servants could be broken down into the following divisions – 575,162 general servants, 99,156 indoor farm servants, 49,885 housemaids, 46,648 housekeepers, 44,009 cooks, 35,937 nurses and 31,902 inn servants.[5]

Although the five top occupational groups for women were clearly linked to domestic crafts (e.g. housework, textile work and childcare), women were also surprisingly found, even if in small numbers, in male-

Table 2.1 Most commonly recorded occupations for employed females in England and Wales, 1851 and 1891

Census classification	1851	1891	Census classification
Domestic service	882,699	1,386,167	Domestic servant (indoor)
Millinery	234,340	415,961	Milliner, dressmaker, staymaker
Cotton manufacture	194,910	332,784	Cotton, cotton goods, manufacture
Washing, mangling and laundry work	133,476	185,246	Bathing and washing service
Silk manufacture	68,342		
Teaching	66,909	144,393	Lecturer, schoolmaster, teacher, professor
		89,244	Tailor

Source: Census 1851, table XXV, England and Wales, pp. ccxxii-ccxxvii.
Census 1891, table 6, England and Wales, pp. xxvi-xxx.

dominated occupations. Thus by the end of the nineteenth century, as table 2.2 illustrates, women were found in heavy manual work as miners, labourers and blacksmiths, as well as in the skilled work of shoemaker.

It is often argued that industrialization brought about a 'separation' between family life and paid work, and that during the nineteenth century women became identified with the private sphere of the home and men with the public sphere of paid work.[6] This demarcation into separate spheres for men and women was not, however, straightforward among the working classes; for one thing, not just working-class men but also single working-class women were likely to look for employment outside the home.

Single women, for example, were drawn into some of the traditional female occupations which expanded, such as domestic service and millinery, and into some of the new occupations, such as factory work and elementary schoolteaching. Yet unlike single working-class men, single working-class women could not separate the two spheres of home and work. Single women earning an income still had family responsibilities, not just in giving all, or part, of their wages to the family 'coffers',[7] but especially in helping in various domestic chores, looking after aged parents or younger brothers and sisters. In particular, it was probably the care and nursing of parents and of siblings that was seen as the responsibility of a single working-class daughter rather than of a single working-class son.[8] Single women were not 'independent' in the same way as their brothers.

For married working-class women, the relationship between the 'separate' spheres was even more complex. Some factories in the early nineteenth century, such as those manufacturing cotton, utilized a family system whereby a husband, wife and children might be employed as a unit, and the patriarchal control of the father/husband over his family was used to maintain work discipline.[9] But such a system was transitional. The majority of working-class women in the early 1800s, did not work in factories but in a range of home-based 'domestic' industries, where wife,

Table 2.2   Some occupations of employed females and males in England and Wales, 1891

Occupation	Females	Males
Shoe, boot, patten, clog-maker	46,141	248,789
Labourer, agricultural, farm servant	24,150	709,283
Clerk, commerical	17,859	247,229
Miner, coal	3,267	513,843
Labourer (general)	1,947	594,128
Blacksmith, whitesmith	500	139,524
Boatman on seas, merchant service, seaman, pilot	389	107,445
Carpenter, joiner	348	220,661
Knacker, catsmeal, dealer, vermin destroyer	152	2,082
Bricklayer	66	130,380
Gamekeeper	3	13,814

Source: *Census 1891*, table 6, England and Wales, pp. xxvi-xxxi.

husband and children might be employed at home, each involved in different and separate activities. In the domestic woollen industry, for example, a husband might buy the wool, while women and children engaged in the unpleasant task of 'picking', i.e., picking tar and dirt from the wool before it was washed. Dyeing was usually a man's job, while women and children might engage in spinning.[10] Homeplace and workplace were united, making it easier, perhaps, for a married woman to integrate the demands of paid work, childbirth, child-rearing and domestic responsibilities.

With the advance of industrialization, however, and the creation of an industrial and commercial system outside the home, the family-based domestic system began to decline. While single and married working-class men and single working-class women increasingly worked outside the home, the working-class woman with small dependent children often had little choice but to remain at home, taking poorly paid work within it. For these women, the public sphere of paid work and the private sphere of the family were integral to each other. The notion of a breadwinner, therefore, became increasingly synonymous with a single working-class man and a working-class husband, not his wife. And the fight of some working-class men, through their trade unions, for a family wage that would enable them to support a wife and children strengthened the concept of the *male* breadwinner.[11] The separation of family and paid work for married working-class women was therefore more ideological than real. In contrast, wives in the bourgeoisie would have experienced such a separation much more acutely; with industrialization these women were unlikely to be involved in any employment other than unpaid, voluntary work and were likely to be supported financially by a husband. Such differences in the lifestyles of married working-class and middle-class women are relevant to Chapter 3, where ideals of femininity and of family life are discussed.

The process of industrialization, then, affected working-class women in different ways. Women with dependents often could not go 'out' into the labour market, and were restricted to a number of poorly paid home-based jobs if they wished to earn an income. Women without dependents had a different range of opportunities outside the home and might even be drawn into some of the better-paid jobs, such as factory work. Whether such changes benefited working-class women is an issue of debate.[12]

The nature of single and married working-class women's involvement in employment was particularly relevant for their participation in education. For our purposes, we should remember that a working-class woman would need time and energy in order to become a student within the mechanics' institutes movement or the working men's college movement. If working conditions were harsh and hours of employment long, it would be difficult for many women to undertake studying, even in evening classes designed specially for them. Since lectures and classes in these two adult education movements were not free, but offered for a weekly fee of perhaps between 1d and 2d in a mechanics' institute and between 1d and 6d in a working men's college, a working woman would also need some spare income in order to pay for her education. The levels of pay in women's occupations would therefore also determine how far particular groups of working-class women could participate in these educational initiatives.

Yet employment conditions were not the only factor influencing a woman's taking up of education; family life, structure and authority, plus working conditions within the home were equally significant in that they could affect the time, energy, income and independence of women. In particular, patriarchal relations within the family shaped a woman's independence and ability to act in her own right. For married women, a husband could be a major factor in encouraging or discouraging a wife's involvement in adult education. For single women, a father might play a similar role. Dependents of any kind, whether children, aged parents or siblings, could make demands on a woman's time and energy, leaving little space for a student's life. In the following sections such issues shall be discussed as we investigate the experiences of single and married working-class women in the nineteenth century.

Single working-class women

Overall, throughout the nineteenth century, single working women were concentrated in particular jobs often characterized by harsh conditions, low status and low wages. Rather than examine the daily lives of single women within the full range of paid work in which they might be found, I shall focus on the five most commonly recorded occupations in which working-class women were located – domestic service, millinery, dressmaking, factory work and schoolteaching.

Domestic service

Life in domestic service, the most common form of employment for working-class girls and single women throughout the nineteenth century, was generally one of hard work and drudgery.[13] Where domestic servants differed from those in other occupational groups was in the fact that many were residential, living in someone else's home. A classic example was Mrs Wrigley, born in 1858, who when about nine years old became a servant-of-all-work to a 'lady and gentleman' in Stockport, Cheshire; this illiterate girl had to get up at six each morning in order to begin her day's hard work. A 16-year-old prostitute, who could neither read nor write, told Mayhew that when she was ten years old and a maid-of-all-work in a small tradesman's family she was frequently beaten with sticks and hands.[14]

Although such physical violence may not have been the experience of all female domestics, the drudgery was common. Hannah Cullwick, as a 26-year-old maid-of-all-work, recorded in her diary in 1860 the daily round of routine manual labour that had to be endured:

Lighted the fires & clean'd the hearth; swept & dusted the rooms. Clean'd 3 pairs of boots. Laid the hearth & got breakfast. Made the beds & emptied the slops. Wash'd the water bottles & lamp glasses; clean'd the bedroom mantle shelf & looking glasses; put down linen for the wash. Clean'd away & wash'd the breakfast things. Clean'd the knives & wash'd up in the scullery... Got the dinner & took it up. Clean'd away & made the fires up; fill'd the scuttles. Swept the passage & pantry & clean'd the kitchen.[15]

For women such as Hannah, the hard physical labour involved in being a general domestic must have used up most of their energy. Not satisfied with extracting almost 24 hours' work from their servants, many employers also attempted to control various aspects of the lives of their employees, including any leisure time they were offered.[16] Indeed, in the 1880s, when no less than one in three of all women between the ages of 15 and 20 were servants, it was claimed that maids were treated like 'children' within the family household, in that 'they had no evenings out unless they had somewhere definite to go and obtained special leave'.[17] By the 1900s, the leisure time allowed servants in the most generous households was usually restricted to a fortnight's holiday each year, plus a half day every Sunday, one day off per month and an evening out weekly; little wonder that one commentator spoke in 1888 of domestic service as the 'last remnant of feudal despotism.[18] Indeed, Davidoff has suggested that the control exercized over female servants was part of a chain of personal subordination in private homes that was a life-time experience for many women. Girls moved from parental control, in their parents' home, into service and then into their husband's home.[19] How many domestic servants would be able to afford the fees, however small, and whether they would have the time and the energy for an adult class is hard to determine, since throughout the century there were wide variations between households and between servants. Generally, housekeepers, lady's maids and cooks would be paid more than those towards the bottom of the female servant hierarchy, such as a general maid, kitchen maid, scullery maid or between maid.

In 1841, for example, a general servant might earn £8 and a lady's maid £40 per annum. Although it has been estimated that the wages of female servants rose by 30 per cent between 1850 and 1870, the amount earned was still low. Figures collected by the Board of Trade in the 1890s reveal that a scullery maid aged 19 could earn as little as £13 per annum, a general maid aged 21 to 24 about £14 18s, and a housekeeper of 40 years old or more about £52; cases of exploitation could also be found in the 1890s of some ex-workhouse girls being paid 1s a week, or £2 10s per annum as general servants.[20]

Overall, then, there can be little doubt that for the vast majority of female domestic servants it would be necessary to scrimp and save on low wages if a few pennies weekly had to be saved for an education class. And the situation was not helped by the fact that many women employed in this occupation, though geographically separated from their parents, brothers and sisters, were often expected to help out in times of family need. In Oxfordshire in the 1880s for example, daughters in service sent home every month at least half of their scanty wages to 'our Mum': in addition, older girls might pay their parents' rent, give them a ton of coal for the winter, and send Christmas and birthday presents as well as parcels of left-off clothing.[21] Such acts of service to the family of origin must have left many a working-class woman short of money.

However, some servants were fortunate enough to have access to a kitchen library and were also allowed to borrow books from their employer.[22] Some too were sponsored by their employers for basic education. In 1822 an illiterate female domestic aged 22 was encouraged by her mistress to find a school where she could obtain free instruction. This young woman attended a day school for children, saying she would 'submit to anything in order to learn to read the Bible'. Over six weeks she learnt not only to read the New Testament, but also to write words of two syllables, work a sum in simple addition and to do high-standard needlework.[23] But many other female servants were not encouraged by their employers to learn to read and write and generally to improve their educational standard. Mr Tapsfield, an overseer and relieving officer of the parish of Farlegh, near Maidstone, was of the view in 1843 that 'the least educated' are the best servants. And such views lingered on, in some households, well into the 1870s. In 1874, for example, it was claimed that there were some 'ladies' who regarded with 'dreadful severity', 'anything like the cultivation of their servants' brains'.[24]

Such ideas may have been based upon a fear that literacy might, especially if combined with the acquisition of certain kinds of domestic knowledge (cooking or management skills, for example), lead to servants' ambitions to move up the hierarchy into such positions as cook or housekeeper. Literacy too might offer some the chance to leave their stations and enter jobs of higher social status, such as in clerical and commercial work. And female domestics seeking mobility through marriage, perhaps to a shopkeeper or artisan, might find literacy skills useful in a family business.[25]

The working-class female domestic servant was removed from the outside world, living in a capsule that involved a high level of personal involvement and exploitation uncommon with other occupations. Employers became their servants' 'new family', often exercising considerable control over their adult women employees. Such control, plus low wages and a sparcity of free time, militated against participation in educational movements outside the workplace. Yet, as we shall later see, some domestic servants did become students within the mechanics' institutes and working men's colleges.

The sewing trades

If the lives of domestic servants were harsh, so too were those of women in a range of sewing trades such as millinery, dressmaking and slop work, although for different reasons.[26] Working-class women would undoubtedly be drawn into these jobs since they probably had to make their own clothes, and were therefore reasonably competent with a needle. There was a diversity of skill and levels of pay within this broad occupational grouping, and whether she was employed, for example, as a milliner in a workshop or a slop worker within her own home would often be determined by whether or not a woman had dependents. The general conditions of life for these women, however, were such that they were hardly conducive to finding space for self-improvement.

Millinery and dressmaking were trades that remained in the hands of women throughout the century; the work was poorly paid and insecure, demanding long hours of labour, often well into the evening when most education classes would be held. Although the standard of skill demanded in millinery and dressmaking varied greatly, three categories of workers appear to have been common – 'apprentices', 'day-workers' and 'improvers'. At the age of 14 an apprentice might be placed with the proprietress of an establishment and, for a premium sometimes as high as 60 guineas, would 'live in' and be taught the trade. Such sums of money were, of course, beyond the means of most working-class women who formed the bulk of the day workers and improvers. In contrast, a day worker usually lived at home, or in lodgings, and would come to the establishment each day: in 1846 she might receive 1s 6d for her long day's work. Since such workers were taken on or dismissed as necessary, their position was precarious. The casual nature of their employment offered little financial security. Even more harsh were the work conditions of the improvers, who were often rural women who came to a town establishment to improve their skills. They stayed six months or longer, paid no premium and received no wages: since they often lived on the premises with their time entirely at the disposal of the dressmaker, they were greatly exploited as cheap labour.[27]

All three grades of workers in millinery and dressmaking shared the burden of excessively long hours of work. In 1863, for example, it was recorded that during the busy season, up to 18 hours a day could be worked.[28] Sometimes, if a special order had to be met, perhaps for a wedding or funeral, the women worked all through the night. Numerous statements can be found recording such facts. In 1846 one apprentice recounted that she had worked, with short intervals for meals, from 5 a.m. until 3 a.m. the next morning; in 1863, another milliner told how she worked without going to bed, from four o'clock on Thursday to ten o'clock on Sunday morning.[29] Such long hours of waged labour in overcrowded, poorly ventilated and badly lit rooms seriously undermined the health of many women and undoubtedly left little time and energy for alternative activities. The low level of pay, if any, meant that little money could be spared for leisure. For these women food and survival, rather than education, were more likely to become priorities.[30]

Economic instability in the 1830s and 1840s caused fluctuations in the millinery and dressmaking trades, and the lack of regular wages would have made it increasingly difficult for women in these jobs to save any money. More and more sewing was put out to home workers, who were cheaper to employ. Women at home, making plain clothes such as shirts, were the most degraded of all ranks of needlewomen and were usually know as 'slop workers'.[31] The essence of slop work was the contract system, whereby an order was given to the contractor charging the lowest price. The continual competition between contractors and the undercutting of prices meant that the system became known as the 'sweating system'. In 1852 it was claimed that three out of every four of all the garments sold in the country were made under the slop system in London or in one of the other large towns; in London alone, in 1849, there were said to be 14,000 female slop workers, 11,440 of whom were under 20 years of age.[32]

If women working in the better-paid sections of the millinery and dressmaking trades endured harsh working conditions, women in the 'dishonourable' slop trade were clearly the most exploited group.[33] Their earnings were even lower than those of the milliners and dressmakers discussed above, so that most lived in a state of acute poverty. Married women and young single women with no other means of employment often did slop work, as well as the more 'vulnerable' groups of single women who were elderly and infirm. All experienced great hardships.

In 1850 an orphan girl without any parental support told how she had worked for eight years at slop work, making trousers and waistcoats for 3d and 4d each and shirts for 1d. She had never earned more than 4s a week, and was left with just 2s 4d to live on after paying for lodgings and 8d for twist, thread and silk.[34] Another single woman who had left domestic service to do waistcoating at home, so that she could look after her elderly parents, found her wages inadequate to buy nourishing food.

I can't have what I ought to have. I think my present illness is from over-exertion ... My greatest earnings are 4s per week – my lowest 2s. 6d. and I generally average about 3s. Many weeks I have been wholly without working – not able to do it ... I never was married.[35]

An 'old maiden woman', 43 years old, living with a widow, told how they worked at their needle from 18 to 20 hours each day, including Sundays. They paid for food by pledging belongings, and if there was nothing to pledge, 'why then ... we starve: yes, we're obliged to it. We'd rather do that than go in debt'.[36]

Prostitution, a form of employment when all else had failed, was, of course, an ever-real threat for all working women who could not earn enough to support themselves.[37] Indeed, one ex-slop worker claimed it was a common way of supplementing inadequate wages:

I am sure no girl can get a living at slop work without prostitution; and I say as much after thirteen years experience of the business. I never knew one girl in the trade, who was virtuous: most of them wished to be so, but were compelled to be otherwise for mere life.[38]

For these women, as for the milliners and dressmakers, the long hours of work, exhaustion, low pay and casual nature of employment would make it difficult to think beyond the next day.

Various kinds of millinery, dressmaking and slop work continued to flourish throughout the nineteenth century, and it is difficult to establish to what extent the working conditions of the women employed in these jobs improved. The greatest advances should have been experienced by those women employed in workshops and sewing establishments, since legislation was passed that related to such employees but not to those women undertaking sweated labour in their own homes. The Workshops Act of 1867, for example, attempted to exercise some control over small establishments and limited the hours for which women could legally be employed. But the law was not always effective. Even in 1896, when milliners and dressmakers were supposed to be working the legal 10 hour day, an extra two hours overtime without additional pay might be demanded by an employer.[39] For women working in their own homes, there was not even the possibility of legal protection, however ineffective. The mass production of cheap ready-made clothing in the second half of the century, plus an increasingly complex subdivision of labour, ensured the survival of sweated conditions of home sewing.[40] For the 234,340 women recorded as milliners in the 1851 Census and for women working in other branches of the sewing trades in the nineteenth century, the cycle of poverty associated with being a needlewoman would have offered few chances to take up an opportunity to educate themselves or to acquire alternative skills. Yet some needlewomen did become adult students.

Cotton-factory work

Compared with domestic servants, milliners, dressmakers, and other kinds of sewing women, women employed in factories, and especially the cotton factories, were relatively well paid and therefore in a better position to afford educational fees. It was estimated in 1834, for example, in selected cotton mills in Lancashire, that the average weekly wage for women in the 36 to 41 year-old age group was 9s 8d.[41] There was, however, considerable variation in wage levels, and the earnings of power-loom weavers could vary according to the kind of cloth woven, the skill and output of the weaver and the number of looms over which she had charge. Female weavers giving evidence to the Factory Commissioners in 1833 included a 20 year-old woman who earned 13s to 15s a week; a 25 year-old who worked two power looms and received 8s to 9s; and an 18 year-old, working four looms, who had 16s, from which she had to deduct 3s to pay the child who helped her.[42]

By the end of the nineteenth century, women weavers working on four looms in Lancashire cotton towns could earn about 25s a week, which was much higher than pay in other jobs open to working-class women; male and female weavers were paid at more similar rates, too, than men and women in other trades.[43] In the 1890s Clara Collett found in the Salford area that the majority (1,120) of female weavers worked two looms and earned 11s 1d a week, though for some (279) on four looms the wage could be as high as 17s 9d.[44]

Women weavers in the silk factories in the 1890s were, on the other hand, poorly paid in comparison with cotton weavers. In 1896 their wages might vary from 7s to 10s in Macclesfield and from 7s to 11s 6d in Congleton but were only 5s a week at Halstead, Essex. Yet 10s a week was considered necessary at this time to keep a woman 'in comfort' and 14s for her to live 'very comfortably' so that she could 'easily lay by a shilling or two every week'.[45]

Women employed in the cotton factories then would appear to have been able to afford to pay for any educational programme that the mechanics' institute movement and the working men's college movement offered. And the majority of these factory women were single. It has been estimated that, in 1851, only 26 per cent of the total number of women in cotton mills were either married or widowed, though this proportion increased to about 33.3 per cent in the 1870s, probably reaching a peak in the 1890s and then declining again.[46]

These women, like all factory women, however, lacked time. Working long hours in noisy rooms with complicated machinery might have lessened any incentive that some factory women had to better themselves. Hours of work were particularly long during the early nineteenth century, when a family was often employed in a textile factory, children as young as five years old working the same 12 to 14 hour day as their parents. Subsequent legislation curtailed the hours that children and women might work. The 1844 Act, for example, limited a woman's working day to 12 hours and forbade night work. Three years later the Ten Hours Bill was passed, but since the time when the ten hours to be worked was not specified, employers often used a relay system which abused the law. It was not until the Acts of 1850 and 1853 that a 'normal' working day of ten hours was achieved for women and children,[47] and even then there were frequent evasions.[48]

During the second half of the nineteenth century, factory work still made heavy demands on the energies of mill women, who, like male factory hands, were described as being physically 'thin and spare, but not emaciated'.[49] Factory work not only required strength and stamina but also the ability to withstand the monotony of the tasks. A poignant comment came from Ada Nield Chew in 1894. When writing as 'a Crewe Factory Girl' to the local press, she asked:

Cultivation of the mind? How is it possible? Reading? Those of us who are determined to live like human beings and require food for mind as well as body are obliged to take time which is necessary for sleep to gratify this desire.[50]

Similarly, Alice Foley spoke of 'the agony of fatigue' endured by standing on her feet from early morning to late evening when, as a 13 year-old school-leaver at the turn of the nineteenth century, she entered Gibraltar Mill, Lancashire, as a knotter for the fringes on counterpane covers. She was so exhausted that she frequently fell asleep over tea or supper, too tired even to eat.[51]

It is little wonder that many factory women were described in 1915 as 'fagged out' by three o'clock in the afternoon; women weavers in particular were said to be doing as much work in a day as in a day and a half 12 or 13 years previously.[52] Such conditions were condemned by trade union representatives, who declared that factory women were so utterly worn out by the end of the day that they were 'generally incapable of any serious work': this accounted, it was believed, for their low numbers in the Workers' Educational Association and other evening classes.[53]

It must be remembered, however, that unlike the working women in other occupations considered so far, factory women who had been employed in the mills as girls may have experienced some schooling, however inadequate, at the workplace. Although provision of education for factory children after the 1833 Act was slow and sporadic and, where established, offered the 'feeblest' instruction[54], educational facilities were available at some workplaces. Some factory owners also offered evening classes for older boys and girls and for adult women. At the mills in Belper, Derbyshire, for example, the school was open four nights a week to any of the young women who wanted 'to improve themselves' in reading, writing and sewing. These mill women were also taught to cut out and make up their own clothes, an amusing book being read while such an activity took place.[55]

Not all of the night schools for factory women offered such a narrow curriculum. At the evening school associated with the Courtauld silk factory at Halstead, Essex, which specialised in producing black crepe for middle-class mourning attire, single women attending the 1847–8 winter session covered a range of topics – biographies, travel, the elements of astronomy, human physiology, the laws governing health, poetry, plants and singing, as well as reading and writing.[56]

The policy of offering female factory employees some education, however basic, on factory premises, continued well into the century. One nine-year-old girl who entered the cotton mills, probably in the 1880s, was expected, after an 11-hour day at the looms, to attend weekly lessons on 'economical cookery' given by the mill owner's daughter. One lecture, she recalled, was on 'three ways of stuffing a cod's head for a penny'.[57]

Attending such evening classes after a day's work on the factory floor was not the only duty that factory women were expected to undertake. Most were also involved in unpaid domestic duties within the parental home. Although married women probably bore the brunt of these tasks, single women did their share too. Alice Foley remembers how her sister Cissy, a 'setter-in' in a Lancashire cotton factory, often acted as 'little mother' in the home. On Friday evenings, after the departure of parents and brothers, a huge cream and brown jug was carried onto the hearth and filled with hot water. Then, in turn, Cissy gave Alice and her sister their 'weekly scrub-down'. Later their hair was fine-tooth combed and neatly braided.[58] Daughters undoubtedly helped with a range of domestic duties which would include not only child care, but also cleaning, shopping and preparing food.

Many daughters also made an important contribution to family income through giving over half of their earnings or more to their parents for board and lodgings. Others, in families where the father was unemployed, earning low wages or generally spendthrift, undoubtedly contributed much more. Cissy Foley's regular weekly wages were depended on at home since her drunken father, who worked as a night caretaker for local foundries, was frequently out of work.[59]

There were different possibilities and constraints for female factory workers, then, in comparison with other groups of working women we have considered so far. The possibilities opened up by higher pay levels and some access to schooling were not shared by other employees. Yet neither were the constraints of heavy physical labour in a noisy environment of machinery shared by domestic servants and needlewomen. But factory women, like all the working women we have discussed, worked long and hard for their wages and must have felt tired in the evenings. In the event, as we shall see, some factory women did become students within the mechanics' institute and working men's college movements. To do so must have required an extraordinary high level of motivation and determination.

Schoolteaching

As the Censuses of 1851 and 1891 show, teaching was a popular occupation for women throughout the nineteenth century, and female schoolteachers were another group of working women who became students within the institutes and colleges. By 1875, 54.3 per cent of all teachers in elementary schools (which catered almost exclusively for working-class children) were women,[60] and it was the female elementary teacher who was regarded as the 'typical' woman teacher of the nineteenth century. Although elementary teaching had an ambivalent status (a theme I discuss later), it was seen as a working-class occupation, staffed mainly by working-class women, especially up to the 1890s.[61]

Unlike other occupations considered so far, elementary teaching involved non-manual work anticipating a varying degree of theoretical knowledge, verbal skills, writing ability and classroom management techniques. And unlike entry into domestic service, millinery, dressmaking, slop work and factory work, entry into schoolteaching was dependent upon a certain educational level.

Many elementary mistresses were the product of the pupil-teacher apprenticeship scheme, initiated in 1846 by Kay-Shuttleworth and offering on the job training. Under this scheme a boy or girl who had completed his or her education to at least 13 years of age and was not subject to any bodily infirmity could compete for a five-year, state-aided apprenticeship. Among other things, candidates for apprenticeships were required to be able to read with fluency, ease and expression; to write in a neat hand, with correct spelling and punctuation, a simple narrative slowly read to them; to write from dictation sums in the first four rules of arithmetic, simple and compound, to work them correctly and to know the tables of weights and measures; to point out the parts of speech in a simple sentence; and to have an elementary knowledge of geography. Candidates were also required to repeat the Catechism, show they understood its meaning, reveal acquaintance with the outline of scripture history in schools connected with the Church of England (in other schools the state of religious knowledge would be certified by the managers), and teach a junior class to the satisfaction of the school inspector. In addition, female candidates only were also expected to be able 'to sew neatly and to knit'.[62]

The length of training could, however, extend beyond the apprenticeship. Thus at 18 years of age, a pupil teacher could sit the Queen's Scholarship and, if successful, become a student at one of the teacher training colleges run by various voluntary schemes (university day training colleges were not founded until late in the nineteenth century). A Queen's Scholarship was awarded only to a minority of very able pupil teachers. In 1863 only 542 pupil teachers and in 1867 as few as 224 were admitted to training colleges.[63]

Elementary teachers also earned more than most of the women in the other occupations described so far. In 1861 the average annual salary of a sample of 1,972 certificated mistresses was £62 4s 11d, though that of uncertificated women fell to £34 19s 7d; and from the 1870s the number of uncertificated women rose – from 13 per cent in 1875 to 41 per cent in 1914.[64] The lower-paid uncertificated schoolmistresses were therefore likely to find it more difficult to raise the fee to attend an evening or educational course, even if ironically they were most likely to benefit from the extra tuition.

One such woman, eking out a miserable existence while also assuming financial and emotional support for an aged parent, was Miss Rose Knowles, headmistress of Thorpe Malsor School, Northamptonshire, from 1882 to 1888. The daughter had to scrimp and scrape on her small salary in order to send sums of money to her widowed mother, a London dressmaker who was frequently without work. Miss Knowles often lacked the means to buy certain things, such as coal for her fire or a black dress and hat for the funeral of the local rector. Even boots could not be bought when needed, as this letter to her mother, dated 30 April 1888, reveals:

I have sent twelve shilling and tea I have not a bit of boot hardly to my feet though I should have been able to get a pair this time but as I have to send this cannot it has taken all again to pay for the tea and send this & pay for other things that I owed.[65]

For lowly paid teachers such as Miss Knowles, participation in any form of extra education would not have been easy. However, other conditions attached to the job reveal many advantages when compared with most other jobs open to working-class women. The hard drudgery of domestic service, the long hours and poorly paid sedentary needlework, and the noise, dirt and pace of life in a factory all compared unfavourably with the relatively clean conditions of the classroom. But, above all else, elementary teaching, since it was not manual labour, offered working-class women the potential for intrinsic job satisfaction and the hope of a limited degree of social mobility, although this was not unproblematic. The working-class elementary teacher suffered from an ambivalent social status. She was often separated from the social class from which she originated and was also unacceptable to those above her; one vicar's wife in the 1880s highlighted the dilemma – should the local schoolmistress be asked to tea in the kitchen or the dining room?[66]

Despite the advantages which seemingly distanced elementary teaching from the other occupations considered so far, there were some broad similarities in the experiences of female teachers and other women workers. For example, the large size of the classes, the overcrowded conditions of the school, the restricted nature of the curriculum with its emphasis upon the three Rs, and the mechanical rote methods of teaching and learning could be exhausting. Clara Grant, an elementary schoolteacher in the 1880s, remembers how the London Board schools established after the 1870 Education Act were built to hold 80 children. 'Classes taught in one large room', she comments, 'were noisy and nerve racking, and large classes with rigid discipline tended to crush out anyone with refined manners or a soul'; the fact that the schools were intended for the 'lower orders' and the children considered 'rough' added to the teacher's problems.[67] Also, even if a teacher felt enthusiastic enough to become an evening student, there was still the fact that time after school was not entirely her own. Lessons had to be prepared, pupil-teachers instructed, administrative duties seen to and pupils' sewing sorted; in addition, some teachers were also expected to teach at night and Sunday schools.[68]

In contrast to other jobs discussed here, then, elementary teaching demanded that its recruits have some scholastic ability. Teachers would clearly have different incentives for entering adult education than would domestic servants, milliners, slop workers or factory workers. They were already literate and would not need instruction in the three Rs. Neither would they need instruction in sewing, since this was a subject they taught to female pupils even before the Revised Code of 1862 made the teaching of needlework compulsory to all girls in schools receiving a government grant. What female elementary teachers might seek in further education was perhaps a general education or more advanced course that might increase promotion opportunities. Although there were few openings for women in the school inspectorate,[69] many may have aspired to headships of elementary schools or to posts in fee-paying, middle-class secondary schools. By 1914 probably about one-fifth of women teachers in grant-earning secondary schools had either begun their careers as elementary teachers or been trained as such.[70]

Other women teachers may have sought further education as a means of moving from a low-status village school to a larger urban institution with opportunities of advanced work. And for some the experience of teaching may simply have acted as a spur to learn more. After all, any new knowledge acquired might not only refresh the mind but also possibly feed into classroom practice. For these women, their own work-setting was an educational environment and this may have made them feel less threatened when becoming students within the mechanics' institutes and various colleges than were women who were domestic servants, milliners, dressmakers, slop workers or factory operatives.

Overall, then, single working-class women in the occupations described here often spent long hours in lowly paid work and some time in unpaid domestic duties. The poverty of their lives undoubtedly caused weariness, yet many struggled, as we shall see, to better themselves educationally. But what about married working-class women? What were the conditions of their lives? How might this influence their participation in education?

Married working-class women

If single working-class women in the nineteenth century led lives that were not particularly conducive towards education, the daily existence for working-class wives and mothers was particularly constrained in this respect. For such women, paid work as well as a range of domestic and childcare duties were an integral part of daily life, especially for those with husbands within the unskilled and semi-skilled sections of the working classes. And it was often within the working-class family itself rather than the work conditions of employees that wives and mothers experienced the most direct oppression. This could have important consequences for any involvement in educational movements.

Agricultural work

Over the course of the century, the pattern of paid work for married women changed. In rural areas, where many mechanics' institutes were subsequently established, many women worked on the land at the beginning of the century, though few were so employed by 1900.[71] For the married woman field day-labourer, work conditions could be extremely hard. Unlike other women discussed so far, the female agricultural labourer worked outside, in all weathers, doing a variety of physically exhausting jobs such as weeding, stone picking, apple picking, potato digging, turnip hoeing, clover picking, hay-making and harvesting. In the 1840s 48 year-old Jane Long of Wiltshire, who had borne nine children, reflected on a life of 35 years in the fields: 'In harvest I have worked nearly night and day, at the time that I had four or five children'.[72] 50 year-old Mary Hunt, who had had 12 children and was expecting her thirteenth, claimed that hard word did her no harm:

... as for hard work I never was hurt by it. I have carried half a sack of peas to Chippenham, four miles, when I have been large in the family.[73]

Others, though, must have suffered aching backs and poor health. Mrs Smart, who had borne 13 children (though six had died), was sometimes so strained with hay-making that she could not get out of her chair. Often, too, she and her children had come home with their clothes wet through. 'I have gone to bed for an hour for my things to get a little dry', she remarked, 'but have had to put them on again when quite wet'.[74]

These examples illustrate how large a number of children these workers might have had and some of the strategies used to integrate children into their patterns of work life. Older children might accompany their mother in the fields, but younger children were usually left at home and looked after by another female, such as a grandmother or hired girl. Sometimes nursing mothers, such as Mrs Britton, who had seven sons, carried the baby with them.[75] Integrating children in this way into one's place of work must have been an additional drain on the energies of many mothers. 'I often come home too tired to do anything', Mrs Long complained, 'but always with a good appetite'.[76]

Yet surprisingly, despite such circumstances, a number of agricultural women workers attended evening classes. That they did so is remarkable, especially in view of the fact that any income earned, however small, was not considered a wife's to spend as she might wish, but as a necessary supplement to a husband's wages. Agricultural women knew that mothers 'must work'.[77] Indeed, while the pay of agricultural workers was considered low, that of female workers, even when they did the same job, was lower still. In rural Wiltshire, Devon and Somerset in the 1840s, the regular wages of a male farm labourer averaged 8s weekly, while that of a woman might vary from 6d a day for weeding to 1s a day for harvesting.[78] Married women generally earned less, too, since their work pattern was more casual, flexible and intermittent than that of men – in order to accommodate domestic responsibilities. Some employers allowed their female hands to work a shorter day or take time off when necessary.[79]

Female agricultural workers who entered adult education were most likely to want literacy classes, since during the first half of the nineteenth century, in particular, many such women, and especially older women, were illiterate. Alfred Austin, when giving evidence to the Poor Law Commissioners in 1843, echoed a commonly held view when he said that a great many women accustomed to work in the fields were 'unable to read and write, or if to do either, it is very imperfectly': this was particularly so, he continued, with women over 30 years of age.[80] A number of the women themselves, presenting their evidence to the Commissioners, validated the claim. 41 year-old Mary Puddicombe, mother of six children, could neither read nor write; Mrs Sculfer, who had also borne six children, confessed that she could read 'a very little'.[81] For women like this, attendance in education may have been promoted by the desire to read. The adult school movement, which flourished particularly in the early nineteenth century, had attracted a number of illiterate mature women, and in some areas such schools had connections with the mechanics' institutes.[82]

Home-based employment

While the number of women employed in agriculture declined over the course of the century, another major change took place in the pattern of home-based employment for married working-class women. As we saw earlier in this chapter, the advance of industrialization with the development of an industrial, commercial and factory system outside the home led to the break-up of the family-based 'domestic' industries. But while working-class men and single women could seek employment outside the home, the married working-class women with small dependent children had little choice but to stay, undertaking poorly-paid casual work that might be divided into two main groupings – first, extended domestic occupations, such as taking in washing, taking in lodgers or child minding, and secondly, tradework, which could be unskilled (as in carding and packeting) or skilled (as in paper-box making, brush making and sewing).[83]

For many a working-class wife and mother there was a notable change in her circumstances over the course of the nineteenth century. Whereas in the past she had been a part of a home-based, mixed-sex, family production unit, now she was employed individually. Although still within her own home, with her children about her, she no longer had the same kind of daily contact with other adult members of her family. In addition, she undoubtedly would have found that her responsibility for the care and rearing of children increased. It was probably women in the unskilled sections of the working-classes who were most disadvantaged in comparison with that minority of women whose menfolk were in the 'better off' artisan stratum. By the mid-nineteenth century, artisans' wives were not expected to engage in waged labour, though many undoubtedly responded to any substantial lowering of the family income by doing so.[84]

Many of these home-based jobs were tiring and could eat into any spare evening time that might be given to self-improvement. Taking in washing, for example, was physically demanding, since everything had to be done by hand.[85] Although, as we saw earlier, washing, mangling and laundry work were the fourth most commonly recorded occupations for women in both the 1851 and 1891 Census, there were undoubtedly many married women workers who escaped the official Census. For some, such as Mary Puddicombe, wife of a labourer and mother of six children, washing was 'harder than working in the field'; others, such as Mrs Woodward, described it 'like washing your guts away'.[86] The demanding nature of the work, which required long hours of standing in damp and steamy conditions, also took its toll on some women's health. A typical example was a 54 year-old Irish widow, living in London in 1851:

I was left destitute with four young children, and had to bring them up as well as I could, by what I could make by washing and charing, and a hard fight it was. . . . My health broke six years ago, and I couldn't do hard work in washing, and I took to trotter selling . . . . I can't either sit, or stand, or walk long at a time, I'm so rheumatic.[87]

Other women with dependents, such as Mrs Layton, born in 1855, whose husband was a night worker on the railway, took in washing to supplement her husband's income. It was a job she could organize in her own time, to fit in with the routine of bringing up a baby and looking after a frequently ill spouse. Even so, she was often washing till four o'clock in the morning, in bitter cold weather.[88]

Married working-class women taking in lodgers might find the work less tiring than taking in washing, but they too might work an extended day, especially if an evening meal had to be prepared. Being a landlady may have been particularly attractive to married women with very young children who were not yet at the stage of taking up much household space, or to married women who missed the income of grown-up children who had left home.[89]

Whatever the job undertaken at home, whether extended domestic occupations or various kinds of tradework, the vast majority of married working-class women received low wages that supplemented a husband's income. In the 1840s, Mrs Houghton, a lace drawer, worked at her trade with her three eldest daughters, Harriet aged eight, Anne, six, and Mary, four. Even though she worked a 13-hour day in the winter and three hours longer in the summer, with just a quarter of an hour for each meal, she earned about a shilling a day. Her husband, a joiner, whose regular wages were 23 shillings a week, was on half-time work.[90] In rural Yorkshire, where many mechanics' institutes were established, the only regular employment for many married women with small dependent children in the 1840s was hand-knitting clothes such as stockings, jackets and caps. Though a mother might earn 6d for a ten-to twelve-hour day, most earned 2s.6d a week.[91] Widows with small children and single mothers, similarly forced into integrating homeplace and workplace as a way of combining the need to earn a living and rear children, faced special hardship, since they alone supported themselves and their dependents. For many, slop work was the only solution in the daily struggle against poverty.

In 1850, for example, a widow with two small sons, left penniless after her husband's death, earned just 5s 6d a week through slop work. Her wages were insufficient to support them all. Her eldest son died of scarlatina. Of her second son, who died some time later of whooping cough, she said:

I loved him as I did my life; but I was glad he was took from me ... he could but have been brought up in the worst kind of poverty ... and God only knows what might have become of him, if he had lived.[92]

Another widow with four children, two of whom were entirely dependent upon her income, often earned in 1849 only 1s 6d a week, and never more than 2.6d.[93] Single mothers too often did slop work, and tales of such parents, forced into prostitution as a way of supplementing a miserable existence for themselves and their children, were common. One such unmarried mother, earning only 2d for each fine full-fronted white shirt told her life story:

I had a child, and it used to cry for food, so, as I could not get a living for him myself by my needle, I went into the street ... I have made pin-cushions and fancy articles, such as I could manage to scrape together, and taken them to the streets to sell, so that I might get an honest living, but I could not; sometimes I would be out in the rain all night, and sell nothing at all, me and my child together; and when we did not get anything that way, we used to sit in a shed; for I was too fatigued with my baby to stand, and I was so poor I could not have even a night's lodgings upon credit.[94]

In large towns, such as London and Birmingham, the range of married women's work might be more varied than lace work, knitting or slop work, but wages were consistently low, mainly because the work was unskilled, casual, overstocked, unorganized by trade unions and unprotected by law.[95] As late as 1906, homeworkers in Birmingham, sewing hooks and eyes onto cards, averaged 3s 3d per week, though those doing skilled work, such as paper-box making, could average 9s.[96]

Overall, then, throughout the nineteenth century married working-class women engaged in a wide variety of low-paid work and unpaid domestic duties that would make any participation in education a carefully planned exercise, both in terms of time and money. All of these women were also involved in a key aspect of a married woman's life, the structure of the family itself, and especially the husband/wife relationship.

The changes that took place in married women's work over the course of the nineteenth century undoubtedly had some impact upon the opportunity and incentive of any wife and mother to participate in education programmes. For one thing the power relations between her and her spouse probably changed. Her increasing confinement to a home world of children and housework, to poorly paid intermittent work that fitted in with the rhythm of family life and her economic dependency upon the main breadwinner, her husband, who increasingly worked outside the home, would probably give her a subordinate status within the marital relationship.[97]

As one writer in 1834 noted, the working man bringing income into the home had 'a right' to do many things, such as drink tea as he pleased, go to a coffee house every night and read the papers. His wife, on the other hand, confined to the home, was :

working from morning till night at housekeeping; she is bearing children, and suffering all the pangs of labour, and all the exhaustion of suckling; she is cooking, and washing, and cleaning; soothing one child, cleaning another, and feeding a third. And all this is nothing; for she gets no wages. Her wages come from her husband; they are optional; he can give her either twenty shillings to keep house with, or he can give her only ten. If she complains, he can damn and swear, and say, like the Duke of Newcastle, 'Have I not a right to do as I please with my own?'[98]

Furthermore, it was 'high treason' for a woman to resist such authority and claim a fair reward for her work.

During the second half of the nineteenth century, the campaign by the male-dominated trade union movement for the withdrawal of married women from paid work outside the home, and for a family wage that would enable them to keep a wife within it, reinforced a wife's material dependency upon her spouse. As Mr Broadhurst proclaimed at the Trades' Union Congress held in Leicester in 1877, male trade unionists felt it was their duty as men and husbands to bring about a condition of things where their wives should be in their proper sphere at home, seeing after their house and family, instead of being dragged into the competition among the great and strong men of the world.[99]

The subordinate status of the wife may also have meant that she could not freely decide what to do with her time and that she had little money to call her own.[100] In particular, a working-class husband may have disliked his wife 'going out' in the evenings. Many examples can be found of this. A tailor in the 1830s suggests that the only way to make a home life attractive for a man was for him to have his wife's company in the evening, after his day's labour. If a wife 'goes out to spout', to attend and speak at meetings, this will drive a husband to the pub. 'In my opinion', he continued, 'none but lazy, gossiping, drunken wives will wish to go to meetings'.[101] Similarly, William Lovett, an artisan and Chartist, claimed that the 'chief duty' of the female homemaker was to gratify the mind and console the heart of man.[102] Not all working-class women of course agreed with these views. One woman, nearly 60 years old, angrily recounted how wives who disagreed with their husbands could experience verbal and physical violence:

she must be insulted with all the diabolical language that man can utter. What a bitter mixture for a poor woman to take! and if she offers the least resistance, it is thrust down her throat with his fist, possibly with the loss of a tooth or the spilling of a little of that blood which he thinks so inferior to his own. As he is lord of his castle, he is master and will be obeyed.[103]

What this woman wanted was for the female sex to be co-equal with man, not in slavery to the passions of either body or mind.

To what extent such attitudes spilled over into a wife's wish to be educated is difficult to determine. But we do find a number of accounts recording the opposition of working-class husbands to attempts by their wives to acquire an education, however basic. One working-class woman who entered adult school in Bath in the first decade of the nineteenth century was threatened by her husband, a sailor, that if she continued to attend he would 'break her bones'.[104] A journalist writing for the radical press in the 1830s wryly commented that the autodidacticism so important in the lives of radical working men was deemed to have little relevance for their womenfolk:

most working men now feel to read a newspaper is a want as urgent as the desire for food ... yet few of them take any trouble to create in their wives this taste for reading.[105]

One working-class wife and mother put the matter in a nutshell, 'Men, in general', she bitterly complained, 'tremble at the idea of a reading wife'.[106]

Some 50 years later, Mrs Layton found that her husband was not entirely happy with her active involvement in various educational classes and activities held by the Women's Co-operative Guild, established in 1883. The guild, he said, was making women think too much of themselves, especially when his own wife asserted her right to have the house in her name. Mrs Layton disagreed. The guild made women think more of themselves than ever before:

It is impossible to say how much I owe to the Guild. It gave me education and recreation. The lectures I heard gave me so much food for thought that I seldom felt dull, and I always had something to talk to my husband about other than the little occurrences of daily life.[107]

Above all else, the guild made her change from a shy nervous woman into 'a fighter'.[108] Another husband within the co-operative movement is reported as saying, 'My wife? What does she want with meetings? Let her stay at home and wash my moleskin trousers!'[109]

For many working-class men throughout the nineteenth century, then, a wife's place was in the home. A working-class wife seeking to enter a mechanics' institute or working men's college might therefore have to contend not only with the poor material conditions of her social class location, but also with the non-supportive attitudes of her spouse. And it was not just married women who might experience patriarchal control. A father or brother might make assumptions about the subordinate status of a single woman within the family structure and similarly discourage her from involvement in adult education. Also, as we saw earlier, a single woman might experience various forms of family control through expectations about her 'duties' in regard to domestic chores and especially the care of parents and siblings.

Conclusion

This survey of working-class women's lives in the nineteenth century has revealed a picture of daily misery, poverty and exploitation. Working-class women tended to be concentrated in particular kinds of employment that was poorly paid, and involved long hours of work and was seen as unskilled. Single working-class women who theoretically were more mobile than married women – without dependents, owning their own income – had access to a different range of occupations than married working-class women. Single women might, for example, become domestic servants, milliners, dressmakers, factory workers and school-teachers. Married working-class women, especially those with young children, were to be found mainly in agricultural work or home-based, lowly paid, unskilled, overstocked, casual work (such as taking in washing, taking in lodgers and sewing) that could be integrated into the daily demands of domestic duties. In addition, both single and married women might find that they had a subordinate status within the family structure – especially a married woman, since she was economically dependent upon the main breadwinner, her husband.

These patterns of life had profound implications for any involvement by working-class women in adult education. As we have seen, single, and especially married, working-class women would have had a struggle against the material poverty of their lives in order to save enough money for any education. Considerable energy and determination would be needed in order to become an adult student. Single women and married women might also find that their efforts to improve themselves were not supported by fathers and husbands, respectively. As many accounts in this chapter reveal, working-class women were aware of these struggles; they worried about poverty, hardship, the upbringing of children, the future. For many, education would have been an escape route.

If so, what might working-class women have sought through education? Did they want vocational skills to improve their occupational prospects, or literacy skills that might remove any stigma attached to being illiterate, or general education that might 'refresh' the mind? How did such goals relate to the aims of those who provided the education – why did they want to educate working-class women?

As noted in the Introduction, the providers of adult education were influenced by the ideological debates about women's place in society, and upheld certain ideals of womanhood and of family life. But how far did these ideals recognize the realities of working-class women's lives?

3

IDEOLOGIES ABOUT WOMEN'S PLACE

Introduction

If an account of the material conditions of working-class women's lives is necessary for any analysis of their involvement in adult education, so too is consideration of the various ideologies about 'women's place' in nineteenth-century society, since these ideologies affected the shape of that educational provision in two main ways. First, they constructed images of women as women and as students, and secondly, they also helped to shape what was considered an 'appropriate' curriculum for women. Ideologies about 'women's place' were influential, then, in determining the range of women's educational experiences and the levels of educational skills that they might be taught.

Within the debates surrounding educational provision we find views expressed about working-class women which were often idealized images of what they should be rather than a description of the daily reality of their lives as illustrated in the last chapter. What also becomes clear is that ideological constructions of women's role in the nineteenth century were not independent of broader social class ideologies and, as class ideologies, were subjected to change over the course of the century. Thus particular definitions of gender, of masculinity and femininity, were historically specific constructions, varying within and between social classes. What is striking is that, despite such class diversity in the ideological assumptions made about women, masculinity was always judged to be the superior gender form, and men the dominant sex.

This relationship between gender and class will be one of the themes of this chapter. I shall concentrate predominantly upon ideas developed by the middle classes, since these interpretations became, in effect, the dominant ideological constructions about women during this period.[1] Also, evidence suggests that it was the 'philanthropic' and industrial sections of the middle classes that were most active in education movements,[2] and particularly in schemes to establish mechanics' institutes and working men's colleges; their ideological assumptions were therefore to affect the form and content of educational provision for the working classes.

In this chapter, I shall focus upon two main constructions which I shall call 'patriarchal' and 'family' ideologies. These two sets of ideologies are both prescriptive and normative: 'patriarchal' ideologies relate to a specific construction of relations between the sexes, while 'family' ideologies relate to specific family forms and structures. Both sets of ideologies appear to have been well-suited to the sexual division of labour within the middle classes, especially towards the end of the nineteenth century.

As we shall see, the middle classes came to identify femininity with domesticity for all women. However, they differentiated between women in different social classes by upholding class-specific ideals of femininity. Thus what was considered appropriate, relevant and attainable for their own womenfolk was often considered inappropriate, irrelevant and unattainable for working-class women.

Patriarchal ideologies and women's place

Within middle-class patriarchal ideologies, male dominance over women was clearly emphasized[3] and justified on a number of grounds: ideas were put forward about how men and women should relate to each other in regard to a whole range of biological-scientific, economic, socio-legal and political relationships. The most fundamental justification for male dominance, one could argue, was that which referred to the biological-scientific domain. Here women's physical and mental inferiority, in comparison with men's, was emphasized and scientific evidence sought in studies of the body and the brain. This 'scientific' justification gave credibility to other 'social' aspects of male–female relations and social commentators apparently accepted these ideas without being sceptical of the evidence.

Thus in 1842, Mrs Ellis, a social commentator and prolific writer on women's place in society, recommended in a highly popular book that the daughters of England should be content to be inferior in mental power to men in the same way that they were inferior in bodily strength.[4] The following year another social commentator proclaimed that, since the head and brain sizes of women were, on average, much smaller than those of men, women's reasoning power was smaller too.[5] The publication of Charles Darwin's *The Origin of Species* in 1859 and especially *The Descent of Man* in 1871 boosted such ideas. In particular, in the latter, Darwin claimed that through natural selection man had become superior to woman in intellect, inventive genius, courage and energy; even those faculties in which women excelled, such as intuition, perception and imitation, were signs of inferiority, characteristic of the lower races, and therefore of a past and lower state of civilization.[6] These books, which offered an evolutionary model for the differences between the sexes, were widely discussed by scientists, anatomists, anthropologists and social commentators. Detailed studies made of the brains of men and women led many to believe that the smaller skull (and, therefore, smaller brain) of women, was indicative of less intelligence, just as a child was considered less intelligent than an adult.[7] In the words of the Darwinian psychiatrist Dr Henry Maudsley, there was 'sex in mind as distinctly as there is sex in body'.[8]

For some, such as Herbert Spencer, the development of women's mental capacities could only have been made at the expense of her reproductive capacity: 'excessive study', he went on to argue, would make girls into 'pale, angular, flat-chested young ladies' who would presumably be unfit to breast-feed any future babies.[9] James Fitzjames Stephen, a QC summed up some of these arguments in 1873 when he asserted:

The physical differences between the two sexes affect every part of the human body, from the hair of the head to the soles of the feet, from the size and density of the bones to the texture of the brain and the character of the nervous system. Ingenious people may argue about anything ... but all the talk in the world will never shake the proposition that men are stronger than women in every shape. They have greater muscular and nervous force, greater intellectual force, greater vigour of character.[10]

The view that women were biologically inferior to men, and that this proposition could be supported by scientific 'proof', provided the rationale for a number of assumptions about the relationships between the sexes. This can be seen, for example, in another important strand within patriarchal ideologies relating, in particular, to socio-legal relationships between men and women.

In social relationships between men and women, the concept of 'woman' was constructed 'in relation to' man – women were defined as daughters, sisters, wives or mothers, rather than as independent and autonomous beings. Closely linked to this idea was the notion of woman as man's 'property', a being who is disposable and may be transferred to another 'owner'. A daughter was a father's property and transferred, in a marriage ceremony, to a husband; when a wife, a woman became a husband's property. Even when not within legal relationships of marriage, common-law wives have been seen as 'owned' by their menfolk.

The 'relative' position of woman in her relations with men was constantly reiterated by a diversity of middle-class commentators throughout the nineteenth century. That popular writer Mrs Ellis reminded the women of England that they were 'from their own constitution, and from the station they occupy in the world, strictly speaking, relative creatures'. John Ruskin, an influential writer, artist and art critic who became a teacher in the London Working Men's College in its early days, emphasized that woman was made to be the helpmate of man, a view echoed by Charlotte Yonge in her highly successful book *Womankind*.[11] Professor Leitner claimed in 1874 that it was the proper sphere of woman to 'excel' as a daughter, sister, wife and mother, while Dr Withers Moore, in his presidential address to the British Medical Association in 1886, asserted that women were made and meant to be 'mothers of men'.[12]

When a woman married, she was frequently assumed to have become an extension of her husband rather than an individual in her own right, and this assumption was reinforced within the law. Indeed one writer commented in 1851 that a married woman

has no legal rights. She is not supposed to exist as a citizen. Her personality is merged in that of man. She is always a minor, never reaching majority. She still takes rank, in the eye of the law, among man's goods and chattels, and is classified with 'his ox and his ass'. The law defines her, in a state of marriage, as belonging to and the property of man.[13]

Though certain changes in family law in the second half of the century improved the legal position of married women[14], the assumption that women had no independent status remained a pervasive element of middle-class beliefs.

A third strand of patriarchal ideologies, and one which grew out of the legal definitions of property ownership, related to economic relationships. The key assumption was that women should be economically dependent upon men. As Bessie Rayner Parkes pointed out in 1865, it was commonly believed that a woman had to rely upon her father, brother or husband for her livelihood.[15] Single middle-class women, for example, might live at home and be financially supported by their parents, while the married middle-class women, like all married women, would find that before the Married Women's Property Act of 1882 any income and property she possessed was transferred to her husband on marriage.[16] Although the notion of female economic dependency might have been a luxury, it had much less meaning, as we saw in the last chapter, among the working classes in the nineteenth century, especially among the poorest sections. The middle classes tended to assume, however, that married working-class women could and indeed should live on a man's earning. Single working-class women, on the other hand, could be expected to work for their living.

Woman's dependent status upon a man might be constructed as emotional as well as economic – a woman was often defined as someone unable to act and make decision on her own. Men, particularly fathers and husbands, could be ascribed the role of deciding 'for her own good' such issues as the appropriate form of education, occupation, maternity conditions and childcare. From this ideological standpoint, men, expecting the women in their lives to be indecisive, helpless and immature, might even have felt the necessity to make the smallest daily decisions for their womenfolk, the 'weaker' sex.

Statements about the economic and emotional dependency of women frequently appeared in the writings of middle-class commentators. Margaret Murray remembers that her father, a managing partner in a firm of merchants, was a 'true' Victorian gentleman in that he believed a lady should live on an adequate income supplied by father, husband or son. Articles in *The Saturday Review*, a conservative newspaper aimed at a middle-class readership, argued that the only 'bond and stay' of domestic life was the consciousness that it was 'the husband's pride and duty' to support his wife; furthermore, the very measure of civilization itself was the extent to which women were relieved from the 'necessity' of self-support.[17] Also, considerable attention was given to the emotional and social dependence of women. Mrs Ellis, for example, told young women that in 'woman's love is mingled the trusting dependence of a child, for she ever looks up to man as her protector, and her guide'. An anonymous writer in *Household Words*, a popular journal edited by Charles Dickens, spoke of the 'instinct' of protection in man and the 'instinct' of dependence in woman,[18] while Mrs Sandford epitomized the idea of the dependent woman, leaning on man, when she told her many readers:

There is, indeed, something unfeminine in independence. It is contrary to nature, and therefore it offends. We do not like to see a woman affecting tremors, but still less do we like to see her acting the Amazon. A really sensible woman feels her dependence ... she is conscious of inferiority, and therefore grateful for support. She knows she is the weaker vessel.[19]

Finally, a wide spectrum of middle-class commentators gave support to another related component of patriarchal ideologies – that of women's subordination to men. The consequences of women's inferiority, their legal, economic and social dependence on men, were to be found in the ideal of female subordination. Within this ideal, the personal politics of male–female relations were defined as male domination; men were seen as responsible for the holding and exercising of power.

One of the popular female writers on woman's sphere in the 1830s announced that female exertions should always be strictly subordinate, that women should never 'act the dictator' and that obedience was but a very small part of conjugal duty.[20] Others warned that to discourage subordination in women was probably the shortest method of 'barbarizing' the race[21] or ending marriage; Professor Marshall of Cambridge, for example, told a disbelieving Beatrice Webb (then Miss Potter) in the 1880s:

woman was a subordinate being ... if she ceased to be subordinate, there would be no object for a man to marry ... marriage was a sacrifice of masculine freedom, and would only be tolerated by male creatures so long as it meant the devotion, body and soul, of the female to the male.[22]

If insubordination in women threatened the foundations of civilized society and the popularity of marriage with men, it could also threaten the traditional orthodoxy of the church. The Rev John William Burgon, Dean of Chichester, who agreed in 1876 to become patron of the Chichester Literary Society and Mechanics' Institute,[23] preached a sermon eight years later, at the University of Oxford, where he felt it was necessary to remind his congregation of the sayings of St Paul:

'Let the women learn in silence with all subjection'. 'I suffer not a woman to teach, nor to usurp authority over the man, but to be in silence' ... St Paul's ... persistent requirement of subordination, submission, obedience, no-one can forget.[24]

It is little wonder that the feminist Maria Grey, who became actively involved in one of the colleges within the working men's college movement, claimed in 1879 that, as a sex, women had always been, and still were, completely subordinate to the masculine gender.[25]

Middle-class patriarchal ideologies in the nineteenth century, then, involved a number of themes – emphasizing both male superiority and dominance over women and ascribing to these relationships a biological naturalness. Contained in the rhetoric also were suggestions that to challenge such a social order would involve challenging the status quo at dangerous levels. The future of the race, of marriage and civilization itself were often represented as the reasons for such sexual relations; rarely were these relationships discussed as ideals pertaining to particular social groupings. The collapse of descriptive and prescriptive statements removed the need for such debate.

Family Ideologies and Women's Place

The constellation of arguments that helped to construct patriarchal ideologies about sex roles in Victorian society were intertwined, and yet also came into conflict, with another set of nineteenth-century beliefs that I shall call family ideologies. Family ideologies related to women's position *vis-à-vis* the home and family and embodied a number of assumptions. It was commonly believed that family life and paid work should be separated, and that women should be located within the private sphere of the home, ideally as full-time wives and mothers. The context of such images, where women were seen as the cornerstone of family life, was that of monogamous marriage, which was upheld as the ideal family form. I shall examine each of these features in turn, and consider not merely their normative aspects but also the ways in which they contradicted assumptions made about male–female relationships as described above.

As we saw in Chapter 2, the development of industrial capitalism created a 'separation' between family life and paid work for the more affluent sections of society. The belief in such a separation, even if it did not always occur in practice, with women being identified with the home and family and men with paid work and economic power, was the central tenet of family ideologies for the middle classes. Davidoff and Hall have shown how evangelical writers such as William Cowper, Hannah More and Thomas Gisborne in the period 1780–1820 were influential in spreading such ideas.[26] Gisborne, for example, pointed out that, while men could be found in a range of professions and employments, female excellence was best displayed in domestic life.[27] Such a theme was increasingly reiterated by a range of people. The French sociologist Comte asserted in 1848 that women's life is essentially domestic, public life being confined to men, while his follower Frederic Harrison, who, like Ruskin, became a teacher at the London Working Men's College, claimed in 1908 that the sphere in which women 'act at their highest' is the family, while the equivalent peak for men was to be found in public life, industry and the service of the state.[28] However, the statement *par excellence* of the notion of separate spheres for the sexes was made by Ruskin himself in his widely acclaimed *Sesame and Lilies*, first published in 1865. For Ruskin, women's true place was in the shelter of home while men battled in the hard world outside:

The man, in his rough work in the open world, must encounter all peril and trial ... often he must be wounded, or subdued, often misled, and 'always' hardened. But he guards the woman from all this; within his home, as ruled by her, unless she herself has sought it, need enter no danger, no temptation, no cause of error or offence. This is the true nature of home – it is the place of Peace; the shelter, not only from all injury, but from all terror, doubt and division.[29]

This idealization of the home and of women's place within it was linked to the prescription that all women should be wives and mothers, often seen as natural functions, a necessary consequence of their biological capacity to bear children. Walker claimed in 1840 that the natural pursuits of women were procreation, gestation, delivery, nursing, care of children, cooking and clothing; W. R. Greg spoke in 1862 of the 'natural duties and labours' of wives and mothers,[30] while that prolific and popular writer Samuel Smiles, who lectured on 'Self help in man' at Leeds Mechanics' Institute in 1852,[31] an event that some of the female members would undoubtedly have attended, pointed out in 1871 that the

respective social functions and duties of men and women are clearly defined by nature. God created man 'and' woman, each to do their proper work.[32]

In sum, marriage, wifehood, motherhood and the management of a home were seen as a woman's vocation or profession. As one writer in *The Saturday Review* eloquently pronounced in 1858, 'the end of a woman's life is the married state.[33]

As wives and mothers, women were also seen as the pivot of family existence, the persons upon whom the quality of family life depended. It was upon woman's shoulders that responsibility lay for providing a well-organized, stable, supportive environment for husband and children. In her attempt to make the home into 'a bright, serene, restful, joyful nook of heaven',[34] it was frequently emphasized that the wife and mother should be self-sacrificing, putting a husband's needs before her own. Mrs Ellis, probably the best-known idealogue of domesticity in the 1840s,[35] advised the wives of England to make 'self, and selfish gratification, subservient to a husband's tastes and enjoyments in all the little items of domestic arrangement'. Similarly, a widow counselled a newly married wife that whenever discord or coldness occurred between herself and her spouse she should remember that 'concession is your duty rather than his'.[36]

Seemingly in contrast to these views, but perhaps giving further support to them, it was also believed by some that women were superior to men in certain respects. In 1865, one writer claimed:

there are certain mental powers with which man has been gifted far more highly than woman. The reasoning faculties are more perfect in him than they are in her. The creative powers belong almost exclusively to him .... But if woman is inferior to man in these gifts, she is as decidedly superior to him in delicacy of perception, subtlety of wit, aesthetic taste, intensity of feeling, depth of religious devotion.[37]

As we can see from this statement, any arguments advanced about 'superior' qualities that women might possess could be very complex. In this case, it seems that a fine line was drawn between qualities men and women were assumed to have and in which they were supposed to excel. For women, qualities that were supposed to make them superior are precisely those attributes which would have made them particularly suited for supportive, nurturing roles as wives and mothers.

Evidence for woman's superiority over man was found especially in relation to her alleged moral influence. She was idealized as an 'angel' by Coventry Patmore and Alfred Tennyson, the Virgin Mary by Mrs Ellis and a 'madonna' by Ruskin.[38] This moral power was closely tied to women's domestic location which, in the view of some, made them generally responsible for the social condition of society. Sarah Lewis, in her widely read *Woman's Mission*, which was first published in 1839 and had gone through 13 editions by 1849, went so far as to suggest that Christian women, especially wives and mothers, could be the main agents in regenerating mankind:

God has pointed out whom he intends for his missionaries upon earth.... Let men enjoy in peace and triumph, the intellectual kingdom which is theirs, and which, doubtless, was intended for them.... The moral world is ours, – ours by position; ours by qualification; ours by the very indication of God himself.[39]

By the second half of the nineteenth century, as Banks has noted, this ideal of female superiority appears to have gained widespread acceptance.[40] Yet this emphasis upon women's moral superiority appeared to conflict with the assumption discussed earlier, that women were inferior to men, a contradiction I shall take up later.

Finally, monogamous marriage rather than a non-legal union was regarded as the ideal family form within middle-class family ideology. Such a form, of course, was sanctioned by the Church. Engels, in 1884, linked the root of this belief to the development of the private ownership of property, arguing that since men wished to have their property inherited by their biological sons this necessitated providing some guarantees that such children were truly theirs and not the offspring of another man; thus sexual fidelity, particularly of women, within monogamous marriage became valued as a means whereby property could be passed on through a male line.[41] Although Engels's analysis has been challenged,[42] it has provided an interesting account into why such value has been placed on monogamous marriage by the propertied middle classes.

The growth of industrial capitalism led to the creation of a propertyless mass of workers who had little to sell but their own labour in order to make a living. Monogamous marriage therefore would seem to have far less economic relevance for this 'new' working class, who owned little property and had little need to concern itself with inheritance. Despite this, legal marriages became increasingly popular among the working classes, especially during the second half of the nineteenth century.[43] Why this should have been so is a matter of debate. Some socialist feminists[44] suggest that ideological pressures were exerted by the middle classes on those in the 'lower' orders to adopt legal rather than common-law marriages. Such pressures are interpreted as part of employers' control over employees – arguably, a married man might have worked harder and become more reliable than a single man, since he would have had to support not only himself but also a growing and dependent family. Also the state and not just employers supported and pressurized individuals into adopting legal marriages through various policies such as poor law provision.[45]

Contradictions and resolutions

A number of conflicts surrounding women's position were created by these patriarchal and family ideologies, since these ideologies were not simple statements but involved many contradictory assumptions and suggestions. As noted earlier, patriarchal ideologies embodied the assumptions that women should be 'inferior' and 'subordinate' to men, while family ideologies stressed, among other things, that women were morally 'superior'. Some nineteenth-century writers were aware of such contradictions and pointed out that a woman's strength lies in her weakness, a tension which an angry writer to *The Englishwoman's Review* in 1869 called 'absurd and mischievous paradox.[46]

A number of attempts were made by various individuals and groups to challenge such ideologies about women's place and to resolve the contradictions inherent in them. Sometimes these view were associated with various political movements, such as Owenism,[47] and especially with the organized women's movement, which gathered momentum from the 1860s. At other times the view challenging the dominant middle-class ideas about woman's role in society were relatively isolated, individual statements.

One of the best-known early challenges had come from Mary Wollstonecraft, daughter of a failed gentleman-farmer. She married William Godwin, a writer and philosopher, and in the *Vindication of the Rights of Woman*, which first appeared in 1792, she asserted that 'the grand end' for women should be 'to unfold their own faculties' rather than merely to fulfil their duties as 'daughters, wives and mothers'.[48] This plea for the right of woman to have an existence of her own, not necessarily independent of marriage, was consistently voiced throughout the nineteenth century and was often couched in terms of a demand for an equal relationship between men and women. William Thompson, a member of the Irish land-owning class who became converted to Owenism in the 1820s, proclaimed in his well-known *Appeal* of 1825 that the home was the eternal prison-house of the wife, who was nothing more than a slave to her husband: he encouraged women to press for 'equal rights', a condition he believed could be achieved only under a new form of society, the system of 'Association, or of Labour by Mutual Co-operation'. Marion Reid's *A Plea for Woman*, in 1843, not only asserted that social equality with men was necessary for the free growth and development of woman's nature but also highlighted the lack of any substantial secondary and higher education for women: 'The grand plea for woman sharing with man all the advantages of education is', she confidently wrote, 'that every rational being is worthy of cultivation, for his or her own individual sake'.[49]

In 1869 the well-known philosopher and politician John Stuart Mill, undoubtedly influenced by the feminist views of his wife Harriet Taylor, who had died one year earlier,[50] argued for the right of women to exist as autonomous beings, stating that the legal subordination of women was 'wrong in itself' and one of the chief hindrances to human improvement.[51] The first feminist journal in Britain, the *Englishwoman's Journal*, founded in 1858, proclaimed in that year that the first duty of women was to themselves, a theme common in the women's movement.[52] Frances Power Cobbe, a writer and active campaigner for women's rights, and also a lecturer at one of the colleges within the working men's college movement, frequently spoke on such an issue. In a lecture given in 1880, she told her female audience:

Laugh at the doctrine that you are a sort of moon, with no *raison d'être* but to go circling round and round a very earthy planet; or a kind of parasite, - ivy, or honeysuckle in the forest. You *may* be, - you probably *are* less strong, less clever, less rich, and less well-educated than most of the men about you. But moral rank does not depend on these things. You are a rational free agent, a child of God, destined to grow nearer to Him and more like Him through the ages of your immortality. As such you are the equal ... with the loftiest of created beings, not one of whom can have a higher destiny.[53]

The issues raised by such individuals were radical, even revolutionary in tone. However, despite this strong minority tradition within the middle classes questioning the way women were defined, and despite the fact that women had won certain legal and social gains by the 1880s, Emma Woodward could still claim in 1885, in an imaginary conversation on *The Woman Question*, that the bulk of writings about the female sex treated her as an appendix to man:

'It has often struck me', said Mr Silverton, 'in looking into articles professedly treating of woman's sphere, how extraordinarily common is the assumption that she was meant to be a mere appendix to man; that collectively, if not individually, he is to be her master, legislator, judge, the unerring and all-powerful Zeus who is the arbiter of her destiny, as if she had no soul, character, or conscience of her own'.[54]

Other attempts to resolve the conflicts within middle-class ideologies about woman's place involved a range of arguments, some of which we have already considered. The inferior/superior dilemma, for example, was often resolved by locating 'inferiority' within the biological/political/ economic domains and 'superiority' in the moral sphere. A woman, as the teacher of morals to a husband and children, might be seen as the conscience of a family, the guardian of law and order whose moral superiority lies in serving others within the limited, private, intimate world of home.[55] There appears to have been little discussion about the conflicts these ideals of subordination and moral superiority would cause in real life.

Other writers resolved the contradictions by arguing that women were equal but different to men or that men were 'more equal' than women. Dr John Thorburn, in a lecture on female education in 1884, remarked:

All the old-fashioned notions of women's brains being in some way inferior to men's are, I am convinced, utterly wrong. My experience shows me that they are equal if not often superior, but that this power is at present being frittered away by foolish attempts to ignore the physiological differences which exist between the two sexes.[56]

Female university students, he claimed, unlike most male students, experienced tiredness and stupidity when engaged in continuous academic study. Samuel Smiles offered, too, a variation on the equal but different theme: education and culture would prove 'equality' wholesome to man and woman, but woman should be educated for 'others' than herself.[57]

Overall, one gains the impression that the attempts to resolve the contradictions within middle-class ideologies about woman's place in nineteenth-century England involved some manipulation of the basic assumptions that women are 'inferior', 'relative' and 'subordinate' to men. Any attempt to challenge the view that women were economically 'dependent' on men appears to have been much rarer: man is usually presented as the main economic provider who supports and protects woman.

One possible interpretation of these ideological assumptions leads to the conclusion that they represented an attempt at the 'domestication' of women, where women would be confined to the home *and* colonized for men's interests. However, as Arnot reminds us, the power of dominant interests has never been total or secure but will have been continually struggled for, won and maintained. Women must have offered unconsciously or consciously their 'consent' to their subordination before male power could be secured. The host of statements about the proper sphere for women in Victorian society may have been used as a means of encouraging women 'freely' to choose their inferior status and to accept their exploitation as natural.[58]

Explanations for such statements may be found in the economic, social and political framework of nineteenth-century society. Changes in the economic structure, especially the development of an industrial, commercial and factory system, increasingly affected a separation between homeplace and workplace for middle-class men by the second half of the century. This had helped to create, for the middle classes in particular, a division between production and consumption, between work and non-work, between public and private spheres. As Eisenstein has noted, the consequences were such that Victorian patriarchal ideology did not recognize domestic labour as work: woman was seen as a non-working housewife.[59] Yet the home-based housewife assumed a new ideological and cultural importance as she provided a stable environment that could offer support to men in their tasks in the public sphere. Within middle-class culture, therefore, femininity became synonymous with domesticity and masculinity with the work of paid work outside the home. However, the assumed cultural and moral power of women as wives and mothers created a basic contradiction for women in a society where economic production had primary status and men held economic, political and ideological power. What is not generally recognized, however, is the extent to which there were class-specific ideals of femininity; it is, therefore, to the class context that I shall now turn.

Class-specific ideals of femininity

Middle-class ideologies about woman's place can also be understood as part of broader social class ideologies. While the identification of femininity with domesticity was something the middle classes believed in for all women, the extent to which they differentiated between ideologies of femininity when applying them to women of the working classes is often not recognized. Contained within patriarchal and family ideologies were class-specific ideals of womanhood where the 'ideals' referred not to descriptions of real women, but to normative constructs against which women of different social classes could be judged. The ideals of femininity upheld by the middle classes for their own womenfolk contrasted in several critical respects to the ideals of femininity upheld for women in the 'lower' social orders. In particular, the ideals upheld for working-class women in various educational programmes offered by the middle classes were intended, or so it was hoped, to support the status quo: working-class girls and women were not to be educated for social mobility, nor to aspire to the leisured lifestyle of middle-class women. It is therefore necessary to discuss the concepts of femininity thought appropriate for middle-class and working-class women, since, in effect, the former helped to shape the latter.

'Young ladies' and 'Ladies'

The feminine ideals usually considered appropriate for middle-class girls and women were, respectively, the *young lady* and the *lady*. A 'young lady' did not engage in paid work but was assumed to be economically dependent upon her father or some other male relative. Since 'winning a husband' was a central goal of her life, her education emphasized those accomplishments which would make her attractive to a future spouse and the future ideal state of full-time wife and mother. The rituals of courtship among the middle classes[60] meant that there was much to be learnt and that one had to 'work at' acquiring a spouse. Often, therefore, a middle-class girl would be sent to a private, single-sex finishing school where she was drilled in a complex ritual of etiquette and decorum.

As Maria Grey complained in 1871, middle-class girls were not educated to be wives and mothers but to get husbands.[61] Confined within the home, where her sphere was the drawing room, carefully chaperoned,[62] the middle-class girl was someone whose life might revolve around the 'faddling twaddling and the endless tweedling of nosegays in jugs'.[63] One writer in 1868 described 'the real English lady' as being a

mixture of purity and refinement, gentleness, tenderness, and elegance ... [who might] faint at the sight of blood ... scream at a spider ... be unable to bear noise or exertion, to ride except at a gentle canter, or to dance anything quicker than a quadrille, while a minuet was more in accordance with dignity.[64]

Consequently, middle-class girls are variously described as 'agreeable toys', 'young ladies who flutter at watering places' and 'sideboard ornaments'.[65]

Over the course of the century, such an ideal of femininity changed. By 1851, various economic pressures were pushing many more young middle-class women into the labour market. There were fewer single men than single women, and consequently not enough future husbands. Incomes in many middle-class families were squeezed as living standards rose, together with family size. In addition, many middle-class men postponed the age of marriage until they were earning enough to support a wife.[66] Even so, some aspects of the concept of a 'young lady', e.g. certain manners and style of speech, were still upheld by the end of the century, even in employment. In 1880, for example, the United Telephone Company decided to employ a few 'young ladies' in their switch rooms.[67] Mrs Peel remembers that as a 16-year-old middle-class girl in the 1880s, her paid employment as a writer of articles for a paper called *Woman* surprised her parents – but 'the money was very useful and even nice girls were now beginning to go about by themselves and to be independent'.[68]

The experience of being 'young ladies' was designed to prepare young women in the middle classes to become 'ladies'. Contained in this adult version were three identifiable characteristics. First, a lady might be the manager of a household, although she would not engage in routine, manual chores – such tasks were undertaken by servants. As Mrs Ellis outlined in 1843:

It can never be said that the atmosphere of the kitchen is an element in which a refined and intellectual woman ought to live; though the department itself is one which no sensible woman would think it a degradation to overlook. But instead of maintaining a general oversight and arrangement of such affairs, some well-intentioned women plunge head, heart, and hand, into the vortex of culinary operations, thinking, feeling, and doing what would be more appropriately left to their servants.[69]

Secondly, although a lady might engage in unpaid, philanthropic work, she did not undertake paid labour. To work for her livelihood was considered a 'misfortune' and 'ungenteel':[70] indeed, by such action she became a 'tradeswoman', looked down upon by friends and relatives as the 'poor relation'[71] who had to provide for herself. Thirdly, being a lady involved following a well-established ritual of etiquette that a woman had learnt in her youth. Thus there were certain unwritten rules in regard to such forms of social interaction as introductions and visiting.

The idea of the 'lady' underwent a number of transformations during the Victorian age. During the first half of the nineteenth century, the model was of the 'perfect wife and mother' providing a well-organized, supportive environment for her husband and children – even if precept did not always match practice.[72] The 'perfect wife and mother' was both a lady and a housewife, undertaking certain domestic tasks such as childbearing. The first duty which apparently nature pointed out to a mother was to be herself 'the nurse of her infant', argued a widow, a sentiment echoed by Mrs Sandford.[73] 'No-one can understand so well the wants of a child as a mother ... therefore, to no-one but a mother, under ordinary circumstances, should the entire charge of a child be committed', argued another writer.[74] As an important moral influence within the home, the 'perfect wife and mother' was expected to be active in child-rearing, though not necessarily to be involved in manual domestic work. How much she did of the latter would depend upon the status and level of income of the family.

Increasingly throughout the century, however, manual labour within the middle-class household was undertaken by a cheap and plentiful supply of servants recruited from the working classes.[75] Such a situation provided the possibility of a new ideal, the 'perfect lady' who was the mistress of a household employing an array of servants. As the 'commander of an army',[76] she led a leisured lifestyle and engaged in an extensive round of social activity, such as visiting and acting as hostess to her husband's guests. Above all else she was economically dependent upon her husband, who supported her elegant and expensive lifestyle. As Havelock Ellis was to point out in 1896, such an apparently 'useless' existence, the outward symbol of the worldly success of the economically active man, could involve both subordination and contempt within the marriage relationship:

In some sense the 'lady' of the period which is just beginning to pass away is the most characteristic product of Commercialism. The sense of Private Property ... turned Woman more and more – especially of course among the possessing classes – into an emblem of possession – a mere doll, an empty idol, a brag of the man's exclusive right in the sex – till at least, as her vain splendours increased and her usefulness diminished, she ultimated into the *'perfect lady'*. But let every woman who piques and preens herself to that fulfilment of this ideal in her own person, remember what is the cost and what is the meaning of her quest: the covert enslavement to, and the covert contempt of Man.[77]

The ideal of the 'perfect lady' was most fully developed in the upper-middle class.[78] However, many families within the broad stratum of the middle classes aspired to such gentility. By the middle of the nineteenth century, no middle-class household was considered 'complete' unless it employed the basic minimum of three domestics – cook, parlourmaid and housemaid, or cook, parlourmaid and nursemaid: and the expansion of domestic service over the years 1851–71 was especially among the specialized kinds of labour rather than among general servants.[79] Lower-middle-class families, though, could probably only afford to employ the one general servant.

In the latter decades of the nineteenth century, the ideals of the 'perfect wife and mother' and 'perfect lady' were challenged by yet another definition of middle-class femininity – the 'new woman'. The 'new woman' challenged custom in many ways by engaging in a wide range of activities outside the sphere of the home; she could be found in paid work and especially in jobs that were the preserve of men (such as clerical work), seeking education, fighting for legal and political rights, challenging the subjection of women to men, even riding bicycles in 'rational' dress like knickerbockers rather than traditional skirts, and smoking.[80]

Such a threat to the traditional relationships between the sexes attracted a good deal of criticism and caricature, especially from the press. Women who sought to enter the male preserves of the universities and the professions, for example, were often lampooned as unsexed and mannish, as in the following comment in *Punch* in 1894:

> Aunt Polly's a marvel of knowledge,
> With any amount of degrees,
> She's Master or head of some college –
> I forget whether Corpus or Caius –
> Aunt Nell is the eminent counsel
> Who pleads at the criminal bar,
> And I feed the canary with groundsel
> For I'm learning to be a Papa.[81]

The dominant ideals of femininity for middle-class females, the 'perfect wife and mother' and the 'perfect lady', derived from and gave support to patriarchal relations in at least two ways. First of all, they supported the notion that women were economically and emotionally dependent upon men. Secondly, they stressed the duty of women to be subservient to and to service men, which was to men's advantage. The 'perfect wife and mother', for example, as an efficient housekeeper, an emotional support to her husband and a caring parent for her children, was of personal benefit to her spouse, while the ideal of the 'perfect lady', the symbol of conspicuous consumption, revealed to the outside world the extent of wealth and worldly success of the husband. In contrast, the advantages for women, as the feminist Frances Power Cobbe remarked in 1878, were few:

It must be borne in mind . . . in estimating a woman's chances of health, that if she neglect to think of herself, there is seldom anybody to do for her what she does for her husband. Nobody reminds her to change her boots when they are damp; nobody jogs her memory as to the unwholesomeness of this or that beverage or comestible, or gives her the little cossettings which so often ward off colds and similar petty ills. Unless the woman live with a sister or friend, it must be scored one against her chances as compared to a man, that she 'has no wife'.[82]

'Good women' of the working classes

If the feminine ideals of the middle classes were a means of maintaining male dominance within these groups, they were not insignificant for working-class women. The definitions of femininity developed by the middle classes were to affect, for example, the women who were the daughters and wives of waged labourers, female waged labourers, or domestic servants within middle-class households. For these women, the middle classes also argued that femininity should be seen as synonymous with domesticity – a relationship that women of all social classes, through the category of their common sex, held in common. But here the common bond between women weakened, since the middle classes proposed very specific ideals of femininity for working-class girls and women – ideals which differed from those they applied to their own social groupings. The effect was one of maintaining class differentiation *between* women.

The ideals of femininity for working-class women were closely related to the image which the middle classes held of 'lower class' women's lives. Such an image would rarely have been based on first-hand knowledge of the actual realities of such an existence, since middle-class people would not be encouraged to venture into poorer districts. The impressions formed would most likely have been gleaned second-hand, from a range of material, such as government reports, novels and newspapers. Although the middle classes had contact with working-class girls and women by employing them as domestic servants, these were particular contexts in which the employees appeared in clean and starched uniforms waiting at table, or wet and dirty when scrubbing the floors. Also, such contact took place within *middle-class*, not working-class, households. From such limited knowledge and limited contact with working-class people, the middle classes drew a picture of a 'typical' working-class girl or women. Selected characteristics of working-class life – poverty, squalor, poor housing conditions, lack of hygiene, intermittent patterns of work – became the characteristics of the individuals themselves. The objective conditions of the lives of working-class people became defined as the qualities of their personalities.

For the middle classes therefore, the working-class woman was someone who was vulgar, coarse, inadequate, ignorant, dirty, incompetent in domestic matters and potentially a source of moral pollution. The assumed vulgarity and coarseness (as well as the physical strength) of the working-class woman derived mainly from the fact that most working-class females were engaged in paid work, especially before marriage, but often after marriage too. As Maria Grey, who was a keen supporter of one of the colleges in the working men's college movement, complained in 1874, the 'genteel classes' saw work as the necessity of 'the vulgar'.[83] For middle-class critics, it was the working-class girls or women employed in 'public' places outside the home, such as the factory and workshop, who were regarded as the most degraded of their sex. Their presence in such places could lead, it was believed, to the worst kind of vulgarity and coarseness in women – sexual knowledge and sexual promiscuity.

This image of factory and workshop women was frequently conveyed in those novels offering portraits of working-class life. Mrs Gaskell, for example, living in industrial Manchester from 1832 until her death in 1865, included a number of working-class heroines in novels such as *Mary Barton* and *Ruth*.[84] However, the chief cause of the 'fall' or sexual weakness of women such as Mary and Ruth is their experience of the factory and workshop. Ruth, for example, an apprentice in a dressmaker's shop, refuses to marry her seducer and the father of her child. As an unmarried mother she is shunned by all, though she eventually redeems herself by working as a nurse during a cholera epidemic, and dying of typhoid. The public generally reacted favourably to the novel, though some adverse criticisms were voiced.[85] For those individuals who had little knowledge and understanding of the reality of working-class women's lives, such fictional characters helped convey an image of what working-class women were like.

Evidence for the vulgarity of the working-class woman might also be found in her apparent lack of etiquette, her poor taste in clothes and use of 'bad language'. When out visiting or shopping, for example, a working-class woman had no need to wear gloves, an item of clothing considered indispensable for a middle-class 'lady'. Hannah Cullwick, a working-class servant who secretly married in 1873 Arthur J. Munby, a barrister, faced the dilemma of what to wear if she should ever accompany her 'gentleman' husband in public. Munby records the following entry in his diary for 6 August 1874:

This morning and last night, Hannah and I had great consultation as to the results of her shopping. She had bought, to please me, a grand new lady-dress for travelling, and a veil, and gloves: and now her mind was that all this costly trumpery was unfit for a servant like her, who was content with her station and its proper costume ... chiefly she was distressed at having had to spend money on gloves and a veil. 'It's a shame of you, Messa', she said, 'to make me wear a veil or gloves, *ever*; things I've never been used to in all my life!'[86]

Employers often believed that their female domestics had a propensity to 'ape' their betters and a wish to dress 'above' their station in life.[87] But working-class women generally were assumed to have poor taste in clothes, which was taken to be indicative of their 'low' character and their tendency to be wasteful. The following middle-class woman undoubtedly voiced the thoughts of many of her class when she claimed in the 1850s that, among all girls who were taught to work for a living, one could find 'the delusive and corrupting cheapness and the preposterous style of dress, which affords every possible discouragement to neat and frugal habits of conversation and repair'.[88] Other commentators noted that working-class females might enter the beer shop or gin shop,[89] and that those women who formed themselves into clubs or associations might not only 'drink, sing and smoke', but also use 'the lowest, most brutal, and most disgusting language imaginable'.[90]

Working-class women were often believed to be 'ignorant', especially in regard to literacy skills, general knowledge and domestic skills. Although there was considerable regional variation in the extent of literacy, various government reports in the 1830s and 1840s revealed widespread illiteracy among factory workers.[91] The information in these reports gave public confirmation to the suspicion – to quote from Engels – that the English working class 'can scarcely read and still less write'.[92] But it was especially the alleged domestic ignorance of working-class girls and women that aroused most horror. In particular, the employment of young girls in factories was said to make them 'utterly ignorant and inexperienced' in household management.[93] As Engels complained:

It is self-evident that a girl who has worked in a mill from her ninth year is in no position to understand domestic work, whence it follows that female operatives prove wholly inexperienced and unfit as housekeepers. They cannot knit or sew, cook or wash, are unacquainted with the most ordinary duties of a housekeeper, and when they have young children to take care of, have not the vaguest idea how to set about it.[94]

Middle-class commentators spoke therefore of the 'slatternly habits' of working-class women, their inability to 'make and mend their own clothes',[95] their inability to make their 'husband's homes comfortable', their 'sheer ignorance' about matters of health and causes of disease in children[96] and their 'waste of hard-earned wages'.[97]

Through middle-class eyes, working-class women were also pictured as potential sources of 'moral pollution' – especially as a result of their 'deficient' habits as wives and mothers. A typical comment was that made by Mrs Austin in 1857:

It is impossible to conceive the waste and improvidence which reigns in the lowest English household. The women buy improvidently, cook improvidently, and dress improvidently. The consequences are, want, debt, disorder, and all that can make a man's home comfortless and irritating, take from him all hope of improvement in his condition, all regard for so useless a partner, and drive him to the alehouse.[98]

Thus working-class women were frequently held responsible for the moral state of their husbands and children.

The other even greater threat of moral pollution – prostitution – was, as we saw in Chapter 2, a form of employment for working-class women when all else had failed. Although the wages of working-class women might give them a certain degree of economic independence, the low pay, semi-skilled, intermittent nature of much of their work meant that destitution was an ever-present threat. When the choice was between destitution and prostitution, many women chose the latter. The public exposure in newspapers such as the *Morning Chronicle* of the wretched conditions of life for such women helped not only to emphasize the vulnerability of working-class women to sexual exploitation but also to add to the idea that they were 'impure'.[99]

Yet paradoxically, even though working-class women were regarded by the middle classes as all these things, such women were also seen as strong and healthy, physically able to undertake hard, manual toil. Arthur J. Munby, barrister and poet, on a visit to Northumberland in 1863, referred to agricultural workers as 'stout strapping' women. Elizabeth Garrett Anderson, daughter of a prosperous merchant, claimed that poor women spending all their available strength in manual work did so, as a rule, without any ill-effect to their health.[100] Other middle-class commentators, such as J. D. Milne and Dr Elizabeth Blackwell, believed that hard work in itself was conducive to good health. Indeed Dr Blackwell, a lecturer at one of the colleges within the working men's college movement, asserted that the 'far better' health of the working classes equalized 'far more than is generally supposed' the conditions between the rich and the poor: the simpler habits of the working classes, their keener enjoyment of life, their greater freedom and engrossing occupation, prevented the miserable 'fragility of the nervous system' which produced so many 'hopeless invalids' among the idle classes, where 'utter weariness of life' checked enthusiasm.[101]

Such comparisons between what Frances Power Cobbe called 'the little health of ladies'[102] and the supposed physical fitness of working-class women served, of course, to maintain the social class differences between women and to justify the relatively 'useless' activities in which ladies might participate and the relatively 'useful' tasks that working-class women might engage in. The 'health' of working-class women was often seen unsympathetically as necessary for the drudgery of hard physical work; indeed, for some (such as Munby) it had connotations of masculinity.

Overall, the image of the working-class woman, as articulated by the middle classes, was that of a degraded human being. A host of phrases were used to describe her, perhaps the most common being 'the drudge'; it was particularly the involvement of working-class women in paid work that tarnished their femininity and made them according to some 'the female mud and dregs of this land'.[103]

In view of the reverence given, within middle-class culture, to the home and the sacred place of women within it, it is not surprising that explanations of disharmony and malfunction in society were concentrated on the working-class family, and especially the wife and mother.[104] Working-class women were often blamed for a host of social problems among the working classes, such as alcoholism, crime, prostitution, spread of disease, a high infant mortality rate, poor educational effort among children and lack of worldly success. The ignorance of working-class women in domestic matters was one of the most powerful arguments used by those who opposed paid work for women. But even more significantly, it diverted attention away from the economic and social causes of 'social ills', such as poverty; solutions were found instead in trying to reform the working-class family itself rather than in economic and political programmes.

Certain inconsistencies and dilemmas also confronted the middle classes as far as working-class women were concerned. They needed and used such women as paid workers within factories, workshops and homes. The middle classes also needed working-class women as domestic servants, especially if the ideal of the middle-class 'lady' was to be made reality. The advantages of employing such 'cheap' and 'expendable' labour were, of course, many – for example, substantial profits could be made, a comfortable and leisured lifestyle upheld. But there were also long-term benefits in stressing the role of working-class women as wives and mothers. Political and economic gains lay in a scheme which guaranteed a well-kept home, cared-for children and a contented husband. The likelihood of the working classes challenging the social order might be reduced and an increased pool of healthy workers for the economy ensured.

How, then, did the middle classes resolve these dilemmas? The solution involved redefining the ideals of femininity upheld for middle-class women into forms more appropriate for their working-class sisters. Thus the dominant ideals upheld for working-class girls were those of the *good worker* and especially the *good domestic servant*, while the dominant ideal for working-class women was that of the *good wife and mother*. As we shall see in subsequent chapters, these ideals were upheld in educational programmes offered to working-class females (though other competing ideals were also to be supported).

In contrast with a middle-class girl, a working-class girl was expected to provide for herself: thus the ideal of the 'good worker' defined femininity in terms of an ability to earn a living. However, since waged labour for women was a fundamental departure from the central belief of middle-class family ideologies that a woman's place was in the home, a particular form of paid work was considered most appropriate for working-class girls – namely domestic service. The 'good domestic servant' was seen as an extension of domesticity, a form of femininity appropriate for girls of the lower orders. This emphasis upon domestic service held, of course, certain advantages for the middle classes. First of all, it meant that the waged labour of working-class girls remained hidden within that sphere most suitable for the female sex – the home. Secondly, such an emphasis might ensure a steady supply of girls who would undertake the drudgery of manual labour within the middle-class household. Thirdly, the skills acquired in domestic service would help to prepare working-class girls for any future role as wife and mother. Indeed, domestic service was seen as the one form of paid work *par excellence* that offered preparation for the future ideal fo the 'good wife and mother'.

Mr Austin claimed in 1843 that any knowledge possessed by the wife of a labourer was generally due to her having, before marriage, lived as a servant in a farmhouse or elsewhere.[105] In 1856, the Rev J. S. Brewer praised those middle-class women, who through training their female domestic servants, helped to raise the standard of housewifery among the lower orders:

The female servants in your household, whom you have taken and instructed in their respective duties – whose manners you have softened – who have learnt from you how to manage a household – who have caught up from you, insensibly, lessons of vast utility, lessons of order, lessons of economy, lessons of cleanliness, lessons of the management of children, of household comfort and tidiness; these women eventually become the wives of small tradesmen and respectable operatives ... in all the ordinary duties of a wife ... the class drawn from domestic servants have advanced as their mistresses have advanced.[106]

The outcome of such arguments was the belief that domestic servants made the best wives.[107]

The ideal of the 'good wife and mother', in contrast, was of someone who was a practical housewife, an efficient housekeeper, a helpmate to her spouse and a competent mother. Like the middle-class 'perfect wife and mother', she was engaged full-time in domesticity, but a much greater emphasis was placed upon obtaining *manual* domestic skills. Unlike her middle-class counterpart, the 'good wife and mother' would not have been able to afford an array of domestic servants and therefore she would not have harboured any pretensions to gentility – hard toil and industry were her lot in her effort to keep a well-ordered, clean home. But industry, orderliness and cleanliness were insufficient in themselves: the 'good wife and mother' would also have to possess personal qualities such as honesty, frugality, thrift, self-sacrifice. She would also have to believe in self-help and demonstrate, in the face of adversity, steadfastness and calm.

Numerous moral tales, written for working-class women, continually reiterate the importance of such personal qualities. The *Annals of the Poor*, for example, probably published by the Religious Tract Society in 1845, contains life stories 'of females in humble life who have been exemplary for their extraordinary perseverance under difficulties, their ingenious industry, and their self-sacrificing benevolence'.[108] One such woman was Nanny Wilson, who managed 'to make all ends meet amid the most trying difficulties': for four years, this 'industrious creature' laboured to support her invalid husband and two small children, yet 'never did anyone hear her utter the voice of complaint'.[109] Another collection of tales, *Household Proverbs for Women*, provided similar moral instruction. For example, 'Wilful Waste makes Woeful Want', tells the story of thrifty housewife Sara Retsam, who informs her neighbour Mrs Sparkes that the delicious soup she has just tasted

is made from bones. I get a few from the butchers, sometimes three penny-worth, and having cleaned them, I simmer them gently with a little salt and pepper, and an onion or two sliced, adding some vegetables if I happen to have them.... The meat I take from the bones when it is done, put it aside till just as the boys are coming home, when I warm it up for them with some potatoes, or put it into the soup, as they like best, and then they have a nice hot supper ready in no time. Why, if a woman did not know how to manage, she and her husband, and three or four children, might have one good hot meal every day, at the expense of from fourpence to sixpence.[110]

Quite predictably, this capable, thrifty, practical housewife has been in domestic service as a cook before her marriage, and she gives Mrs Sparkes the list of rules that make her a good manager:

Look forward.
Never buy what you do not want.
Make the most of what you do buy.
Turn everything to account.
Waste nothing.

Forethought, cleanliness, punctuality; these are my three helpers, and capital helps I find them.[111]

Above all else, such tales emphasize that the 'good wife and mother' was the cornerstone of family stability, since her success determined the 'good' behaviour of her husband – a theme explored in 'A Man is What a Woman Makes Him'. Through providing material and emotional comforts for her husband, e.g. a cheery home, clean floors, a bright fire, a hot meal, the wife could expect a good-tempered husband who was not tempted to go to the pub.[112] However, the husband who came home after his day's work to find the fire out, the room in a mess, the children crying, and his wife hurrying in 'perhaps, from a gossip with a neighbour, a-wasting the time that she ought to have been spending in getting everything right and tight for her good-man's coming home'[113] will become ill-tempered, seek the comfort of the public house and spend his wages on drink. The ideal of the 'good wife and mother', as is evident in nineteenth-century writings, therefore stressed the same basic contradiction that is found in the ideal of the middle-class 'perfect wife and mother' – namely, that a wife was subservient to her husband, serving his material and emotional needs, while at the same time exercising considerable moral power over him.

One can understand such ideals perhaps as an attempt by the middle classes to impose not just a particular concept of womanhood but also a specific family form upon working-class life – that of a wage-earning husband and an economically dependent wife. Statements such as that made by the Rev James Booth in a lecture given on 20 March 1855 at the Mechanics' Institute, Wandsworth, gives credence to this view:

Now, when we are speaking of the home of the working man, and of the influence of home and of good example set at home, we refer almost entirely to the wife or mother. The working man but seldom sees his children on weekdays. He goes to his daily work in the early morning, before his children are out of bed, and by the time he returns late from his day's labour they will have gone to skeep.[114]

Since men went out to work each day, he continued, they could exercise very little influence or control over their children. Upon the mother evolved the 'moral duties' of both parents: she is the centre of home influence, the one who sets the 'guiding example, of sobriety, thrift, industry and cleanliness', and she ought, therefore, to have a fair share of skill in household matters and sufficient knowledge to be able to answer 'the prattling questions of her little ones'.[115] As we saw in the last chapter, economic and industrial changes that began to occur around the middle of the nineteenth century helped to make possible the family form of a wage-earning husband and an economically dependent wife. The development of an industrial and commercial system also aided the 'separation' of workplace and homeplace: working-class men increasingly went outside the home to work while their wives, especially those with dependent children, were increasingly located within it.

Conclusion

Middle-class ideologies about a woman's place in nineteenth-century society became, to a large extent, the dominant ideological assumptions about the female role. Patriarchal ideologies which emphasized male dominance over women were intertwined, and yet came into conflict, with family ideologies which emphasized that women should be located within the private sphere of the home, ideally as full-time wives and mothers. A range of compromises were made by commentators in an attempt to resolve the contradictions in these gendered ideologies. Overall, it would appear that this involved some manipulation of the assumptions that women were 'inferior', 'relative' and 'subordinate' to men and, more rarely, of the view that women were 'dependent' upon men.

While the identification of femininity with domesticity was seen as common for all women, the middle classes also constructed class-specific ideals of femininity which helped to maintain social class differentiation. The dominant ideals for their own womenfolk ranged from the 'young lady' and the 'perfect lady' to the 'perfect wife and mother'. For working-class girls and women, however, the ideals were those of the 'good worker' (especially the 'good domestic servant') and the 'good wife and mother', respectively. Since the middle classes were particularly active within the mechanics' institute and working men's college movements, these ideological assumptions were to influence both the form and content of the provision offered to working-class women.

Also, middle-class involvement in elementary education for children of the 'lower' orders helped shape such provision. Working-class women had already been exposed to such ideals of working-class femininity supported by their social superiors. When young girls attended the schools organized for them by the middle classes, such experiences contributed not merely to their education but also to their self-image and to their educational needs as adults. In the next chapter, such school experiences are outlined, together with a brief account of the education offered to working-class girls by their own communities.

4

SCHOOLING AND WORKING-CLASS GIRLS

Introduction

Although material and ideological factors were relevant to working-class women's lives in the nineteenth century, perhaps of more direct significance for their involvement in mechanics' institutes and working men's colleges is the form and extent of their schooling. There would be legacies and outcomes for women from this schooling which would relate not only to skills learnt, such as reading and writing, but also to ideologies encountered about what women can and cannot do in society.

The nature of schooling for working-class girls from 1800–1870 is particularly relevant, since this was the period in which the mechanics' institute and working men's college movements were founded – the former in the 1820s, the latter in 1854. Yet discovering the educational past of working-class girls in this period is a complex task, since most historians[1] offer little original research about girls' education and tend only to provide general overviews of schooling for the 'lower' orders. In particular, there have been few attempts to discuss the experiences of working-class girls in the range of educational institutions that existed before 1870.[2]

The available research suggests that class and gender are central issues in the history of women's education.[3] Middle-class girls from 1800–1870 were taught mainly in familial, domestic settings, such as home and/or a small private school managed by middle-class 'ladies'.[4] The principle of sex segregation was not always adhered to when the pupils were young, when home-based education might be undertaken by a parent, a governess or both; however, once the boys were old enough to be sent away to public school, a middle-class girl usually continued her education in the cloistered environment of home and/or a small, private, single-sex establishment.

Most historians stress the effects of gender differentiation among such boys and girls; while public schools aimed to 'mould' the character of middle-class boys and prepare them for success in professional and public life,[5] middle-class girls tended to be educated as potential wives and mothers who would be supported economically rather than as independent salary earners. The curriculum they studied therefore stressed forms of ornamental knowledge that might be 'useful' in attracting a husband.[6] Thus 'snatches of disconnected information' in subjects such as English, history, geography and Latin, and 'trivial or showy accomplishments' in subjects such as French conversation, fancy needlework, singing, piano playing and the use of the globes were commonly taught.[7]

In contrast, working-class children, as we shall see, were taught in a different range of educational institutions during the period 1800–1870, though there is no consensus about how far gender differentiation shaped such institutions. Some writers, such as Delamont and Turnbull, have tended to assume a homogeneity in the content of education for both sexes, while others, including Purvis, Digby and Searby, Beddoe and Gomersal, have stressed that this was not the case.[8] Despite such disagreements in interpretation, it is apparent that there was a marked difference between, on the one hand, schools founded and managed by the working classes themselves, integral to the working-class community (e.g. dame schools) and, on the other hand, other groups of schools founded by, for example, national religious agencies such as the National Society for Promoting the Education of the Poor in the Principles of the Established Church (the Church of England) and the British and Foreign School Society (supported largely by religious dissenters). Although working-class children attended National and British schools, the ethos and support for such institutions came from organizations that were 'outside' the working-class community; such externally imposed public schooling was viewed as 'suspect' by the working classes, especially that offered by the 'overwhelmingly dominant' Anglican National Society.[9]

Clearly it is difficult to generalize about the education of working-class girls in such a range of institutions. Instead I would like to focus on a few central issues – such as how many working-class girls attended schools; their length of attendance; whether the debates about working-class femininity identified in the previous chapter impinged on this provision; and what were the kinds of curricula offered.

A Little Schooling

Before 1870, working-class girls, like their brothers, might receive the basic rudiments of education within a diversity of institutions – such as dame schools, Sunday schools, plait and lace schools, charity schools, factory schools, workhouse schools, ragged schools, schools of industry, Roman Catholic schools and the day schools of the National and British and Foreign societies. Such a range of institutions constituted a hierarchy where the National and British schools (which from 1833 received government grants and from 1839 were subjected to government inspection) were often seen as offering an allegedly 'superior' form of schooling. This was especially the view of those 'middle-class people ... puzzling about the schooling of the children of the working-class'[10] whose ideas are found in such profusion in nineteenth-century educational reports.

These various reports also give the impression that schools that were not inspected and not in receipt of government grants were seen as offering a 'lower' standard of education. A typical comment was that made by the Rev Richard Dawes, who believed that such schools were 'inferior in teaching power and efficiency'.[11] In particular, it was those privately organized working-class forms of schooling, dame and gaffer schools run by untrained, necessitous working-class women or men in their own homes, that bore the brunt of the inspectors' criticisms. Kay-Shuttleworth, Secretary of the Supervisory Committee of the Privy Council on Education, quoted with relish a report of 1834–5 which claimed that dame schools were

in the most deplorable condition. The greater part of them are kept by females, but some by old men, whose only qualification for this employment seems to be their unfitness for every other. Many of these teachers are engaged at the same time in some other employment, such as shopkeeping, sewing, washing, &c., which renders any regular instruction among their scholars absolutely impossible. Indeed, neither parents nor teachers seem to consider this as the principal object in sending their children to these schools, but generally say that they go there in order to be taken care of, and to be out of the way at home.[12]

Sunday schools, Roman Catholic schools and ragged schools would also have been placed, claims Aldrich, at the 'lowest' end of the school spectrum: plait, lace and factory schools were similarly to be found at the bottom of the school hierarchy.[13]

It is impossible to determine with any degree of accuracy the number of working-class girls who attended such schools, and for what period of time. As Gardner has noted, there was no agreed currency in the nineteenth century as to what constituted a 'scholar' (i.e. school pupil) or a 'school'.[14] Officially inspected schools might be included in government statistics but private schools often escaped the official eye or were even ignored. As one officer of the Children's Employment Commission working in the Potteries in the early 1840s complained, 'small private schools are very bad and not worthy of investigation'.[15] Despite these problems, the nineteenth-century government reports do give us some indication, albeit limited, about the pattern of working-class schooling.

The 1851 Census, for example, estimates that in England and Wales there were 4,908,696 children of an age appropriate to day school (i.e. three to 15 years old), but that as many as 968,557 of those between five and 12 were absent from school for reasons other than 'illness, occupation, professional home instruction, or legitimate excuse of parents'.[16] And there was a marked inequality in the number of male and female pupils. Of the

Table 4.1 Number of public weekday schools and scholars, 1861

Description of school	Weekday Schools i.e. departments	Male	Female	Total	Average number of scholars in a school
Class 1					
Church of England	19,549	624,104	562,982	1,187,086	60.7
British	1,131	89,843	61,162	151,005	113.5
Roman Catholic	743	41,678	44,188	85,866	115.5
Wesleyan (Old Connexion)	445	35,887	23,986	59,873	134.5
Congregational	388	18,143	15,020	33,163	85.4
Baptist	144	5,102	4,286	9,388	65.2
Unitarian	54	2,105	1,983	4,088	75.7
Calvinistic Methodist[a]	44	1,759	1,170	2,929	66.5
Jews	20	1,908	1,296	3,204	160.2
Society of Friends	33	1,674	1,352	3,026	91.7
Presbyterian Church of England[a]	28	1,675	1,048	2,723	97.2
Primitive Methodist[a]	26	643	699	1,342	51.6
Presbyterian (undefined)[a]	17	1,528	1,064	2,592	152.4
Methodist (New Connexion)[a]	14	1,096	755	1,851	132.2
United Methodist Free Church[a]	11	656	520	1,176	107.0
Total	22,647	827,801	721,511	1,549,312	–

Class II					
Ragged schools	192	10,308	10,601	20,909	108.9
Orphan and Philanthropic	40	2,116	1,646	3,762	94.5
Birkbeck schools	10	1,088	339	1,427	142.7
Factory schools[a]	115	9,000	8,000	17,000	147.8
Total	357	22,512	20,586	43,098	–
Class III					
Workhouse	869	18,313	16,990	35,303	40.6
Reformatory	47	2,198	485	2,683	57.0
Naval[b]	13	1,476	15	1,491	114.6
Military[c]	70	6,852	1,419	8,271	118.1
Total	999	28,839	18,909	47,748	–
Class IV					
Collegiate and superior or richer endowed schools[a]	560	32,000	3,000	35,00	62.5

[a]These returns are taken from the Census of 1851.
[b]Not including ships' schools.
[c]Not including regimental schools.

Source: PP (1861) XXI, I (*The Newcastle Report*), pp. 592–3.

estimated total population of 8,781,225 males and 9,146,384 females, only 13.2 per cent of the former (1,157,685) and 10.8 per cent of the latter (986,693) apparently attended day school. If the 1,177,071 male and 1,017,307 female scholars being educated at home are added to these figures, the proportion being educated at this time would be raised to 13.4 per cent for boys and 11.1 per cent for girls.[17] As noted earlier, home-educated girls were likely, however, to be daughters of the middle classes.

The inequality in day school attendance between girls and boys was seen as regrettable by the compilers of the 1851 Census. In particular, concern about the lower number of female pupils was couched in terms of a family ideology that stressed the moral importance for society of girls being educated for a future state of wifehood and motherhood. Since female character apparently exerted such a vast influence upon 'the general disposition of society', it was considered important that 'the future wives and mothers of the people should be qualified by sound and healthy education, continued for the longest practicable period, to exert a softening and an elevating influence upon their partners and offspring'.[18]

Such arguments may have held little sway with working-class parents, since there are indications that they might have considered the education of their daughters as less important than that of their sons. As early as 1814, Thomas Pole had wryly commented that in the education of children, 'a preference seems to be generally given to boys'.[19] The preponderance of boys in almost every London school for the poor in the 1820s was owing, Samuel Wilderspin believed, to the fact that it was particularly common among labouring families for girls aged seven or eight years old to be earning a living.[20] And girls might have been kept from school for domestic reasons too. In the 1850s in the Tottenham Court Road area of London, Anna Swanwick frequently met young girls carrying babies. When asked if they went to school, the invariable reply was, 'Oh, no, the boys go to school – mother wants me to mind the baby!' Since school fees in the neighbourhood were high, parents may not have been able to afford to send both boys and girls, and it was likely that the boys were given preference.[21]

Ten years later, national statistics collected for the Newcastle Commission (1861) revealed again that more boys than girls attended public weekday schools, especially the inspected National and British schools, as table 4.1 shows. The data also revealed a further inequality between the sexes in that girls were in the majority only in those weekday schools which were considered by some to be at the bottom end of the school hierarchy – Roman Catholic schools and ragged schools.[22] However, in another allegedly 'inferior' educational institution, the Sunday school, girls and boys seem to have been more equally represented, as table 4.2 demonstrates.

However, the number of working-class schoolgirls was likely to be much larger than these official statistics indicated. Dame and gaffer schools were widely used by the working classes, yet such schools, as noted earlier, were not likely to be recorded accurately by the official enumerator.

Table 4.2   Number of Sunday schools and scholars, 1861

Description of school	Schools i.e. departments	Male	Female	Total
Class I				
Church of England	22,236	540,303	552,519	1,092,822
Wesleyan (Old Connexion)	4,311	224,519	229,183	453,702
Congregational	1,935	128,081	139,145	267,226
Primitive Methodist	1,493	68,273	68,656	136,929
Baptist	1,420	77,153	82,349	159,502
Calvinistic Methodist[a]	962	60,025	52,715	112,740
Methodist (New Connexion)	336	24,943	26,574	51,517
United Methodist Free Churches	402	30,540	32,069	62,609
Roman Catholic	263	15,768	19,690	35,458
Unitarian	133	6,940	6,202	13,142
Non-denominational	23	1,537	1,125	2,662
Jews (Sabbath)	2	18	70	88
Total	33,516	1,178,100	1,210,297	2,388,397
Class I				
Ragged schools (Sunday and Sunday evening)	356	11,625	11,532	23,157
Total	33,872	1,189,725	1,221,829	2,411,554

[a]The numbers of the Calvinistic Methodist Schools and scholars have been taken from the Census returns of 1851. Circulars and forms in the Welsh language were issued from the Office of the Education Commission; but the returns were so imperfect that it has been thought advisable to adopt the numbers of the Census returns.

Source: PP (1861) XXI, I (*The Newcastle Report*), p. 594.

Consequently we find little agreement between the nineteenth-century sources about the number of working-class children attending such places. The 1851 Census, for example, identifies a minimum of 13,879 private schools designed primarily for working-class use, with 225,000 pupils; the 1861 Newcastle Report only ten years later, on the other hand, quotes a much larger figure of 573,576 children.[23] Aggravating these statistical problems, it also appears that those working-class girls and boys who became 'scholars' were likely to be only intermittent attenders. Indeed, the 1851 Census suggested that such irregularity could cut in half the estimated four and a half years of schooling that, on average, children of the labouring classes might receive.[24] School attendance was affected by a number of factors as diverse as the level of family income, the amount of the school fee, gender roles, time left free from paid work, bad weather, distance from school, inadequate clothing, illness and local events.[25] Probably the two most important factors preventing regular attendance or any attendance at all were the low income of parents and gender roles of the children; these two would have affected the other factors listed above.

The family standard of living would affect how much could be allowed for school fees and how much free time could be allowed for children who were needed to contribute to family income. As we saw in Chapter 2, the poverty of many working-class families during the course of the century meant that sons and daughters would be expected to support themselves, or to contribute to a family wage, or to help in some way those who were economically active. Under such circumstances, the cost of any schooling was likely to be prohibitive. Even as late as 1887, most working people found it hard to acquire 'the necessaries of life, indispensable to existence'.[26] It was especially those working-class parents with low wages and large families who were forced to utilize the wage-earning capacity of their offspring.[27] A fancy-cabinet maker in London, for example, told Henry Mayhew in 1851 that most men in his trade had five or six children and had no choice but to send them to work:

The most on us has got large families. We put the children to work as soon as we can. My little girl began about six, but about eight or nine is the usual age ... she works regularly every day from six in the morning till ten at night. She never goes to school. We can't spare her. There's schools enough about here for a penny a week, but we could not afford to keep her without working. If I'd ten more children I should be obliged to employ them all the same way.[28]

This interlocking of the necessity for paid work and the extent of schooling was also found in agricultural districts. As late as 1866, the Rev W. W. Howard, in a report on schools connected with the Church of England in Devon and Dorset, blamed the poor attendance records of the pupils on the economic plight of the parents and their indifference towards their children's education. With wages ranging from 9s to 11s a week one can hardly wonder, he suggested, that agricultural labourers sent their children out to work as soon as they could earn a few pence.[29]

Yet even within this general pattern, working-class girls experienced particular difficulties which made their irregular attendance even more intermittent than that of working-class boys. Learning various domestic skills, such as nursing children, household cleaning and sewing, was seen as a necessary and natural part of the socialization of a working-class girl. Mrs Layton, born in 1855 in Bethnal Green, London, whose father's wages from 'a government situation' were insufficient to support a family of 14 children, remembered that she and her fourth sister always stayed away from school on washing day to mind the babies. Mary Merryweather observed that even when the young women employed in the Halstead factory in Essex had been at a day school in their younger days, it was rare for them to remain pupils once they were old enough to nurse a baby.[30] In rural areas, where girls might have remained at school longer than their brothers who were employed earlier in the fields, their attendance was much more broken, especially when the mother was engaged in agricultural work away from home.[31]

Such demands upon the time of working-class daughters extended well beyond the 1870 Education Act. In some Derbyshire schools in the 1870s, for example, there are frequent references in the school log-books to the involvement of schoolgirls in housework – 'several girls absent, it being wash day at home', 'cleaning time and the militia being in the town the girls required for extra work where they are lodging', 'Wakes cleaning', 'Spring cleaning' and 'Autumn cleaning': Friday afternoons were the most common time in the school week for absence for such activities.[32]

The experiences of one working-class girl shows some of the constraints on their lives. Hannah Mitchell, born in 1871 to poor farming parents in the Peak district of Derbyshire, enjoyed only a fortnight's schooling. The journey to school was long and rough, and when winter arrived and Hannah and her sister fell ill, they were kept at home. Hannah never returned to school again, despite her deep desire to do so. She recounts how her mother resented the daughter's wish to be a scholar. So Hannah was kept at home, doing a host of household chores until she became an apprentice seamstress. She bitterly remembers this time in her life:

It was a hard life for us all, especially the girls, as my mother was a harder taskmaster than my father. She never seemed to realise how small and weak we were. She made us sweep and scrub, turn the heavy mangle on washing days and the still heavier churn on butter-making days. Stone floors had to be whitened, brasses and steel fire-irons polished every week. On winter evenings there was sewing by hand, making and mending shirts and underwear. At eight years old my weekly task was to darn all the stockings for the household, and I think my first reactions to feminism began at this time when I was forced to darn my brothers' stockings while they read or played cards or dominoes. Sometimes the boys helped with rugmaking, or in cutting up wool or picking feathers for beds and pillows, but for them this was voluntary work; for the girls it was compulsory, and the fact that the boys could read if they wished filled my cup of bitterness to the brim.[33]

Examples like this illustrate how working-class girls could not attend school because they were expected, in Elizabeth Roberts's phrase, to act as 'their mothers' apprentices'.[34] Femininity might be represented to working-class girls as involving the sacrifice of their own interests for service to others, especially boys and men. Being 'servants' within their own families[35] may have left working-class girls little free time for self-improvement.

Such experiences suggest, therefore, that gender differences between working-class girls and boys were to be found not only in terms of access to schooling, but also in terms of the pattern and length of school attendance. Working-class girls were likely to face particular constraints in attending and staying at school; in addition only a minority of them were to be found in National and British schools, though larger numbers did attend lower-status privately organized institutions, and it is to the latter that I now turn.

Dame schools

As noted earlier, one such range of private schools for working-class children consisted of the dame and gaffer schools organized by working-class women and men in their own homes. Although relatively small in size and often short lived,[36] such schools appear to have been numerous. In Bristol in 1841, for example, 217 of the 446 private schools that were listed seem to have been dame schools; sometimes, as in the working-class community of Burslem in 1852, two dame schools would be found in every street.[37]

Women in particular entered dame teaching and such a job was often seen as an extension of a woman's part in bringing up her own children as well as providing additional, home-based income.[38] Indeed some authorities claim that dame schools were little more than baby or child-minding establishments where the untrained 'teachers' exploited a situation in which an increasing number of mothers went out to work.[39] It appears that many dames, such as Mrs Collinson in the East Riding of Yorkshire in 1868, took in young children and babies; sometimes too a dame might have taken on more children than she could manage, with the result that babies were neglected and even died.[40]

The more children a dame took into her home, the more she could earn. Fees might be charged weekly or daily, and could vary considerably. In the 50 dame schools in Rutland in 1839, the average weekly fee was 3d, but in other cases, as at Burslem in 1852, as much as 6d weekly could be charged.[41] The fact that many working-class parents were willing to pay more for their children to attend a dame school than the few pence necessary for the allegedly 'superior' church schools has been interpreted by one present-day historian as indicative of the class consciousness of the poor, who wished to avoid being tainted with middle-class philanthropy.[42] But it was much more than class consciousness that made the dame schools so popular with working-class parents. These schools bore a relationship to the realities of working-class life that made them much more convenient than many of the 'provided' day schools. Dame schools were likely to be closer to home, cosier and warmer than National and British schools. Above all else, they did not try to impose rules about fixed hours of attendance, clean clothes and short or tidy hair.[43]

Working-class parents did not just use dame schools for the child-care facilities they might offer: some dame schools might also have provided a basic education, though the quality varied enormously. While it is difficult to decipher a clear pattern of educational provision or objectives,[44] or to estimate the extent of gender differentiation in such institutions, we can glimpse, from various sources, some of the features of such provision.

The main task of dame schools appears to have been teaching boys and girls to read, though some also offered spelling, sewing and knitting.[45] To what extent a common curriculum was taught to both boys and girls is hard to establish but examples can be found of gender differentiation in both mixed-sex and single-sex dame schools. Thomas Cooper, for example, born in 1805, was a pupil at a dame school where both boys and girls were taught to read and spell but knitting was taught to girls only; similarly, the Rev John Allen found that the majority of dame schools in Derby in the early 1840s taught sewing to girls.[46]

However, gender differences in curricula provision were probably most pronounced in single-sex dame schools. Mary Smith, born in 1822 in Cropedy, Oxfordshire, whose father was a boot-maker and whose mother died after the birth of the fifth child, was sent, when seven years old, to a dame school solely for the purpose of learning to knit and sew. The dame was unable to move from her chair or lift her hand to her mouth and her knowledge

was very small. The girls had a lesson once a day in the New Testament, and the little ones read out of the 'Reading Made Easy'. But knitting and sewing occupied nearly the whole time of the girls, who perhaps might average from nine to ten.[47]

In contrast, the gaffer schools kept by men may have concentrated much more on teaching writing. The pupils in such schools were most likely to be boys, especially older boys. However, by the late 1830s girls were allowed in some cases, as in Westminster, to enter gaffer schools to learn writing and ciphering.[48] Male teachers in gaffer schools did not have a monopoly upon teaching writing, though, since many women also ran 'writing schools'.

The educational plight of working-class girls in rural areas where cottage industries such as straw plaiting, glovemaking and lacemaking flourished may have been particularly acute, since in some villages the only dame schools available were those teaching work skills. In the straw-plaiting counties of Bedfordshire, Buckinghamshire and Hertfordshire, where it was believed that in order to become a good plaiter a girl had to begin the work at about three years old,[49] the educational standard of the plaiting schools was low. The pupils might learn a hymn to relieve the monotony of the work, or learn to read or chant a few verses from the Bible. Young girls in lace schools fared no better. Though some women who ran the lace schools may have tried to teach their young charges to read as well as to make lace, the majority were very probably like Mrs Sarah Mitchell of Oakley in Bedfordshire, who in the late 1860s stated quite openly, 'I can't learn them much, I can't read much myself, but I do the best I can.' She had 12 pupils in her school, eight of whom were not yet eight years old.[50]

By 1870, when the state-aided day schools of the National and British societies were providing over 90 per cent of voluntary school places,[51] the popularity of dame schools had declined, though some survived into the early years of the twentieth century. Dame schools had reached their peak during the first half of the nineteenth century and were, at that time, a common form of schooling for working-class children. The literacy level of working-class girls taught only in such schools, therefore, was unlikely to be high. But it must be remembered that in some geographical areas, though not all, such an education might also have been combined with attendance at a Sunday school.

Sunday schools

Sunday schools supported by a number of religious denominations, e.g. Dissenting, Unitarian, Wesleyan, Church of England and Quaker, were another form of educational provision in which the working-class community was involved. The motives of those who established such institutions were varied, but overall it would appear that the Sunday school movement, at least in its early years, was seen primarily as an attempt to rescue and save poor children from the corrupting influences of their parents and society by teaching them to read the Bible.[52]

Sunday schools have been interpreted by some historians, such as Jones, as growing out of a voluntary movement, financed by the subscriptions and donations of the middle classes.[53] In contrast, Laqueur has suggested that, by the early nineteenth century, the Sunday school was fundamentally 'a local, even neighbourhood, organisation' in which a distant authority could play only a minimal part. Sunday schools must not be seen, he continues, 'as a weapon in an allegedly bourgeois assault on working-class culture.... The schools were effective in large measure because they worked from within and because they were not merely organs of middle-class propaganda.' Furthermore, many of the founders and teachers were from the same social strata as their pupils.[54] For Laqueur, Sunday schools were 'strange half-way houses' between the private dame schools that were integrated into the working-class community and the externally imposed 'public' day schools of the two main religious societies.[55]

In the early nineteenth century in particular, more working-class children could be found in Sunday schools than in weekday schools. One estimate for 1818 suggests that, in England and Wales, 452,000 children attended Sunday schools, 168,000 charity schools and another 53,000 dame schools.[56] Although the relationship of Sunday to weekday schooling varied from region to region, from 1834 to 1843 the majority of children in Sunday schools in industrial and mining areas of the North and Midlands received no weekday schooling.[57] By 1861, nearly two and a half million working-class children were enrolled as Sunday scholars, the majority being girls (see table 4.2). Here, especially during the first half of the nineteenth century, a girl might have acquired the rudiments of an education. After all, Sunday schools were free and held on a day which was less likely to interfere with paid and unpaid work. The curriculum appears to have covered mainly the teaching of reading, especially of the scriptures, and religious instruction. The teaching of writing, seen by many providers as secular rather than religious education, was a controversial issue and, therefore, often confined to a weekday class. Whether writing was taught on the Sabbath or not appears to have been related to the aims of a school and its denomination; the Anglican Church was especially hostile to the teaching of writing, the dissenting denominations less so.[58] The controversy over writing faded during the second half of the nineteenth century as religious instruction became more systematic in the Sunday schools and secular instruction less common;[59] the latter task was increasingly under-taken by elementary day schools which could offer a grounding in the three Rs.

It is difficult to assess the degree of gender differentiation in Sunday schools as so little research has been conducted into this issue. However, gender differences may have been very pronounced when single-sex group-ings were found. At Stockport Sunday School, for example, there were separate seating arrangements for boys and girls. When Andrew Ure visited here in the 1830s, he witnessed 'the very gratifying sight of about 1,500 boys, and as many girls, regularly seated upon separate benches, the one set on the right side, and the other on the left'.[60] But in addition to this, the reading material used in either single-sex or mixed classes could contain hidden gender messages. Mary Anne Hearne, born in 1834, the daughter of a village postmaster, particularly remembered how the reading material published by the Sunday School Union contained no refer-ences to 'great' women:

My father gave us two monthly magazines published by the Sunday School Union, the 'Teacher's Offering', and the 'Child's Companion'. In one of these was a series of descriptive articles on men who have been poor boys, and risen to be rich and great. Every month I hoped to find the story of some poor ignorant *girl*, who, beginning life as handicapped as I, had yet been able by her own efforts and the blessing of God upon them to live a life of usefulness, if not of greatness. But I believe there was not a woman in the whole series. I was very bitter and naughty at that time. I did not pray, and was not anxious to be good.[61]

Some of the books and tracts that were given as prizes and other literature that could be borrowed from the small libraries attached to many Sunday schools may also have contained similar gender messages. If Rutland is representative of other areas in England in 1840, between a half and three-quarters of urban and probably a quarter of rural Sunday schools had libraries.[62]

Just how effective Sunday schools were as educational institutions during the nineteenth century is debatable. Claims have been made that many scholars left unable to read, victims of the worst kind of emotional bullying about the confession of sins and coming to a sense of salvation: one little girl told a commissioner investigating child labour in the mines, 'If I died a good girl I should go to heaven – if I were bad I should have to be burned in brimstone and fire: they told me that at school yesterday, I did not know it before.[63] Many children too were ill-informed; another Sunday school pupil, Mary Read, told a commissioner in 1842, 'The man in the sky made me, but I do not know who he is: never heard of Jesus Christ'.[64]

In contrast, it has also been asserted that the three to five hours instruc-tion each Sunday, over an average of four years, using specialized text-books in small classes graded according to scholastic ability rather than age, may well have had a significant impact on the creation of mass literacy in nineteenth-century England.[65] Such a statement is clearly a generalization. The working-class girl attending a Sunday school might have had no other form of education during the week. Consequently, many lacked the opportunity to build systematically, day by day, upon their knowledge base. Also, although many may have learnt to read at Sunday school, this skill might have become rusty or lost in later years, especially if few books were available or there was little free time for such pursuits.

Those educational institutions in which the working classes were likely to be involved as providers, namely dame and Sunday schools, embraced a diversity of provision and an unevenness in the quality of education for working-class children. Despite this, such institutions it seems performed an important educative function, especially for those working-class boys and girls who experienced no other form of schooling, in that they offered access to a little learning, especially reading and perhaps writing. Yet, at the same time, working-class girls who only attended dame and Sunday schools were unlikely to acquire a high level of literacy. Those who later became students in the mechanics' institutes and working men's colleges might want to improve certain skills, such as reading, and possibly acquire new ones, such as writing and arithmetic. How far their experiences differed from those of working-class girls who were taught under the allegedly superior day schools organized by the middle classes is a difficult question to answer.

Middle-class provision

In contrast to dame and Sunday schools, day schools organized by the middle classes for working-class children were much more co-ordinated and planned, being part of a centralized bureaucracy. In these educational movements, despite their different traditions, the experiences of working-class girls commonly differed from those of working-class boys. There appears to have been an emphasis upon preparing girls for certain kinds of 'useful' work in typically feminine occupations, such as domestic service, and in unpaid, practical, routine, household tasks that might be undertaken as a wife and mother. These concerns derived from middle-class family ideologies which, as we saw in Chapter 3, constructed an image of working-class women as incompetent and ignorant in domestic matters even though, paradoxically, they were also seen as physically strong. Such ideas about womanhood had consequences for the schooling of working-class girls, not least in the desire to train each pupil to become a 'good worker', and especially a 'good domestic servant', whether as an employee or as a competent wife and mother in her own home. These ideas, it seems, permeated the rhetoric surrounding the education programmes offered to working-class girls and the curriculum content of their elementary schooling. Here I shall investigate the impact of such ideals on charity schools, schools of industry and the weekday schools of the two main religious societies – the National Society and the British and Foreign School Society.

Charity schools and schools of industry

Charity schools for the poor, founded by middle-class philanthropy, had been established since before the Reformation. However, the charity school movement reached its heyday during the middle of the eighteenth century, when it was educating some 30,000 children.[66] By the beginning of the nineteenth century, many schools had disappeared or merged with new institutions, though some were to survive for many years yet.

The intentions of the founders were to provide a moral, religious and useful training for poor children through a curriculum of religion, literacy and some practical skill that had vocational value.[67] The concern with training in religious and moral principles was expected to sustain the pupils and to guide their lives once they left school. Indeed some schools, such as those organized by Hannah and Martha More in the Mendip Hills, even offered rewards or inducements to past female pupils to encourage desirable behaviour:

In order to encourage chastity and good morals in the single woman, the patronesses present every young woman 'of good character', who has been educated in their schools, and continues to attend religious instruction there, with five shillings, a new Bible, and a pair of white stockings on the day of marriage.[68]

The concern with conduct was closely intertwined with an emphasis upon usefulness and busyness, also regarded as good in themselves for the 'lower orders'. By a combination of 'useful labour' and 'mental stimulation', it was hoped that poor children would be brought up to habits of 'early industry' that would prepare them for those 'subordinate positions in society to which they may be called'.[69] Charity schools were expected therefore not only to socialize poor children into 'appropriate' conduct and to teach industrious habits and skills by which they could earn a living, but also to preserve, rather than change, the existing social hierarchy.

For girls, however, the articulation of such aims was set in a different context to that for boys, in that the aims usually related to the teaching of domestic skills. At a charity school in York, for example, the girls were taught to read, write, sew, knit, spin worsted, wash clothes and do general household work. And when their schooldays were over, the girls were 'to be bound apprentices for four years to any decent family who might be desirous of taking them'.[70] Similarly, at Leeds Charity School, moral and academic education were integrated with real work. Thus for 49 weeks of the year, eight hours a day, 120 children, aged eight to 13 years old, were taught English, writing and the spinning of worsted, the girls also being taught 'to sew, spin, line and knit and to wash and clean a house'.[71] Of course, teaching domestic skills could not only prepare girls for typically female work in domestic service but also fit them for being 'useful daughters' and 'good wives'.[72] In such schools, girls tended not to be offered the range of curricula available to boys. Indeed, Gordon claims that in charity schools generally, writing was rare and arithmetic rarer still for female pupils.[73]

It is highly significant that the closer the tie of working-class education to employment, as in those charity schools called schools of industry, which directly prepared working-class boys and girls for paid work, the greater the degree of gender differentiation. The vocational element of training for girls was to become 'good domestic servants' – as well as unpaid helpers within the home. The following statement, made by the Rev Henry Moseley about the Royal Schools in the Great Park at Windsor, which 50 boys and 50 girls attended, epitomizes these views:

It being understood to be Her Majesty's wish that the girls should be so trained in the school as to fit them for service, and to enable them to discharge in after-life the duties of wives and mothers, to the usual instruction in religious and secular knowledge a great deal of useful teaching in domestic economy is added. Besides making their own clothes and those of the boys, they do (assisted by one maid-servant) all the housework of the schools – the cleaning, cooking, washing and baking.[74]

In contrast, many schools of industry prepared boys for a wide range of occupations, including agriculture and handicrafts. At Quatt Industrial School, for example, where there were 32 boys and 19 girls, the girls were occupied in household work, dairy work, washing, ironing, baking, making and mending their own clothes, while 15 of the boys, with the assistance of the master, cultivated the land and looked after the cows, pigs and pony.[75] Among the 112 children at the schools of industry in Kendal, 30 of the elder girls were employed in spinning, sewing, knitting and general house-work, including the preparation of breakfast and the washing of utensils. It was claimed that cooking will not only be 'very useful in training girls for the station of servants, but will also supply a vast essential qualification for the wife of a cottager'.[76] 38 of the boys, on the other hand, were taught card setting and another eight shoe-making.[77]

At Cheltenham School of Industry for Girls, where the aim was to educate the pupils for much needed 'under servants' who would 'quietly and properly' do 'all sorts' of household work, the girls were taught baking, milling, washing, ironing and every 'other kind of household work' – to spin wool, flax and hemp; to knit; to sew; to plait whole straw for baskets; and to cut out and make clothing which afterwards was sold at reduced prices to the poor. Such a curriculum, it was hoped, would prepare girls for that sphere of life within which they would in future move as 'servants, wives, or daughters'. Also, in this context, socialization into an appropriate form of conduct and behaviour was an important aim of the school, i.e. attention to religious duties, to order, to neatness, to cleanliness and to earning an honest living were stressed.[78]

Preparing girls for an honest living in domestic service meant a prohibi-tion upon teaching one of the basic literary skills – writing. Again, writing seems to have been considered a dangerous skill, since 'ignorant parents' attached to it the idea of 'scholarship' and 'capacity', ideas which might encourage a rejection of manual work and the low levels of income in domestic service.[79] Acquiring the skill of writing tended to be seen as a potential lever for occupational mobility and hence a threat to the clearly stratified social class hierarchy.

Interestingly, while the evils of writing and even of reading are mentioned in relation to girls, no such reference is made in the case of boys. Thus the sketch of a plan for a School of Industry for Boys at Cheltenham involves a curriculum of reading, writing, spelling and cipher. Here, even though the boys were to be trained to be farmers' servants and to take up other types of service, they were to be instructed in an entirely different range of skills - skills that could be utilized both within and outside the private sphere of the home, e.g. weaving, basket-making, the making and mending of shoes, the making of ropes, twines and sacking, gardening, assisting in making hedges and ditches, the occasional mending of roads.[80] Examples such as these illustrate vividly how a sexual division of labour could be created and reinforced by the differential educational experiences offered to working-class boys and girls.

Certain aspects of middle-class patriarchal and family ideologies seem to have been institutionalized in curriculum content in both charity schools and schools of industry. In particular, the idea of separate spheres for the sexes, especially the notion that the female sex should be located primarily within the private sphere of the home while males engaged primarily in activities outside the home, meant that girls and boys were offered a gender-specific curriculum that reflected their respective spheres.

National and British schools

Gender differentiation in schooling for working-class children is particularly clear in the day schools organized by the National and British Societies, which by 1870, as noted earlier, offered over 90 per cent of voluntary school places.[81] Here patriarchal and family ideologies seem to be most evident. This is not surprising. The patrons of both societies were drawn largely from the middle and upper strata that possessed both the time and level of income to support such philanthropic activity. The committee and officers of the National Society, for example, included the Lord High Chancellor, the Archbishop of York, three earls, 27 bishops and five lords.[82]

The aims of the National Society, stated in its first annual report of 1812, were to communicate to the poor such knowledge and habits that were sufficient to guide them through life 'in their proper stations, especially to teach the doctrines of Religion, according to the principles of the Established Church and to train them to the performance of their religious duties by early discipline'.[83] As in charity schools, the concern here was to offer working-class children basic knowledge, discipline and conduct considered appropriate for their class and gender location. However, by 1841 the aim of female education was clearly differentiated from that of boys, in that female pupils were to be taught 'to be sober, to love their husbands, to love their children, to be discreet, chaste, keepers at home, obedient to their husbands that the word of God be not blasphemed'; by 1861, it was made quite clear that any academic honours to which girls might aspire were not to take precedence over domestic skills:

> it is to be hoped that no desire to make girls little Newtons, little Captain Cooks, little Livingstones, little Mozarts and Handels, and little Sir Joshua Reynoldses, will ever take us too low for keeping in sight the object of teaching them to make and mend shirts, to make and mend pinafores, and darn stockings and socks. If it does then from that day the Society will go back.[84]

Initially, most National schools charged no fees, but from 1824 a small weekly charge was recommended since the society's funds had become exhausted.[85] Significantly, some schools charged boys and girls differential rates, as at Aston National School, Derbyshire, in 1860, where boys paid from 1½d to 8d and girls 1½d to 3d.[86] Despite the fact that its schools were fee paying, the National Society sought through a system of rules to exercise organizational and ideological control over parents and pupils. It was stipulated that parents 'must' send their children regularly to schools 'at proper hours, clean, washed, and combed' and never keep them home except in cases of sickness or when permission had been granted; regular Sunday school attendance was expected, too.[87]

Parents, it would appear, had little client control in terms of participating in those decision-making processes that determined what was taught in the schools. Such schools were established not as a result of popular demand but as institutions conferred by those who 'knew best'.[88] Similarly, the rules stated that pupils 'must' behave respectfully towards the teachers, obey instructions, be diligent, behave with reverence during prayers, be kind to one another, and 'never tell a Lie, Cheat, Steal, or Swear'.[89] Not surprisingly, there are frequent references in the log-books kept by National schools to occasions when such rules were broken. For example, at Northam Girls' School, Hampshire, Mrs Elizabeth A. Davies (the mistress in charge) recorded in the log-book entry for 9 September 1864, 'I was obliged to send Eliza Fryer home this morning, because she was so impudent and unruly, that she upset the whole school'.[90]

Gender divisions were evident in inequalities in admission and attendance and in the various types of curricula provision. Initially, boys and girls were admitted at different ages to National schools – five years old and upwards for the former and seven years old and upwards for the latter.[91] Such a practice would have been advantageous for boys in that they experienced a systematic schooling at an earlier age than girls. It would also appear that greater priority was given to places for boys, since it was several years after the foundation of the National Society before concern was expressed about the scale of provision for girls: even by 1861, there were fewer female than male pupils – 562,982 girls and 624,104 boys respectively.[92]

In addition to these inequalities in admission, gender differentiation was also to be found in separate provision – either in single-sex schools or in separate divisions, separate departments or separate rooms in mixed schools. At the Central Schools of the society, at Baldwin's Gardens, for example, we find both a girls' and a boys' room.[93] At Watton, Norfolk, the boys and girls were taught in one large room, but in separate divisions; at Norwich, we find a boys' school and a girls' school.[94] The Rev Tregarthen claimed, in 1867, that separate schools for girls were more likely to be found in the towns rather than the villages.[95] This is not surprising. The catchment area of village schools might not have been large enough to support the expense of single-sex schools and, in addition, there may have been prejudice against schooling working-class girls in the more traditional, rural areas. Within any one county, therefore, a variety of educational forms would have been possible. For example, in Yorkshire in the 1860s the Church of England schools inspected by the Rev Charles Routledge included 39 boys' schools, 35 girls' schools, 123 mixed schools, 35 infant schools and 80 evening schools.[96]

Sometimes a girls' school would be mixed with an infants' school. This was the case at Whitby in the 1860s and at Bramshaw School, Hampshire, from 1819.[97] Where this occurred, girls usually suffered an educational disadvantage in comparison with boys. Infants and girls would often be in one room, taught simultaneously by a female teacher and her assistants. As late as 1870, the Rev W. J. Kennedy, Inspector for Church of England schools in Lancashire, Cheshire and the Isle of Man, pointed out the handicaps of such a system:

The chief defect I have to regret in the organisation of school is, that schools for boys and girls are too much crowded with infants. This is especially the case in some girls' schools, and the evil is rather on the increase I fear, because in my district some managers are attempting to reduce the expense of the schools by having one certificated mistress for both girls and infants.... It is not only that infants in the same room with girls are noisy and interfere with good order and discipline, but the infants themselves require the care and teaching of a trained and experienced mistress, and ought neither to be neglected nor regarded as little more than a means of bringing a certain amount of grant to a school by swelling the average attendance.[98]

In addition, if the earlier advice of inspectors of the 1840s and 1850s was adopted, those limited subjects taught to girls were directed towards domestic tasks; arithmetic, it was argued, could be taught by adding up shopping bills and calculating the amount of material necessary for dress-making, while writing could concentrate upon themes such as how to boil a leg of mutton, general duties of a cook or parlourmaid.[99]

Not surprisingly, the educational standard attained by girls often appears to have been inferior in comparison with that attained by boys, especially boys educated in a single-sex school. The Rev Allington claimed that in the Church of England schools inspected by him in Suffolk, the girls failed much more frequently than the boys in 'all subjects' and in 'all standards', though the differences in educational attainment between boys and girls was less noticeable in mixed schools; the Rev Barry's observations as Inspector for the Counties of Gloucester and Somerset suggest, however, that the mixing of some boys' and girls' schools under one master resulted in a 'great improvement' in the arithmetic of the girls.[100] Where girls could be taught by the male teacher who taught the boys, less time was given to needlework[101] and there was always the possibility that they could reach that higher standard in the three Rs (especially in arithmetic) that the boys traditionally attained. Further, some were of the opinion that parents preferred a mixed school and a male rather than a female teacher, especially since the master of a mixed school might be able to discipline the boys more successfully than could a mistress.[102] As Arnold claimed in 1852, when girls learnt with boys and were taught by a male teacher, their schooling gained that 'very correctness and stringency which female education generally wants'.[103] The issue of mixed or single-sex schooling for working-class girls plus the question of the sex of the teacher appears, therefore, to have held crucial consequences for educational standards and educational attainment.

Gender differentiation was also evident in the Central Schools founded by the National Society, in Baldwin Gardens, to train teachers. Here there were two rooms, one to hold 600 boys and the other to take 400 girls. Even though both sexes participated in prayers, ciphering, religious exercises, writing and reading in the morning, in the afternoon the boys continued with ciphering, writing, reading and arithmetic tables while the girls were taught knitting and needlework till half past four and then arithmetical tables till five o'clock.[104] Many other National schools appear to have established similar schemes. At Bampton National School, Oxfordshire, both boys and girls were taught spelling, reading, the Church Catechism and the first principles of religion. Boys who had made sufficient progress and behaved well were to be taught writing and arithmetic. Furthermore, it was intended that they should be employed in some handicraft 'for the purpose of training them up in the habits of industry'. The opposite sex, however, were to be treated rather differently:

Those Girls, who have made sufficient progress and have recommended themselves by their good behaviour, will also be instructed in Writing. Needlework, Knitting &c. will form part of their constant employment for the purposes of training them up in habits of useful industry, and contributing to the support of the School.[105]

Girls, it seems, were not taught arithmetic like boys. The 'useful' skill of sewing taught to them brought some financial benefits to the school in that articles of clothing were made for sale – including men's fine shirts at 2s each, night shirts at 10d, a girl's coarse shirt from 3d to 6d, and a pair of pillow cases from 2d to 4d.[106] Gomersal estimates that in 1851 43 per cent of all female pupils in public schools were learning to sew, though by 1862 the proportion had increased to 75 per cent.[107] However, sewing did not, perhaps, give girls the employment opportunities the boys received.

Interestingly, though the quality of education varied greatly within National schools, we can find complaints by contemporary critics that such a schooling only prepared working-class girls for superior kinds of paid work (such as housemaid and mantua maker) rather than the more mundane dairymaid.[108] An alternative view would be that National schools prepared working-class girls for entry into a typically low-status feminine range of occupations (albeit more skilled than would have been possible without such a schooling). Such limited occupational mobility still prepared working-class girls for women's work – either in low-paid jobs or in unpaid domestic tasks within the home.

By the 1850s, National schools outnumbered British and Foreign Society schools by about 17 to one.[109] Despite the fact that the British and Foreign Society was largely supported by dissenting religious groups such as the Quakers, its aims, provision and curriculum for girls were similar to those of the National Society. In particular, both societies had ladies' committees which were concerned with female education. However, it would appear that the Ladies' Committee of the British Society was especially persistent in its demand that an equal number of school places should be offered to boys and girls.[110]

The aims of the British Society were similar to that of its rival, namely to offer poor children the 'rudiments' of education and to provide a training in 'morals and good conduct'.[111] A basic curriculum of reading, writing, arithmetic and needlework was recommended for girls, the lessons for reading to include extracts from the Holy Scriptures.[112] Sometimes, too, knitting was taught to girls, as at Sheffield and Portsea.[113] A small fee was charged, often one penny a week, though by the 1860s this could be as much as fourpence.[114]

Statements made by the Ladies' Committee of the British Society show that desirable education for working-class girls was seen in terms of teaching them 'useful knowledge' that would qualify them as 'industrious servants' who would eventually become 'the wives and mothers of industrious and intelligent mechanics'.[115] Yet despite the number of such statements concerning the importance of education for poor girls, fewer places were available for females than for males. Priority appears to have been given to boys, who were the target clientele. As the Ladies' Committee complained, the expense of building boys' schoolrooms and raising sufficient subscriptions for their support meant that little attention was given to expanding female education.[116] Consequently schools for girls were 'a very small proportion' of the total number.[117]

We find that in the British schools both boys and girls were taught the three Rs and religious instruction, but again only girls learnt the skill of sewing. The following list of clothes, made in the 1820s by girls at the Portsea School, Hampshire, vividly illustrates the range of items to be produced:

HALF PRICE CLOTHING PLAN
Articles made and sold from October 1823 to October 1824. 207 pincloths; 156 shirts; 11 aprons; 6 boys' shirts; 3 women's caps; 217 girls' caps; 30 infants' bedgowns; 54 infants' caps; 24 infants' shirts; and 5 women's bed-gowns.[118]

Similarly, at Worcester Girls' School in 1824, 42 frocks and various other 'useful articles of clothing' had been made and were distributed as 'rewards' according to the 'merit' of the children.[119] Sometimes, too, the girls were involved in cleaning duties within the school. This was the case at Tottenham, where the elder girls were employed to keep the schoolroom clean and assist the mistress a little in her apartment.[120] The British schools, then, were not different from other forms of schooling provided by the middle classes in their formulation of male and female education.

The level of education attained by pupils in National and British schools would have been affected by the monitorial method of teaching, used especially up to the 1840s, whereby pupils instructed their peers in a mechanistic, repetitive, chanting manner.[121] Memorization of dates, verses from the Bible and other books, poetry, lists of sovereigns etc., became a key feature of the learning process, rather than an understanding of what was taught, and was much criticized by the various school inspectors. The Rev Cook, for example, commented on the long list of mistakes, omissions and mispronunciations of main words: even when the Lord's Prayer was recited, it was common to hear the pupils say, 'Our Father charter heaven'.[122] Some mistakes were not even noticed, let alone corrected.[123]

Both National and British schools, too, during the first half of the century, began to use secular reading books that included subjects such as political economy, history and geography.[124] However, the impact of this greater range of subjects for girls, in comparison with those offered in dame, Sunday and charity schools, is unclear. The new subjects were apparently often 'scraps' taught by 'tacking them' on to spelling lessons that often evolved round the Scriptures.[125] Girls' schools appear to have fared worse than boys' schools in this respect. One observer in 1838 noted that, in many girls' schools:

Writing on paper is confined to half a dozen or so of the principal monitors, in others it is not permitted at all; and in arithmetic, they are nearly all most lamentably and miserably deficient. We find in a few schools the dry rigid rules of grammar attempted, and the barren definitions of geography; but the children rarely enter into the spirit of what they are about for want of the required books, maps, etc.[126]

In addition, the retention of plain needlework as a gender-specific subject for girls meant that there was less time for other less practical areas.[127] This is not to deny that some girls might have had access to a broader curriculum, and especially in the model schools of the two societies. By 1854, for example, at the Girls' Model School of the British Society, the curriculum included modern geography, practical arithmetic, object lessons, English history, reading, spelling, dictation, English grammar, Scripture reading and interrogation, domestic economy every Friday morning from 9.15 to 9.45 and needlework every afternoon from 3.15 to four o'clock.[128]

For the majority of working-class girls in National and British schools by 1850, though, it would appear that education was a daily grind in reading, religious instruction and sewing, with less frequent lessons in writing and arithmetic. The 1862 Revised Code introduced a 'payment by results' scheme whereby a government grant of 12 shillings per child could be earned if attendance was regular and a satisfactory standard attained in the annual three Rs examination conducted by an HMI.[129] It was likely that these reforms led to more attention being paid to writing and arithmetic. Plain needlework, however, remained an examinable obligatory subject for girls only. From 1867, a higher grant could be earned if extra 'specific' subjects, such as geography, grammar and history, were taught and in 1871 the list was extended to include alegebra, geometry, natural philosophy, physical geography, the natural sciences, political economy and languages, together with any definite subject of instructions approved by the Inspector.[130] But the number of working-class girls who had access to this broader curriculum was likely to be small, since in 1875 only 3.7 per cent of all children enrolled in elementary schools were examined in any of these 'specific' subjects.[131] Further efforts to widen the curriculum, as in 1875, when geography, grammar, history and plain needlework were converted to 'class' subjects (whereby the grant earned related to the proficiency of the whole class rather than the individual pupil) made little impact, especially in rural areas. Up to 1890, claims Horn, the three Rs examination, combined with average attendances, formed the main basis of state grants.[132]

Conclusion

During the period 1800–1870 there was a considerable variety of educational provision for working-class girls, though only a minority attended formal schools, especially the allegedly superior day schools of the National and British societies. The picture of girls' schooling within this diversity of institutions is not entirely clear, but the experiences of girls indicate that working-class girls and boys were not receiving the same education. The gender of working-class children structured their learning experiences at the same time that their social class background helped determine the kind of schooling they should receive.

One can see ideological influences impinging on this schooling, especially in the charity, National and British schools. Working-class girls within such schools would receive particular messages about woman's place in society, namely that they should become good workers, especially good domestic servants as well as competent wives and mothers. Working-class girls would also receive messages about the kind of knowledge and skills considered suitable for girls. Although it is difficult to generalize about the content of their education, three traditions of schooling were apparent. In dame and Sunday schools, the main emphasis was upon learning to read, though some dame schools also offered spelling, sewing and knitting. In charity schools and schools of industry organized by the middle-classes, girls were expected to acquire useful vocational skills that would prepare them for typically feminine employment and for women's work within the home. A similar emphasis was to be found in National and British schools, though here the curriculum might include not only the three Rs, plain needlework and religious instruction, but also, for a small minority of schoolgirls, a wider range of subjects.

Overall, the kind of knowledge and skills considered suitable for working-class girls were limited, framed around their expected destinations in life and shaped by their economic circumstances. Like middle-class girls, working-class girls were linked to a domestic ideal, but, in contrast to the former with their accomplishments curriculum, working-class girls had access only to the most basic 'useful' knowledge. And there were many who had no formal schooling at all.

The most important questions to come out of this brief overview of working-class girls' schooling between 1800 and 1870 lie in deciphering the links between this schooling and the education women received within the mechanics' institutes and working men's colleges. One of the key issues we will have to consider is whether the education provided by these adult education institutes built on the basic knowledge that working-class girls might have received or whether it compensated those who had no schooling at all and were probably illiterate. After the passing of the 1870 Education Act, when a state system of national elementary schooling became possible, there was no guarantee that working-class girls would be literate, since school attendance was not made compulsory until 1880 and free until 1891;[133] even then many pupils slipped through the net. The drawing of working-class girls into elementary education influenced the mechanics' institutes and working men's colleges in various ways, as we shall see in Part III.

Part III

EDUCATING WORKING-CLASS WOMEN

INTRODUCTION

Part II, which looked at the context of working-class womens' lives, revealed that the conditions of employment and family life for working-class women were such that for the majority, the cycle of poverty was likely to be reproduced over a generation; working-class daughters, with few 'escape' options for a 'better' lifestyle, were also likely to become working-class mothers who struggled to bring up their children in conditions of economic hardship. Although industrialization brought some increased employment opportunities for women, especially in non-manual jobs such as elementary schoolteaching and in 'relatively' well-paid jobs in cotton factories, the hours worked were long and the conditions tiring.

In contrast, middle-class ideologies about a woman's place in nineteenth-century society being within the home, ideally as a full-time wife and mother, were far removed from the realities of working-class women's lives. In particular, the romantic notion of the family bore little relation to the daily grind of working-class women's everyday existence. The emphasis upon domesticity for working-class women helped to shape educational provision offered to working-class girls, especially in those forms of schooling organized by the middle classes. Working-class girls were unlikely to receive the same schooling as their brothers.

The full impact of these middle-class patriarchal and family ideologies will now be explored in Part III, where we investigate women's participation in two major adult educational movements of the nineteenth century – the mechanics' institute and working men's college movements. As discussed in the Introduction, it is the impact of social class rather than gender aspects of these educational movements that has received the attention of scholars.

When we focus upon women's involvement in these movements, we, shall concentrate upon two key themes. First, in Chapters 5 and 7, we shall examine the conditions of entry for women, the scale of their participation and the social backgrounds from which they were drawn. How far the founders of these movements took women into account, and how far their ideas about a woman's place in society influenced the status accorded female students within the institutes and colleges, will also be explored. Second, in Chapters 6 and 8, we shall examine the kinds of knowledge to which women were given access in these movements and, in particular, discuss in what ways those patriarchical and family ideologies investigated in Chapter 3 helped to shape the curriculum offered.

A discussion of these themes will help provide an assessment of these two educational movements and their impact on the lives of their female clientele. For example, did the providers understand the lives of their potential female students? Was the education offered to working-class women more suitable to their daily existence than that schooling offered to working-class girls discussed in Chapter 4? Did the mechanics' institutes and working men's colleges offer working-class women something more extensive or more 'radical' than what they had experienced educationally in the past? Was the curriculum in these adult educational institutions as gender differentiated as the forms of education offered in schools? The themes outlined will be discussed first in relation to the mechanics' institute movement (Chapters 5 and 6) and then to the working men's college movement (Chapters 7 and 8).

5

WOMEN AND THE MECHANICS'
INSTITUTE MOVEMENT

Introduction

Although there is some dispute as to when the mechanics' institute movement actually 'began', it is usually seen as dating from 2 December 1823, when the London Mechanics' Institution was founded.[1] The aims and objectives of each institute were usually formulated by individual founders or by a committee of directors. The founders were nearly always men, mainly from middle-class backgrounds, especially from 'the employing class'.[2] For example, Edward Baines, proprietor of the *Leeds Mercury*, and other influential businessmen, such as Benjamin Gott and John Marshall MP, both textile manufacturers, were involved in founding the Leeds Institute.[3] John Smith Wright, head of a banking firm, was a key figure in establishing the Nottingham Institute. The origins of the Manchester Mechanics' Institution are attributed to a conversation between three prominent middle-class men – William Fairbairn (an engineer and employer), Richard Roberts (a mechanical inventor) and Thomas Hopkins; Benjamin Heywood, a banker, became the main patron. At Portsmouth, mechanics who wanted to see an institute established were encouraged to leave their names at the residence of two surgeons, Henry and Julian Slight.[4] At Sheffield, the initiative for a mechanics' institute came from artisans, but it was the town's middle-class leaders, such as James Montgomery, a journalist and poet, Thomas Ward, a Unitarian cutlery merchant, and Arnold Knight, a medical practitioner, plus a sprinkling of dissenting ministers and Anglican clergy, who established, managed and monitored the institute.[5]

Historians have revealed that only a minority of institutes, as at Keighley, Halifax and Bradford, appeared to have been founded by men 'in humble circumstances': at Keighley, John Farrish, a reed-maker, John

Bradley, a painter, William Dixon, a tailor, and John Haigh, a joiner, were the founders.[6]

The social class background of the founders and governing committees was significant in influencing the policies and aims of the institutes, which were both class and sex specific. The focus of most institutes, on the whole, was the diffusion of scientifically useful knowledge to working-class men. As Duppa noted in 1839, the persons for whom the institutes were originally designed were 'Mechanics or Workmen'.[7] The issue of admitting women, whatever their class origins, does not appear to have been considered by the early founders.[8] The institutes, as originally conceived, did not see women as a target clientele, and equality of access between the sexes does not seem to have been discussed until the movement was well established.

Since many of the middle-class founders donated large sums of money to the institutes and sat on the governing committees, there was always potential for conflict between the educational goals they set and those of the working-class men they hoped the institutes would attract. It is not surprising, therefore, that the issue of class control arose early, and was to recur regularly, in the movement. The policy within early institutes of avoiding political or religious controversy, the attempts to ban newspapers, and the belief that free discussion was undesirable[9], were deeply resented by radical working-class men. It seems that the struggle by the working class to control their own education and not simply to be recipients of what middle-class patrons wished them to receive opened a debate also about the right for women to have access to the institutes. It is significant that in the mid–1820s individuals associated with various radical movements, such as Owenism, were outspoken on this issue. In 1826, for example, William Thompson, a prominent Owenite, urged all members and managers of mechanics' institutes:

Let your libraries, your models, and your lectures ... be equally open to both sexes. Equal justice demands it. Have not women an equal right to that happiness which arises from an equal cultivation of all their faculties that men have? ... Long have the rich excluded the poorer classes from knowledge: will the poor classes now exercise the same odious power to gratify the same anti-social propensity – the love of domination over the physically weaker half of their race?[10]

To what extent Thompson's words were heeded is difficult to say. Certainly some working-class men, contemptuous of middle-class control, left a local institute to establish alternative institutions or an Owenite Hall of Science,[11] and permitted women access to, and education in, such institutions. At Manchester, for example, the absence of working-class involvement in the government of the institute led, in March 1829, to a 'New Mechanics' Institution' being founded, controlled by working-class men and offering classes for working-class women. But the reasons advanced by the working-class president of the new institute, Roland Detrosier, for supporting women's education were in terms of the advantages to men, as husbands of 'educated' wives, and to children, as offspring of 'competent' mothers. Thus he told his fellow institute members in 1829:

> Be assured the condition of the industrious artisan can never be permanently improved, until the daughter of the poor man be educated to perform with propriety and decorum the important duties of a wife and mother.... Is it of no moment to the working man that he should have a partner who has the ability to administer to his comforts and his wants ...? Is it of no moment that the few comforts which are still left to him should be served up with cleanliness? Or would it ... detract from the charms of home, if, when returning from the labours of the day, he found his little cot the blessed scene of cleanliness, good sense, and cheerfulness? ... With whom are passed the first years of those who are to become the future parents of a future race? ... From woman, in the sacred character of mother! But if that mother be ignorant, brutish, and uncleanly in her habits, what rational hope have you that her children will make either good mothers, good wives, good husbands, or good fathers?[12]

Such ideas about woman's place in society were not dissimilar to those patriarchal and family ideologies held by the middle classes, as discussed in Chapter 3. Indeed, it is often difficult to differentiate *between* the views of men from the different social strata when they spoke about women's education within the institutes.

In the vast majority of institutes where the middle classes were much more active in management and policy-making, women's education when spoken of at all was usually advocated in terms of their assumed roles as wives and mothers. For example, Thomas Wyse MP, in his speech at the opening of the New Mechanics' Institution, Liverpool, in 1837, reminded his audience that the education 'best befitting Englishmen' could be pursued with full advantage 'in the gentle converse of the domestic hearth at night'. What better protection, he questioned, 'than the mother's wing – what better guide than the mother's hand?' In particular, he told the 'Mothers and sisters of Englishmen' in his audience that they they were entrusted with 'noble duties' and 'awful responsibilities', namely 'to lead up to their high place amidst the nations, the future men of England!'[13] George Searle Phillips, a journalist and writer who became secretary of the Huddersfield Mechanics' Institute from 1846 to 1854 and agent for the Yorkshire Union of Mechanics' Institutes from 1854 to 1856, also argued that women should be educated to be housewives, not scholars:

> A 'blue stocking' – that is, a female literary pedant – is certainly no desirable person to know either in private or public; but there is no necessity to manufacture this kind of hosiery in our educational looms.... I do not see why a woman should not be as good a housewife, and as prudent, virtuous, and honourable in all her relations with a furnished as with an unfurnished mind.[14]

James Hole, a foreign correspondent and clerk in a Leeds firm and also a writer, regarded as a key figure within the mechanics' institute movement in Yorkshire,[15] seemed to hold a similar view. Thus while condemning those women in the labouring class who 'from want of knowing how to improve a leisure hour' spent their time on their knees, 'cooking, washing, scrubbing, and rubbing, from Monday morning till Saturday night', Hole also advocated their 'elevation', through education, in order to become companions (rather than drudges) for their husbands.[16]

Not surprisingly, the middle-class ideal of femininity for working-class women, that of the 'good wife and mother' (see Chapter 3), was frequently reiterated as the main aim of the various educational programmes that were eventually offered to working-class women. This ideal is epitomized in Duppa's *A Manual for Mechanics' Institutions*, which was published in 1839 and offered advice on how to organize an institute successfully, including classes for women. The rationale for such provision was justified, in Duppa's view, in terms of the deficiencies of the working-class wife and mother; only through education could she become the capable, thrifty, practical housewife, the 'ideal' companion for her spouse and the 'ideal' mother for her husband's children:

The instruction of adult females has been hitherto unprovided for. In Mechanics' Institutions, women, if not excluded, have at least been wholly lost sight of. There appears, however, no good reason why one-half of the working-classes, in whose moral and intellectual elevation the other half have the deepest interest, should be overlooked. A happy and well-ordered home, valuable in every situation of life, is especially so to the working man of all ranks; whose increased skill and knowledge, and his cultivated tastes, are likely only to be sources of disappointment, if the companion of his home and the mother of his children is deficient in the habits and knowledge befitting her sex, and essential to the due performance of her duties. The absence of a systematic provision for female instruction is a fertile source of improvidence and domestic unhappiness. The difficulties, whatever they may be, in the way of introducing female education into Mechanics' Institutions, are those of detail merely, and may be obviated by judicious superintendence.[17]

Since this statement was made in a footnote, rather than incorporated in the main body of the text, it suggests that even by 1839 working-class women's education was still seen as marginal to the main educational concerns of the period. It was only in the later development of the mechanics' institute movement that women became part of some mainstream activities within the institutes. And in this later development we can uncover more detail about the educational ideologies at work in curricular provision (Chapter 6). In this chapter I shall look at the admission of women to the mechanics' institutes, female recruitment, women students, their second-class membership, the access of women to newsrooms and reading rooms, and their right to vote and hold office.

The reluctant admission of women

The rapid expansion in the number of mechanics' institutes in the early 1820s had slowed down by the early 1830s; other phases of advance seemed to peak about 1839, about 1850 and about 1860.[18] As Kelly has pointed out, the movement was not even and continuous, either geographically or chronologically. By 1841, 261 institutes are recorded, with the largest concentration, about 22 per cent being in Lancashire and the West Riding of Yorkshire.[19] However, the greater number of institutes in these two northern areas did not necessarily mean that more women would be found here than elsewhere.

We begin to hear about the entry of women into the institutes from 1830, since it was a move that often aroused much opposition from the male membership. As institutes were founded by men, controlled by men, and for the use of men, it was hardly surprising that women's admittance was regarded with suspicion. At a general meeting held in March 1830 at the London Mechanics' Institution, for example, the motion to allow women as members was passed only against considerable opposition, one man pointing out that it would lead to the admission of 'females of a very questionable character'; another man suggested that the institute would be brought into 'very great dispute', since 'female mechanics' would have to be taught the arts they practise such as the getting up of linen and the chronicling of small beer![20]

Such debates highlight the assumption then made that 'male' and 'female' spheres were clearly distinguishable and could not be brought together without polluting both. At this time the word 'mechanic', as far as it had any precise meaning, meant a skilled artisan, a craftsman or a tradesman,[21] though the term was often extended to cover all male manual workers. Women, therefore, were not seen as 'skilled' workers in the same way as male mechanics.[22] Once the two categories of workers were mixed, female students interested in joining the institute were redefined as being of a dubious character. It has not been unusual historically, as Rowbotham[23] has pointed out, to find such accusations of sexual abandon or, alternatively, sexual frigidity, made against women who oppose male orthodoxy. In this case, female membership implied that women wanted to gain access to male forms of knowledge and skills. But scientifically useful knowledge in the hands of women might be subversive – they might try to enter men's occupations and become socially mobile. To keep women out of the institutes would be seen by some as clearly in men's interests: to allow women to enter was to challenge the male ordering of the world.

The objections raised about the admission of women also highlighted another issue – what and how they should be taught. Although these matters are discussed in detail later, at this point it is significant to note that the objections indicated that women would have a number of battles to fight if they wanted equal access to the same courses and same facilities as men. The issue of allowing women to enter the institutes was a political, not just an educational, question. And many instances can be found of the struggle women encountered.

At Lewes in Sussex, for example, in 1834, after 'many resolutions and counter-resolutions' women were allowed to attend the lectures and to use the library.[24] At Birmingham in 1840, a group of women petitioned the institute for classes. Their request was not granted – 'Such a thing would ruin the Atheneum in a month', the middle-class directors told them. So the women looked elsewhere, to the local Owenite branch, which not only met the request but also delighted in the fact that they could provide something which their middle-class competitors could not.[25] At Bingley Mechanics' Institute, on the other hand, a deputation of young factory women was successful in 1850 in having their demands for a class met,[26] and at Holbeck, in the same year, another group of women were granted permission to become students, though only after some deliberation by the all-male committee:

About Christmas, application was made by several females to be allowed to attend in the evening, saying they needed instruction as much as the young men, and were as anxious to get it, and pay for it too. After long and serious debate about the difficulties and liability to abuse, &c., it was at last agreed, that the benefits of the society should be open to females; and 50 joined at once.[27]

As these examples show, the decision whether or not to admit women to the institutes was in the hands of men. However, the available sources rarely clarify the reasons why men allowed women entrance. Undoubtedly in some instances, as at Holbeck, it was because the women's case was considered reasonable. But women might also have been admitted for social reasons[28] or because their numbers would boost a failing membership or dwindling finances.

For some women, the fight for entry was resolved by attending one of the few women-only mechanics' institutes in the north of England. Again sparse records reveal no clear reasons why such institutions were established. Perhaps the founders believed in single-sex education for adult men and women; perhaps they though that women trying to enter 'male' institutes would encounter many obstacles. The Huddersfield Mechanics' Institution discussed in 1844 the 'propriety of endeavouring to afford to the female portion of working-class society advantages similar' to those offered to the men: there was no reason against, and every reason for, the wife and daughter 'sharing' the social, literary and educational privileges of the husband and son.[29] However, the plan for educating women was delayed for two years, since the institution had enough work to do in 'educating the sons of toil'.[30] No reasons are given why a separate Huddersfield Female Educational Institute was established in January 1847 by Samuel Kell, a local businessman, with the aim of attracting young women of the working classes.[31]

Whatever the rationale for the foundation, the women-only institutes were usually attached to the main local 'male' institute and had a large number of men in influential official positions. Thus both the separate female institutes at Huddersfield and Keighley were regarded as 'under the wing' of their local 'male' institutes.[32] The Bradford Female Educational Institute, founded in 1857 by the same Samuel Kell,[33] after he had moved to that area, had a system of government that gave men considerable power in this women-only college: the governing committee was composed of eight men, five women and four elected student representatives – but all the prestigious official posts were held by men, as figure 5.1 shows. Similarly, at the Huddersfield Female Institute, men held the

BRADFORD
Female Educational Institute.

OFFICERS AND COMMITTEE FOR 1860.

President.
Mr. ALDERMAN BROWN.

Vice=Presidents.
Rev. Dr. BURNET (Vicar).   Mr. S. C. KELL.

Treasurer.
Mr. WILLIAM D. HERTZ.

Hon. Secretary.
Mr. A. ILLINGWORTH.

Auditors.
Mr. A. ENGELMANN.   Mr. WILLIAM WHITEHEAD.

Bankers.
Messrs. HARRIS & CO.

Committee.

Mrs. W. R. HAIGH.	Mr. CHARLES HASTINGS.
„ W. D. HERTZ.	Dr. HEINGAERTNER.
„ S. C. KELL.	Mr. ALFRED ILLINGWORTH.
Miss KELL.	„ THOMAS STEPHENSON.
„ PESEL.	„ JULIUS WOLFFSOHN.
Mr. W. R. HAIGH.	„ F. WETZLER.
„ JAMES HANSON.	

Elected by the Pupils.

Miss Grace Bastow.	Miss Elizabeth Kay.
„ Jane Hartley.	„ Esther Ann Schofield.

Secretary.
Mr. J. H. RAWNSLEY.

BRADFORD:
PRINTED BY GEORGE HARRISON, CHEAPSIDE.

Figure 5.1   Bradford Female Educational Institute: officers and committee for 1860 (from *Rules of the Bradford Female Educational Institute*, 1860).

offices of president, vice president, treasurer and honorary secretary.[34] As elsewhere in the history of women's education in the nineteenth century, male support and patronage was often found in 'new' educational ventures.[35] Such support could come, however, not only from influential middle-class men but also from their families.

The Kell family, for example, was not only on the governing body of the Bradford female institute but also actively involved in running the institution. Mrs Kell taught the needlework class, while Miss Kell, who had managed the library at the Huddersfield Female Institute, now also undertook such a task at the Bradford centre.[36] Mr Kell donated 64 books to the library in 1860 and another five volumes a couple of years later.[37] The involvement of a husband, wife and daughter in this way may have helped to create that familial atmosphere so prized in small private schools for middle-class girls.[38] Another husband and wife team on the committee were Mr and Mrs Hertz. Fanny Hertz, a middle-class woman with a keen interest in education, established the Bradford Ladies' Educational Association in 1868; she was also on the central committee of the National Union for Improving the Education of Women of All Classes,[39] an organization which Maria Grey founded in 1871 to strengthen and combine the efforts of all those involved in promoting the education of women and girls. Fanny Hertz also helped to publicize the idea of mechanics' institutes for working women when she gave a paper on the topic at the 1859 meeting of the prestigious National Association for the Promotion of Social Science.[40]

Female recruitment

Trying to determine the number of women who entered the institutes is no easy task, partly because by the mid-nineteenth century the institutes were so numerous and so varied in name, form and function that they almost defy classification.[41] For example, Kelly includes under the title 'Mechanics' Institutions' organizations bearing that precise name as well as mechanics' literary and scientific institutions, lyceums, institutions or societies for the diffusion or advancement of knowledge and similar bodies intended for the working classes (though mutual instruction societies are excluded). He distinguishes these institutions from a second group, usually titled 'Literary and Scientific Institutions', which were more middle-class in character, though admitting working people to membership and seeking to provide for their education.[42] However, the differences between the various types of educational institutions existing at this time were by no means as clear-cut as the name might indicate. As Kelly notes, mechanics' institutes changed into literary and scientific institutions; mechanics' libraries and mutual improvement societies developed into mechanics' institutes; mechanics' institutes and literary and scientific institutions not infrequently declined into libraries or mutual improvement societies; and these changes of function were not always accompanied by a change of name.[43] While acknowledging the complexity of the situation, and especially the lack of documentation about the literary and scientific institutions,[44] I am mainly concerned in this research with that group of institutions that Kelly puts under the heading 'Mechanics' Institutions'; and I shall refer to these as 'institutes' or 'mechanics' institutes'.

In view of the fact that any statistical computation of the number of mechanics' institutes is inevitably arbitrary, calculating the number of women members is a difficult task. Nevertheless, the 1851 Census does offer a national picture of women members at a time when the mechanics' institute movement was considered vigorous.[45] Since I will refer only to statistics that relate to institutions that include the word 'Mechanics' or 'Mechanical' or use the shorthand letter 'M' in their title, and to lyceums and institutions or societies for the diffusion or advancement of knowledge or useful knowledge, the following calculations are probably an under- rather than an over-estimate of women's participation in the mechanics' institute movement.[46]

The first broad trend we find in table 5.1 is that the number of women in the institutes was highest in Yorkshire and the north-western counties of Cheshire and Lancashire, and lowest in the west midland counties and in Wales.[47] This geographical distribution may be partly explained by the

Table 5.1 Membership by sex of the mechanics' institutes in England and Wales, 1851[a]

	Male students	Female students	Females as % of total membership
Division I: London (includes parts of Middlesex, Surrey and Kent)	2,329	672	22.4
Division II: south-eastern counties (includes parts of Surrey and Kent, and counties of Sussex, Hampshire and Berkshire)	5,223	547	9.5
Division III: south midland counties (includes parts of Middlesex, Hertfordshire, Buckinghamshire, Oxfordshire, Northamptonshire, Huntingdonshire, Bedfordshire and Cambridgeshire)	2,348	191	7.5
Division IV: eastern counties (includes Essex, Suffolk and Norfolk)	2,981	444	13.0
Division V: south-western counties (includes Wiltshire, Dorset, Devonshire, Cornwall and Somerset)	3,690	760	17.1
Division VI: west midland counties (includes Gloucestershire, Herefordshire, Shropshire, Staffordshire, Worcestershire and Warwickshire)	2,711	129	4.5
Division VII: north midland counties (includes Leicestershire, Rutland, Lincolnshire, Nottinghamshire and Derbyshire)	3,566	285	7.4
Division VIII: north-western counties (includes Cheshire, Lancashire)	10,827	973	8.2
Division IX: Yorkshire (includes West Riding, East Riding with York, North Riding)	14,782	1,399	8.6
Division X: northern counties (includes Durham, Northumberland, Cumberland and Westmorland)	4,770	173	3.5
Division XI: Monmouthshire and Wales	2,012	137	6.4
	55,239	5,710	9.4

[a]In the few cases where no division of membership by sex is given, I have assumed that all members are men.

Source: Census 1851, Education (England and Wales), pp. 215–58

greater availability of access to institutes in these areas: there were 104 institutes in Yorkshire, 45 in Cheshire and Lancashire, 26 in the west midland counties and 18 in Wales.[48] The higher number of women in the northern counties may also be partly explained by the fact that the Yorkshire Union of Mechanics' Institute advanced in the 1840s, among other things, 'the cause of female education'.[49]

Looking at the number of women tells us little about their representation *vis-à-vis* men. Analysing female membership as a proportion of total membership reveals another broad trend – women formed a much higher proportion of total membership in southern than in northern counties – 22.4 per cent in London, 17.1 per cent in south-western counties, 13 per cent in eastern counties, 8.6 per cent in Yorkshire and 8.2 per cent in north-western counties.

Data from the 1851 Census also reveals that the number of female members is related to the size of an institute. By the mid-nineteenth century, institutes could be divided into three broad divisions: large institutes with a membership of more than 500 (e.g. Manchester, Leeds and Liverpool), medium-sized institutes of 200–499 members (e.g. Woolwich, Barnsley, Newcastle-upon-Tyne), and small institutes of 199 and fewer members (e.g. Royston, Grassington, Paignton).[50] Large numbers of female students (such as 100 or more) are concentrated mainly in that minority of *large* institutes. For example, at Manchester in 1851 there were 350 women and 1,500 men, at Leeds 290 women and 1,558 men, and at Chelmsford 330 women and 450 men; female membership represented 19 per cent, 16 per cent and 42 per cent respectively of the total membership in these institutes.[51]

In none of the small institutes, which make up four-fifths of the total number,[52] do we find a female membership of 100 or more, though the number did vary widely – for example, in 1851 there were 60 women and 116 men at Royston, no women and 22 men at Grassington and one woman and 17 men at Paignton.[53] In these instances the proportion of women members was 34 per cent, 0 per cent and 6 per cent respectively.

These statistics indicate, then, that women might form as much as nearly a half of the total membership of any one institute. Female students dominated the student body only in that handful of women-only institutes. Yet one of the most important of these, the Huddersfield Female Institute, established in 1847, is not even recorded in the 1851 Census – despite the fact that it had 127 members in 1850.[54] The Census also suggests that in England and Wales in 1851 there was a huge difference in male and female recruitments – 55,239 and 5,710 respectively. Although women formed only a small proportion of the national membership – approximately 9.4 per cent – the proportion of members who were women in any region varied from between 22.4 per cent to 3.5 per cent.

Overall, the 1851 Census reveals that numerically women were distributed unequally between regions and within regions, the large institutes recruiting the greatest numbers. Proportionately, women appear not to have exceeded men in any one institute (except the women-only institutes), and nationally they were a minority group. Yet as a minority group of 5,710 persons, they were not insignificant. As we shall later see, many of these women were working class. Given the circumstances of their lives, as described in Chapter 2, it is remarkable that they succeeded in becoming institute members. It is also significant that, since only 10.8 per cent of the estimated number of 9,146,384 girls aged three to 15 years old in 1851 attended day school,[55] a proportion of the female non-attenders became students within the mechanics' institutes.

Women students

It is difficult to establish accurately who the women students were, since, in the various sources, female membership is not always recorded in terms of occupation but often in categories such as 'female subscriber', 'lady member', 'wives, daughters and sisters of members'. Table 5.2 shows a common method of classification.[56]

Such a record makes a number of assumptions. First of all, while men are categorized as 'men', women are called 'females' and, like 'youths', are categorized as 'other' to the male student; it was the male student who defined the norm. In such a male-ordered world, females and children had much in common, especially in the way their membership was defined.

Women students and male youth tended, for example, to be presented as homogeneous categories, undifferentiated by any criterion, whether it be age, occupation, marital status. The subdivision by occupation for men, but not for women, was also significant in that it implied that men worked, while women were not engaged in any 'productive' work, despite the fact that throughout the nineteenth century so many of them were employed in a wide range of jobs. For example, in Nottingham, noted for its hosiery and lace industries, the male students at the mechanics' institute employed in these trades were listed as lace- and stocking-makers; but the 64 women were not so classified – despite the fact that many were likely to have been employed in this work.[57]

Table 5.2   Classification of membership at Nottingham Mechanics' Institute, 1850

Professional men and manufacturers	16
Shopkeepers and tradesmen	80
Clerks, warehousemen, shopmen	236
Lace and stocking makers	38
Joiners, masons, plumbers, painters	10
Smiths, engine and bobbin and carriage makers	35
Handicraft trades not specified	20
Servants, labourers, gardeners	10
Artists, schoolmasters, excisemen	14
Youths	56
Females	64

Source: Nottingham Journal (1 February 1850), quoted in D. Wardle, *Education and Society in Nineteenth-Century Nottingham* (Cambridge, Cambridge University Press, 1971), p. 178.

The classification of students' occupational status is also useful to the historian for indicating social class origins. We know, for example, from the classification of the male membership at Nottingham that the men were drawn mainly from the upper-working classes and lower-middle classes. Such evidence is rarely available for women – though when it is, it appears that the mechanics' institutes often failed to attract large numbers of working-class women in much the same way as they failed to attract large numbers of working-class men.[58] At the large institutes at Manchester and Liverpool by 1851, for example, it seems that female membership was mainly middle class.[59] Indeed, at some institutes, such as Manchester, a deliberate attempt was made by the directors in 1845 to attract women of particular sections of the middle classes and to *exclude* those in the working class. Thus the institute hoped to attract the daughters of 'shopkeepers', 'respectable classes of artisans', those who had 'risen in the world a little' and those who had been 'reduced in circumstances' and could no longer afford an expensive school; working-class daughters were specifically *not* the target audience:

The working classes, perhaps, find a sufficient education for their girls in the Sunday schools, and small schools in their neighbourhood – or, perhaps, what they consider a sufficient education.[60]

A middle-class clientele was largely assured at Manchester, since the female classes were held in the daytime when only women who could afford not to undertake paid work would be able to attend. The cost of the classes – £1 per quarter to study ten subjects, or 8s to study one plus 5s for each additional subject – would have been prohibitive for most working-class women.[61] In 1863, however, the institute offered two evening classes for 'young females engaged in business avocations during the day' and was surprised to find that the courses attracted students of a 'higher social grade' than intended; by 1866, though, the majority of the 80 evening students were 'of a class whose benefit was contemplated'.[62] The number of female students attending evening classes, however, never reached the level of women students attending the 'Ladies' Day Classes' (where 421 women are recorded in December 1865).[63]

Evidence from the large mechanics' institute at Leeds suggests that here the social class intake of women seemed to have been much more varied.[64] Women admitted in 1845 to classes for 5s a year were described and classified as 'Ladies, the Wives, Mothers, Daughters, and Sisters of Members and Subscribers'.[65] By 1847 another category of female members had been introduced – 'Ladies at 10s' – raising the social rank of students, as table 5.3 shows.

This categorization of women into two groups was clearly based on the relation/non-relation of women to male members. Female membership was largest in those categories which referred to relatives of men – wives, mothers, daughters and sisters. As discussed in Chapter 3, a key element in middle-class patriarchal ideology was that women were defined in relation to men, and here the same principle seems to be operating. Rather

Table 5.3 Membership of Leeds Mechanics' Institute, 1844-7

	1844	1845	1846	1847
Life members	5	5	5	4
Proprietary members	132	125	120	133
Subscribers at 15s	245	301	340	377
Subscribers at 12s	228	299	412	432
Subscribers at 8s	206	305	404	435
Ladies at 10s	–	–	–	13
Ladies – the wives, mothers, daughters and sisters of members and subscribers at 5s	–	20	40	157
Day school pupils at 8s	–	–	146	150
	816	1,055	1,467[a]	1,701

[a]The total given was 1,466, but since the figures add up to 1,467 I have listed the latter number.

Source: Report of the Yorkshire Union of Mechanics' Institutes (Leeds, Edward Baines and Sons, 1847), p. 56.

than offer a special fee for a married couple or a family, men are taken as the norm and a cheaper entrance fee is charged for women 'of' male members and subscribers.

The few 'Ladies' not categorized in this way were presumably 'independent' members, charged double the fee of their sisters. The majority of women, however, paid a fee of 5s – which was much lower than that paid by men. This fee may, of course, reflect women's financial dependence or the lower income they might earn in comparison with men. An alternative and more benevolent view of this fee policy might be that the management committee wished to bring women into the institute, and give them a chance to acquire the same opportunities as their menfolk. The problem with this latter interpretation is that, as we shall see in the next section, those women who paid less also had access to far fewer facilities than male members. Women were usually buying a specially reduced service rather than the same service at reduced cost.

The categorization of women at Leeds, once again, is not very helpful when trying to find out about their social background. The historian wishing to define the class position of these women students could, if necessary, use as an indicator the social class background of their menfolk, especially since the majority of women were relatives of male members. The men, it seems, in the case of Leeds, were probably mainly of the aristocracy of labour and lower-middle classes: few men at Leeds were factory workers, though the drawing class in 1850 apparently included masons, bricklayers, joiners, cabinet-makers, engravers, carvers, mechanics, mill-wrights, and blacksmiths.[66]

In the 1850s, the Leeds Institute made a deliberate attempt to attract more working-class women, and by the 1860s two distinctive sets of classes for women were well established. Thus a 'Ladies' Educational

Institute' offered a wide range of day courses, while the section called 'Evening Classes for Adult Females' offered instruction that was 'ordinary and practical, being limited to the elements of an English Education'.[67] The evening classes ran over five evenings a week in order to give young women who were engaged in employment a maximum choice of times that might be convenient. The fees were kept low, and reduced by 33 per cent in 1859 in order to attract more students.[68]

In institutes in the south of England, where a middle-class clientele predominated, working-class women appear to have attended intermittently.[69] At Basingstoke Mechanics' Institution, it was not until the winter session of 1856-7 that a serious attempt was made to attract 'the adult working classes of the town' by offering free elementary classes in reading, writing and arithmetic. Yet despite the fact that a large number enrolled, the committee decided that the venture was too costly.[70] Unless such classes were provided free or at a substantially reduced rate to the 8s yearly or 1s 6d quarterly tickets charged to women, few working-class women would be able to attend. Women working in the fields as day labourers, for example, who wanted to become literate or improve basic reading skills, would have to look elsewhere in rural Hampshire.

At Alton Mechanics' Institute in the Hampshire countryside, they would also have found little consolation. As late as 1886, the all-male committee decided to invite 'ladies' to attend, but with fees of 10s for an afternoon class in art and evening classes costing 3s or 4s, for institute and non-institute members respectively, only the more affluent women would be able to attend.[71] During the 1890s, though, working-class women who were elementary schoolteachers seeking further training might have been drawn to the Saturday afternoon art and cookery classes specially organized for them in collaboration with the county council: the fees were two pence per lesson.[72] But for the majority of working-class women who were not teachers, the Alton institute offered little. Like most southern institutes, it probably funtioned as a literary and scientific society for its literate middle-class clientele. The emphasis upon instruction in classes rather than in lectures, so common in northern institutes, was less frequent in the south.

It is in the many institutes in the north of England charging weekly fees of 1d, 2d or 3d that a reconstruction of the class position of female students is possible, since frequently the occupational status and other relevant information about the women has been recorded. We know, for example, that factory women attended mixed-sex institutes in the north. At Kirkstall in 1846, women working in the local mills were included in the membership of 106: at Holbeck in 1847, where three evening classes for 50 women were organized, it was claimed that 'ignorant factory girls have been trained fit for Sunday School Teachers'.[73] At Bingley in 1850, 'great numbers' of young factory women solicited the committee to join the institute and swelled the female membership to 63 out of a total membership of 243.[74] But it is especially the records of the two main female institutes at Huddersfield and Bradford that yield most information about the social backgrounds of their students.

At Huddersfield Female Institute in 1862, 112 students were enrolled, 61 being over, and 51 under, 15 years of age; the age range could be wide, since in 1866 the youngest student, Hannah Eastwood, was only eight while the eldest, Ann Wood, a lodging-house keeper, was 44 years old.[75] Each student paid 3d a week, or 1d under the 'presentee' system whereby a subscriber could nominate a young women for every 10s given annually. The presentee scheme may have been particularly used by middle-class philanthropists anxious for the welfare of poor young women, and by employers interested in 'the intellectual and moral well-being of the young women engaged in their service'.[76] In 1859, 23 of the 45 fatherless students attended as presentees, and in 1876, when membership rose to 367, one mill-owner sent 20 of his factory hands for instruction.[77] However, not all the students were young single women. In 1864, eight married women attended classes in reading and writing and were praised for their efforts:

it is much to their credit that, feeling their want of education, they have the moral courage to come to the institute, and, taking their places by the side of the young women, endeavour to make up for the loss of opportunities of school training either neglected by or denied to them in their youth.[78]

Other married women, such as the 27 year old who ran a small shop, came to learn arithmetic; she had lost pounds 'in oddments', she claimed, through her inability to count.[79]

The students at Huddersfield seem to have been mainly milliners, dress-makers, domestic servants or daughters living at home with their parents.[80] However, a number of factory workers also attended, as table 5.4 illustrates.

Table 5.4   Huddersfield Female Education Institute: some of the student entries for 1866

Entries	Parent		Student	
	Name	Occupation	Age	Occupation
Mary Hodgkinson	Hannah	Knotter	13	Factory
Alice Dufton	Samuel	Coach builder	11	Mill
Emma Burton	Ester	Burler	16	Factory
Mary Teale	Mary	Shop	12	At home
Ruth Witham	Mary Ann	Weaver	16	Weaver
Ellen Whitehead	William	Shoe-maker	15	Service
Henrietta Parr	Benjamin	Butcher	11	Service
Alice Shaw	Eliza	Lodging house	11	At home
Jane Elizabeth Banks	John	Shoe-maker	13	Warehouse
Eliza Jane Cawthray	William	Ginger beer man	20	At home
Sarah Elizabeth Hallas	Charles Frederick	Organ builder	14	At home
Harriett Binns	–	–	13	French Polisher

Source: Huddersfield Female Educational Institute Book of Pupil Entries (1866).

In contrast, at Bradford Female Institure, where the fees were 2d weekly or 1s 6d a quarter,[81] the students appear to have been drawn from an even wider range of occupations. The 570 students recorded in 1862 included 129 weavers, 267 spinners and other factory workers, 122 nursemaids at home, 6 dress-makers, 2 assistant teachers, 10 piece-board paperers, 17 domestic servants, 1 cigar-maker, 1 employee in a chemical works, 3 employees in a paper warehouse, 4 shop workers, 2 stay-makers, 2 uphol-sterers, 2 bookbinders, and 2 stitchers in a dye-house. The majority (367) of these students were aged 13 to 18 years old, with only 17 women being placed in the eldest age category of 30 to 34 years old.[82]

From such limited data we begin to locate the working-class women who were students within the mechanics' institutes. The students at the Huddersfield and Bradford female institutes, for example, were drawn from those occupations in which, as we have seen in Chapter 2, working-class women were often found. The struggle these working-class women faced in studying part-time must have been considerable. To afford even the weekly fees of many northern institutes must have involved much scrimping and scraping. And of course, in times of unemployment working-class women would be unable to save. The complaint from the Pudsey institute in 1862 is typical of many small institutes struggling to survive with a working-class membership:

Our members – which are males 120 and females 40, total 160 ... (belonging) chiefly to the operative classes, have decreased considerably in numbers, owing, no doubt, to their not being able to pay the subscription of 2d. weekly, consequent upon the scarcity of employment.[83]

Three years earlier, the number of students at Pudsey had been almost double – 230 members, of whom 70 were women.[84]

For the working-class women students, and especially the wives and mothers, the effort and motivation required to attend a class must have been enormous, especially if the institute was a long distance from home. We find frequent references to the way the double burden of long hours of paid work and domestic duties could interfere with the demands of being a part-time student. Mr McCollom, writing master at the Bradford Female Institute, spoke of the restrictions that hard manual labour imposed on the physical capacity of working-class women learning how to write:

It is highly gratifying to any one who takes an interest in the education of the working classes to observe the patience and assiduity with which these girls, after long hours of wearisome toil,   try, with hands cramped and stiffened by daily labour, 'to guide the pen obedient to the will' and very pleasing to see the neat copies many of them have to show.[85]

Miss Mercer, reading teacher at the same place, regretted that many of the students in one of her classes were regularly absent because of domestic responsibilities – despite the fact that they were keen to learn:

About four months since, I had the 2nd adult elementary class placed under my care – out of this class I cannot say much as to the progress made, on account of the irregular attendance of many of the members, very few of whom have attended more than two evenings each week; being all young women, they have had home duties to perform that prevented them from coming so often as they could have desired; but when they are present they manifest great anxiety for their improvement.[86]

The presence of working-class women as students within the mechanics' institutes appears to have been affected by a number of factors. An institute keen to encourage such a clientele would need to have adopted a clear admissions policy. It would have to recognize that working-class women could only afford to pay low fees for their education, on a weekly basis. The timing of a class would also be a potential barrier or aid to attendance. While some married working-class women might be able to attend a daytime class (if fees were low), the vast majority of working-class women would only be able to attend in the evening. The presence or absence of these conditions made a critical difference to an institute's recruitment.

Second-class membership

Although there was some variation between institutes in regard to terms of membership for women, the general trend in the majority of mixed-sex institutes was that women rarely, if ever, attained full membership with equal access to all facilities and privileges granted to men. Winning the struggle to enter the institutes and attend courses never necessarily meant that women had won the battle to remove that host of cultural assumptions about 'woman's place' in society, discussed in Chapter 3. Women as a whole in the nineteenth century were a group of citizens who held secondary status in comparison with men. It was not unexpected perhaps, therefore, to find that women within the institutes were given a membership category that was inferior and unequal to that given to men. Women were offered only restricted use of facilities, limited or no voting powers, and hardly any opportunities to hold official positions.

The unequal membership status of women and men was partly reflected in the different fee and subscription rates for each sex and partly in the different methods of classification. In 1857, the Yorkshire Union of Mechanics' Institutes advised all those wishing to establish an institute in a small town or village to offer yearly, quarterly or weekly fees, the latter to be 3d for men and 2d for women (though it was recommended that men and women pay the same entrance fee of 6d).[87] To what extent the advice about differential weekly fees was heeded is impossible to determine, since the necessary records to not exist. At the institutes at Addingham, Churwell, Gisburn, Slaidburn and Stanningley in Yorkshire in 1852, for example, men and women alike paid one penny a week.[88] And, as noted above, it was in the small northern institutes which charged weekly fees of 1d, 2d or 3d that most working-class women were likely to be found. A weekly fee would, of course, help weekly waged working-class women who would probably not have a capital of, say, 4s 6d for a yearly subscription. On a weekly basis, a working-class woman could buy education as needed and when she could afford it. She could also not attend, when necessary, without losing money.

The greatest disparity between the amounts charged to women and men is evident when payment is quarterly, half-yearly or yearly. In these instances, the subscription rates for women were usually much lower than those for men, as at the medium-sized institute at Colchester, where in 1851 the 205 men paid 8s per annum and the 15 women 5s per annum.[89] The small institutes too, which formed the majority, usually charged women considerably less per annum, as table 5.5 shows.

Table 5.5 Yearly subscription rates in some small mechanics' institutes, 1851

	Males	Females	Youth	Total membership	Number of females
Ashford	13s	6s	8s	96	11
Falmouth[a]	10s	4s 9d	–	190	80
Farnham[a]	6s	4s	–	150	30
Guiseley	5s	4s 2d	–	119	5
Kendal[a]	6s	4s	4s	83	4

[a]Quarterly payments are listed in the Census, which I have multiplied by four for a yearly amount.

Source: Census 1851, Education (England and Wales), pp. 215–58.

The advantages of a yearly subscription were that it gave an institute a regular income and a continuity of membership in the way that a weekly fee could not. Paying a long-term subscription also implied that a member had a commitment to the institute, a vested interest in it, and might be granted access to certain facilities. Yet, as we shall see, female and male subscribers were treated differently.

Women often paid about two-thirds, and sometimes half of the subscription fee that men might pay, though rates could vary enormously and were specific to individual institutes. The lower fee for women was not in itself a predictor of the number of females who would become students, but it does have a symbolic value in that it denotes a particular status for women that was different from that for men. It implied at the very least that men and women *should* be treated differently. The male governing bodies decided the amount of fee to charge women and therefore women's degree of access to institute facilities.

We can date restricted access for women from the 1830s, when they were being admitted to the institutes. A common pattern was for women to be admitted *only* to the library and lectures, and not to men's classes. This was the case, for example, in 1830 at the London Mechanics' Institution, where female relations and friends of members were admitted to the lectures and circulating library. Similarly, at Lewes in 1834, as noted earlier, women were admitted only to the lectures and library. And at Manchester in 1838 'ladies' could 'avail themselves' only of the lectures and library for 5s per quarter and of lectures only for 6d per lecture.[90] What women students bought for their reduced fee was reduced access, a different service from that offered to men. For example, at Andover Mechanics' Institution for the Diffusion of Useful Knowledge in 1840, women were admitted to the library, museum, lectures and readings for 2s per quarter. At Holmfirth, a decision was made at the annual meeting held in 1845 to give to the all-male board of directors the authority to admit only to the library and lectures 'the wives, the unmarried and widowed daughters and sisters of members' at the rate of 6s per annum, payable quarterly in advance.[91] At Ripley, women were admitted 'to the privilege of reading and attending lectures' for 3s per annum or 3d a month.[92]

What is significant at this time, however, is that, having paid for access to libraries and lectures, women were still denied entrance to newsrooms and reading rooms as well as the right to participate in certain management issues.

Newsrooms and reading rooms

In addition to a library, most institutes tried to establish a newsroom where magazine and newspapers could be read. Sometimes there was also a separate reading room. Smaller institutes, of course, might combine a library, reading room and newsroom all in one. But in the early days of the admission of women it appears to have been common to exclude them, particularly from newsrooms and reading rooms. This was the case at London, Manchester and Colchester.[93] Even in the Manchester lyceums, those mechanics' institutes of a more popular kind aiming particularly to attract working-class men and women, women were admitted to 'all the privileges of the institution *excepting* the reading rooms'.[94] Such restrictions extended well into the 1850s and even into the 1860s, as table 5.6, about West Hartlepool Mechanics' Institute, illustrates.

In this instance, women were given the same status in regard to institute facilities as youths and apprentices: yet 'captains and strangers' (presumably men) could use the newsroom if they put one penny at each visit into the 'stranger's box' in the newsroom.[95] It was not unusual for men who

Table 5.6 Use of newsroom related to subscription rate at West Hartlepool Mechanics' Institute, 1860

	per quarter	number
First Class, for Newsroom, Library and Institute	4s	94
Second Class, for Newsroom, Library and Institute	2s6d	144
Third Class, for Library and Institute only	2s	23
Fourth Class, for Library and Institute only (ladies)	1s6d	11
Fifth Class, for Library and Institute only (youths and apprentices)	1s	18

Source: Report of the Yorkshire Union of Mechanics' Institutes (Leeds, Edward Baines and Sons, 1860), p. 87.

were not members to be admitted to an institute's newsroom, while women who were members could be barred. Interestingly, at the two main women-only institutes at Huddersfield and Bradford, we find no reference even to the provision of newsrooms for working-class women who formed the bulk of the clientele.

So what made such facilities particularly unsuitable for women? One feature of the early days of the mechanics' institute movement was the exclusion of topics of religious and political controversy from the curriculum. Therefore when some institutes introduced newsrooms with newspapers, periodicals and magazines for their students, the policy was contentious. Opponents argued that newspapers would not just be expensive, but would introduce an 'undesirable class of members' and lead to 'political discord'; supporters suggested that newspapers would educate members, encourage them to read and prevent the 'working-man' from having to go to the public house to find one.[96] The supporters won the day, and by 1840 Birmingham, Cheltenham, Coventry, Glasgow, Leeds, London and Manchester all had newsrooms: within a few years they were commonly found in most mechanics' institutes.

Such debates undoubtedly played a part in the exclusion of women from newsrooms. As we saw in Chapter 3, politics was a part of the 'public' world of men, and women were assumed to have little or no interest in it. Women disliked politics, claimed the editor of *The Poor Man's Guardian* in 1833, since it made their husbands neglect their homes and families for the club-room and the public house. In 1839, a male resident in Manchester uttered a familiar theme – 'Woman's sphere is *home*. When she enters into the strife, contention, and animosity of politics, she is out of it'.[97] Whether this anonymous letter writer was a member of any of the institutes in the Manchester area we do not know, but here, as in other parts of the country, attempts were made to make the reading rooms and newsrooms into comfortable retreats for men. Indeed some middle-class officials, such as Benjamin Heywood, the banker and president of the Manchester Mechanics' Institution, hoped that a social club atmosphere for men in primarily working-class institutes, such as that at Miles Platting, would prove an alternative to the public house:

We are endeavouring to make our reading-room there very popular – to have in an evening a blazing fire, red curtains, easy chairs – a capital cup of coffee – chess – pictures; now and then a good story read aloud – now and then a good song; in short, to see if we cannot make it a match for the public house, as a place of resort for the working man after his day's work.[98]

The introduction of women into such 'male' clubs would obviously be obtrusive and restricting for men.

Gradually (and particularly during the 1860s) we hear about the admittance of women to reading rooms and newsrooms. At Manchester, the new rules of 1861 stated that every member, on paying 'his or her subscription', shall receive a non-transferable ticket giving 'free admission to the Library, Newsroom, Lectures, and to such Classes and other privileges as the Directors may from time to time determine.' Traice, in his advice in the

MANCHESTER MECHANICS' INSTITUTION

The following is a List of the Newspapers and Periodicals regularly supplied to the News and Reading Room.

NEWSPAPERS.

Daily.

Times (four copies)
Daily News (two copies)
Morning Chronicle
Morning Herald
Sun
Globe
Standard
Manchester Guardian (eight copies)
Manchester Examiner & Times (six copies)
Liverpool Mercury

Tri-Weekly.

Leeds Mercury

Semi-Weekly.

Scotsman

Weekly.

Aris's Birmingham Gazette
Builder
Courier de l' Europe
Despatch
Dublin Advertiser

Economist
Examiner (two copies)
Engineer
Gardeners' Chronicle
Illustrated London News (two copies)
Illustrated Times
Inquirer (two copies)
Liverpool Albion
Leader
Manchester Courier (three copies)
Manchester Advertiser (two copies)
Manchester Weekly Guardian
Manchester Review
Manchester Weekly Times (two copies)
Mark Lane Express
Midland Counties Herald
Mining Journal
Nonconformist
Observer
Saturday Review
Spectator
Ulverstone Advertiser
Watchman
Weekly Chronicle
Wesleyan Times

AMERICAN & AUSTRALIAN PAPERS.

New York Herald
New York Times
Washington Globe
Washington Intelligencer
Philadelphia North American Gazette
Philadelphia Evening Bulletin
Philadelphia Press
Pensylvania Inquirer
Boston Commercial Bulletin
Boston Advertiser
New Orleans Picayune
New Orleans Daily True Delta
New Orleans Crescent
New Orleans Courier
New Orleans Commercial Bulletin
New Orleans Bee

New Orleans Delta
St. Louis Missouri Republican
St. Louis Missouri Democrat
Memphis Daily Appeal
Charleston Mercury
Charleston Courier
Pittsburg Gazette
Columbia Banner
Cleveland Herald
Sacramento Union
San Francisco Herald
San Francisco Daily National
The Valley Tan (Gt. Salt Lake City)

Melbourne Argus
Melbourne Age

MAGAZINES & PERIODICALS.

Weekly.

All The Year Round (two copies)
Athenæum
Chambers' Journal
Lancet
Leisure Hour
Mechanics' Magazine
Notes and Queries
Once a Week (two copies)
Punch (two copies)
Society of Arts Journal
Welcome Guest

Monthly.

All The Year Round
Art Journal

Bentley's Miscellany
Blackwood's Magazine
Chambers' Journal
Civil Engineer
Cornhill Magazine
Cottage Gardener
Dublin University Magazine
Englishwoman's Journal
Family Friend
Family Herald (two copies)
Frazer's Magazine
Gentleman's Magazine
Macmillan's Magazine
National Magazine
Newton's London Journal
Pharmaceutical Journal
Tait's Edinburgh Magazine

Reviews.

| British Quarterly | National | Quarterly |
| Edinburgh | North British | Westminster |

Figure 5.2   Manchester Mechanics' Institution: list of newspapers and periodicals, 1861 (from *Thirty-Seventh Annual Report of the Directors of the Mechanics' Institution*, 1861).

1860s to all affiliated institutes of the Yorkshire Union, recommended that every member should receive a ticket entitling 'him or her' to all the advantages of the institute. But such advice was not universally heeded. For example, it was not until 1888 that Colchester Mechanics' Institute decided to admit women – on condition that they left by 5 p.m.[99]

The facilities available in the newsrooms and libraries to which women eventually gained access varied considerably, but at the large institutes in particular the range could be wide. The 268 women and 1,210 male members at Leeds in 1861 could consult more than 6,300 periodicals and more than 1,000 newspapers: in addition, the newsroom housed 'telegraphic dispatches', a service designed particularly for those with business interests.[100] At Manchester the 272 women members in 1861 would find the reading material listed in figure 5.2 in the news and reading room.

The range of material at Manchester reflects middle-class tastes and interests, nor surprising in an institute where the clientele was mainly middle class. The overseas papers might mirror business interests and connections, while journals such as *The Cornhill Magazine, Macmillan's Magazine* and *Tait's Edinburgh Magazine* would be read by the well educated. Among the more popular periodicals to be found is *The Family Herald*, regarded as the most successful of the new 'family' journals, with a circulation of 125,000 in 1849, mainly among sections of the lower-middle and upper-working class; its content was largely fiction, especially 'affairs of the heart'.[101] Particularly significant for women at Manchester at this time was their right of access to magazines devoted primarily to women's issues – such as the *Englishwoman's Journal*. Begun in March 1858, with its offices at 19 Langham Place, London, the journal contained regular articles by well-known middle-class feminists such as Bessie Rayner Parkes, Barbara Leigh Smith (who married Dr Bodichon in 1857) and Jessie Boucherett.[102] Like the radical working-class press earlier in the century, this journal was an important forum whereby feminist concerns (such as the right of middle-class women to remunerative employment) could be debated before the women's movement became consolidated into political organizations.

It is highly probable that the 272 women at Manchester at this time were drawn from the middle classes, and possibly the more affluent sections of the working class,[103] since no evening, but only day classes were available. For these women, the possibility of reading a woman's journal that debated women's issues may have aided feminist consciousness. But for that vast majority of working-class women in small institutes in the north, such a journal was not available, nor was the range of reading material wide. At Eccleshill, for example, with a total membership of 80 in 1861, the 19 women paying 3d per week or 8d per month could read *The Illustrated London News, The Manchester Examiner and Times, The Leeds Mercury, The Bradford Observer, The London Journal, The Family Herald, Punch* and *The British Workman*.[104] It is rare to find a journal aimed at a female readership in these institutes.

By the mid-nineteenth century the restrictions imposed upon the entry of women into newsrooms and reading rooms were gradually being lifted. In another important area of inequality between the sexes – the right to vote and hold office – change was equally contentious.

Voting and holding office

Trying to assess the extent to which women could vote within the institutes on policy matters and for the election of officials is highly problematic, since the nineteenth century sources do not always clearly specify whether women could or could not vote. However, since the terms of entry for women were usually clearly defined, one could assume that if those terms do not include voting rights, then women were excluded from these.

The right to vote at various meetings, particularly the right to participate in the election of members for official positions, was not an automatic right for *all* male members. A key factor was the organizational structure of any one institute, a structure that could range from oligarchic to democratic, and also change over time. The Manchester Mechanics' Institution, when originally founded, was a good example of an oligarchic structure. Here the property of the institute was vested in the hands of the honorary members, who were wealthy enough to afford the ten guineas necessary for a life membership or one guinea per annum for a yearly membership. These honorary members annually chose 21 persons out of their own number to form a board of directors.[105] However, from 1829 this structure was democratized so that, by February 1834, the directors were elected by and from all the male members eligible to vote.[106] But women were still excluded. It was not until 1861 that female and male members alike could vote in elections for officials: the only members who could not vote were those whose subscriptiuons were in arrears, those whose subscriptions had not been taken out at least three months before the 24th December preceding the day of election, and those under 17 years of age (who might include a large number of the young women in the day classes).[107]

The events up to this change of policy at Manchester are not recorded, but the 1850s were times when the 'woman question', as it was often called, was actively being debated. In July 1851 an article on the enfranchisement of women was published in the *Westminster Review*: in 1855 a pamphlet titled *The Right of Women to Exercise the Elective Franchise* appeared. In 1856 a committee of middle-class women, which included Bessie Rayner Parkes, Barbara Leigh Smith, Mrs Bridell Fox and Mrs Howitt, agitated for support for a Married Women's Property Bill which would extend property rights and the power to make wills to married women. In 1859 a society for enhancing the employment prospects of middle-class women, the Society for Promoting the Employment of Women, was formed; since its administrative centre was at the offices of the *Englishwoman's Journal*, at Langham Place, there was close co-operation between the two ventures, and the women involved became known as the 'Langham Place Group' – Barbara Leigh Smith Bodichon being a key figure.[108] All these changes probably helped to create a certain awareness about women's issues within the Manchester institute itself.

The oligarchic structure of government found initially at the Manchester Institution was also encountered in a number of other institutes in their early years, e.g. at Leeds, Stockport, Hull, Tyldesley.[109] But not all of those institutes with an oligarchic structure refused women voting rights. For example, the revived mechanics' institute that was established in 1852 at Worksop, Nottinghamshire, which was probably managed by those who could afford a guinea subscription, allowed women to 'vote by proxy'; indeed such a right had also been written into the rules of the earlier institute, established in 1831.[110] This is the earliest statement I have found that says clearly and unambiguously that women could vote, by proxy, at any meetings. Such a rule, nevertheless, preserved the 'political' arena of the institute as a male sphere from which women were physically removed.

Not all institutes, when initially founded, used such a structure of decision-making. At the other end of the spectrum were those institutes where the working-class male membership had some control over management and the government was democratic. Crayford Mechanics' Institute, though founded by the gentry, was run by a committee of operatives; Deptford, Hackney, Poplar, Ashton-under-Lyne, Carlisle 'and probably many others' adopted the London model where two-thirds of the committee were working men.[111] But even these more democratically controlled institutes did not *necessarily* give women the vote on policy issues. Indeed, those institutes which allowed female suffrage stand out as the exception rather than the rule. At the more popular institutes called lyceums, where middle-class patrons stayed in the background regarding committee decisions, women could vote: this was the case, for example, at the lyceums founded at Ancoats, Chorlton-on-Medlock and Salford in 1838.[112] At some of the small institutes, too, we read of women being given 'all' or 'the same' privileges as men, as at Guiseley in 1848 and Honley in 1845.[113] Yet these were not representative of the movement as a whole. Much more common was the situation where women were prevented from voting because of their unequal membership status.

At London, women were excluded from voting rights, since they were put with girls in the undifferentiated, apparently homogeneous category of females or ladies and shared the same conditions that applied to 'sons' and 'apprentices'.[114] To equate women with female and male youths was perhaps to imply that all shared, in comparison with adult men, certain characteristics, e.g. innocence, vulnerability, dependence, subordination. In particular, it implied that women were not perceived as responsible for their own circumstances and lives. The unequal membership status given to women automatically excluded them from the right to vote in many institutes, just as it could exclude them from reading rooms and newsrooms. At Thornton, near Bradford, for example, where a new building necessitated in 1871 an increase in subscription rates, the all-male committee re-asserted a familiar pattern:

(a) For honorary members, a subscription of not less than 10s. per annum.
(b) For members under 18 years of age and for women members, a payment of 5s. per annum entitling subscribers to all the privileges of the Institute except use of the refreshment room and the right to vote for the election of officers.

(c) For all other members, a subscription of 7s.6d. per annum.[115]

If women within the mixed-sex institutes did not fare too well in regard to voting rights, were they given suffrage within the women-only institutes? It is important to emphasize a point made earlier, that, despite the 'separateness' of these institutes, they were not free from male control or middle-class influences. However, it was perhaps disappointing for women that the organizational structure of the two main women-only institutes at Huddersfield and Bradford were less democratic than that of either 'parent' institute.

At the Huddersfield Female Institute, the teachers appear to have been a key force in managing affairs, since the management committee was composed of all the 'lady teachers', such of the 'gentlemen teachers or subscribers' who might be elected by the institute, and six students or 'pupil' representatives selected by the female students themselves.[116] Such 'lady' and 'gentlemen' teachers were likely to be middle-class persons who had the necessary level of education plus the motivation and leisure time to engage in such an activity. In 1848 there were about 30 'Ladies' and six 'Gentlemen' who gave their teaching services free, together with another three paid male teachers.[117] By the 1860s, student representation was reduced to four. In 1864, for example, Maria Miles, Hannah Schofield, Mrs Hudson and Jane Dufton were elected from the student body.[118] Whether such women found it difficult to speak in the presence of so many 'educated' and 'superior' persons, we do not know; but if, as girls, they had attended that range of schools organized by the middle classes, e.g. charity schools, schools of industry, National and British schools, they would have been taught deference to those 'above' them.

The Bradford Female Institute, which attracted nearly double the number of students to that at Huddersfield, also had four student representatives on its governing committee:

The affairs of the Institute shall be managed by a Committee of not less than Twelve Members; of whom four shall be pupil members entitled to vote; the remainder shall be elected from Subscribers or Honorary Members at the annual meeting, when all the officers shall be appointed.[119]

Those entitled to vote at the annual or general meeting were female students above the age of 18 who had been 'uninterruptedly connected' with the institute for three months prior to such a meeting.[120] The phrase 'uninterruptedly connected' is unusual in the rules of a mechanics' institute, although the insistence upon a minimum amount of time as a member upon attaining the age of 18 were common as prerequisites for the right to vote. The main Bradford Mechanics' Institute, established in 1832, initially allowed all members over 21 to vote, and then all those above 18.[121] But no stipulation was made about being 'uninterruptedly connected' with the institute.

The policy of the Bradford Female Institute, of allowing eight officers to be elected by subscribers paying a half or one guinea per year and by those honorary members who were the voluntary teachers and librarians[122] –

persons who were likely to be drawn from the ranks of the middle classes – meant that such individuals could decide the composition of two-thirds of the governing body. The claim, therefore, made by Fanny Hertz, that the female institutes at Huddersfield and Bradford were based on 'principles of self government' must be questioned. The views of the working women students on such matters may have differed from the perspective of Mrs Hertz, who hoped that the contact the students had with 'superior and more developed minds' might bring about a 'taste for self-improvement'; her view of women students suggested a need to control them rather than to allow self-government.[123]

The sparse records about some of the smaller female institutes indicate that such places had little or no student involvement in management and were organized mainly by middle-class persons, sometimes 'ladies'. At Netherton, the female institute was 'under the management of several ladies residing in the village, assisted by two paid teachers', and 58 young women were students there in 1861. At Meltham, also in the Huddersfield area, the female institute was 'under the able superintendence' of a Mr Lawford.[124]

With the exception of the female institutes at Huddersfield and Bradford, women within the mechanics' institutes appeared to have had few voting rights, although in the 1860s some women, as at Manchester, were accorded the vote. In 1863, Traice, in his influential *Hand-Book* for mechanics institutes, advised that voting rights should be linked to the level of subscription and, in particular, that no member paying less than 2s 6d a quarter or being under 18 years of age should have the privilege of voting at a general meeting.[125] Institutes following this advice offered only the more affluent women paying 2s 6d per quarter or more the right to vote. The weekly fees that Traice recommended of 3d for men and 2d for women would automatically exclude the latter, since 2d a week for 52 weeks of the year would make only 2s 2d per quarter. Evidently, the struggle of working-class women to enter the institutes did not guarantee equality of treatment.

Not surprisingly, therefore, it is rare to find women in official posts within mixed-sex institutes. When women succeeded in obtaining such posts they were usually appointed as the head or 'lady-superintendent' of a separate female department (as in the institutes at Manchester and Leeds) or, in even less common cases, as a librarian (as at Lincoln).[126] Such posts were likely to be held by middle-class women. Working-class women found employment in the institutes in poorly paid, low-status jobs such as charring and housekeeping.[127] In contrast to the mixed-sex institutes, *more* women at the main women-only institutes at Huddersfield and Bradford appeared to hold official positions, especially, as we have seen, on the governing committees. Such committees were one of the few spaces within the mechanics' institute movement that gave working-class women, through their student representatives, a chance to express an 'official' voice.

It is difficult to determine whether women were actually debarred from standing for office in any one institute. Traice, in his advice to institutes about eligibility of members for office, consistently refers to the male gender of 'he'.[128] Whether 'he' refers to both men and women or men only is debatable: if the former, then 'he' eclipses women who had secondary membership within the institutes: if the latter, then any institute could argue that women were ineligible to stand. Such issues were important in the nineteenth century when women struggled to enter male preserves.

In 1891, when Harriet Smith made an unsuccessful application for membership of the Institute of Chartered Accountants in England and Wales, she was told that the use of the words 'he' and 'his' in the profession's charter could not be interpreted to include women.[129] How many women struggled to hold office within a mechanics' institute we do not know. But some did. At Manchester Mechanics' Institution in 1878, when elementary evening classes for working women were well established, Miss L. E. Willis was nominated for election as director. Since the rules stating the grounds upon which members were eligible for election made no reference to 'he' or 'she' but simply to 'members' and 'persons',[130] Miss Willis and her supporters thought she could stand. The all-male governing board declared her nomination ineligible on the ground that 'male persons only were entitled to serve'.[131] Dr Richard Pankhurst, a keen supporter of women's rights and, by this time, honorary secretary of the Lancashire and Cheshire Union of Mechanics' Institutes, and Lydia Becker, secretary of the Manchester National Society for Women's Suffrage and also a member of the institute, took up the issue.[132] At an annual general meeting they met the opposition of Mr Davies, who argued:

it would be inexpedient to elect a lady to the directorate ... it would be a means of causing much confusion and of interrupting proceedings (Laughter). There were a number of young men connected with the Institution who – would be glad of the opportunity of filling the directorate with ladies, and even the offices of president and vice-presidents. ('No, no', and 'Hear, hear'.)[133]

Lydia Becker, who was loudly cheered on rising, argued that Miss Willis's name should remain on the voting list, while Dr Pankhurst pointed out that it was not a question of privilege or expediency but of substantive right; Lydia Becker and Dr Pankhurst carried the meeting. Mr Davies was defeated, only about a dozen members voting in his favour. Miss Willis did not become director, however. Having won the right to be nominated did not mean that she would be elected to what was seen as a 'male' post. Sylvia Pankhurst, another key figure in the women's suffrage movement, recollects that Miss Willis received fewer votes than any of her male competitors.[134]

Such a debate at Manchester Mechanics' Institution in 1878 would have been linked to agitation for women's rights, both nationally and locally. In February 1874 a Tory government was elected to power and met a constant stream of petitions for women's suffrage: by the close of parliament's first session, 1,272 petitions with 415,622 signatures had been presented. Lydia Becker was active in Manchester and elsewhere for women's suffrage, while Dr Pankhurst not only supported this cause but was also trying to attract women students into the mechanics' institutes.[135] Other changes were occurring, too, especially in regard to the entry of middle-class women into that preserve of men, higher education.

In 1869 Emily Davies established a small college for women at Hitchin with the aim of preparing the students for examinations of Cambridge University. In 1871 Anne Jemina Clough took charge of a house in Cambridge for women students, preparing them for special women's examinations. These two ventures were to grow into Girton and Newnham colleges, at Cambridge University. Although a number of the activists for women's higher education were wary of speaking publicly in favour of women's suffrage, lest it should hamper their cause, the two issues were not unconnected, as Maria Grey recognized in 1877: 'I have felt more and more that we should never get justice in education without the suffrage, and, on the other hand, the suffrage movement has helped that for education.'[136] Similar ideas may have fuelled the debate about Miss Willis's nomination for the directorship at Manchester. Whether any of the working-class women who were students at this time were involved in this debate or in suffrage activities is debatable; the demand by working-class women in Manchester for the vote appears not to have become mobilized until the 1890s, though both Lydia Becker and Emmeline Pankhurst were to make sporadic efforts to link the suffrage campaign with the interests of working women.[137]

Conclusion

The mechanics' institutes were nearly always founded by men, especially middle-class men, with the aim of diffusing scientifically useful knowledge to working-class men. Histories of the mechanics' institute movement have focused on these social class dimensions, especially issues of class control and class conflict. The involvement of women in the movement has been largely ignored. Yet, as we have seen, women struggled to enter such male institutions, often against considerable opposition. For some women, however, the struggle to enter was resolved by attending one of the few women-only mechanics' institutes, especially the two main female institutes at Huddersfield and Bradford.

By the middle of the nineteenth century, nearly 6,000 women were members of the institutes and formed about 9.4 per cent of the national membership. Numerically, they were distributed unequally between regions – Yorkshire, Cheshire and Lancashire attracting the largest numbers. As a proportion of total male/female membership in any one region, however, women achieved their largest representation in the London area and the south-western counties.

Some institutes, especially in the south, appear to have attracted mainly middle-class women, while many northern institutes, and especially the women-only institutes at Huddersfield and Bradford, attracted working-class women in a great variety of occupations. The struggle of these single and married working-class women to study part-time in the evenings, given the material and social conditions of their lives, must have been enormous. Saving the few pennies for an institute's fees must have necessitated a high level of determination. Yet having made the effort to become a 'spare-time' student did not mean equality of treatment with male members of institutes.

The status of women within the institutes was that of second-class members. They often paid two-thirds and sometimes half the subscription fee that men might pay, and for this reduced fee they bought reduced access to institute facilities. When women first entered the institutes in the 1830s, it was common for them to be admitted only to the lectures and library, not to men's classes. Entrance to newsrooms and reading rooms was usually denied also, though during the 1860s this ban was gradually lifted. The secondary membership status of women within the institutes usually prevented them from voting in elections for institute officers and representatives. And it was rare to find women in official posts in mixed-sex institutes, especially in senior posts.

The two main women-only mechanics' institutes at Huddersfield and Bradford had organizational structures that were less democratic than that of the 'male' institutes in both cities. Nevertheless, these female institutes did offer working-class women students the right, under certain conditions, to vote for the election of officers and the opportunity to stand for office themselves. In contrast to the mixed-sex institutes, therefore, the women-only institutes offered their female clientele an 'official' voice; in addition, more women, especially among the middle-classes, held official posts in women-only institutes than in those of mixed sex. Throughout the nineteenth century, the majority of mixed-sex institutes remained male spaces where women were tolerated. It was only in the women-only institutes that women were not seen as unusual. In the following chapter we shall consider the nature of the education provided in such institutes and in those institutes in the mainstream.

6

AN INSTITUTE EDUCATION

Introduction

The entry of women into the institutes created a dilemma for the organizers. How should women be integrated into the traditions of the institutes, given that they were a different sex from the main clientele? As we have seen, a few radical institutes largely ignored sex differences and allowed women access to facilities enjoyed by men – but no woman ever became president of an institute. In the vast majority of cases, women were classified as a separate category of student whose marginal and secondary status brought them an inferior service. In this chapter, we shall investigate how such a secondary status affected women's educational experiences and the kinds of curricula offered to them. How were women students taught, and for what ends?

Over the course of the nineteenth century, changes are evident in the curricula offered to women within the mechanics' institutes, whether organized in day or evening sessions. Nevertheless certain patterns in curricula provision emerge over this period of time. Two major features of the mechanics' institutes were sex segregation in curricula and social class differentiation; thus male and female students and women of different social classes were offered different curricula. Also, within the institutes, the curriculum transmitted certain messages to women students. This could include, as we shall see, messages about women's traditional place within the sphere of the home, the political ideas of the nineteenth-century women's movement, and images of women's 'public' role.

Sex segregation

The physical segregation of male and female students within the mechanics' institutes reinforced and confirmed the need for different curricula for men and women, who were seen as distinct educational populations with separate needs. Sex segregation as a principle was strongest in the provision of male and female institutes, but it also permeated mixed institutes.

Overall, two main tendencies seem to have shaped teaching within the institutes – on the whole, men and women tended to be separated for small-group class work, though they were allowed, and expected, to attend lectures together. As early as 1839, Duppa had recommended:

It is desirable, of course, as far as circumstances allow, to keep the male and female classes distinct; and this is easily done by means of separate entrances, and by varying the hours and evening of attendance.[1]

Most of the mixed institutes organized single-sex classes. In at least 30 towns in Lancashire and Yorkshire during the 1840s, for example, separate classes for women were established.[2] In mixed institutes, where men and women were in the same building, sex segregation could be maintained by setting up separate classrooms, separate evenings, separate departments and separate entrances.

Separate classrooms for men and women or, as at Wakefield, for 'Adults, Boys, and Females' appear to have been common.[3] At Kirkstall, where frequent attempts to establish women's classes during the late 1840s met with repeated failure, it was decided that 'a separate room, which will be shortly supplied, is necessary, as ladies do not like to attend to conduct their education in the place where the males are receiving instruction'.[4] Sometimes, when the demand by women exceeded the supply of rooms, the principle of sex segregation could limit the number of female, rather than male, classes. At Manchester in 1863, for example, when evening classes for working women were held in rooms set aside for the purpose 'without the chance of collision with the members of any other Department of the Institution', the arrangement limited the meetings to two, rather than three, a week.[5] At other times, an institute accommodated the demands by women for instruction by letting them use a non-teaching room (such as a newsroom), extra rented accommodation or another building.[6] If these arrangements failed to meet demand, women could be turned away, as at Southowram in 1857, where more than a dozen women were refused admission 'for want of room'.[7]

Separate evenings for men and women was another common feature of class provision. At Pudsey, where 96 women and 100 men were members in 1852, the women attended two evenings a week and the men 'the remaining'; similarly, at Bingley in 1850, when young factory women entered the institute, the committee decided upon separate nights for attendance.[8] At Lockwood too in 1857, the 45 girls and women attended classes on Tuesday and Thursday evenings, while the 212 males met on different nights of the week.[9] At some of the larger institutes, keeping the sexes separate was less of a problem, since women were contained in their own department. This was the case at Leeds, where the women's day classes were organized by the 'Ladies Educational Institute'; a similiar arrangement operated at Manchester, where the committee organizing the day classes for females made a monthly report to the board of directors.[10]

How far Duppa's recommendation of separate entrances for men and women was implemented within the institutes is difficult to determine, since the issue is not always mentioned in the various texts. But some institutes thought it desirable. At the London Mechanics' Institution, where women were first admitted in 1830, the 'propriety' of allowing them to use 'the front entrance' was still being debated some three years later.[11] At Woodhouse, where the institute was established in 1848 by 12 young working men who belonged to the temperance movement, there was one entrance 'intended for young men, the other for young women'.[12] If an institute was purpose built, according to the recommendations of the Manchester District Association of Literary and Scientific Institutions for a plain but substantial building costing about £1,700 in 1840, then separate entrances and other features of sex segregation would be integral:

The 2nd., or principal storey, would contain the news room and library, to be entered by a door to the front of the street, and a large room for the females' department, with a distinct entrance for their sake at the side of the building. Between this and the other parts of the institution there would be no internal communication; and the requisite separation of the sexes would be still more completely preserved by means of a door opening into the library, behind the librarian's partition, through which alone the female members would enter from their room to procure books. This would obviate all possible objections to connecting female instruction with Mechanics' Institutions, as well as the necessity for a regulation sometimes adopted to setting apart certain evenings for females only.[13]

Although separate classes for men and women were the predominant pattern in mixed-sex institutes, some mixed classes could also be found. For example, at Wakefield in 1850, with 522 male and 25 female members, 47 men and women were taught together in the reading, writing and arithmetic classes; at Keighley in 1850, with 319 male and 101 female members, men and women shared the class taught by Mr Leach, the 'eminent Teacher of Ornamental Writing'.[14] At the institute established in 1849 for male factory hands at the Courtaulds Silk Factory, Halstead, young women were invited to share the essay, discussion and botany classes.[15] The practice adopted at Halstead does not appear to have been common elsewhere. When joint classes were held in the institutes, they were used mainly in recreational activities, such as singing.

Joint singing classes, common in a large number of institutes, often formed the backbone of a concert or other form of entertainment. At Nottingham, where the singing class had more than 50 members, a concert in 1852 included a five-part glee, 'When Winds Breathe Soft', in which the Misses Stafford and Challand, and Messrs Ward, Elliott and Granger all took part. At Huddersfield Mechanics' Institute, where women attended the singing class, a concert in 1857 included contributions by Mr Hartley, Miss Crosland, Miss Hirst, Miss Parker, and the Paddock Choir. In the musical society formed at Plymouth for entertaining institute members, recruits were still being sought in the 1890s.[16]

In marked contrast to the policy of separate classes in mixed-sex institutes was the provision of lectures which women could attend jointly with their menfolk. It is not clear from the records, though, why the classes and lectures were organized in this way. However, if a separate female curriculum was advocated in the 'serious' work undertaken in the classes, then this would necessitate separate class provision for women and men. Lectures, on the other hand, might have been seen as a leisure activity, and it would be more acceptable in Victorian society for men and women to attend such recreational events jointly: indeed, there were educational precedents for this, since from 1828 women could attend the lectures with men at both King's and University College, London, and both sexes also attended lectures at the numerous literary and philosophical societies.[17] The different nature and characteristics of lecture and class teaching may also help to explain why they were organized differently. The specific nature of class teaching, which involved intimate, face-to-face interaction over a period of time, could be more threatening to social relationships between men and women than the more formal, public nature of a one-off lecture. However, there also may have been deeper, underlying reasons why separate rather than mixed classes were favoured, reasons that could be sought in the conventions and ideologies of the period.

Although working-class children might have attended a range of co-educational schools, it was commonly assumed that the 'best' model for educating working-class men and women was single-sex classes, as in the adult Sunday schools.[18] The principle of sex segregation in education was evident also among the middle classes; as discussed in Chapter 4, though young brothers and sisters might be educated together, a son would be sent away to school as soon as he was old enough, while a daughter would be taught at home and sometimes also in a small private girls' school. For an institute to oppose the practice of single-sex classes for adults would have been radical and daring.

Single-sex classes in mixed institutes might also be supported on grounds of principle, namely that men and women were different and had different educational needs. As we saw in chapters 2 and 3, over the course of the nineteenth century women became increasingly identified with the private sphere of the home and family, and men with the public sphere of business, paid work and politics. Such differences are reflected in statements about the educational needs of men and women within the institutes. Men's education was advocated in terms of its relevance for vocational skills, the creation of new technical knowledge, self-improvement and value as a worthwhile leisure hobby.[19] As Linnaeus Banks, a popular songwriter, said in his address at Harrogate Mechanics' and Literary Institute, the aim of the institutes was to make the man a better mechanic and the mechanic a better man.[20] In contrast, women's education within the institutes, as we saw in the previous chapter, was usually advocated in terms of their assumed roles as wives and mothers.

The idea that the female student might be mentally 'inferior' to the male was rarely expressed directly, though statements about the different mental capacities of the sexes was common. While the male students might be referred to as a 'thinking man', extending 'the universe of mind',[21] it was commonly believed 'it is not good that the minds of women should have liberty to expand in all directions'; in particular, it was assumed that certain 'avenues of knowledge' should be closed to women in the humble ranks of society.[22] Indeed some writers believed that working-class women, especially wives, had interests only in the satisfaction of material wants – 'she is apt to consider as prodigal every outlay that does not directly administer to some physical want'.[23] Overall, the assumption is that the abilities of the female student lent more to the practical than the mental and intellectual, and that her range of talents was more limited than that of the male. Such supposed differences between men and women could easily be used to justify sex segregation in the organization of class teaching.

Another possible reason why separate rather than mixed classes were held in the institutes relates to fear of sexual relations. Although the issue of co-education for children had been discussed early in the nineteenth century,[24] the value of co-education for adult students appears to have become an important subject of debate only by the 1860s. And sometimes fears about 'affairs' between male and female students were openly expressed, as in 1868:

It was prophesied in America that when young men and women were brought together in colleges, there would be many love affairs, and that these would be often imprudent, and lead to the neglect of studies. The experience of the American college shows that though there were fewer cases of this kind than had been anticipated, they rather incited those concerned to better conduct and more earnest study. Both man and maid aspire to make the best appearance in the eyes of those they love, and not to be surpassed by others, and why should such attachments be imprudent? ... to a thoughtful man or woman it will be no disparagement of the co-educational plan that it may lead to attachments which, surviving the tests of years of associated study, may end in marriage.[25]

Within the mechanics' institutes, fears about the mixing of the sexes rarely eluded to 'love affairs'. What is common is to find 'worthy people' objecting to both sexes visiting an institute at the same time, since 'they would go home together, and that would be improper, perhaps dangerous!'[26] Whether male students objected to sex segregation in the classes, we do not know; and in the few cases where women apparently asked for separate provision, as at Kirkstall in 1848, there are no records of their reasons.[27] It should not be forgotten that many of the institute students were under 20 years of age (and even as young as 14) and therefore at a time of life when courting might be common. This helps to explain the emphasis upon 'the strictest decorum'[28] prevailing in the mixed classes that were held. Unless such assurances were given, married women might be reluctant to attend, too, and their husbands unwilling to support their part-time studies.

Sex-segregated teaching obviously influenced the women's experiences of being students within the institutes. But this was not all; sex segregation also held significance for the curriculum that was taught.

Curriculum differentiation

Theoretically it was possible to teach the *same* curriculum to men and women, separately. However, the principle of sex segregation in this instance was based more on the notion of *different* curricula provision for the sexes than on a common curriculum. This division of knowledge by sex into 'male' and 'female' shaped the kinds of subjects taught, the standard of teaching and the forms of assessment thought appropriate for men and women students.

It is not easy to derive, from the records, a national picture of this differentiation, since many institutes appear to have been autonomous, differing in size, income, location and degree of local influence. However, it is possible to focus on one or two case studies in order to identify some of the factors that influenced the policy of gender-differentiated curricula. Another difficulty when trying to generalize about curricula provision is that there were different types of curricula for women, based upon the assumed social class background of the clientele. As we have seen, evening classes charging a small weekly fee aimed to attract working-class women, while day classes, with a much higher fee, hoped for a middle-class audience. In these different forms of provision, the curriculum was differentiated by social class. Here we can find the impact of class-specific ideals of femininity, for example, those of the working-class 'good wife and mother' and the middle-class 'lady', discussed in Chapter 3. One cannot, of course, rule out exceptions to such generalizations, given the inadequacy of information on the class background of the women students.

In this book the main concern is with working-class women who were unlikely to attend day classes, given the conditions of their daily lives. However, the day classes are of interest also since they provide a model with which to compare working-class women's education; in particular, they help us to evaluate the quality of education offered to women of the 'lower' orders.

The curriculum of middle-class women

As noted in the last chapter, the women at the large institutes at Liverpool and Manchester were drawn mainly from the middle classes. Although

Manchester Mechanics' Institution is not a typical institute, it does offer a case study of the way the social class background of middle-class women could be the most important factor shaping the female curriculum. In the Manchester Institute there were even two different strands of middle-class female education – afternoon classes for adult women and day classes for young women.

Although no information is given about the social background of the women in the afternoon classes in the 1860s, it is probably that, since attendance was in the daytime, women in the more affluent sections of the working-class and in the lower middle-class would be the most likely source of recruits; the fee of 3s per quarter would be beyond the means of most working-class women.[29] The number of adult women paying this amount for an afternoon class at Manchester, though, was never large – 30 in 1866 and 38 in 1870.[30]

These afternoon classes appear to have been aimed at two main groups of middle-class women: 'those ladies whose early education has been neglected' and 'those who can give only a part of their time to study'.[31] Compensatory education appears to have been a main motive of the providers: the women were offered a general education plus access to some subjects studied by the more numerous younger women in the day classes, e.g. English literature, music, dancing, botany, drill and drawing.[32] Since explicit reference is made to offering these adult women, through education, an 'intellectual culture'[33] rather than any preparation for home life, the majority may already have been wives and mothers whose attendance at the classes was seen as a kind of 'culture raising'. However, instruction was not solely confined to non-examinable liberal subjects.

By the 1880s some of these women were sitting examinations organized by the Union of Lancashire and Cheshire Institutes. In 1881, six adult women gained passes, in different grades, in a range of subjects that included arithmetic, history, dictation, geography and needlework.[34] Such success might, of course, have a vocational value. With such general knowledge, a married woman might set up a small private school, while a single woman might enter clerical work or elementary schoolteaching. And it may have been particularly the less affluent middle-class women who sought such jobs, since in 1863 reference was made to the way 'the pressure of the times' had brought about a 'diminution' in the number of adult women students who were able to devote only 'a small portion of their time' to their studies.[35] Overall, the curriculum for adult women at the Manchester Mechanics' Institution appears to have offered the opportunity both to study liberal subjects and to acquire knowledge that had a vocational value.

However, the afternoon classes for adult women at Manchester were of marginal interest to the institute and not representative of the curriculum in the day classes for young women. The day classes were the really interesting provision for middle-class women, offering a model of the way a young ladies' curriculum might develop over the nineteenth century.

When the directors at Manchester decided in 1845 to attract daughters

HIGHER DAY CLASSES FOR FEMALE EDUCATION,

ARE NOW IN ACTIVE OPERATION.

Lady Superintendent .... MISS WOOD.

Branches Taught.

1. English Reading, Grammar, Geography, Arithmetic, and Writing	Miss WOOD, Miss ASKEW, Miss POLLITT, Miss GELL, and Miss PILCHER.
2. Plain and Fancy Needlework	Miss WOOD, Miss HORDERN, and Miss ASKEW.
3. Cutting-out and Making-up of Dresses, &c...........	Miss HORDERN.
4. French Language and Literature	Mons. MORDACQUE.
5. Biography and Criticism of English Literature	Mr. DANIEL STONE, Jun.
6. Landscape, Flower, and Figure Drawing	Mr. H. H. HADFIELD.
7. Music—(Instruction on the Piano Forte)—first class..	Mr. M. CONRAN.
8. Music ditto ditto	Mr. M. CONRAN.
9. Department of Modelling and Casting—(Flowers, Fruit, &c.).............................	Mons. BALLY.
10. Natural Philosophy and Chemistry	Mr. DANIEL STONE, Jun.

Hours of Attendance at the Classes.

The English Department	Miss WOOD, Miss ASKEW	Daily, from 2 to 5 o'clock.
Plain and Ornamental Needlework	Miss WOOD, Miss HORDERN, & Miss ASKEW	Mon. & Thrs. fr. 2 to 4 o'cl.
Cutting-out & Making of Dresses ..	Miss HORDERN	Tuesday, 11 a.m.
French Department	M. MORDACQUE................	Saturday, 4 p.m.
Biography and Criticism of English Literature..............	Mr. D. STONE, Jun..............	Thursday, from 4 to 5 o'cl.
Modelling of Fruit, Flowers, &c. in wax and plaster	M. BALLY......................	Friday, from 3 to 5 o'clock.
General Drawing	Mr. H. H. HADFIELD	Saturday, from 2 to 4 o'cl.
Music (the Piano-Forte)...........	Mr. CONRAN	Wednesday, 11 a.m.
Music..........................	Mr. CONRAN	Wednesday, 3 p.m.
Class Lectures on Natural Philosophy and Chemistry	Mr. D. STONE, Jun.	Tuesday, from 4 to 5 o'cl.

Figure 6.1 Subjects offered to females at Manchester Mechanics' Institution, 1846 (from *Twenty-Second Annual Report of the Directors of the Manchester Mechanics' Institution*, 1846).

of the lower-middle class,[36] the subjects offered to these young women in day classes were as in figure 6.1.

Such a curriculum attempted to transmit the knowledge and skills considered appropriate for a 'young lady'. The majority of students on these courses appear to have been young girls and women; in 1851, for example, 162 of the total number of 253 were 14 years old and younger. The curriculum thought appropriate for this clientele consisted of such subjects as English, where considerable attention was given to the spoken word and art of conversation and writing, which included not only letter writing but also writing bills, keeping cash accounts, sealing letters and pen-making.[37] Such skills might help young women become competent in middle-class rituals of 'calling' as well as in managerial skills as a future mistress of a household.[38] Other subjects studied might fill the leisure hours of the 'young lady' and embellish her femininity, e.g. playing the piano, drawing, making flowers, fancy needlework. The subsequent inclusion of morning dancing classes (established by 1851) probably also taught middle-class rituals of etiquette; after all, in nineteenth-century society dances and balls were important social functions where young ladies might meet suitable future husbands.[39]

In 1861 the inclusion of drilling in the curriculum helped promote the physical well-being of the student.[40] Drilling, and other forms of exercise (such as callisthenics, a kind of gentle gymnastics), were often taught as a means of promoting healthier growth in the more 'academic' private schools for middle-class girls established in the second half of the nineteenth century.[41] More academic subjects, such as Latin, were also available, though by 1861 classes in domestic chemistry and natural philosophy had been dropped.[42] Periodic attempts were made in the 1860s to re-introduce classes in philosophy or science and short courses were given on the 'Philosophy of Common Things' and on astronomy,[43] but overall the curriculum for young ladies in 1870 remained very much the same as it had been in 1846, with its emphasis on social rather than academic subjects. What is remarkable over this span of time is its continuity.

It was claimed in 1847 that such a curriculum would make the female students 'better wives, sisters, mothers, and members of society'; emphasis, however, was also placed on its 'practical value', especially for women 'desirous of educating for the office of governesses'.[44] That such a vocational aim was stressed at this particular time was unusual (though not unique in the history of girls' and young women's education). For many girls, such as these, education was normally provided at home or in small private schools where the curriculum was decided by 'social priorities'[45] rather than vocational skills. However, some training institutions for women were being established.

For example, the first women's teacher-training college, Whitelands, which aimed to recruit young women between 17 and 25 years old, was founded in 1842. The early records reveal that the students included daughters of respectable artisans and tradespeople as well as of clergymen and surgeons.[46] In 1848 Queen's College, London, was founded for 'any young ladies' of 12 years old or more who wished to come. Although it was originally intended that the college should be for governesses or intending governesses, the plan was abandoned. Nevertheless, a series of free evening lectures for governesses was organized.[47] That a predominantly male, vocational institution, such as a mechanics' instititute, without the title 'college', could find space for educating 'young ladies' *and* stress the vocational usefulness of the course, was undoubtedly unusual and perhaps stigmatized the education offered. To associate a governess with the working class and with practical education was to downgrade even further her already ambivalent middle-class status. Although many single middle-class women without financial means became governesses, they experienced status incongruence in that, in such a 'ladylike' occupation, they were engaging in that very activity that was anathema to a lady – paid work.[48]

On the other hand, since being a governess was considered a suitable

LIST OF THE TEACHERS AND OF SUBJECTS TAUGHT.

Commercial and Scientific School for Boys.

The following subjects are included in the School Fee : Reading, Writing, Arithmetic, Grammar and Analysis, Geography, History, Physiography, Theoretical Mechanics, Mathematics, Magnetism and Electricity, Drawing, Latin, French, English Literature, Animal Physiology.

Head Master	Mr. R. F. BREWER, B.A., London.
Assistant Masters {	Mr. G. F. FARRAND.
... ...	Mr. F. W. TUCK.
... ...	Mr. F. H. WEST.
Drawing (Landscape and Figure)	Mr. H. H. HADFIELD.
„ *(Second and Third Grade Art)*	Mr. W. E. CROWTHER.
Pianoforte and Singing	Mr. JOSEPH VAREY.
Dancing	Mons. P. H. PARIS.
Drilling	Captain LOVELOCK.

Young Ladies' Day Classes.

The following subjects are included in the School Fee : Reading, Writing, Arithmetic, Grammar and Analysis, Geography, History, Latin, French, English Literature, Botany, Animal Physiology, Needlework, Domestic Economy.

Lady Principal	Mrs. K. R. SMITH.

Figure 6.2   Classes at the Manchester Mechanics' Institution, 1881 (from *Fifty-Seventh Annual Report of the Directors of the Manchester Mechanics' Institution,* 1881).

occupation for a woman of gentle brith who had fallen on hard times,[49] the Manchester Mechanics' Institution, in providing courses for those who wanted to enter the occupation, may have attracted the 'right' sort of clientele. The 'female' knowledge taught to 'young ladies' at Manchester would, of course, prepare them for such a female and class-based occupation. And we can see how predominantly 'female' this knowledge was if we look at the alternative curriculum provided for middle-class boys at Manchester.

By the 1860s, a 'Commercial and Scientific Day School for Boys' had been established as part of the Manchester Mechanics' Institution, probably for an equivalent age group to that of the young ladies in the day classes.[50] The aim of the boys' school was to offer a 'sound English education, especially adapted to the requirements of this commercial district'.[51] Not unexpectedly, the major difference between the curriculum studied by these boys and that studied by the 'young ladies' was most marked in regard to the greater range of scientific and mathematical subjects, as the advertisement for the school in 1881 (Figure 6.2) shows.

On the other hand, that these young men could study subjects such as landscape and figure drawing, the piano, singing and dancing shows that the skills were *not* just considered accomplishments for 'young ladies'. 'Young gentlemen' also needed socialization into graces that would make them competent in rituals of etiquette and in courtship. However, it seems as if caution needs to be maintained here, since the popularity of such subjects was never high.[52]

Although the curricula for 'young ladies' never included the range of scientific and mathematical knowledge available in the boys' classes, changes took place. During the early 1860s, the 'Young Ladies Day Classes' began to suffer fluctuations in membership, so that by 1864 there were only 181 members compared with 242 three years earlier. The decline in recruitment was attributed to the financial pressures facing many middle-class parents, who were having to send their daughters into the labour market.[53] However, other factors impinged on the curriculum at this time, helping to mould it into a new form that may have seemed more relevant for the lives of young middle-class women.

During the early 1860s, the issue of admitting girls and women to various educational examinations was debated in certain feminist circles. Thus Emily Davies, who had founded in Durham and Northumberland a local branch of the new Society for Promoting the Employment of Women, attempted, under its auspices, to win approval for women to sit Church and mechanics' institute examinations.[54] Then in October 1862 she set up a committee to press for the admission of females to the local examinations of the ancient universities of Oxford and Cambridge. Success came first at Cambridge, where girls were admitted to the local examinations on an experimental basis in December 1864, and then permanently, on the same terms as boys, in March 1865. The aims were not only to bring women into a national system of examination that would improve their educational standard but also, in Emily Davies's words, to 'let female education be *encouraged* – let it be understood that the public really *cares* whether the work is done well or ill'.[55] The debate about the standard of education for middle-class girls was further fuelled by the Schools Inquiry Commission, which suggested that undue time was given to accomplishments and that the low standard generally was due to lack of thoroughness, foundation and system.[56]

The Manchester Institute, with its declining number of female day students, seems to have been aware of these debates. In 1869 the retiring board of the institute urgently recommended its successor to consider the desirability of presenting annually a number of female candidates for the Cambridge Local or London University Examinations, since such a test would give 'point' and 'definiteness' to the pupils' work as well as instil a 'greater amount of public confidence' in the institute.[57] The advice seems to have been adopted, since gradually we hear of successful entrants.

In December 1879 Henrietta Mears passed the Junior Cambridge Local Examinations in English grammar and analysis, arithmetic, history, geography, English literature, botany and scripture with distinctions in French and Latin; the following year she successfully sat the Senior Cambridge Examination.[58] In 1881 Miss Zanetti and Miss Caldwell passed the Senior Oxford Local Examination.[59] Nor were these the only qualifications that young women might gain, since examinations were also held by other bodies – the Society of Arts, the Science and Art Department and the Union of Lancashire and Cheshire Institutes.[60] Miss Zanetti gained a prize of £1.10s. in the commercial English examination of the union and Miss Stern one for the same amount in commercial French.[61] The directors at Manchester were keen to encourage these developments and especially to 'draw the attention' of parents to the university local examinations which 'afford a valuable test of the attainments of the pupils'.[62]

Such changes were undoubtedly linked to 'increasing competition' from other educational institutions in the Manchester area.[63] The 1870 Education Act aimed to provide a national system of elementary schooling for children by establishing school boards in districts where there were no efficient and suitable schools. Although middle-class girls were educated largely outside this state sector, some attended state schools, especially the superior board schools and those elementary schools called 'higher grade schools' which attempted to offer some form of secondary education. The middle-class girls attending these 'superior' and 'higher' elementary schools were likely to come from the impoverished sections of the middle classes.[64] There was also some pupil movement from the state elementary sector to the fee-paying grammar schools, which offered the more impecunious a secondary education via the scholarship system; in 1887 the chair of the Manchester School Board claimed that it was mainly the children of the 'labour aristocracy' and the better-paid 'upper strata' of the working class who benefited from such an opportunity.[65] Some of the girls in these social groupings might therefore be using the state scholarship system rather than the comparatively 'expensive' fee-paying education of the Manchester Mechanics' Institute.

However, a much bigger threat to the viability of the day classes for young women at the Manchester Institute may have been posed by the Manchester High School for Girls, a fee-paying institution established in 1874, largely through the efforts of the Manchester Association for Promoting the Education of Women. One of the educational aims of the new high school was to offer a sound education, which would meet the requirements of the university local examination, while not neglecting the preparation of girls to become 'intelligent companions and associates for their brothers, meet helps and counsellors for their husbands, and wise guides and trainers for the minds of their children'.[66] On the first day of its opening, 19 January 1874, parents 'poured in' to pay the fee and 60 pupils were enrolled.[67]

By the early 1880s, when the mechanics' institute movement was in decline and the number of students at Manchester had fallen to 1,639 (of whom 326 were females paying 3s per quarter),[68] the curriculum in the 'Young Ladies' Day Classes' had changed from that in early 1846, but had also retained a number of similar characteristics. The main continuities were to be found in the teaching of general subjects, such as reading, writing, arithmetic and geography, and in 'accomplishments', such as French, needlework, piano playing, landscape and figure drawing. The main changes we can identify were in the inclusion of additional subjects, such as science, and especially in the methods of assessment. Not only were the students entered for various 'public' examinations, there were also a number of prizes and scholarships that were offered in the institute.[69] Of particular interest in this context are the Pochin Scholarships, worth £10 each, offered through the generosity of H. D. Pochin to young women who did well in certain examinations. Henry Pochin and his wife were active in the women's suffrage campaign. In 1868 Mr Pochin, Mayor of Salford, had presided over the first public meeting on women's suffrage, held in the Free Trade Hall, Manchester. Lydia Becker, who (as we saw in the previous chapter) would become involved ten years later in the nomination of Miss Willis for the post of director of the Manchester Institute, proposed a resolution supporting women's suffrage, while Mrs Pochin expressed approval of the aims of the National Society for Women's suffrage; Dr Richard Pankhurst, another advocate of women's rights, was also at this public meeting and later involved also with Miss Willis's right to stand for office.[70] It was Mrs Pochin who had written the pamphlet *The Right of Women to Exercise the Elective Franchise* under the pseudonym of 'Justitia', published in 1855, and to her, along with Mrs Jacob Bright, Mrs Wolstenholme Elmy and Mrs Duncan M'Laren, is attributed the passing of the first Married Women's Property Act and the Guardianship of Children Act.[71] In view of the interest of Mr and Mrs Pochin in the 'women question', it was not surprising that they offered scholarships for able young women at a local mechanics' institute. Their gesture showed that men and women active in the women's movement could also be involved in institute affairs and see a link between the improvement of standards in the education of young women and the improvement of the social position of women in society generally. Many more such connections in the mechanics' institute movement are probably hidden in history.

The curriculum model for young middle-class women at Manchester Mechanics' Institution has revealed, then, that while lady–like accomplishments were taught throughout the period, increasing emphasis was also given to academic excellence through public examinations. Delamont claims that such contradictions were common in girls' private schools in the nineteenth century, especially those attempting to improve their educational standards; such schools, dependent for survival upon the fees that parents would pay, had to supply what parents wanted or else close down.[72] At Manchester Mechanics' Institution, the directors seem to have faced similar dilemmas: they offered accomplishments that would enhance the femininity of the students and possibly increase their prospects in the marriage market, while also preparing them for academic success that might lead to employment. It was an attempt to cover all eventualities; if a young middle-class woman failed to find a husband, her education was not 'wasted' since she had marketable skills. After all, by the 1880s, 'young ladies' might be found in paid work.

By the end of the nineteenth century, as we have already seen (Chapter 3), a new ideal of femininity for middle-class women was also emerging – that of the 'new woman' who moved outside the sphere of the home to seek, among other things, a sound academic education and the right to employment. It would appear that a mechanics' institute, such as that at Manchester, attempted to respond to these changes in middle-class lifestyles by reformulating the curriculum for young, middle-class women.

The curriculum of working-class women

In contrast with the curriculum for middle-class 'ladies' in day and afternoon classes at Manchester, working-class women attending in the evenings, usually for a weekly fee of a few pence, were offered different kinds of knowledge. The working-class female curriculum in most institutes covered a much narrower range of subjects, namely reading, writing, arithmetic, plain sewing and some limited general knowledge. If the education of 'young ladies' in the institutes had much in common with the secondary schooling of middle-class girls, the classes for working-class women derived from the developing elementary schooling offered to working-class girls. As we saw in Chapter 4, that minority of working-class girls who attended National and British schools were taught the three Rs, sewing and, if lucky, some history and geography. And whereas middle-class young women within the institutes might be prepared for both domesticity *and* employment, paradoxically it seems that the working-class women's curriculum was very much orientated towards the former rather than the latter. The class-specific ideal of working-class femininity discussed earlier, that of the 'good wife and mother', seems to have dominated the curriculum for working-class women. It is somewhat ironic that, given the appalling conditions of working-class women's lives in paid work, so little attention appears to have been bestowed on improving their employment prospects. In contrast, the education of working-class men in the institutes, as we shall see, was often orientated towards such vocational 'improvement'.

Not surprisingly, it was particularly in the northern institutes, where the proportion of women from working-class backgrounds was much greater than in the southern institutes, that the limited curriculum for working-class women was well established. In 1857 the Yorkshire Union advised those wishing to establish an institute in a small town or village to include female classes for reading, writing and plain needlework.[73] In 1859 Mr Barnett Blake, agent and lecturer of the union, reiterated such views adding that such a curriculum, was 'so necessary' to the comfort of the working-class *man*'s household; furthermore, he pointed to

the great importance of female education as one of the surest means of achieving social amelioration. As the first lessons of instruction, whether or good or evil, are derived from the mother, it is evident that our young females should not be neglected. Upon their training depends much of the future.[74]

For Mr Blake, as for many other people, the education of working-class women was justified in terms of her future life as a practical, efficient housewife who served the interests of a husband, children and society.

In 1846 evening classes for working women were established in the small Yorkshire institutes at Kirkstall, Holmfirth and Honley. At Holmfirth, for example, for two pence per week (which also included access to the library and lectures), 23 women were taught writing, arithmetic, sewing and knitting. At Kirkstall, special mention is made of a 'lady' teacher who read to the students in the sewing class, 'giving in familiar language such explanations as they need; thus instructing and amusing their minds' while skill with a needle was acquired.[75] At Wakefield and Holbeck in 1847, 33 and 50 women, respectively, attended classes in reading, writing and arithmetic.[76] It is rare to find an institute such as that at Wilsden, with 62 female members out of a total membership of 196, claiming that its classes for women, as for men, are 'for the improvement of their minds'.[77]

The division between male and female knowledge, so common in the schooling of working-class children, were also to be found in the education of working-class adults. At Holmfirth, where working-class women were limited to the three Rs and knitting, men could attend classes in the three Rs and general knowledge, the latter offering a range of topics such as the atmosphere, geology, China, electricity, galvinism, the properties of water, electrotype and phrenology.[78] Even in the large women-only institutes, where working-class women were offered a wider range of curricula than in the small mixed-sex institutes, the subjects were distinctly different in comparison with the local 'male' institutes. At the Huddersfield Female Institute in 1848 the 240 women could attend classes in reading, writing, arithmetic, mental arithmetic, dictation, grammar, needlework, singing and geography over the five nights of the week.[79] The mainly working-class male students at the Huddersfield Institute, on the other hand, had a much more varied programme. The 52 classes included courses on the three Rs, vocal and instrumental music, singing, elocution, composition, phonography, geography, history, architectural drawing, mechanical drawing, design, ornamental drawing, French, German, grammar, geometry, ornamental writing and literature.[80]

The working-class female curriculum, however, like that for middle-class women, did not remain static over the course of the nineteenth century. In particular its content widened to include subjects other than the three Rs and sewing. Ironically, at the same time, gender differentiation in the subject offered to working-class men and women became further pronounced.

This widening of the curriculum was already evident in some institutes by the middle of the nineteenth century. By 1850, classes in the three Rs, singing, drawing and grammar were offered to both men and women at Thorp-Arch; at Pudsey in 1852, women could study English grammar, dictation, drawing and phonography as well as the three Rs.[81] At Halifax in 1861, the women students were taught the three Rs, sewing, dictation, grammar, geography and history, while the women at Northowram could also study geography and 'correspondence', presumably letter writing.[82] Such a rather arbitrary collection of additional subjects might indicate that some institutes were moving towards including more liberal subjects within the curriculum for working-class women.

The women-only institutes at Huddersfield and Bradford were also involved in curricula change. At Huddersfield in 1859, history and composition had been added, as Table 6.1 shows.

Table 6.1 Number of classes, class activity and number of students attending Huddersfield Female Educational Institute, 1859

Number of Classes	Class activity	Students attending
10	Reading	157
14	Writing	157
11	Arithmetic	157
5	Geography	110
4	History	97
3	Dictation	85
3	Grammar	68
1	Singing	64
2	Sewing	51
1	Composition	30

Source: *Report of the Yorkshire Union of Mechanics' Institutes* (Leeds, Edward Baines and Sons), 1859, p. 93.

As we can see, the women at Huddersfield were offered ten different subject areas, though they were concentrated in the three Rs and geography. At the Bradford Female Institute we find a similar curriculum: the 570 female students in 1862 were offered nine classes in subjects such as the three Rs, sewing, history, English grammar, geography, domestic economy and dictation.[83] However, the advanced class in 'the elements of natural science', which was functioning in 1859, had disappeared by 1862.[84]

Although no explicit reasons are given for the widening of the curriculum for working-class women in some of the institutes, it could have been related to a number of factors, such as improved levels of literacy, the increased availability of teachers, the broadening of knowledge that was available, changing ideas about the kinds of occupation and training appropriate for working-class women, and demand from the students themselves for new areas of of knowledge once they could read and write. We have already noted in Chapter 4 that, by 1850, some of the

National and British schools that working-class girls attended had widened the curriculum to include subjects such as political economy, history and geography; the education of working-class women within the institutes may have reflected this change too.

As we have seen, by the 1860s, some institutes were also offering women the opportunity to sit examinations and compete for prizes. On 3 December 1858, Charles Dickens, a guest speaker at the annual meeting of the Institutional Association of Lancashire and Cheshire (a union of 114 local institutes and mutual improvement societies), praised not only those working-class men who struggled against many hardships to acquire knowledge but also the working-class women who sought self-improvement and even took examinations:

The women employed in factories, milliners' work, and domestic service, have begun to show, as it is fitting they should, a most decided determination not to be outdone by the men: and the women of Preston in particular, have so honourably distinguished themselves, and shown in their examination papers such an admirable knowledge of the science of household management and household economy, that if I were a working bachelor of Lancashire or Cheshire, and if I had not cast my eye or set my heart upon any lass in particular, I should go to Preston in search of a wife.[85]

While these women were studying subjects traditionally linked to their sex, some of the other institutes were beginning to acknowledge that women might be educated for spheres other than the home. In 1859 the Huddersfield Female Institute lamented the fact that so much was said about educating women for 'the advantages of others ... [in] her social relations as wife or mother, as mistress or servant' and so little about education for self.[86] But this appears to have been a relatively isolated complaint.

As the state became increasingly involved in the provision of elementary education, the demand for the teaching of the three Rs in the institutes declined. The Revised Code of 1862 and the 1870 Education Act helped to decrease illiteracy among working-class children, though it is important *not* to over-estimate this influence. As we saw in Chapter 4, only a minority of working-class girls before 1870 attended National and British schools, and attendance at any form of schooling was usually irregular. A high level of literacy among working-class women cannot be assumed. The records for the Bradford Female Institute in 1861, for example, show that of the 114 new members, 43 could neither read nor write, 26 could read indifferently but could not write, 21 could read moderately well and write a little, 15 could read well and write moderately, 10 could read and write well, and not more than 32 could work a simple addition sum correctly.[87]

However, by the late 1870s, many surviving institutes had adapted to a 'higher order' education than the three Rs.[88] At Manchester, for example, women could attend vocational classes. From 1881 the Union of Lancashire and Cheshire Institutes organized commercial examinations which included a Certificate in Commercial Knowledge, for which the obligatory subjects were handwriting, arithmetic, English and book-keeping, and in

1882 the 'Female Elementary Evening Classes' intended primarily for working-class women included not only instruction in elementary subjects but also in book-keeping, shorthand and foreign languages.[89] At Nottingham in the 1880s, classes were established in shorthand too.[90]

Just how many working-class women participated in these 'new' developments is difficult to determine. But changes were occurring. In Lancashire, for example, there was a dramatic increase in white-collar jobs towards the end of the nineteenth century. As Liddington and Norris have noted, firms needed women clerks (who were cheaper to employ than men) to handle the growing column of paperwork; new department stores and shops needed an army of shop assistants; successive governments had passed many statutes which needed day to day administration, and the new Education Acts, by making schooling compulsory, created a massive demand for elementary teachers. Such new openings attracted both middle-class girls for whom previously no jobs had been seen as 'suitable' and some of the more ambitious 'refined' working-class girls who hated the noise and dirt of the mill and the social stigma of clogs and shawls.[91] Institutes in other parts of England also responded to these social changes: as we saw in the last chapter, in the 1890s the institute at Alton, in collaboration with the county council, organized art and cookery classes for elementary teachers.

Interestingly, although the female working-class curriculum changed, it appears not to have kept pace with the developments in the curriculum offered to working-class men or to have expanded into technical areas of male knowledge. Gender divisions between women and men were already well marked by the late 1850s and the 1860s. At Lockwood in 1857, women were taught the three Rs, grammar, knitting, sewing and marking, while the men could study the three Rs, algebra, mensuration, history, geography, grammar, music and freehand and ornamental drawing.[92] At Sheffield 'junior' males were offered only the three Rs, but in contrast 'senior' males could choose from a wide selection – grammar, geography, Roman history, elocution, book-keeping, drawing, literary and philosophical topics, French, German, fencing, chess and vocal music; 'females' could study only the three Rs and dressmaking.[93] The gender differentiation in mechanics' institutes' curricula was especially pronounced in regard to the advanced arithmetic and technical subjects which were usually offered only to men and in the sewing and knitting classes that only women attended.

Clearly, such differentiation reflects ideas about the respective 'spheres' of men and women in Victorian society, discussed previously. Education for working-class men would be justified for its value for employment, as at Northwram, where a class in mechanical and freehand drawing was seen as being 'very serviceable' for the young men in their respective trades – joiners, masons, mechanics and designers.[94] In contrast, the education of working-class women is usually justified in terms of an improvement in their domestic knowledge and performance. If there was one subject more than any other than epitomized this version of working-class femininity and domesticity it was that of sewing.

While middle-class 'ladies' within the institutes, as at Manchester, might be taught both plain and decorative needlework, working-class women were taught, as were working-class girls in National and British schools, plain 'useful' sewing.[95] As noted earlier, such a skill implied not only femininity but also a concern with thrift.[96] Sewing, needlework or dressmaking classes were found especially in the northern institutes where most of the working-class female students were concentrated. At Kirkstall in 1846, where a dressmaker assisted the needlework teacher by explaining 'the best methods of cutting and arranging', sewing was described as an 'apparently very humble art, but one, nevertheless, on which much of domestic comfort and decency depends'. At Northwram in 1861, 15 young women in the Thursday evening needlework classes were restricted 'entirely to plain sewing, such as useful articles of clothing, which they are also taught to cut out for themselves'. Similarly at Ripon in 1857, young working-class women were taught plain sewing, one evening a week, by 'ladies'; while the work was going on, 'an instructive book' was read and discussed. Here, as elsewhere, an attempt was made 'to inculcate right principles' so that the 'Daughters of the poor' would tend to the 'better ordering, comfort, and economy of the poor man's home'.[97]

Although both the women-only institutes at Huddersfield and Bradford offered classes for sewing, it was especially at the latter that its importance was stessed. As we saw in the previous chapter, a much higher proportion of young factory women were to be found at the Bradford than the Huddersfield Female Institute, which attracted more women who were milliners, dressmakers and domestic servants. Milliners and dressmakers in particular earned their livelihood with the needle and were therefore unlikely to 'need' sewing classes, but for factory women this was not so. As we saw in chapter 3, factory women were especially seen by middle-class commentators as making 'wretched wives'[98] since, among other things, it was believed they could not sew. In addition, their higher rate of pay in comparison with other women workers was thought to give rise to a 'thousand wants' such as 'dress, amusements and gaieties'.[99] In particular, factory women in Bradford were described as being of a 'slatternly appearance'.[100] All these factors may help to explain the greater importance given to sewing at the Bradford Female Institute. It was undoubtedly a matter of pride when in 1862 this institute recorded that many of the students attended classes wearing 'dresses and other garments' made in the sewing classes.[101]

Such developments would be praised by the Yorkshire Union, which, in its annual report for 1860 had spoken yet again of the ignorance of young working-class women, stressing the need for sewing and cooking skills which could help them to become 'good wives and mothers':

it is quite certain that among young women of the working classes, a lamentable degree of ignorance prevails. Few of them comparatively know how to cut out and make their own clothes, cook, to keep an account of domestic expenditure, or to discharge properly all the manifold duties of household management. To their ignorance of the nursing and treatment of infancy may be fairly attributed in no

HUDDERSFIELD
FEMALE EDUCATIONAL INSTITUTE.

BEAUMONT STREET BOARD SCHOOL.

COOKERY CLASS

Arrangements have been made to give a series of

TWELVE

LESSONS IN PLAIN COOKING

IN THE ABOVE SCHOOLS

ON FRIDAY EVENINGS,

Commencing on FRIDAY, October 13th, 1882.

Tickets for one Lecture 2d. For the Series 1s.
Members of Institute Free.

THE ELEMENTARY CLASSES

Meet on Four Evenings of the Week, from 7-30 to 9, and
are conducted by Certificated Teachers.

Monday.—Needlework. Arithmetic, Dictation, and Grammar.
Tuesday.—Reading, Writing, Arithmetic (with Mental do.)
Wednesday.—Reading. Writing. Dictation. Composition, and Geography.
Thursday.—Reading. Dictation and Composition, Domestic Economy.

ONE CLASS ROOM IS SET APART FOR ADULTS.

A cordial welcome is given to all, however much their Education
has been neglected.

FEES—MEMBERS, 3d. PER WEEK.

Presentees (those recommended by a Subscriber) **1d. per Week.**

ROBERT DENISON, SECRETARY.

J. WOODHEAD, PRINTER, "EXAMINER" OFFICE, HUDDERSFIELD.

Figure 6.3 Advertisement for the cookery class at Huddersfield Female
Educational Institute, 1882

slight degree the well known fact that, half the children born die before reaching the age of five years ... however great the necessity for Mechanics' and similar Institutes, that for the establishment for females is far greater.[102]

Teaching cookery, of course, would have been relatively expensive since kitchens would need to be installed. The Huddersfield Female Institute appears to have been one of the few institutes organizing such provision, though this was not until the 1880s, when cookery classes were offered in conjunction with the local board school (see figure 6.3). Teaching sewing, on the other hand, was relatively inexpensive, especially if the teachers were middle-class 'ladies' who gave their services free. No attention appears to have been paid, though, to the issue of whether sewing skills were necessary for working-class women in an increasingly differentiated society where shop-bought clothes were often cheaper and better made than home-made ones.[103] Competence with a needle had 'symbolic' importance beyond its practical value.[104] It implied that working-class women would sit quietly at home, being industrious and thrifty, 'making do' with mending and repairs rather than 'wasting' their family income. Indeed, for some, needlework was seen as 'that most effectual sedative, that grand soother and composer of women's distress'.[105] There are indications, however, that the institute sewing classes were not always as popular as the organizers wished.

At Halifax in 1861, despite the services of an 'excellent teacher', the sewing class was not well attended, since more women wanted to learn writing and arithmetic; at Sheffield in the same year only five women were in the dressmaking class, though 18 were learning the three Rs.[106] At the women-only institutes at Huddersfield and Bradford, the numbers in the sewing classes were usually well below the numbers enrolled for the three Rs.[107] Similarly, the evening dressmaking class at Manchester, which attracted only seven scholars in 1880, was not a 'marked success'.[108]

Many reasons could be advanced for the greater student popularity for classes in the three Rs. It is very probable that large numbers of working-class women were already competent with a needle, though still unable to read, write and do sums well. Under such circumstances, the few pennies that could be spared for self-improvement would be spent on eradicating the stigma of illiteracy. The teachers also may have used dress patterns that the students did not like. At one sewing school at Leeds in the 1850s a working-class woman complained, 'Noo, then, ye laadies, ye reckon t'teach sewing, whoy, thou know'st no more nor babbies how to cut ott orr things'.[109] Women within the institutes may also have resented the 'improving' tone of the literature that was often read while they sewed.

Gender differentiation in the curriculum was further strengthened during the second half of the century through assessment procedures. From the 1850s the institutes began to make use of various examining bodies, especially the Society of Arts: its examining system, plus the demand for technical and scientific education helped save the institutes from 'educational bankruptcy', since they became increasingly identified as a means of 'getting on in life'.[110] But 'getting on in life' appears to have especially linked to the paid work of men, not women. More men than women entered for examinations and in subjects that reflect the division between 'male' and 'female' knowledge.

For example, at Leeds in 1857, the institute welcomed the scheme whereby the Society of Arts developed contact with large manufacturing and other local firms, but this related only to 'the instruction of males (youths and adults)'.[111] This is not surprising. The majority of subjects in which candidates might be examined fell into the technical/scientific category, regarded as 'male' knowledge: the one examinable subject that was likely to be studied exclusively by women was domestic economy.[112] Gradually during the 1860s and 1870s we hear of successful female entrants in this subject.

At Manchester, in the Female Elementary Classes attended mainly by working-class women, seven Society of Arts Certificates were gained in 1881 – five in cookery, one in clothing and one in house-keeping and thrift.[113] Manchester also developed its own 'Special Certificates' for awarding to students: in 1871, for example, first class 'Special Certificates' were awarded in domestic economy to Priscilla Smethurst and Maria Robinson and in machine calculations to William Dodgson and Thomas Mills.[114] Such locally based assessment procedures, as well as the national Society of Arts examining system, legitimated the gender differentiation within curricula within the institutes.

The Union of Lancashire and Cheshire Institutes (UCLI) was another influential examining body, especially for working-class students, since its tests were especially for 'sifting the knowledge obtained in Elementary Evening Classes'.[115] But in addition to this task, the UCLI also reinforced the gender differentiation between working-class men and women, since while all candidates at both lower and higher grade levels were expected to show proficiency in arithmetic, writing, spelling, reading and grammar, only women 'must' also be examined in needlework and only men in scripture, history or geography.[116] The entry and success rate of women candidates, however, appears to have been much lower than that of men. At Manchester in 1866, 26 of the 29 men entered for higher and lower grades obtained passes but none of the nine female entrants: all the women failed the arithmetic paper.[117] It is not until the following year that for the 'first time' women entrants were successful – Selina Garlick, Susannah Howcroft and Ellen Tunnicliffe gaining lower-grade certificates.[118]

The experience of women in other mixed-sex institutes that used examining bodies was probably very similar. The scheme for elementary examinations conducted by the West Riding Educational Board endorsed the gender differentiation found in the UCLI in that at both junior and senior levels women only 'must' be examined in needlework.[119] The number of women passing such elementary examinations was always lower than the number of men. In 1862, for example, only 14 of the successful 78 candidates were female: since 13 of these came from the Leeds Female Educational Institution, as the women's department at the

Leeds institute was now called, this indicates that working-class women wishing to pass examinations in elementary knowledge might fare better in mixed-sex institutes with a larger, separate women's department. Under such conditions, like-minded students could offer each other mutual support and teachers could direct their efforts on examinations preparation.

The two main women-only institutes at Huddersfield and Bradford did not link up with the various examining bodies, and the curriculum here appears to have been even more stereotypical. The female institute at Huddersfield restricted its activities 'exclusively to the simply useful' and rarely went beyond 'the merely elementary', while that at Bradford aimed at 'training its pupils to an acquaintance with the simplest and most necessary elements of knowledge'.[120] Whether such limited aims worried the 590 and 157 women students who passed through the Bradford and Huddersfield Institutes, respectively, during 1859–60, we do not know.[121] But over the next 20 years, large numbers of young working-class women were still in need of elementary knowledge, despite the passing of the 1870 Education Act.

In Huddersfield in 1879, for example, there were said to be 'hundreds of girls and young women ... who know comparatively nothing of even reading, writing and arithmetic', since a number of girls in the elementary day schools were compelled, 'through domestic circumstances', to leave school at the earliest possible time.[122] For these young women, now too old for day school, the female institute offered a 'second chance' education, the opportunity of becoming literate. Yet progress might have been slow. When an HMI examined 70 of the women students in the three Rs in March 1878, 64 passed in reading, 45 in writing and only 26 in arithmetic.[123] Many of the older women in the adult class were frightened away by the threat of examinations.[124] Overall it would appear that single-sex institutes for women were less advantageous in giving working-class women access to higher-status examinable knowledge and possible access to male knowledge.

Significantly, the divisions between male and female knowledge appear to have become more pronounced after the 1870 Education Act, when many institutes, in order to survive, moved away from elementary to technical knowledge. At Manchester, as elsewhere, such provision benefited working-class men rather than the womenfolk. In 1881, under the auspices of the City and Guilds Institute, Manchester offered classes relating to cotton manufacture, coachbuilding, mechancial engineering, the steel and iron industries, fuel, telegraphy, bleaching, printing and dyeing. At once, a number of 'artisans' joined the classes.[125] Working-class women at Manchester, it seems, did not share this expansion into technical education. Although by 1882 the female evening classes included book-keeping, shorthand and foreign languages, besides the teaching of the three Rs, the scale of the new departure was much smaller and in a different direction – mainly towards clerical and commercial work.[126]

In conclusion, although the examination system may have improved the educational standard and employment prospects for some working-class women within the institutes, it also legitimated the gender divisions within the working-class curriculum. In particular, it seems that working-class women became increasingly unequal in comparison with the menfolk, since they did not share the expansion into scientific and technical 'male' subjects.

The overall picture of the curriculum offered to working-class women within the mechanics' institutes reveals the impact of social class and gender differentiation. The curriculum for both working-class women and men had a lower status than that offered to middle-class people. However, the working-class female curriculum was also inferior in depth and breadth to that offered to working-class men. In particular, those organizing provision for women of the 'lower' orders saw their task within a narrow framework – the preparation of women for wifehood and motherhood. Yet for many working-class women, an institute education offered the chance of remedial schooling, a second chance, especially in those skills such as writing that might have been neglected in elementary schools.

Lecture programme

It would be a mistake to conclude our account of the mechanics' institutes without analysing one final aspect of educational activity – lecture provision. Although the bulk of the teaching within the institutes was in classes, to concentrate upon this to the exclusion of lectures is to give a one-sided account of the benefits or constraints of an institute education; the lectures offered an alternative route or access to knowledge. Once women had won the struggle to enter the institutes they could usually attend the lectures jointly with the male members. The lectures were of two main types – a talk given by a speaker and a 'manuscript' lecture, i.e. a written talk that could be read to an audience. As early as 1826, sets of lecture notes were read to members at Newcastle and Newport; when the supply of local dignitaries, such as doctors and clergymen, ran out, and professional lecturers charged three to five guineas a time, a manuscript lecture was a cheap alternative.[127] Although some of the large institutes in urban areas, e.g. at Manchester, Leeds, Liverpool and London, were successful in organizing a lecture programme, not all institutes, especially small institutes in rural areas, were able to do so. Sometimes no speaker could be found, sometimes the audience was lacking.[128]

Nevertheless, where lecture programmes could be offered, the proportion of women attending was not insignificant. At Manchester and York in 1839, women formed nearly one-fifth and one-third, respectively, of the lecture audiences.[129] The weekly lectures at Sheffield in 1843 drew average audiences of about 300, of whom, once again, about a third were women.[130] At Lewes, the presence of women at lectures was felt especially after 1846. At the anniversary celebrations, it was noted that the

attendance of ladies was 'very numerous, far more so, we regret to say –
ungallant as it may appear – than that of the mechanics'.[131] At Wakefield in
1846, where the average audience at lectures was about 200, two-thirds of
the attenders were women; at Beverley in the same year, where the
average lecture attendance was 100, one-third of these were 'ladies' who
were admitted free.[132] The number of women appearing at the lectures
suggests a high level of demand for education which had not necessarily
been satisfied by class provision. At the two main women-only institutes,
however, lecture provision appears to have been sparse. The Huddersfield
Female Institute from the mid-1850s offered an occasional lecture: from
1857 to 1860, for example, Mrs Balfour spoke on 'Thoughts on Female
Education', Mr Barnett Blake on 'Common Things', Joseph Batley, vice
president of the institute, on 'Preparation for Life' (this lecture was read by
the president), Mr Dore on 'Heavenly Bodies' (a talk that was illustrated
with the magic lantern), the Rev Bruce on 'The Importance of Little
Things' and John Moody on 'Topsy, or the Power of Kindness'.[133] The
female institute at Bradford appears to have offered no extensive lecture
programme. Women at both institutes, of course, may have attended
lectures at the local 'male' institute.

It is often difficult, in retrospect, to discover the social class background
of the women who attended lectures. The cost of attendance and the
lecture topics would obviously be critical. At Manchester, for example, a
middle-class audience was largely guaranteed, since 'ladies' had to pay 5s a
quarter to attend the lectures and library or 6d only for each lecture.[134]
Such charges would be beyond the means of most working-class women.
However, where lectures were free or for a small fee, working-class
women might attend. The lecture topic would also make a difference.
Working-class women schooled, if lucky, in the three Rs might have little
interest in specialized topics, such as science;[135] middle-class women who
could afford to employ domestic servants might not be drawn to topics
that focused on self-improvement through measures such as thrift or
penny savings banks.[136]

Those institutes which organized lecture programmes often offered a
variety of topics. Initially, the main emphasis was upon scientific
subjects,[137] regarded as 'male' knowledge, but gradually the focus
broadened to include the arts, history, and literary, social and musical
themes. The women attending the lectures at York during 1839–40, for
example, could choose between chemistry, phrenology, the philosophy of
sleep, the civilization of Africa, the uses of horn and bone in manufacture,
pneumatics, the manners and customs of London during the eighteenth
century, substitutes for capital punishments, the fine arts, music and
British poets.[138] Women at the lectures at Manchester in 1839 had the
advantage of hearing mainly scientific themes.[139] Other institutes in the
Manchester area at this time, including those institutes called 'lyceums'
which (as noted in the previous chapter) aimed particularly to recruit both
working-class men and women by offering education and entertainment at
much cheaper rates, offered an even wider range of themes.[140]

Of particular interest to women may have been the lectures on 'Education and Capabilities of Women' and 'Female Education' delivered in 1840 by Mrs Martin at the Ancoats and Oldham lyceums respectively.[141] Although the women students at Ancoats were likely to be working-class while those at Oldham belonged primarily to the middle-class,[142] all were likely to hear a feminist message from Emma Martin. She was one of a small group of female lecturers within the Owenite movement who in the later 1830s and early 1840s spoke on the rights of women in education, marriage and divorce.[143] The daughter of small tradespeople in Bristol, she was aware of the inadequacies of female education, even within the lower-middle class, and of the disabilities which women suffered. 'The degraded social condition of women', she proclaimed, might be helped by 'improved education and better employment'.[144] By the time Emma Martin was speaking on female education in the Manchester area, she had apparently abandoned Christianity and become a freethinker and feminist. As Taylor notes, from being an evangelical in Christ's cause, Emma Martin became one of the leading evangelizers of 'infidel Socialism'.[145]

Whatever Emma Martin said to her audiences at Ancoats and Oldham was not likely to conform to those dominant middle-class ideas about woman's place in society, discussed in Chapter 3. Like other Owenite feminist lecturers, she linked the struggle for women's rights and emancipation to the struggle against patriarchal Christian orthodoxy.[146] But the fact that such an 'infidel' lecturer was speaking within the mechanics' institute movement reveals that in the early 1840s 'space' was given to discussion of feminist issues.

Throughout the 1840s in fact, lectures on women, usually given by women, were a regular feature of many institute programmes. The speakers, though, were usually of a more 'respectable' hue than Emma Martin. At York, Mrs J. W. Hudson, whose husband was assistant secretary of the Leeds Institute and honorary secretary of the Yorkshire Union, spoke in 1846 on 'Female Education' and, one year later, 'On Distinguished Englishwomen'.[147] In 1848, Mrs Clara Balfour, a prolific moral writer and religious and temperance lecturer, spoke 'On the Influence of Women' and 'On Distinguished Female Sovereigns', while two years later Miss G. Bennet gave two lectures on 'Woman'.[148] But it was Mrs Balfour who was the key female lecturer on topics about women within the mechanics' institute movement. Her lecturing career spanned some 40 years,[149] and in 1847 she was one of a group of people engaged upon reduced terms by the Yorkshire Union of Mechanics' Institutes. Although it is impossible to give an exact figure of the number of her talks, there were at least 27 different occasions when she spoke on the following themes within the institutes – 'The Moral and Intellectual Influence of Women on Society', 'Female Sovereigns of Europe', 'The Obligations of English Literature to Females', 'Remarkable Women of the Present Century', 'Thoughts on Female Education', 'The English Female Poets of the Present Century' and 'Charlotte Bronte'.[150]

Mrs Balfour's popularity with programme organizers in the institutes may not just have been related to her reputed competence as a lecturer. As a Christian and temperance speaker, she also probably encapsulated and supported many of the middle-class ideas thought appropriate for working-class men and women, e.g. a prudent, happy home life, and self-improvement. She saw women as the most influential moral teachers of society, with a responsibility to promote virtue and to reform husbands and children.[151] Although she welcomed the advances in elementary schooling for girls during the nineteenth century, she warned those who wished to become 'really cultivated and intelligent women' that they must not fall into the danger of depending too much on what was done for them: self-training, self-culture and motivation were still important.[152] If Mrs Balfour expressed such views within her lectures at the institutes, women who heard her speak may have been motivated to improve themselves; but in common with those middle-class ideologies discussed earlier, Mrs Balfour advocated women's self-improvement primarily for others.

As the organized women's movement gathered momentum in the 1860s and 1870s, demanding, among other things, access to higher education and the right to vote, such topics appear to have been largely ignored within lecture programmes. Mrs Balfour did not speak on the suffrage issue, but there are a few isolated cases where the topic was covered. On 20 May 1870 Lady Kate Amberley spoke on suffrage for women who were householders, paying rates and taxes, at the Subscription Rooms in Stroud, at the request of the mechanics' institute there. The meeting apparently was badly chaired by the vice president of the institute, a Tory squire, who did not agree with what was said. The 'respectably dressed' audience offered hardly any applause after the talk, and generally 'it seemed to fall very flat'.[153] A petition supporting female suffrage was placed in another room, and few signed it.

However, the talk attracted the interest of the national and local press. *The Times* expressed some sympathy but reiterated that well-worn cliché that woman's 'natural sphere of duty' was marriage and that for women who had to work, because they had no husbands, nothing would be gained by giving them votes and turning them into 'politicians and agitators'.[154] But the response of a person signed 'A He-Critter' in a letter to the *Stroud Journal* was more explosive:

The 'claims of women' as interpreted by modern Blue-Stockingdom, to participate in the rough public and political work of men, utterly ignores the home principle, the essentially feminine characteristics.... Men are to be elbowed out of every department of life by the new order or Amazons. Female doctors, female preachers, female lawyers, female judges, are to be the order of the day.... What in the meantime is to become of the home, and what of the domestic occupations? If the house is to be deserted for the exchange and mart, who is to mind the nursery? or – necessary question – will there by any nurseries to mind? And when such a vulgar thing as 'housekeeping' is discarded by the emancipated woman of the future, are the present duties of chambermaid and laundress to be performed by men, or to go undone altogether.[155]

It was not unusual for male opposition to certain demands made by women to be couched in terms of the 'unsexing' of women and the supposed harmful effects upon marriage, the birth rate and motherhood. Whether any women in the audience responded in the same way to the lecture we do not know, but many listeners were apparently 'converted' to Kate Amberley's views.[156]

Another institute lecturer on women's rights was Florence Fenwick Miller, a journalist and writer on feminist issues who was not afraid to take up 'unpopular' causes.[157] In December 1876, after her election to the London School Board, she spoke on 'The Woman Movement' at Basingstoke Mechanics' Institute and the following year on 'Women Warriors' at the Chichester institute.[158] Her talk at Chichester was held in October, just four months after the trial of Charles and Annie Besant for issuing an 'indecent, lewd, filthy, bawdy and obscene book'[159] that advocated birth control. Florence, who was single at the time, had supported the accused by writing a letter on their behalf to the newspapers. Whether such a bold stance on such a controversial issue drew people to hear her speak, we do not know. But her message, probably addressed to principally middle-class men and women at the Basingstoke and Chichester institutes, was likely to be unorthodox. She was a pioneer suffragist who defined the 'new woman' of the late nineteenth century as someone who wanted to earn a living, take a degree, exercise the franchise and serve her generation by working in public affairs.[160]

Of course not all the women lecturers within the institutes spoke on topics relating to their own sex. Mrs Noyes spoke on 'The Wind', Mrs Ware on 'Music', Mrs de Lancy on 'Elocution' and Mrs Bonwell on 'The Life and Origins of the Gipsies'.[161] Mary Kingsley, the explorer, gave a lecture on 'West Africa' at Basingstoke in 1899. One wonders how her probably middle-class audience responded to her cockney accent! As Mary, daughter of a doctor and female cockney servant, jokingly complained, a newspaper account of one of her lectures criticized her for dropping her g's 'when I am trying so hard to hold on to the 'hs''.[162] Neither was it only women who spoke on woman's place in society. Mr John Bennett offered a rare theme, on women and paid work, when he spoke at Leeds in 1857 on 'Women and Watchwork, with a view to the introduction of Female Employment'. Dr Henry McCormac similarly expressed an unusual view within the institute context when at the mechanics' institute in Belfast in 1830 he advocated that working-class women should be educated on their own accout. 'Are not women', he asked, 'made subordinate in their powers of action to man in almost every public and private capacity? ... let them have the same voice in society which men have'.[163]

What was more common was for men speaking on women's issues to see women, especially working-class women, in a domestic light, serving the needs of their menfolk. The Rev James Booth, speaking on 'The Female Education of the Industrial Classes' at the Wandsworth institute in 1855, condemned 'those scraps of book-learning' taught to working-class women.[164] But like so many middle-class men of his time he advocated a

practical curriculum for working-class women that would teach then to be
'good wives and mothers':

Why should not 'young women' be taught a knowledge of those common things
with which she will have to deal the whole residue of her life? Why should she not,
for example, be taught to light a fire, to sweep a room, to wash crockery and glass
without breaking the half of them, to wash clothes, to bake bread, to dress a
dinner, to choose meat or fish or vegetables, and to know how to keep them when
bought; what clothes are most economical – cheap, showy, tawdy rags, or those
which are perhaps more expensive but cheaper in the end? Why should she not be
taught the use of savings banks and the results of thrift?[165]

We do not know the response of the women who listened to these
various lectures about their own sex. But it is important to emphasize that
the lecture programme brought into the institutes various contentious
political ideas and controversies. Socialist, feminist and traditional views on
the women question were presented. Whereas the educational work
undertaken in classes may have reinforced women's views of themselves
as inferior, relative and subordinate to men, as well as dependent upon
them, the lectures may have inspired other thoughts. Emma Martin's
ideas, contrasting with those of Clara Balfour, show the diversity of
ideological input as well as the strength of the institutes in allowing such a
range of views. In addition, the presence of women lecturers may have
acted as role models for some students, offering an alternative context to
that with which women were usually identified – the home and the family.
It should not be forgotten that in the 1830s and 1840s in particular, the
'very idea' of a woman lecturer was so unusual and different that it was
'sufficient to draw a crowd'.[166] As late as 1870, when Kate Amberley
spoke on women's suffrage at the request of the mechanics' institute at
Stroud, 'people expressed surprise ... to see that a woman could lecture
and still look like a lady!'[167]

The lectures on topics relating to women were just one strand of the
total lecture programme that women might attend. By the 1840s, as
already noted, the trend away from scientific towards literary and general
subjects was pronounced. This is in marked contrast to the later
development of class provision in those institutes that survived into the
later decades of the nineteenth century: as we saw earlier, after 1870 class
provision increasingly moved in the direction of technical and vocational
knowledge. The shift in the opposite direction, in the lecture programmes,
was evident in one analysis, made in 1850, of 1,000 lectures recently given
in 43 institutes: thus 572 of the lectures were on literary, 340 on scientific
and 88 on musical (excluding concerts) themes.[168] Public readings by
famous people were also common around this time. Fanny Kemble, a
noted actress, gave readings from Shakespeare at Nottingham,
Manchester and Basingstoke institutes.[169] Charles Dickens, the famous
novelist, was another well-known speaker in the institutes. On 27
December 1853 he gave, on behalf of the Birmingham and Midland
Institute, a reading of his own work *A Christmas Carol* to nearly 2,000 people
who packed the Birmingham Town Hall to hear him and his remarkable

mimetic powers; some three days later 'a large assemblage of work-people' listened to his second reading of this work. In 1855, three days before Christmas the members at Sheffield Mechanics' Institute had a chance to hear another reading of this story.[170]

Sometimes a penny was charged for entry to readings. Indeed 'Penny Readings', aimed at bringing more people and extra income into the institutes, became regular features in some, especially in southern England. Chelmsford Mechanics' Institute, for example, where 275 women are recorded out of a total membership of 827 in 1852, organized a series of Penny Readings from the 1860s. At other institutes in Essex, such as that at Coggeshall, Penny Readings took place almost weekly and increasingly became a key source of income. At Halstead, too, where men and women factory workers shared certain classes, the Penny Readings were the only successful events in the lecture programme over the years 1860–5.[171]

Figure 6.4   Entertainment at Plymouth Mechanics' Institute, 1894 (from *Plymouth Mechanics' Institute Prospectus, First Half of Session*, 1894–5).

The trend towards lectures on general cultural issues and entertainments of various kinds continued throughout the 1870s and subsequent decades of the nineteenth century, though we must not forget that in many northern institutes, in particular, valuable compensatory education for working-class women was still being conducted in the classes. The lecture programme at those institutes that still survived and could organize activities was not unlike that billed for the 1886–7 session at Chichester; thus interspersed with talks on themes such as 'The Life and Writings of Lord Macaulay', 'Our Glorious Colonies: a Cruise under the British Flag', 'Jerusalem: the Buried City' and 'Heroes of British India: the Men who Conquered, Ruled and Saved it' we find an entertainment by an illusionist and ventriloquist, a lecture on light and colour that was illustrated with experiments and a dramatic and musical recital.[172]

Entertainers at this time included a number of women, a tradition going back at least to the 1840s when women of lesser renown than Fanny Kemble played the piano and perhaps sang. At the Leeds institute in 1857, for example, Mr William Spark 'assisted by Miss Whitham and Miss Newbound' gave a lecture on 'The Ministrelsy of Old England'.[173] But it was especially during the latter decades of the century that female entertainers such as Miss Nora Hastings, billed to appear on 19 October 1894 at Plymouth Mechanics' Institute (see figure 6.4), became more numerous.

Conclusion

In the previous chapter we saw that working-class women had become students within the mechanics' institutes and in this chapter we have discussed the kinds of knowledge to which women might have access. Although a final evaluation of this involvement will be offered in Part IV, especially in relation to the context of working-class women's lives, a few observations may be made here.

There was a marked difference between lecture and class provision within the mechanics' institutes in regard to content and access to ideas. In the various lecture programmes, men and women shared access to a range of knowledge that could cover science, the arts and general subjects – as well as recreational activities. Some lectures were also a form of entertainment and recreation, offering, in addition, access to the famous. At a lecture, a woman might have a chance to hear a paid, middle-class professional, in contrast to many of the 'amateur', unpaid female class teachers within the institutes. In particular, the lectures could bear a crucial relation to important nineteenth-century debates outside the institutes, such as 'the woman question', and bring into an institute new ideas and new ways of thinking. In this respect, the lectures could be of much value to working-class women whose lives were likely to be occupied with the daily business of earning a living, inside or outside the sphere of the home, and who therefore had few other chances to reflect critically on their lives and the relations between the sexes and society in general.

At the same time, however, social class and gender differentiation was evident within the institute curriculum, and this is seen most clearly in class, rather than lecture, provision. The knowledge taught to working-class women and men had a lower status in comparison with that offered to a middle-class clientele. In particular, women of different social classes were offered a curriculum considered appropriate for their social position and gender. While for all women attending institute classes the curriculum could relate to paid work (as in the case of becoming a governess for middle-class women or taking up clerical and commercial work for working-class women), it was also strongly associated with female domestic roles. And it is here, in the emphasis upon a domestic 'vocation', that the class differences between women are emphasized. The dominant ideal of femininity upheld by the middle classes for young women in their own social stratum was that of the 'young lady', and an accomplishments curriculum was considered appropriate. The dominant ideal upheld for working-class women was that of the 'good wife and mother', who needed a practical, household curriculum. The shaping of these two main forms of female curricula involved the teaching of class-specific domestic and social skills. Therefore, while it might appear that middle-class and working-class women had much in common in that they both had a domestic/cultural curriculum, this was not so.

This social class differentiation between women was affected by a number of other factors, especially gender differentiation. Gender differentiation within the curriculum contained the limits of female development and shaped women's educational interests. In particular, though some subjects were common to both working-class men and women, in general working-class women were taught different curricula to that taught to their menfolk.

Working-class women were usually offered the three Rs, plain sewing and some limited general knowledge, while working-class men had access to a much wider range of subjects that included the three Rs, advanced arithmetic, and scientific and technical knowledge. This tendency to differentiate on the basis of scientific/technical 'male' knowledge and domestic/cultural 'female' knowledge reinforced the divisions between the sexes and ideas about a woman's place in nineteenth-century society.

Changes in educational provision during the nineteenth century, the development of a public examination system and the rise of the women's movement all helped to alter the pattern and content of the gender-differentiated curricula. The development of elementary schooling at one end of the educational spectrum, and of university education at the other, put pressure on the mechanics' institute to change their role much more in the direction of technical education. Women, especially working-class women, did not share equally in these changes with men.

The development of examination boards in association with the institutes increased the pressure for 'examinable', high-status knowledge. While this may have broadened the curriculum for women in each social class, at the same time it reinforced the gender division between male and female knowledge; in particular, the examination of elementary knowledge of working-class men and women often specified compulsory gender-specific subjects, such as needlework for women.

7

WOMEN AND THE WORKING MEN'S COLLEGE MOVEMENT

Introduction

The working men's colleges, though never attracting the number of students recorded for the mechanics' institutes, formed another major adult education movement of nineteenth-century England. They developed partly in response to criticisms from working-class men about the 'inadequacies' of the mechanics' institutes. It was alleged that the institutes failed to attract large numbers of working men; the management was not in the hands of mechanics; politics and religion were excluded; there was usually only one institute in each town; institutes were closed on Sundays; the instruction given was desultory, unconnected and more scientific than elementary; and weekly payments were not always available.[1] However, although such criticisms were widely voiced, most historians claim[2] that the main catalyst for the working men's college movement was the fear and unrest caused by working-class agitation for radical change, evident especially in the activities of the Chartists in the 1830s and 1840s.

Although Chartism was a diverse movement, it was the allegiance to the six points of the Charter – universal male suffrage, annual parliaments, vote by ballot, equal representation, abolition of the property qualifications for members of Parliament and payment of the latter – that united large numbers of working-class men and women.[3] Demands were also made for a free press and for a national system of education. Indeed, it appears that the 'strong educational trend' of the Chartist movement was derived partly from the disappointment that many working-class men felt with the mechanics' institutes: in particular, they were critical of middle-class involvement in the management of the institutes and the refusal to allow newspapers and other 'controversial' literature into institute reading rooms.[4]

The Chartist movement suffered a number of setbacks and its final organized rally took place on Kennington Common, South London, on 10 April 1848, when thousands of people demonstrated in favour of a third National Petition that was to be presented to Parliament. That evening, a small group of middle-class men who were later to become very influential in the working men's college movement met at the house of the Rev F. D. Maurice, professor at King's College, London, and discussed the demonstrations of that day. Present at the meeting with Maurice were John Malcolm Ludlow and Thomas Hughes, both barristers, and the Rev Charles Kingsley. All four men sought a solution to the turmoil and upheavals so evident in society in Christian socialism – a system of beliefs that was to inspire many of the founders and early students of the most famous of the working men's colleges, the London Working Men's College.[5]

Christian Socialism represented an attempt to knit together the principles of Christianity with the socialist principles of co-operation.[6] Followers of this tradition, who tended to be ethical and educational reformers rather than politicians,[7] tried to apply such ideas to a number of practical ventures that they organized, such as evening schools, infant schools, house-to-house visiting, Bible classes and working men's and working women's co-operative associations. Many of the ideals of Christian Socialism, especially that of co-operation, permeated the working men's college movement. The stress upon co-operation between the voluntary teachers, mainly drawn from the educated middle classes, and their less well educated students, who were often drawn from the skilled manual classes, was a key feature of the college. Such co-operation which cut across social class boundaries was seen as more conducive to learning and, much more importantly, to the stability and cohesion of society.[8] In this chapter I shall investigate the development and aims of the working men's college movement, the access of women to the colleges, the recruitment of female students and the terms of their membership.

Development and aims of the movement

The London Working Men's College, founded in 1854, is usually regarded as the impetus for the working men's college movement, though a People's College, originally intended for 'working youths' and 'young men from the age of 13 upwards', had already been established by the Rev Robert Slater Bayley in 1842 in Sheffield.[9] After the foundation of the London college, working men's colleges were established in Cambridge in 1855, Halifax and Sheffield in 1856, Ancoats and Wolverhampton in 1857, Manchester and Salford in 1858, Oxford by January 1859, Boston and Ely in 1858, Liverpool and Ayr in 1860, Birkenhead in 1861, Leicester in 1862 and South London in 1868.[10] Hull, Huddersfield, Edinburgh, Prestwich, Huntingdon, Ipswich and Cheltenham also had colleges – though little appears to be known about them.[11] Unfortunately, the records of many of the provincial institutions have not survived. Some of the colleges, such as those at Ancoats, Cambridge, Wolverhampton, Ely, Ayr and Prestwich, disbanded within ten years of their foundation,[12] others, as at Manchester, lost their identity when they merged with a local institution.[13]

From the existing records it would appear that the founders were nearly always men and, in particular, men from a particular stratum within the middle classes – the professional stratum. Thus clergymen, barristers, doctors and university lecturers were overwhelmingly represented among the founders, and especially at the London Working Men's College.

The foundation of the London Working Men's College has usually been attributed to the work of a group of eight professional men[14] – the Rev Frederick Denison Maurice, who had been expelled in the autumn of 1853 from his posts of Professor of English Literature and History and Professor of Theology, both held at King's College, London; John Malcolm Ludlow, a barrister and scholar; Thomas Hughes, barrister and author of *Tom Brown's Schooldays*, later to become a Liberal MP and county court judge; Frederick James Furnivall, a barrister, philologist and scholar of Early and Middle English literature; John Westlake, a barrister and, from 1888, Professor of International Law at Cambridge University; Richard Buckley Litchfield, a barrister who, in 1859, entered the service of the Ecclesiastical Commission; the Rev John Llewelyn Davies, brother of Emily Davies who later fought in the 1860s and 1870s (as we saw in chapter 5) for the entry of women into the all-male preserve of Cambridge University; and C. Lowes Dickenson, a portrait painter, print seller and member of the Pre-Raphaelite Brotherhood. Many of these men were Christian Socialists. In addition, five of them were Cambridge men, four – Maurice, Westlake, Litchfield and Llewelyn Davies – being from Trinity College. Thomas Hughes, who had studied at Oriel College, was the only Oxford man. Among all these it was Maurice in particular who was regarded as the key figure and the London college bore the stamp of his ideals more than those of the other seven founders.

Existing records indicate too that professional middle-class men were active in establishing colleges elsewhere. Dr Harvey Goodwin, later Bishop of Carlisle, was influential in founding the college at Cambridge, while the college at Ancoats, Manchester, was established 'under the auspices' of the Rev Canon Richson.[15] The Manchester Working Men's College was founded mainly through the influence of Professor Greenwood and other members of staff of Owens College.[16] The Rev David Vaughan, formerly a Fellow of Trinity College, Cambridge, and a friend of one of the founders of the London college, the Rev John Llewelyn Davies, founded the Leicester college.[17]

Few of the colleges seem to have been established by wealthy manufacturers, though this was so at Halifax where Edward Akroyd, a local mill–owner, founded and supported the college.[18] Only a small number of colleges, such as those in Wolverhampton, South London and Boston, appear to have been founded by working men: the 'moving spirit' behind the South London Working Men's College, for example, was

William Rossiter, a portmanteau worker who had been a student at the London Working Men's College and its first fellow.[19] Overall, the working men's college movement began mainly as a phenomenon created by the middle classes rather than arising out of working-class sponsorship and leadership.

The social class background of the founders and governing councils would undoubtedly shape the policies of any one college. But what united the various institutions was their status as 'colleges' rather than 'institutes'. This concept was meant to convey an ideal of 'humane culture', based on 'democratic comradeship'; consequently, the main aim was not just the transmission of knowledge but 'enrichment of personality'.[20] This diffuse goal was to be attained through a collegiate structure that offered a liberal, humane curriculum and emphasized the importance of fellowship and mutual help between teachers and taught.[21]

The majority of founders appear to have held one view in common – that the working men's college movement was, as its name implies, both class and sex specific, i.e. the education of working men was taken to mean working-class men. The circular printed to attract students to the London College, for example, stated:

Any Working Man above sixteen years of age who can read and write, and knows the first four rules of Arithmetic is eligible as a student. The College is established especially for Manual Workers: but we shall refuse no one who is not ashamed to be called a Working *Man*, to whatever class *he* may belong.[22]

Similarly, at Salford the aim was to give 'working men' the opportunity of advanced culture, and to help those whose early education had been neglected to acquire the rudiments of knowledge.[23]

This emphasis upon working-class men is, perhaps, hard to understand when one considers that the working men's college movement began as a response to political agitation by Chartists, who included within their ranks a large number of working-class *women* as well as their menfolk.[24] Yet the involvement of women in Chartism often attracted comment by the very stratum within the middle classes that became active in the working men's college movement, the professional classes. In 1839, for example, the Rev Francis Close of Cheltenham bitterly attacked those women who 'used their influence' over their husbands, brothers and fathers to 'foment discord' and, not content with that, became 'politicians' themselves:

they leave the distaff and spindle to listen to the teachers of sedition; they forsake their fireside and home duties for political meetings, they neglect honest industry to read the factious newspapers! and so destitute are they of all sense of female decorum, of female modesty and diffidence, that they become themselves political agitators – female dictators – female mobs – female Chartists![25]

These women were a curse to their country, he acidly remarked. Their children, taught revolution at home, would grow up to be revolutionaries.

The working men's college movement had a number of features that contrasted with the mechanics' institute movement. First, its philosophy was both Christian and socialist as opposed to the vocational aim of the institutes. Second, the founders of the working men's colleges were largely academics and clergymen rather than the industrialists and employers who were active in establishing institutes. Third, whereas the working men's college movement aimed to break down the barriers between the social classes, the mechanics' institutes did not. Fourth, while the former planned to offer a liberal, humane curriculum, the original aim of the institutes was to offer scientifically useful knowledge. Finally, the working men's college movement, concentrated as it was in urban areas, was not as large as the movement to establish mechanics' institutes.

In view of such differences between these two major adult education movements of the nineteenth century, we should, perhaps, expect to find diverging opinions about women within the institutes and colleges. Yet what is remarkable is the consistency of arguments voiced by founders of both kinds of educational institution. Like those responsible for the mechanics' institutes, the majority of founders of the working men's colleges appeared not to have considered the education of women as an important objective. The tensions and contradictions between different conceptions about women's roles in Victorian society are also discernible. The ideas of F. D. Maurice, for example, generally regarded as the 'father' of the colleges,[26] were particularly influential and perhaps best exemplify such attitudes.

Maurice's ideas about women can be interpreted as part of a broader world view upholding not only the supposed 'natural' hierarchy between the sexes but also the established hierarchy between social classes. Although a Christian socialist, he has not been represented as a democrat but as a Tory paternalist,[27] someone who believed in the authority of the upper classes over the lower classes. One male student recollected from his days at the London Working Men's College that Maurice was 'Christian first, and certainly no Socialist at any time'.[28] In addition, Llewelyn Davies claimed that Maurice did not believe in equality between men and women: 'order and relation, not sameness' were part of his view of the 'characteristics of the Divine Creation'.[29] Nevertheless, Maurice's views about men and women did not preclude him supporting the extension of improved educational facilities for middle-class girls and women. He was regarded as the founder of Queen's College, London, which, as we saw in the last chapter, was established in 1848 for 'young ladies' of 12 years old or more. Maurice was also an advocate of improved educational facilities for governesses[30] and a committee member of the Governesses' Benevolent Institution.

While Maurice often clearly acknowledged the necessity of educating single middle-class women for an occupation such as being a governess, when referring to the education of working-class women he usually spoke in terms of an 'improvement' in their domestic roles, as wives and mothers. He supported the education of working-class women from the viewpoint, as he perceived it, of their menfolk, emphasizing the benefits such as education might bring to their husbands, their children and to society rather than to the women themselves:

If I did not believe that the education of working men would lead us by the most direct road to the education of working women, I should care much less for it. But I am sure that the earnest thoughtful man who is also a labourer with his hands, instead of grudging his wife the best culture she can obtain, will demand that she should have it. He will long to have a true household, he will desire to bring up brave citizens. He will understand that his country looks to the wives and mothers, in every one of her classes, as the best security that the next generation of Englishmen shall not make her ashamed.[31]

With such views, it was hardly surprising that Maurice supported different kinds of education for women in different social classes, based upon particular concepts of femininity.

Maurice was not alone among middle-class founders in holding such views, particularly about working-class women. Another founder of the London Working Men's College, Richard Litchfield, believed that the place of working-class women was in the home, improving the social and domestic comforts of their families. He condemned the employment of working-class females outside the home, since he believed it was detrimental to their *husband's* happiness and to the well-being of their *husband's* children:

Is the working man's home too happy; his children too well educated? Has his wife so little to do, that we must send her off to the factory to make cotton prints for the Fans of Central Africa? Which is best, that his children shall learn something to do them good as human creatures, or that the Queen of Madagascar shall have a Birmingham teapot?[32]

Professor Thomas Huxley, Principal of the South London Working Men's College, also believed that the 'wife of a poor Englishman' lacked habits of frugality and method and was ignorant of domestic economy. The remedy to alleviate the misery and waste that her ignorance caused was to be found in the instruction of working-class children, 'and especially of girls', in the elements of household work and domestic economy.[33] The industrialist and philanthropist Edward Akroyd, founder of the Halifax Working Men's College, saw the young women's section as aiming 'to fit the females to discharge the important duties of after-life in a more intelligent way than they could without such help'.[34] Other reports from Halifax make it quite clear that the 'important duties of after-life' were domestic duties, as wives and mothers.[35]

As these examples illustrate, the working men's college movement was traditional in its views about working-class women – despite being radical in terms of socialist principles. Also the issue of admitting women to the colleges in the 1850s was as contentious as it had been for the mechanics' institutes in the 1820s and 1830s.

Debates about admitting women

It is not surprising to find that, as far as the existing records indicate, it was rare for women to be students in a working men's college. When the issue of female student recruitment arose, it usually provoked much controversy and debate. In the case of the London Working Men's College, for example, the plan submitted by Maurice, on 7 February 1854, for the proposed college made it clear that the education of women *was* considered, but only as a vague future goal:

It was agreed that adult males (that is to say, males, at all events, not younger than 16) should be contemplated first and chiefly in our education; thought it was thought very desirable that provision should in due time be made for the teaching of boys and of females.[36]

As in the case of the mechanics' institutes, females could refer to both girls and women since no age differentiation was given: in addition, 'females' were linked with 'boys' in a way that implied juvenile and dependant status.

It was 'safer', claimed Maurice, to defer the admittance of working-class women until 'the experiment with the men had been fairly made', since the presence of women would have created 'great difficulties'.[37] The extent to which working-class women protested about this, we do not know. But the issue was controversial and protests were forthcoming from a number of people, including some 'ladies'. Maurice remembers that he and the other men involved in the initial planning were told:

we should do nothing with our scholars unless we could improve the character and the knowledge of their wives and daughters; that they were already less instructed than the males of their own class; that if we succeeded at all, we should make the distance between them wider and more hopeless. It was impossible not to listen to these remonstrances, especially when they proceeded, as some of them did, from ladies who were using great exertions to raise their own sex, which they accused us of neglecting.[38]

Such arguments illustrated how the supporters of women's education in the colleges justified provision for women in terms of the benefits it would bring to the male students, rather than to the women themselves. But other arguments, opposing the entry of women, were also voiced. Working men could become jealous, ran one such line of thought, if their womenfolk were educated.[39]

The council of the London Working Men's College held a meeting to allow male students to express their views on the issue and, in particular, on the time that would be most convenient for women to attend classes and the propriety of teaching men and women together or separately. The prospective female students were not consulted. When the male students expressed support for the admittance of women, the decision-makers faced a dilemma: they felt they had made a 'pledge' to provide education for women 'if their husbands and brothers were not opposed to it' and yet, on the other hand, they felt 'not ready' for such a move.[40] Some felt the success of the college itself would be jeopardized if women were admitted. But another consideration weighed more heavily with Maurice – the problem of whether a sense of fellowship would develop in the college among male students if women were present:

Our object in founding a college for working men had not been only or chiefly to given them instruction on certain subjects. We had wished to adopt them into a society with ourselves, to give them that sense of fellowship with us which exists between members of colleges and universities, however accidental circumstances and pursuits may divide them. Now, it did not seem possible to create such a fellowship with the working women. We might teach them things which it would be worth their while to know; but that would be nearly all. And so, while attempting to influence a larger circle, we should really be making our objects with respect to the smaller one less intelligible and so should be doing harm rather than good.[41]

For Maurice, education for fellowship was primarily a form of male culture and male bonding in which women could not participate.

The council of the London college held to its initial decision, claiming that they were not competent to offer education provision for women. Maurice favoured the setting up of a separate college for working women where the managers and teachers were 'ladies'. The 'ladies' with whom the proposal was discussed were keen for the college to be a training institution where they might learn the principles and methods of teaching. But Maurice hoped that a wider range of activities might be undertaken, including the teaching of nursing and district visiting to the poor. His aim was that the new 'College for Working Women', as it was to be called, would reduce class differences and make way for a 'real living communion between the upper and lower classes, – between the lady and the working woman ... in London'.[42]

The controversy about whether women should be admitted to the London college during the first year of its establishment illustrates the strategies and stance taken by an all-male governing body. In this particular case, women students were seen by the governing council as 'outsiders' who might disrupt the main college activities. The solution was to suggest, as Maurice did, that women's education be offered in a separate institution. But this proposal was not implemented, nor was it accepted as an appropriate strategy by all participants to the debate.

There had always been those in the London college, such as Frederick James Furnivall, one of the founders, who favoured the entry of female students. In the event, the advocates of this view must have won the day, since from January 1856 separate afternoon classes for women were organized (the governing council was not able to support the wish of the male students for co-educational classes).[43] The 'woman' question, however, continued to attract notice. In 1859 a male student complained that he only supported women's presence if their teaching could be conducted 'without detriment of the present real usefulness' of the college.[44] The controversy never resolved itself. As late as July 1911, at a meeting of the college council, Mr A. Hepburn moved that a plebiscite of the students be taken on the question of admitting women students – a suggestion that was rejected by 17 votes to two. It was decided that women could become students in the elocution class but should not be admitted to the college, since, apart from 'other reasons', the buildings were not large enough for any great increase of numbers.[45]

In other colleges which had not included women among their target clientele, similar struggles were probably encountered by women seeking to become students. Although Furnivall urged the committee at the Salford college to open its doors to women, this only happened in 1859, when, merging with the local mechanics' institute, the college agreed to maintain the institute's existing class provision.[46] At Lancaster, promoters of the working men's college movement distributed 400 questionnaires to working men to try to find out what they might want if a college were founded. No working women seem to have been consulted. Indeed the very absence of any discussion about classes for women provoked the following comment from one male respondent:

If we obtain and attend these places of recreation, what have the fair sex to do? Have they to be left at home by themselves? They appear to have been entirely over-looked; can't there be no means provided for their instruction and amusement as well?[47]

Examples like this show, as at the London college, that not all working men were against their womenfolk being educated. At the Leicester college, established in 1862, the all-male singing class presented a memorial to the college committee 'begging that the introduction of female voices might be permitted'; the committee decided it was 'not advisable to sanction the request'.[48] The controversial issue of women's admittance arose again at Leicester at the fourteenth annual meeting, held in May 1876, when Henry Newton expressed a wish for a women's college to be established.[49] To what extent working women themselves were pressing for this or for admission to the male college, we do not know. But either way they were to have a long wait. On 3 May 1880 the president told the members of the annual meeting that, though they were planning a working women's college, he believed in 'slow ground and widely directed effort, and not flashes in the pan'.[50] It was not until October of that year that women were admitted, 18 years after the college was founded. Despite such opposition to women as students within the working men's college, a range of arguments as advanced to support women's cause. These arguments may be grouped into three broad camps – those emphasizing the improvements women would experience with education, those stressing the advantages for the quality of college education, and those focusing upon the benefits to social life, both within and outside the college.

What is significant about arguments centreing around the 'improvement' of women through college attendance was that they were rarely couched in terms of the improvement of women's minds, the expansion of knowledge generally and any possible 'enrichment' of personality. What was emphasized was the improvement of woman for her role in the home. The views of founders such as Maurice are frequently reiterated – that an 'educated' woman would be a 'better' wife and mother and a 'better' companion for her husband. The lack of managerial household skills among working-class wives was probably the key factor, argued one man, in making their husbands dissolute.[51] An educated woman would have a better chance of getting married than an ignorant woman, ran another argument. She would also be a better companion for her husband:

How often do you hear of an educated female without the opportunity of marrying? No, men are too glad to embrace the opportunity of uniting themselves for life with partners with whom they can enjoy some hours weekly of pleasant and instructive conversation, instead of the next-door neighbour's gossip, to allow such occasions to slip by.[52]

It is rare to find a statement suggesting that education might help women overcome any of the disadvantages they might experience as women. If such views were expressed, they were usually linked to the hope that educated women would still respect their menfolk, especially those who were skilled workers. A typical comment was that of a member of the London college who suggested that one means of relieving women 'of the burdens that oppress them' was to 'Educate the female sex, and let them when educated not despise a mechanic'.[53]

Other arguments were advanced concerning the advantages for the quality of college education if women were present. In some cases it was suggested that both male and female students would benefit from the natural rivalry between the sexes:

The young men naturally wish to keep ahead of those who conventionally have been esteemed intellectually inferior; but the quickness of women in matters purely nemonical and mental gives them an advantage; and these two causes combined would stimulate both to put forth all their energies.[54]

In other cases, mixed classes for men and women were advocated in terms of the benefits it would bring to men. The presence of women would, argued Roebuck, motive men to work harder; men would naturally desire to distinguish themselves in the eyes of their 'fairer class-mates', and, for the honour and reputation of their sex, they would strive not to be outdone by them.[55]

Another group of arguments supporting the entry of women into the colleges focused around the benefits to social life, both within and outside the colleges. In one northern town, it was believed that the mixed-sex social activities organized by the local working men's college (such as conversaziones, occasional lectures, prize-givings and soirees) helped create 'brotherly and sisterly sympathy', which was the main way of 'humanizing and softening' the rugged and selfish manners of the young men, and 'elevating and rendering more stable' the social conditions of the women.[56] In other cases it was the supposed civilizing influence of women upon men that was stressed. A student at the London college claimed that the presence of women would do much to 'refine the men'; another spoke of the 'softening and refining' influence women would have upon the 'naturally rugged characters of the men'.[57]

As in the mechanics' institutes, therefore, women were allowed to enter the working men's colleges, but on terms that were defined by men. Women students were not necessarily fully integrated into a college structure or welcomed by the male students. In 1859 the editor of *The Working Men's College Magazine* spoke of the 'greater shock' which women's classes offered to 'common prejudices about education' and, as late as 1900, a member of the London college complained about the rising 'wave of femininity' that was threatening to submerge 'our bachelor domain'.[58] In 1905, on the death of Mrs Tansley, a woman who had been active in the working men's college movement, another member of the London college commented:

She understood exactly the limits of women's work in an institution like ours. The education and the daily social life belong to the men alone.[59]

Undoubtedly attitudes such as this, which lingered on during the second half of the nineteenth century, helped to fuel the formation of a group arguing for separate women's colleges.

Separate women's colleges

The group supporting separate women's colleges was based in southern England and developed as a response to the inadequate class provision offered to women at the London Working Men's College. There had always been uncertainty about the future of the women's classes, first offered in London in 1856. During 1860, when the classes were discontinued, the problem of what to do for women 'remained on the consciences' of those at the London college.[60] The issue was resolved not by those men who held power within the London college but by a separatist women's college faction.

A key figure in this development was Elizabeth Malleson, a middle-class woman who was an active campaigner in the women's cause and a friend of Barbara Bodichon.[61] In 1856, for example, a ladies' committee was formed to press for changes in the legal position of married women, and Elizabeth Malleson gave her name and address as the headquarters of the society to which all communications should be sent. She had a long interest in education and is believed to have helped in various schemes to improve the higher education of women, such as the foundation of Queen's College in 1848 and of Bedford College in 1849.[62]

Through contact with teachers at the London Working Men's College, the male students and their female relatives, Elizabeth Malleson became aware of the relative educational deprivation that such women experienced in comparison with their menfolk; the plight of women who earned their own livelihood especially stirred her, and she decided to organize 'the same sort of educational advantages for them that the men enjoyed'.[63] On 5 February 1864 interested friends and relatives gathered at a meeting which included Mr and Mrs Malleson and their two daughters, Professor Seeley of Cambridge, Richard Litchfield, Mr and Mrs George Tansley, Arthur J. Munby, and six 'young ladies' who had offered to be teachers.[64] A provisional committee for the proposed college was formed, with Elizabeth Malleson as the honorary secretary. In this capacity, she sought gifts of furniture, books, pictures and money from a number of well-known people, including John Stuart Mill, George Eliot, Madame Bodichon, Dr Martineau, Harriet Martineau, Vernon and Godfrey Lushington and Anna Swanwick.

In October 1864 a Working Women's College at 29 Queen Street, Bloomsbury, offering evening rather than day classes, was officially opened. It was not established under any doctrine that education separate from men was necessary or best for women – it was simply that circumstances 'made it expedient at that time'.[65] The discontinuation of the women's day classes at the main London college (which working women could not have attended anyway), may have been an important factor in influencing alternative strategies.

Unlike the concerns with wifehood and mothering that seemed to permeate the rhetoric about women within 'male' colleges, the aims of the Working Women's College were couched in terms of a broad general education that was more in tune with the diffuse goals of the working men's college movement:

It was decided that the college should be open to all comers, the serious desire to learn being the only guarantee of fitness for admission. We intended to set up a standard of education in its widest sense, and we believed that the pleasure of learning would be inducement enough to ensure good intellectual effort.[66]

Social mixing between teachers and taught was to be encouraged so that 'small narrowing class distinctions' could be eliminated; it was also hoped that a 'community' could develop where the 'magic of genuine companionship and friendship prevailed.[67]

However, not everyone thought of the new women's college in these terms. Some 39 years later, a male member of the London Working Men's College claimed that the Working Women's College had been founded in order to 'fit' women to become the 'wives of intelligent working men'.[68] An indignant Elizabeth Malleson contested this view, arguing that the education offered was not to fit women to become wives any more than the education of men at the London Working Men's College was to fit them to become husbands of intelligent women, though she hoped that both colleges indirectly helped the students to become good husbands and wives; the aim of the women's college was to provide the widest and most liberal education then attainable, 'without limiting it to any special employment or destiny that might follow upon their students' life'.[69] The exchange illustrated how some men might interpret any education offered to working women, irrespective of its aims, as beneficial to men within a domestic context. Ironically, by the early 1870s the council of the Working Women's College discussed whether or not men should be admitted as students. Somewhat surprisingly Elizabeth Malleson supported co-education rather than single-sex education, arguing that men and women were created not to live in separate worlds, nor to have separate interests, nor to have separate aspirations. The inspirational force for her ideas, she pointed out, came from Maurice's educational thinking.[70] Not everyone agreed with her. Litchfield protested that such a scheme would not have met with Maurice's approval (Maurice had died in 1872). His was not the only dissident voice. A minority of the council of the Working Women's College strongly disapproved of a co-educational college where the sexes would be taught together and a collegiate life encouraged. The Working Women's College was the only institution in London devoted exclusively to the improvement and culture of working women, they protested: to close it would be a retrograde step.[71] The issue split the council in half.

The majority of the Working Women's College supported Mrs Malleson and the college became, in 1874, a College for Men and Women. The minority of the council who had deplored such a decision formed a rival College for Working Women, in Fitzroy Street. The issue of separate spheres for men and women and of single sex or co-education were therefore diversive issues within the working men's college movement. But it is ironic that it was the problem of whether to admit men to a women's college that caused such major divisions and not the admission of women to men's colleges! By 1874 the pattern of provision for women within the working men's college movement consisted of classes in some men's colleges, a co-educational college and a women's college.

Despite its mixed education, the new College for Men and Women continued to support the wide, liberal educational aims of the original Working Women's College. Thus it hoped to give to men and women, 'occupied' during the day, a higher education than was generally within their reach; again, an emphasis was put upon the development of mutual help and fellowship between teachers and taught.[72] In particular, the education offered was to be 'an end in itself', irrespective of 'all worldly or commercial aspects'.[73] Such aims for a co-educational institution were supported by some, though not all, feminists who were active in the women's movement. Maria Grey, for example, a tireless campaigner for improvements in women's education, spoke in favour of the mixed college on its opening night.[74]

Other middle-class women involved in the various changes taking place in women's education were against the co-educational college from the start. This was the position taken by Frances Martin, the founder of the rival institution, the College for Working Women. Miss Martin's supporters included Charles Kingsley, Erasmus Darwin, Mr and Mrs Tansley, the Rev Llewelyn Davies, John Lubbock, Harriet Martineau, Elizabeth Garrett Anderson, Lady Paget, Millicent Garrett Fawcett and Sir Francis Morris.[75] Harriet Martineau was a well-known writer who, though refusing to become closely identified with the early women's movement, nevertheless wrote many articles supporting the advancement of female education. During the 1860s, however, she supported the newly formed suffrage movement and the campaign to repeal the Contagious Diseases Acts, while in 1870 she personally petitioned Parliament to admit women into the medical profession.[76] Elizabeth Garrett Anderson was the first woman in England to pass a recognized course of medical training.

She had been greatly encouraged in her struggle to enter the all-male profession of medicine by Emily Davies, sister of the Rev Llewelyn Davies, one of the founders of the London Working Men's College. Her sister, Millicent Garrett Fawcett, emerged during the 1880s as one of the leaders of the women's suffrage movement.[77]

Frances Martin was one of those relatively privileged middle-class women who, like Mary Buss, Dorothea Beale and Julia Wedgwood, had once been a pupil at Queen's College, London. From 1853 to 1868 she held the post of superintendent of a girl's school attached to Bedford College, London. It was in this capacity that she gave evidence to the Schools Inquiry Commission in 1866, where she made it clear that she did not believe in co-education for adult men and women.[78] After her contact with Bedford College was discontinued, Frances Martin became actively involved in the Working Women's College, in which she had been interested from its establishment in 1864.[79] She is generally regarded as the founder, in 1874, of the College of Working Women.

The aim of the College for Working Women was to offer 'improvement and culture' to women in employment who, either from their own scruples or those of friends, 'objected to mixed evening classes'.[80] And just as Elizabeth Malleson had asserted that the inspirational force for mixed education was to be found in Maurice's educational thinking, so Frances Martin claimed that Maurice had supported single-sex education! The new college, Miss Martin pointed out, was a living monument to Maurice and his efforts on behalf of women.[81]

The issue of separate women's colleges created, then, a number of divisions and conflicts within the working men's college movement. It revealed the dilemmas involved when trying to equalize educational opportunities for women and men without changing the power structure of 'male' colleges. It also illustrated how separate women's colleges, offering opportunities for women to become founders, teachers and students, were accommodated within an essentially male orientated movement.

Recruitment of female students

It is impossible to give exact figures for the number of women students within the colleges in any one year, since, as noted earlier, records are often not available or are inadequate. In addition, even when documentary evidence about any one particular college does exist, there is often little information about female students. And any statistics relating to women are often difficult to interpret, since the number of entries per class per term may be given rather than the total female membership. Since any one woman may have been a student in more than one class each term, there is always the danger of over-estimating the extent of their membership in a college. Despite these difficulties, the sources do reveal some interesting information.

During the course of the nineteenth century, some of the colleges reached a membership of more than 1,000 as at Ipswich, Leicester and the London Working Men's College.[82] The College for Men and Women and the women-only colleges in London never recruited such large numbers. The size of any individual college, however, did not determine the size of the female membership. As in the mechanics' institutes, female students were often clustered in particular regions – London, the Midlands and the north.

The London area had one of the largest concentrations of women students, hardly surprising in view of the number of colleges established there. However, not many women students were found in the London Working Men's College; in 1856, when women's classes were first offered, about 40 women enrolled, though by 1858 his had risen to about 70 each term, each student participating on average in three classes per week.[83] By this time women constituted over one-third of the total student membership (as in the October to Christmas term, when 242 men students were enrolled).[84] However, during 1860 the women's classes were discontinued. For the rest of the century, the London college offered no provision for women other than a few joint classes in singing and participation in various recreational activities. The separate Working Women's College established in 1864 in Queen's Street, London, attracted 157 students during its first term, and over the next ten years this number increased to between 200 and 300.[85] Of the two colleges that developed from the collapse of the Queen Street institution, the single-sex College for Working Women rather than the co-educational College for Men and Women attracted the higher number of women; 369 students were recorded here in 1874, rising to 579 during the 1879–80 sessions.[86] However, over the next decade the popularity of this single-sex college declined. By the 1885–6 session, 416 students were registered,[87] a membership decline of 28 per cent in comparison with six years earlier.

It is highly probable that in the late 1870s no other area in England had as many women students enrolled within the working men's college movement as the London region. Of all the provincial colleges, that at Leicester was the most successful and also the only one to survive into the twentieth century.[88] At a comparatively late date, October 1880, 175 women became the first female students at the college, forming approximately 13 per cent of the student body.[89] Towards the end of the century, however, the number of women students increased both absolutely and proportionately, as table 7.1 illustrates.

By the end of the nineteenth century, the 698 female students at Leicester formed about one-third of the total student body. This is the highest recorded number of women I have been able to find in any of the mixed-sex colleges.

In the north, the number of female college students never reached the totals reported for London or for the Midlands, though women might form a third or more of the total student population in any one college. At Salford Working Men's College, women were first admitted towards the

Table 7.1   Student numbers at Leicester Working Men's College, 1884–1902

	Men's dept.	Women's dept.	Youth's dept. (males)	Total	Females as % of total student body
1884	1,075	470	310	1,885	25%
1892	1,075	453	171	1,699	27%
1898	1,083	698	324	2,105	33%
1902	1,209	799	343	2,351	34%

Sources: A. J. Allaway, *Vaughan College Leicester 1862–1962* (Leicester, Leicester University Press, 1962), pp. 21, 38. *Working Men's College Journal* (August 1892), p. 112. *Working Men's College Journal* (February 1898), p. 27.

end of 1860, too late for the first term of the academic year; eight women joined the classes in the second term, 12 in the third and 18 in the fourth. Even if we assume that all these women in each term were different women, that gives only 38 female students for three terms in 1861. Since male membership for 1861 was 327, women on initial entry formed about 10 per cent of the total membership.[90] During the 1870s, when the college flourished, enrolments by women students never rose beyond an average of 25 per year.[91]

Sheffield Working Men's College was a much smaller institution than that at Salford. Over the three-year period from 1856 to 1859, its total membership declined from 100 to 50, though the number of women members increased absolutely from 20 to 25 and proportionally from 20 to 50 per cent.[92] A larger number of women were to be found at the Halifax Working Men's College, where the Young Women's Institute, housed in a separate building, enrolled 165 students in 1858. Since 176 men were students in this year, women formed nearly half of the total membership. Want of space, it was claimed, was the only thing that prevented the number of women 'increasing amazingly'.[93] But such a prediction was inaccurate. Over the next four years female membership at Halifax steadily declined, while that of males rose. By 1862, 67 women and 223 men are recorded, making women now 23 per cent of total membership.[94]

It is difficult to establish whether women were admitted or not, and if so in what numbers, to other colleges in the north of England, in places such as Birkenhead, Hull and Ancoats in Manchester. The Ancoats report for 1859, for example, contains no references to any women students.[95] Neither were women admitted to the Manchester Working Men's College, which existed as a male-only institution until its absorption into Owens College in 1861.[96]

The available sources reveal, then, a somewhat patchy representation of women in the various colleges within the working men's college movement. Although they obviously made up the total membership of the women-only colleges, in other institutions they could form as little as none or as much as 50 per cent of student numbers. The statistics reveal also variations between regions and between colleges within regions. In the north in 1859, for example, no women were registered at the colleges of Manchester, Ancoats and Salford, though 28 were enrolled at Sheffield and 115 at Halifax.[97] On the other hand, in the London area in the 1870s, no women were enrolled at the London Working Men's College, though more than 600 were studying at the Working Women's College and its rival institution, the College for Men and Women.[98] Overall, it would appear that during the second half of the nineteenth century the colleges, with a few notable exceptions, were mainly places of study for men.

Recruiting 'working women'

It is not always possible to say what sort of women students were recruited into the colleges, since, as in the case of the mechanics' institutes, the available sources rarely state women's occupations. In contrast, the occupations of male students were often given. Such a discriminatory or arbitrary practice was particularly common in mixed-sex colleges, where separate statements about the men's and women's classes were offered in official college reports. The fourth annual report of the London Working Men's College, for example, includes an analysis of the occupational status of the male students (see table 7.2).

Table 7.2   Occupations of male students at London Working Men's College, 1858

Operatives: Building trades (carpenters etc)	15
Cabinet makers, upholsterers, pianoforte makers, gilders, frame makers, decorators	14
Jewellers, goldsmiths, watch & clock makers, opticians, instrument makers	17
Draughtsmen, lithographers, engravers	8
Wood turners, wood engravers	5
Printers, compositors, bookbinders	25
Bootmakers, tailors	6
Miscellaneous	19
	109
Clerks	
Tradesmen, tradesmen's assistants and warehousemen	25
Schoolmasters, teachers	6
Sundry occupations	24
	242

Source: Supplement to the Working Men's College Magazine (1 April 1859), p. 78.

The section of the report that deals with the 'Women's Classes', however, gives no information about the occupational background, marital status or age of the students.[99] Similarly, the 1861 annual report of the Salford Working Men's College contains just eight sentences about the female

evening classes; comments are made about the small number of women
students and thanks are expressed to two 'lady' teachers, Mrs John Plant
and Mrs Pochin – but no details are given about the background of the
students.[100] On the other hand, the occupations and ages of the male
students are given, as shown in table 7.3.

As this table reveals, the male membership at the London and Salford
Colleges was drawn largely from the lower-middle classes and from skilled
workmen in the upper-working class/aristocracy of labour.[101] Such patterns of male membership tended to be repeated elsewhere.[102] Finding out
about the social class origins of the female membership, however, is much
more problematic without such occupational data. We have to look at other
indicators of social class background – such as the target groups of women
that the colleges wanted to attract, their age, the timing of a class and its
cost.

Table 7.3 Age and occupation of male students at Salford Working Men's College,
1861

Age	Number	Occupation	Number
16–19	143	Mercantile clerks	63
20–9	150	Warehousemen	56
30–9	40	Printers	20
40–9	4	Decorative artists	7
	337[a]	Shopmen	11
		Teachers	7
		Handicraftsmen	51
		Labourers, millhands and sundry miscellaneous occupations	112
			327

[a]The original gives this total as 327. However, since the figures add up to 337, I have given the
latter total.
Source: The Working Men's College Magazine (1 June 1861), pp. 78–9.

We find in the available records frequent reference to one group of
women whom colleges hoped to attract – 'working women'. The use of this
term is interesting, not least because it is not found in the mechanics'
institute movement, where women were referred to as 'females', 'ladies' or
'women' or in terms of their particular occupation, e.g. factory work. The
term 'mechanic' had, of course, a more specific connotation than the term
'working man' within the working men's college movement. Although, as
pointed out in Chapter 5, there was some limited discussion about the
term 'female mechanic', it was seen as a frivolous issue, a juxtaposition of
two contradictory words. On the other hand, there was a female
equivalent to the much broader term 'working men' – 'working women'. If
the working men's college movement wanted to attract 'working women'
as opposed to 'ladies' or 'females', then this implied that it would aim much
more at a specific group of women who were in paid work rather than
those, for example, who were leisured housewives or single women at

home. A college seeking to recruit such a clientele would need to offer evening rather than daytime classes.

Such issues were aired particularly in the 1850s at the London Working Men's College, where the afternoon classes for women were more likely to recruit those full-time housewives or daughters at home in the relatively affluent sections of the working-class/lower-middle class than those women engaged in full-time paid work. As one teacher of the afternoon classes said in 1859, the students were not those 'commonly called Working Women. That is to say ... paid workers, engaged in trades or crafts'.[103] But then she went on to question the definition of the term 'working women' as applying only to those in employment:

Is it right ... to apply the name 'working women', exclusively to these hired workers in shops or factories? Are we not unnecessarily narrowing the class by so doing? Why not rather acknowledge all London as being one great factory in which 'women' are 'working', – working at housekeeping for the men of their families? In London, surely the number of paid working women must be very small in comparison with the number of women belonging to the working classes, – wives, sisters, or daughters, of working men. I suppose, then, that these women, who are working, not for wages, but in the houses of their own relations, can find time to attend the afternoon classes.[104]

The debate at the London college continued well into the following year. Some of the teachers and students argued for evening classes to be opened to women, since this would allow 'working women' to become students if they so desired.[105] A member of the women's afternoon classes who was a full-time wife and mother and called herself 'A Student's Wife' questioned the wisdom of such a move. 'Do we require the same training,' she asked, 'that our husbands need?' Husbands have two lives, one in the world, one in the home; they have to set up 'a temple' of which women were the 'priestesses' and protect their womenfolk from the rougher world. The training for the 'outer battle of life' needed by husbands could be found in the evening classes in Latin, trigonometry and political economy. It was only in regard to the 'inner life of home' that man and wife needed the same education, the women's afternoon classes in drawing and music being immensely valuable here. The connection between the 'beauty of a drawing and the neatness of a home', between the 'harmony of a part song and the harmony of kind word and loving looks' was more real than imaginary, she continued. Rather than admit women to evening classes, the male students should teach their womenfolk the value of a college education. 'Make us your companions; do not hand us over to class teachers; be our teachers yourselves', she implored.[106]

This plea appeared in *The Working Men's College Magazine*, whose editor hoped that 'some unmarried sister' would tell his readers what she thought. 'A Working Woman' took up the challenge:

Sir, – Permit a working woman – one who has had to depend on her daily labour for daily bread – to thank you and the other gentlemen of the College for the interest you evince in the education of women. I believe much good has resulted from the afternoon classes; still more would accrue from the establishment of evening classes for those who cannot spare time in the afternoon. Your correspondent, 'A Student's Wife,' appears to me to mistake the position of working women altogether: it is not they who are the 'Priestesses of the Temple;' that is only the position of the favoured few. I cannot help envying the dear lady who 'has an armed guard to protect her from the rough hands of the outer world.' Unfortunately the majority of working women have to encounter for themselves the battle of life, not unfrequently to compete with men for the means of earning their daily bread. God help us if the contest unfits us for the amenities of home! 'Music and Drawing,' why crowns and coronets seem scarcely more beyond our reach than these ladylike accomplishments. All honour to the generous men who are willing to teach us even Algebra and Trigonometry, not that we may become thereby more fit Priestesses of the Temple, but in order that we may be better qualified to do our duty in that state of life in which it may please God to place us, whether it be His will that we fight the battle of life singly, or, like many a widowed mother, we have to perform the duty of father and mother towards our orphan children. I will not intrude longer on your valuable time. You will see that the pen is not a familiar tool to me, but as you have invited all those to speak who have serious thoughts or honest convictions, I rely on your goodness to excuse the blunders of

A WORKING WOMAN.[107]

Whether this correspondent was unmarried (or perhaps a single parent) we do not know. But the tone of her letter offended 'A Student's Wife', who reiterated her views, expressed earlier.[108]

At the very least, such an exchange of letters illustrates that women were debating, in a public forum, the form female education should take. Ironically, despite the support of *both* groups of women, the women's daytime classes were discontinued in 1860 – the evening classes never set up. These facts help to put the debate in context; women could argue about the term 'working women' and the timing and content of women's class but in the event they had no control over provision.

Besides the limitations of the timing of the women's classes at the London Working Men's College, the cost also was clearly going to exclude certain types of women. The termly fees of 2s for one day per week, 3s 6d for two, 4s for three and 5s for four would be beyond the means of poor women.[109] The South London Working Men's College in Blackfriars Road, charging a flat rate of 4s per term for its afternoon women's class,[110] probably attracted a similar female clientele to that found at the main London college. By November 1868, however, the social background of the women was likely to be much more mixed since both day and evening classes were operating for 2d to 4d per week.[111]

Most detail about the social background of the female students can be found in the separate women-only colleges and the new co-educational college. The Working Women's College, for example, offering only evening classes and charging fees to meet 'the lowest wages of working women', attracted during the first term of its opening every 'class of workers', claimed Mrs Malleson – 'teachers of all kinds, sick nurses, dressmakers, domestic servants, and representatives of so many handicrafts that until we saw them on our registers we did not know that even London offered so many employments to women'.[112] This range of background of the students can also be gauged from the entries in the college book for 1865, where we find Kate Appleton, a telegraph clerk, Emily Holdsworth, a corrector of the press, Charlotte Frank, a medical student, Jane Orris, a tobacconist, Louisa Cooke, a bootmaker, Emma Wilson, a barmaid, Lucy Gearing, a waitress, and Anne Smith, a domestic servant; the majority of the students, apparently, were single but 'not a few' were married.[113]

The single-sex college established after the collapse of the Working Women's College attracted women in a similar range of occupations. The 434 women attending the College for Working Women from October 1882 to July 1883 apparently included 107 milliners, needlewomen, dress-makers, mantle-makers and tailoresses, 52 shopwomen, 37 teachers and pupil teachers, 32 book-keepers, clerks and law copyists, 26 domestic servants, 21 hospital nurses, superintendents and housekeepers, 16 machinists, 16 upholsterers and bed-makers, 15 blind brush-makers and chair-caners, nine artificial flower-makers, toy-makers and feather cleaners, nine gilders, china-painters, artists etc., nine embroiderers, lace milliners etc., nine stationers and fancy trades, and four book-binders and compositors.[114] In addition, 72 were of 'no occupation stated', a category where nearly all the women were employed in housework or needlework in their own homes.[115] All of these women, who had to be above 15 years of age in order to enter the college, would have to pay termly fees varying from 1s to 3s, according to the subject studied.[116]

One forms the impression that the majority of students at this college were young single women. Since one-third of the students in the 1870s were learning to read and write, they were probably working-class women who had experienced little or no schooling as girls. We are told that many were 'ashamed' of not possessing basic skills.[117] One, a domestic servant, the eldest of ten children whose father had died when they were all young, described how she entered domestic service at eight years old, and had 'very little schooling as a child, and quickly forgot what she had learnt'. Until she came to the college, it was a kindly mistress or a fellow-servant who had helped her.[118]

At other colleges scattered in the Midlands and north of England, again one forms the impression from the records that the female students were working women, though probably in a much narrower range of occupations than in the London area. Since the occupations of the students are not always stated, one cannot distinguish between 'working women' and 'working-class women'. At Leicester Working Men's College, although no explicit information was recorded concerning the background of the women students, we might surmise that, as their classes were mainly in the three Rs and domestic subjects, most of the students were working class.[119] The low fees charged, one penny per class, also reinforces this view.[120] Prize lists reveal that the students were both single and married women; at the annual meeting held on 10 April 1890, for example, Dr and Mrs Vaughan distributed prizes and certificates to, among others, Mary Anne Briggs and Emily Sharpe from the reading and writing class, Sarah

Perkins and Mrs Murdoch from the backward readers' class, Clara Jordon from the grammar and letter-writing class, Mrs Clulow and Kate Palmer from the sewing class, and Rachel Biggs from the ambulance and French class.[121] Examples like this show that, even towards the end of the nineteenth century, women were still learning literacy and domestic skills. From 1899, however, when a shilling entrance fee was introduced for all women's classes, except for those in elementary and domestic subjects,[122] the clientele probably became much more mixed in social origin.

Northern colleges at Sheffield and Halifax appear overwhelmingly to have attracted young working women to the evening classes. At Sheffield in 1857, the 20 women recorded out of a total membership of 100 would have paid 3d per week for mainly elementary subjects.[123] At Halifax, most of the women were factory workers under 18 years of age; in 1858, 45 of these students were from 13 to 15 years old, 50 from 15 to 18 and 40 from 18 years old and upwards.[124]

What is not recorded in the official college documents is the struggle all these women must have faced in order to study in their spare time. As we saw in earlier chapters, single women could work for long hours on low pay and married women were likely to be involved in home-based, poorly paid jobs such as needlework, as well as a range of domestic and child-care tasks. To find the energy for adult classes, plus a fee of 2d per week or termly fees of 1s to 3s, must have been no easy task. Married women in particular may have felt guilty at spending money on themselves that could be spent on their children and home.

Attendance at a class must have involved a high level of financial sacrifice and commitment. Frances Martin, founder of the College for Working Women, spoke of the 'sharp economy' women had to practise in order to become students[125] and how, once they entered the college, they had little money to spare for any 'extras' that college life might offer:

They don't smoke, and they don't want anything to eat or drink. Women have not acquired the habit, or have not got the means, of spending money on superfluous stimulants or food; and a cup of tea or coffee with bread and butter for three-pence does not tempt them. They 'have meals at home', they say, and an occasional 'exception' only 'proves this rule'.[126]

In comparison with the mechanics' institutes, then, the working men's colleges appear to have put much more emphasis upon offering evening classes and upon attracting working women – though the total number of women recorded as college members never reached the number to be found in the institutes. In addition, the fees of the colleges were lower than those in many institutes. Consequently, the women in the working men's colleges were probably more likely to have been recruited from the working class than those in the mechanics' institutes: in particular, middle-class 'ladies' and 'young ladies' are rarely referred to.

Second-class membership

Again, one critical aspect of female student recruitment into the colleges appears to have been their status as students and consumers. The available information reveals marked differences between the mixed-sex colleges and the separate colleges in regard to the terms of membership for women. In many mixed-sex colleges, and especially the London Working Men's College, women rarely enjoyed equal access to all the facilities open to male students. Like the mixed mechanics' institutes, such places were controlled by men and for men, reflecting aspects of influential ideologies about woman's place in Victorian society (see Chapter 3). The subordinate position of women within the wider society was reflected in their inferior membership status, the limited use of facilities, the limited voting powers and the few opportunities to hold office.

The unequal membership status for women within mixed-sex working men's colleges was not always based on differential fees for men and women. It would appear that an equal fee for both sexes was charged mainly in colleges in the north of England. At the Sheffield college men and women paid the same weekly fee of 3d, while 2d was charged to both sexes at Haley Mill.[127] However, in other colleges there was a marked difference in the amounts charged to men and women. At South London, men paid 6d weekly for an evening class and women, as noted earlier, 2d to 4d weekly for evening and day classes.[128] But it was at the London Working Men's College that differential rates were most marked. In 1861 male students paid an entrance fee of 1s 6d, a term fee of 1s, and a range of class fees varying from 2s for one hour per week, 3s for two hours and 4s for drawing classes, irrespective of duration. Yearly course tickets in algebra, geometry, history, French and Latin could also be obtained for 10s for two hours a week or 6s for one. To enter the afternoon classes in 1859 however, women paid no entrance fee and, as pointed out previously, the termly class fees were based upon the number of days attended per week – 2s for one day, 3s 6d for two, 4s for three and 5s for four.[129] The lower fee charged to women may have resulted from the assumption that, as in the case of the mechanics' institutes, women were economically dependent upon men and had little money of their own, that 'working' women earned less than 'working' men and that women could not be members of the institution in the same way as men. However, as in the mechanics' institutes, women were also buying for their lower fee a different and reduced service to that offered to men.

Clearly the issue of differential fees did not apply to the two separate women's colleges, though it is interesting to note that the level of fees were lower than those charged to women in the London Working Men's College. The women's colleges appear to have charged a range of weekly and termly fees. The Working Women's College presumably charged weekly fees, since the amounts levied, as noted earlier, were designed to meet 'the lowest wages of working women', while the College for Working Women charged termly fees from 1s to 3s, according to subject.[130] The

College for Men and Women included both weekly and termly fees; those studying the three Rs paid 3d to 6d weekly, while the termly charges for arithmetic and book-keeping were 2s and for drawing, French, Latin and German, 3s.[131]

As we saw in Chapter 5, in many of the mechanics' institutes female members were categorized in terms of their relationship to male members (as wives, mothers, daughters, sisters) or as females or ladies. Within the colleges, on the other hand, the most common categorization for female members is 'women'. However, some differences between the sexes are still maintained, since men are often categorized also in regard to age, while females are not. At Halifax, the three divisions among the members were 'Senior Men', i.e. those aged 18 and above, 'Junior Men', thosed aged 13 to 18, and 'Women'. Similarly at Leicester, the divisions were 'Men', 'Women' and 'Youths'.[132] The homogeneous category 'women' implies that it was not necessary to differentiate female members along the same lines as the males – who were the prime clientele. Nevertheless, it *is* significant that the word 'women' rather than 'ladies' was commonly used in the colleges.

The categorization 'women' might indicate, of course, that the working men's college movement attracted more females of working-class background than middle-class 'ladies'. It might also reflect changes in the status of women within Victorian society generally. From the late 1840s, many single middle-class daughters were forced, from economic necessity, to enter the labour market and thus to lose that coveted title 'lady', a being who did not engage in paid work (see Chapter 3). By the time the working men's college movement 'began' in 1854, such changes in the lifestyle of middle-class daughters were well pronounced. And it is significant that even the London Working Men's College, which attracted the more affluent working-class women and those from the lower-middle class, referred to its female members as 'women'.

The second-class membership given to women within the mixed-sex working men's colleges was especially reflected in the unequal access to college facilities. For example, although most mixed-sex colleges seem to have had libraries, common rooms and clubs, women did not necessarily have access to these facilities on the same terms as men. At the London Working Men's College the library was free to male members, who could study there every day (except Sundays and the holidays in September) from 7 till 10 p.m. and borrow books during the vacation.[133] Women, on the other hand, only had access to a circulating library that was specially established for them, at a cost of 1s extra fee per quarter.[134] Women students at this college, therefore, were considerably disadvantaged in comparison with men. They had no access to the library as a quiet place for studying and for consulting books. Secondly, the range of books that they might borrow was probably much more limited than those available to men. And, perhaps even more unjustly, women had to pay extra for this service.

At the working men's colleges at Halifax and Leicester, where women formed a much larger proportion of the membership, the segregation of the women into separate female departments could also mean that access to the full range of library facilities was limited. At Halifax, where the Young Women's Institute was separate from the Young Men's Institute, the library and reading room appear to have been open to male and female members alike, as well as to subscription-paying non-members.[135] Whether female members could just borrow reading material, rather than read in these rooms, we do not know. But it is probable that the former was the case, since chess and draughts might be played in both rooms, coffee and tea drunk and smoking permitted. Such activities were very often associated with 'male' spaces, rather than spaces where both men and women might mingle.

The Leicester Working Men's College, originally begun as a reading room and library for working men, developed the former into such a comfortable social room for men, where games of chess, draughts and dominoes might be played, that during the Christmas holidays the place was kept open.[136] When women were finally admitted to the college, they were contained within their own separate department. No mention is made of a library for them. Presumably they used, when necessary, the free public library that was established in Leicester about 1870. When a new college building was opened in 1908, the library was located, yet again, in a place where women were denied access – the men's common room. The lack of library facilities for women is described, as late as the 1912–13 session, as a deficiency which ought to be remedied at once.[137]

However, despite this lack of access to reading material at Leicester, the women members had available to them that rare commodity in a mixed-sex college – a common room of their own. Here women could meet together, before and after classes. Here too they might be given some light refreshments, such as a cup of cocoa and a bun, as they came into the college after a day's work, perhaps tired and rushed.[138] Although there is no mention of women organizing games and sing-songs in their common room, the place offered women a space of their own, an opportunity to develop bonding as members of an educational venture. Such places, as at the London Working Men's College, were usually reserved for men.

At the London college, the unequal and marginal status of women was particularly symbolized by the fact that they were barred from the common room. The only qualification necessary for entrance was 'to have the appearance of being a man'.[139] Yet in many ways the common room was the 'heart' of the social life of the college, where contact between male students and between teachers and taught were cemented. After 10 o'clock, when the evening classes had ended, the students and teachers might go to the common room for tea and light refreshments. Here, although beer was not permitted, pipes could be lit and friendly discussion on a wide range of social and political issues could take place. If the discussion got too heated, the chairman would call for a song to restore the peace and conviviality.[140] One old student particularly like the Wednesday evenings, when we had a kind of 'smoking concert', over which our well-loved teacher, companion, leader, and friend, 'Tom' Hughes presided: while Furnivall and Litchfield (who had added the teaching of vocal music – part-singing – to that of mathematics) could be depended on to share in our social enjoyment. I can almost hear again our 'Jim' Fisher roaring out 'The Saucy Arethusa' and 'Come cheer up, my lads, 'tis to glory we steer', or some other of Dibdin's sea ditties; and Litchfield's 'Leather Bottel', and Hughes's rendering of Thackeray's 'Three Sailors of Bristol City' were always thoroughly enjoyed.[141]

Here, then, 'good fellowship'[142] might be formed. But it was male fellowship, in a male space, which made men feel a part of 'their' college. Women were outsiders and could never be 'proper' members in this sense.

Women's marginal status was further underlined by their lack of access to various club activities. The clubs that are mentioned in most of the mixed working men's colleges seem to have been designed primarily for men. At Halifax, for example, all the clubs appeared to have been located within, or linked to, the men's department, and women in the separate women's department were therefore probably excluded.[143] Three of the clubs founded early in the history of the London Working Men's College – the Boxing Class, the Cricket Club and the Volunteer Rifle Corps – were all male societies.[144] Some of the clubs admitted women, but since they were convened at a time after the women's classes had disbanded, the women were usually relatives or friends of male members or members of the separate women's colleges that later developed. The Furnivall Cycling Club, for example, included women from the women's colleges.[145] Similarly, female students at the College for Men and Women were eligible for membership of the Economic Club – which had Sidney Webb as its president.[146] And the Musical Society, formed in 1895, was said to be one means of bringing within the walls of the college 'the women folk of its members and making them known to each other'.[147]

Another critical aspect of membership status was the right to vote and hold office. As in the case of the mechanics' institutes, the existing records of the mixed-sex colleges are not always clear on the issues with regard to women's rights. However, when women entered the colleges some reference was usually made to the conditions of their entry and the facilities to which they had access. And from these sources we can build up a picture of the political rights of female members.

It is important to note that, despite the pervasive influence of Christian Socialism within the working men's college movement, the government of the colleges was 'very various'.[148] Some colleges allowed student representation on the governing council and gave the student body certain voting rights, while other colleges were much more oligarchic. A number of important factors would help to shape the formal structure of a college, e.g. the views of the founders, the supposed requirements of the respective district, the demands of the students.[149] Despite this variety, it would appear that women in mixed-sex working men's colleges had few opportunities to hold official positions. In particular, the pattern of government at the London Working Men's College was such that student representation was sparse, especially during the years when female students were present.

At its inception, the London college allowed for no student representation on its governing body. Such a policy was largely due to Maurice's influence. In his original plan of a 'College for Working Men', drawn up in February 1854, he made it quite clear that the power of decision-making in the proposed institutions should lay in the hands of the founders, though at some later date students might be involved.[150] A number of people, including Furnivall and Ludlow, criticized Maurice and argued for an equal representation of working men and teachers on the all-male governing body. But Maurice's views prevailed, and it was decided that only teachers should form the council of the college, though gradually working men might be admitted, to the extent of one-third of their total number.[151]

I have found no evidence that female students representation was even discussed at the London college, despite the fact that women were students in the college from 1856 to 1860. This is not surprising. Even male student representation was low. In 1860, only two of the 28 members of the college council were students; in 1870 this number increased to six, though the council itself had expanded to 53 members. It was not until after Maurice's death, in April 1872, that student representation was substantially increased – though by then there were no women's classes.[152] The only committee on which women might be found during their time at the college was the dancing committee!

During the summer of 1859, male and female students had greatly enjoyed the various mixed encursions, organized largely by Furnivall, and with the onset of winter it was proposed to continue mixed social gatherings indoors in the form of dances. A committee was set up, which included two married women and two single women, some of whom had once been members of the women's classes, as well as six male students, three teachers and two compositors.[153] The committee was, however, marginal to the main committee structure within the college. Indeed, the very issue of the dances was controversial and frowned upon by men such as Maurice, Ludlow and Litchfield, who believed such frivolities detracted from the main work of the college. In one scathing attack, Litchfield suggested that, while all dancers were not fools, a large proportion were 'silly people'; in particular, 'dancing' men were certainly not 'working' men. But, above all else, he stressed that the main business of the college was not play and heels but work and heads.[154]

The whole issue came to a climax in two special conferences on 'The Amusement Question', as it was called, held in January 1861. All members of the council, except Furnivall, were against continuation of the dances. Some male students, including two who had been members of the dance committee, pointed out that if it was a choice between the college and dances, then the dances must go.[155] The views of women members of the dance committee were not recorded; no mention was even made to the presence of women at the conference. If women were attending, they would have had a sharp reminder from Litchfield of their marginal place within the college and of their marginal role on the dance committee:

It would not do to listen to the arguments urged on behalf of the young women, for the simple reason that we are a College for men, not for women. If we could take in hand the entire question of female education, we might also deal with that of female amusement. To touch just that part alone of this great problem, which least concerns us, while we shrink from the attempt to bring women within the action of the serious influence of the College, would be plainly absurd. Till they are allowed to share our work, let us at least keep them clear of our frivolities.[156]

The outcome of the meetings was that the council formally condemned the dances. Every teacher at the college and every member of the council was urged to discourage their formation. The dance committee disbanded. And with its loss, the small voice of women within the committee structure of the college disappeared.

The women students at the London Working Men's College had also been denied attendance at the general meeting that male students could attend. As Octavia Hill, a teacher of the women's classes, noted in a letter dated 11 January 1856, 'I hear that at one meeting it was proposed that women should be admitted to the General Meeting. The idea was laughed at'.[157] To air views at such a gathering was a privilege for men only.

However, the pattern of government that prevailed at the London Working Men's College does not appear to have been adopted generally elsewhere.[158] At Salford the governing council included trustees, a president, six vice-presidents, a treasurer, an honorary secretary, the unpaid teachers of each class and elected student representatives, in the following proportions: one representative to each class of ten and not more than 20; two representatives to each class of 21 students; and one additional representative for each additional 20 students.[159] At Halifax Working Men's College from 1859, two students were elected to sit on the committee.[160] And at Leicester, the college was governed by a committee consisting mainly of students and teachers, plus a number of sub-committees.[161] To what extent women at the provincial mixed-sex colleges were a part of this student representation on governing committees is difficult to say. Presumably the female students at Salford were assured of at least one representative on the committee, provided there were ten of them in the class.

At both Halifax and Leicester, the wife of the male founder of each college was also head of the female department. Such women might, therefore, by virtue of the position they held and by virtue of their professional relationship to the founder, sit on the governing body. This was the case at Leicester, where Mrs Vaughan, wife of the president and head of the women's education committee, was a member of the council.[162]

In the latter decades of the nineteenth century we find some isolated cases of women being members of governing bodies in other mixed-sex colleges. At the South London Working Men's College in 1881, Anna Swanwick and Miss Helen Taylor were both members of the council.[163] Anna Swanwick, a middle-class woman who had been a student at Bedford

College, London, was regarded as one of the most learned women of her day. She was a scholar of Greek, Hebrew and German and one of the first women to receive a Doctor's degree – the Hon LL.D of Aberdeen University.[164] She was enthusiastic about the attempts to establish colleges for working men and working women and actively supported other movements to improve women's education. Helen Taylor was the daughter of Harriet Taylor, who, late in life, had married John Stuart Mill. She was an active campaigner for women's suffrage and wrote many of the letters which her stepfather signed in aid of the cause. In 1876 she was elected to the London School Board, and repeated her success in 1879 and 1882.[165] The presence of both of these campaigners on the governing body of a mixed-sex college would undoubtedly ensure that issues relating to women students would be aired and discussed at policy-making meetings. Their fellow members on the council apparently included another staunch supporter of the women's movement, Professor Henry Fawcett MP.[166]

THE COLLEGE FOR MEN AND WOMEN,

WITH WHICH IS INCORPORATED

THE WORKING WOMEN'S COLLEGE,

29, QUEEN SQUARE, BLOOMSBURY.

~ ~ ~ ~ ~ ~

The Council.

*Professor Sheldon Amos, M.A. Cambridge.	Miss Murray.
Mrs. Sheldon Amos.	Miss Mondy, C.S.
Miss Braine.	*Mr. F. Murray.
Mdlle. Blancard.	Miss Alice Malleson.
The Hon. Dudley Campbell.	Mr. Wm. T. Malleson, B.A. University College, London.
Mr. E. Cooke.	Mr. H. A. Nesbitt, M.A. University College, London.
Miss Ellen Drewry.	
*Mr. A. Grugeon (Certificated Teacher of Botany, Science and and Art Department of Privy Council).	Mr. Reginald Stuart Poole, British Museum.
	Miss C. Scott.
Miss Hertz.	*Mr. A. Sonnenschein.
*Mr. Hytch.	Mrs. Sonnenschein.
Miss Justice, C.S.	Mrs P. A. Taylor.
*Mr. Edmund Maurice, B.A. Christ Church, Oxford.	Mr. Harry Taylor.
	Miss Madeline Whitehead.

* Members of the Council of Teachers of the Working Men's College.

Mr. F. R. Malleson, *Treasurer.*   Mrs. F. R. Malleson, *Hon. Sec.*

Lady Superintendents—Mrs. SITWELL and Miss GOTTO.

Figure 7.1   Members of the council at the College for Men and Women, 1874 (from College for Men and Women, *Report of the Council*, 1874).

who, in 1867, had married Millicent Garrett Anderson.

It is interesting to consider the governmental structure of the separate women's colleges and the new co-educational college, since all three opened up opportunities for women in key posts of responsibility in a way never possible in the mixed-sex colleges. At the Working Women's College, the figurehead was Mrs Malleson. Yet she never adopted the title 'President' or 'Principal', usually found in the working men's colleges, but chose instead the much humbler one of 'Honorary Secretary'.[167] The governing body of this single-sex college was composed of 'teachers and workers', who were 'distinguished by their educational fitness only, and possessing no other advantage of rank or position'.[168] However, teachers on the committee greatly outnumbered the two student members; in addition, the student members were not elected by the total student body, but just that small section of it that had passed certain examinations.[169] It is highly likely, therefore, that the female representatives were drawn disproportionately from the more educated students rather than the semi-literate.

When the Working Women's College split in 1874, the institution with which Mrs Malleson was intimately involved, the College for Men and Women, continued the tradition of the 'old' college of drawing staff and students into the governing body. But some changes were thought necessary for the more efficient government of the new institution. Thus it was stipulated that at least one-third of the members of the council should be teachers holding classes in the college. In addition, student members were increased to six and elected by all the student body.[170]

What is particularly interesting about the composition of the council of the College for Men and Women was that the majority of the members were women, something that I have found in no other institution within the working men's college movement. As figure 7.1 shows, alongside Elizabeth Malleson on the council sat 13 other women, some of them relatives. One wonders whether Miss Hertz was related to Mrs Fanny Hertz, who was active in the female mechanics' institute at Bradford.[171]

Although Elizabeth Malleson was the driving force behind the co-educational college, once again she did not take the title of president or principal, but that of honorary secretary. Her husband, who 'worked equally hard' for the college, held the official position of treasurer.[172] As we saw in Chapter 5, husband and wife teams were not uncommon in institutions offering education to working-class women; both the female mechanics' institutes at Bradford and Huddersfield had such 'family' arrangements.

When the Mallesons left London in 1882, we find, however, that the Rev Stopford Brooke was invited to become 'President' of the College for Men and Women.[173] Perhaps the title was not used earlier, since it was considered inappropriate for a woman. After all, Emily Davies, a much better known figure in the movement to improve women's education, was known as 'Mistress' of Hitchin College, established in 1869, a title she kept when the college moved to Girton, Cambridge, in September 1873; Miss

Clough, however, who was the head of Newnham College, Cambridge, which developed in 1880 from an earlier hall of residence, was known as 'Principal'.[174]

Little information is available about the mode of government at the rival institution to the College for Men and Women, the College of Working Women, Fitzroy Street. One forms the impression, however, that it was less democratic than the co-educational college and tended more towards the paternalistic model that Maurice adopted. A key figure at the College for Working Women was Miss Martin. Yet she, like Mrs Malleson, took the position of honorary secretary, a task that was initially shared with Mrs Lionel Lucas.[175] Other members of the governing council in its early years included George Tansley and Dr Storrar, its chair.[176] How many of the female students had the right to stand for office or vote in elections, we do not know.

The key position at the College for Working Women during the nineteenth century was that of chair of the council, a post held by the mid-1880s by the Rev Llewelyn Davies,[177] a man with an interest in women's education and in favour of granting women university degrees as well as the franchise. Not unnaturally, he was a keen advocate of Girton College, where his sister, Emily, was Mistress. Perhaps it was these connections, together with his involvement in the London Working Men's College, that made him a 'suitable' candidate to head an all women's college; after all, in the 1870s Llewelyn Davies had been the principal of another educational establishment for women, Queen's College, London. Perhaps also it was considered 'necessary' for a father figure to head a college aimed primarily at working women. It was not until the early twentieth century that a woman, Miss Martin, headed the college, in the new post of principal; on her death in 1922, the college was renamed the 'Frances Martin College' in honour of her memory.[178]

Conclusion

What becomes clear from this account is that there were similarities between the working men's college movement and the mechanics' institute movement. Thus in order to become students within the working men's colleges as in the mechanics' institutes, women had to struggle to gain access to male-orientated institutions. Male founders of the colleges expressed similar views about the function of women's education as male founders of the institutes. The goals of female education, especially for working-class women, were primarily for wifehood and motherhood. Once admitted to the colleges, as to the institutes, women were usually given secondary status in terms of membership category, limited access to facilities and restricted rights of voting and holding office.

However, there were also marked differences between these two major adult education movements. Whereas the founders of the mechanics' institutes were often industrialists, the founders of the working men's colleges were mainly drawn from the professional classes and included clergymen, barristers, doctors and university lecturers. These professional men were infused with the ideals of Christian Socialism, while the founders of the institutes were primarily concerned with the transmission of scientifically useful knowledge. Also, within the working men's college movement there was a much greater emphasis upon reducing class differences between the middle-class providers and the intended working-class clientele. This was especially reflected in the much greater concern with recruiting 'working women' and in the debates about the provision of evening classes. It is probable, therefore, that the women entering the colleges (though small in number in comparison with those entering the institutes) were much more likely to be working class than those in the institutes.

In contrast to the mechanics' institute movement, the issue of single sex or co-education also became a key debating point within the working men's college movement. Whereas the women-only mechanics' institutes had been founded by men, the London-based separate women's colleges and the new co-educational college were founded by women: these separate colleges offered women the possibility of holding key influential positions in a way that was not possible within 'male' mixed-sex colleges. In addition, such institutions also made it possible for women students to vote and hold office.

The conditions of entry for women into the colleges were not the only important issues, however. Once within the colleges, women were offered certain kinds of curricula which were influenced both by Christian Socialism and by ideological assumptions about women's role in Victorian society.

8

A COLLEGE EDUCATION

Introduction

As in the mechanics' institutes, the admission of women into working men's colleges posed a number of problems for the organizers. As we saw in the last chapter, the aim of the colleges was to offer working men a liberal, humane education where fellowship and brotherhood could be developed between the voluntary teachers (drawn mainly from the educated middle classes) and the less well educated students. It was unclear, however, how such models could be applied for women – could women be taught according to the same principles? What kinds of educational experiences were women to be offered? In this chapter, I shall answer questions such as these by examining the way teaching was organized, the class provision and lecture provision. I shall look at both mixed-sex colleges and the separate colleges.

Sex segregation

The general pattern of curriculum provision appears to have been similar to that provided in the mechanics' institutes – namely that men and women were separated for classes, though both sexes might attend lectures. As in the institutes, the specific nature of class teaching might have appeared more threatening to the social relationships between men and women than attendance at formal lectures. As we noted earlier, classes were more intimate and private activities than lectures and involved continued contact between students over a period of time; there was, therefore, more potential for men and women to mix. But other reasons relating to convention, principle and the fear of sex relations may have had just as much force in the different context of the 1850s in the working men's colleges as in the 1820s when the first mechanics' institutes were founded.

As we saw in Chapter 6, it was conventional practice in educational institutions to educate men and women separately rather than in mixed classes. And this practice extended into the second half of the nineteenth century, well after the foundation of the working men's college movement in 1854. In 1878, for example, when London University conferred degrees on women, the junior classes of women were mainly distinct from those attended by male students, though senior classes were more generally open to both sexes.[1] For mixed classes to be offered in working men's college would then have been a radical suggestion, a marked departure from well-tried and established practice.

However, the Rev F. D. Maurice, when proposing in 1854 the foundation of a college for working men, suggested that men and women might share joint classes in languages, drawing and music.[2] Maurice changed his mind on this issue, though, and, as we saw in the last chapter, came to favour a separate college for working women (which did not materialize) rather than allow them to enter the London college, let alone partake in mixed classes. The only co-educational class that was offered at the London Working Men's College was the singing class.[3] When the idea was first mooted in August 1859 that occasional meetings between the male and female singing classes should be arranged, it was supported in terms of the gains for the men, not the women:

It is needless to say how much interest such a combination will add to the ordinary practice of the classes. Our men's class at least cannot help being benefited by associating with such a well-trained body of fresh voices as entertained us at our late 'conversazione'.[4]

After 1860, when the women's classes were discontinued, we find sporadic attempts to bring female students from other institutions into the London college. Some 'tentative' mixed classes[5] in algebra, geometry, astronomy, geology and law were set up with the female students at the Working Women's College, established in 1864, but the venture failed. And by 1896 female students of the College for Men and Women could attend certain joint classes that were offered mainly in recreational activities, such as walks and excursions.[6] In 1911 the executive committee of the London Working Men's College rescinded a previous decision that had barred women from joining the elocution class: it was claimed that although the teacher and students of the class were not strongly in favour of admitting women, it was now hoped that the new proposals would remove 'the practical inconvenience at present caused by the exclusion of ladies to other classes in the Musical section, and their exclusion from this particular class.[7]

Since the London Working Men's College followed the conventional pattern of separate education for male and female students, it is hardly surprising that, when the women's classes were discontinued in 1860,

Elizabeth Malleson argued and worked for a single-sex college for women; yet when the Working Women's College was opened in 1864, she pointed out, as we saw in the last chapter, that it was not established under any doctrine that an education for women should be separate from men or even that it was best for women, but that circumstances 'made it expedient at that time'.[8] She firmly believed in mixed education, and when the question of the renewal of the lease on the buildings used by the women's college arose in 1871, she supported a merger of her college with the London Working Men's College. Representatives from the latter, however, had little faith in any benefits that might result, and opposed an amalgamation.[9] For Elizabeth Malleson, however, the issue did not die. When she and her supporters finally established the co-educational College for Men and Women, where mixed classes were the order of the day, the decision was controversial.

Some attempts were made to bring closer contact between this unique co-educational college and the London Working Men's College. In 1887 the Trustees of the City Parochial Charities offered an annual grant of £400 to a joint committee of both institutions on condition that lectures and certain classes were open to male and female students alike.[10] But, despite the wishes of the trustees, a merger between the colleges did not occur. The very existence of the co-educational college within the working men's college movement was too radical, and the prospect of one large co-educational institution would seem to have threatened the male ethos and male culture of the London Working Men's College.

A secure future for the College for Men and Women was not therefore guaranteed. It had to live in the shadow of the illustrious London Working Men's College and also compete for students with its rival institution, the College for Working Women, plus the other educational institutions that developed in the London area during the latter decades of the nineteenth century. In 1901, 37 years after its foundation, this mixed college closed its doors. Interestingly, it was the College for Working Women, offering only single-sex education, that survived well into the twentieth century and merged with the London Working Men's College in 1966.[11]

In other mixed-sex colleges outside London, separate classes for men and women appear also to have been the predominant pattern of organization of the teaching. This was so at Halifax, Leicester, Sheffield and Salford. When two young women at Salford, for example, who had made 'great progress' in the women's classes, asked to be admitted into the men's classes, their application was refused. The hope was expressed, however, that 'some arrangement' could be made which would secure for the women the 'advantages' occupied by the men; whether this happened or not, we do not know, but the editor of a local paper undoubtedly expressed a common view when he uttered that 'the principle of a mixed class would break down in a week'.[12]

In a few of the mixed-sex colleges in the provinces, we find isolated joint classes, again usually for singing. Thus at Halifax in 1861, 'great additional life and vigour' was given to the vocal music class by the singing class from the Young Women's Institute joining the men's class at practice. Similarly at Leicester, female students joined the men's singing class in 1909, though this time it was because the preparation of a cantata for the annual concert 'necessitated the admission of women'.[13] The 'experiment', as it was called, led the committee of the Leicester college to open some of the other men's classes to women when the subject to be studied could not be found in the women's department. By 1912 Leicester had mixed classes in drawing, advanced book-keeping, German, English literature, English history, harmony, botany, horticulture and choral work.[14]

Classes for men and women within the various colleges might also be separated on the grounds of principle, mainly that male and female students had 'different' destinations in life and that this differentiation should be maintained educationally. The idea was often expressed that the 'needs' of female students were different from those of the male. In particular, as we saw in the last chapter, the 'needs' of working-class women were often seen as related to the world of the home, husband and children. Maurice's comments, for example, that the schooling of the working-class wife would help her to bring up 'brave citizens' who would not make England ashamed,[15] may be interpreted as a 'moral panic': working-class women were so deficient in domestic skills that they needed an education in domesticity, separate from their menfolk, who could be taught a different range of curricular subjects.

A third possible reason why separate rather than mixed classes were found in the colleges relates, as in the case of the mechanics' institutes, to fear of sex relations. Such a fear may have been particularly reinforced by widespread public discussion about prostitution in the 1860s, a way of life especially associated with poor women. Under the Contagious Diseases Acts of 1864, 1866 and 1869, any woman suspected of being a prostitute in areas where the laws operated (ports and army towns) could be subjected to a compulsory examination for venereal disease.[16] Working-class women generally were thought by the middle classes to flaunt their sexuality,[17] and such ideas, though not openly expressed, may have worried many providers of classes for 'working' women in male colleges. Thus it is common to find various terms used to hint that certain 'undesirable' activities might occur. The euphemism 'not advisable', for example, was used by the governing council of the London Working Men's College in 1857 in regard to the issue of mixed classes and by the president of the Leicester Working Men's College in 1870 when the men in the singing class asked for female participants.[18]

Occasionally the words used to describe such fears about what might happen if men and women were educated together were more forceful. At Halifax Working Men's College in 1859 the senior tutor considered it an open question as to whether the 'moral and disciplinary effects' of mixed classes would be 'good or bad'. At another college, a male student dared to say that what gave most anxiety in the admission of women to the men's evening classes was, he presumed, 'the fear that unpleasant things might occur from the levity of students of either sex'.[19] The issue of whether women should be educated in separate or integrated classes within the college was a crucial one, with profound implications for the female students, since separate education generally meant a separate curriculum.

Organization of the curriculum in classes

From the available sources about mixed-sex colleges, we may discern two key variables shaping curricula for women. First of all, as in the mechanics' institutes, the assumed social class background of the female students played an important part in determining the kinds of knowledge offered. In particular, different forms of curriculum were offered to women in the more affluent sections of the working class/lower-middle class than to those in the ranks below them. This differentiation, though not as extreme as in the mechanics' institutes, was reinforced by holding classes for the former in the daytime and for the latter in the evening, as well as by differential levels of fees. Secondly, these two main forms of curriculum were also clearly influenced by the class-specific images of femininity, that of the middle-class 'lady' and that of the working-class 'good wife and mother', discussed in Chapter 3.

The curriculum of 'ladylike' women

Some of the mixed-sex colleges that drew their female clientele primarily from the ranks of the labour aristocracy and the lower-middle classes appear to have constructed images of the 'ladylike' woman. The London Working Men's College and the South London Working Men's College provide illustrative case studies of the way this ideal influenced curricula content.

As indicated in the previous chapter, the separate daytime classes for women first offered from January 1856 at the London Working Men's College were likely to attract those in the more affluent sections of the working class/lower-middle class, such as full-time wives and daughters at home, rather than full-time paid workers. As a teacher of these classes commented:

I suppose, then, that these women, who are working, not for wages, but in the houses of their own relations, can find time to attend the afternoon classes. Their business in this world is to clean rooms, to cook, to mend clothes, to tend children; – dreary mechanical work, even that last mentioned can become, if their minds are not now and then aroused out of the thoughts connected with its routine, if they are not occasionally allowed to feel that they belong to another world besides the world of pinafores and perambulators.[20]

For these women, the curriculum embraced a relatively wide range of subjects that might broaden general knowledge as well as teach a few 'ladylike' and 'good wife and mother' skills.

The afternoon classes in reading, writing, arithmetic, English, geography, history, natural history and the Bible might extend general knowledge, though the level in some of these subjects appears to have been very basic.[21] The English class, for example, was restricted to the teaching of grammar, with no attention to the essay writing and literature that men might study; similarly, the elementary classes, especially in writing and arithmetic, were more popular than the advanced lessons.[22]

'Ladylike' accomplishments could have been learnt in the classes in drawing, singing and botany,[23] but other forms of knowledge ensured that the students aimed more for the image of the 'good wife and mother'. The lectures on household economy, for example, included the topics of home-ventilation, stoves, fuel, lighting apparatus, washing, cleaning and the principles of economical cookery; in addition, plain and not fancy needlework was taught[24] – though such classes were not very popular.

Elizabeth Rossiter, a married student at the London Working Men's College, claimed that the women's classes deepened her understanding of her family duties. Geography, history, and singing did not improve her cooking skills or efficiency in scouring pots and pans, but then, she asked:

Do the names of 'wife' or 'mother' convey only the notion of a scrubbing, cooking, and nursing animal? ... Would it be fair to estimate a wife only by her ability to do domestic work? ... For myself, I feel thankful that the College Classes have made me understand the true nature of a wife's position in her family; to know that domestic work is all-important in itself but is quite subordinate to the higher duties of a woman in her house; to feel that rooms are not built merely to be scrubbed, nor children sent into the world merely to be nursed and dressed. I believe the more this is understood the happier will our homes be.[25]

To what extent other married women students had similar feelings, we do not know.

The single female student might, of course, have evaluated the classes less in terms of any domestic benefits than in terms of preparation for employment. By 1860, the year when the women's classes were discontinued, the curriculum, as table 8.1 shows, was one which might have encouraged women to enter jobs such as clerical worker and sales assistant. A similar experience may have been shared by those girls and young women too old for a day school, who were attending, in the late 1860s, the afternoon classes at the South London Working Men's College in French, drawing, book-keeping, reading, grammar, arithmetic, writing from dictation, history, geography and the Bible.[26] But for the young

Table 8.1   Classes for women at the London Working Men's College, 1860

	3–4 p.m.	4–5 p.m.
Monday	Reading	Writing
Tuesday	Bible class	Book-keeping
Wednesday	Arithmetic	Grammar
Thursday	Writing	Reading
Friday	Geography	History
Saturday	Natural history of plants	Arithmetic

Source: The Working Men's College Magazine (1 October 1860), p. 164.

women at both colleges, the female curriculum was far less extensive in terms of diversity than the men's curriculum, and was clearly differentiated from it. At the London Working Men's College, for example, men were offered not only a larger number of classes, 25 in all, but also a much wider range, including algebra, geometry, mechanics, physiology, geology, chemistry, botany, drawing, Latin, Greek, French, logic, politics and the history of the working classes of England.[27]

Working-class women and the curriculum

We can see within the mixed-sex colleges not only a marked division between male and female knowledge but also a clear demarcation between women within the different strata of the working classes. Thus women within the poor and poorest sections of the working classes were offered, as in the mechanics' institutes, evening classes for a small fee that usually involved the teaching of the three Rs, plain sewing and some elementary knowledge.

This basic female curriculum was established in mixed-sex colleges in different parts of the country – for example, at Halifax and Sheffield in the north, at Leicester in the Midlands, and at the South London Working Men's College. At Halifax, which has been described as more akin to a 'fairly advanced night school',[28] the young factory women who became evening students could study writing and geography on Tuesdays, sewing on Wednesdays, and reading, dictation and arithmetic on Thursdays.[29] The emphasis in the sewing class was upon teaching the students 'only what is useful, vis., making and mending their own dresses, &c.'.[30] By 1859 a cookery school had also been established for the teaching of 'plain cooking' which would increase the comforts of the home of the working man and economize his limited means.[31] It was also stressed that the young women were instructed how to cook for the sick, which would teach them both a lesson in charity and how to care for those who became ill in their own homes.

The senior male tutor of the Halifax college asserted that such a curriculum was meant to make the young women practical managers of households – efficient, thrifty wives who would save their husbands from dissolute lives:

The young women, too, have prizes awarded for proficiency in homely dressmaking and millinery, and are taught the art of simple cookery. Nor are these last by any means unimportant matters. Perhaps more of the dissoluteness and recklessness of living among husbands in the working class is produced by want of good management in their wives than by any other cause. Hence, what can be more important than to teach young women neat and thrifty modes of turning everything to the best account, whether it be the print or stuff for their own dresses, or the small joint for the family dinner? No one who is not practically acquainted with the matter, would credit the necessity in such matters that exists among the young women employed in mills.[32]

In contrast, in the case of male students, no mention was made of education for becoming a husband or father. Indeed, the range of subjects men could study in evening classes was much wider than that for women – covering, for example, reading, writing, arithmetic, dictation, composition, parsing, algebra, geometry, English history, geography, drawing, French, chemistry and theology.[33]

At Sheffield, young working-class women in 1857 might have studied a wider range of subjects that their counterparts at Halifax, since the curriculum included not only the three Rs and English grammar but also singing, drawing and literary discussion.[34] The two latter subjects in particular were often associated with the broad, humane educational aims of the working men's college movement, but whether this was met in the women's classes at Sheffield is doubtful. The committee of the college appeared to have been keen to attract those young working women considered deficient in domestic skills. In 1858 it expressed the hope that a needlework and domestic economy class would be established, since there were, in the area, a large number of young women employed in the factories and warehouses who, 'when called upon to change their situations in life, are totally ignorant of the important duties which will devolve upon them'.[35] Whether the intended clientele responded to this rhetoric, we do not know.

In the Midlands by the 1890s, working-class women attending the separate Women's Department at the Leicester Working Men's College could study a familiar range of subjects – the three Rs, needlework, dressmaking, cookery, and singing – as well as the less familiar topics of drilling, sick nursing and French.[36] How this particular combination of subjects arose is difficult to determine, but one key figure who may have shaped the female curriculum here was Mrs Vaughan, wife of the Rev David James Vaughan, founder of the college. She took an active part in planning the women's classes and appears to have been a deeply religious woman who, like her husband, saw the education of working-class adults as a mission and a means of establishing mutual understanding and co-operation between the middle-class providers and the 'lower'-class recipients.[37]

The male curriculum at Leicester reveals a similar diverse pattern of curricular subjects to that found in other working men's colleges. In 1867 the men had classes in the three Rs, book-keeping, mensuration, English grammar, history, geography, drawing, shorthand and discussion; by 1869, music and French had been added.[38] Then, during the 1876–7 session, it was decided to extend the men's classes both 'upwards and downwards' in the social scale; this, it was hoped, would attract men in business, who would study Christian Evidences, English history, music and essay writing, as well as men in the lower social strata, who could study the three Rs – an elementary education already offered at the college, on a Sunday evening.[39] Such a range of curricular subjects, and such a range of weekday and Sunday times, were not available to women. In addition, it was only in the Men's Department that advanced classes were offered.[40]

A similar pattern of gender-differentiated curricula was to be found at the mixed-sex college in South London. The evening classes for females over 14 years of age covered only the three Rs, and were probably intended to compensate for the previously inadequate schooling of many working-class girls. The evening classes for men, however, covered English, French, Latin, grammar, arithmetic, algebra, geometry, physics, chemistry, animal physiology, mensuration and book-keeping.[41]

As in the mechanics' institutes, the extent of differentiation between the sexes became even more pronounced in mixed colleges if students were entered for examinations. From its beginnings, the London Working Men's College had included examinations and honours in the programme offered to men, since Maurice and the founders thought such a scheme would be security against the 'danger of dilletantism'.[42] However, Maurice also favoured entering students for examinations of external bodies, such as the Society of Arts. When in 1860 the Rev H. Chester, who pioneered the society's examinations, wrote to him suggesting such a move, Maurice urged the council of the college to accept the proposal – but the council rejected it.[43] Earlier fears had been expressed that such a link would forfeit the right to the very name 'College' as distinct from that of 'Mechanics' Institute'; 'Our own distinctive character', it was emphasized, must be retained.[44] And that 'distinctive' character was the offering of a broad, liberal education, teaching the student how to think rather than how to 'get on' in the world. The annual report of the college for 1862 justified the decision not to join the Society of Arts in the following terms:

we have feared lest our own pupils and those who many concern themselves in our proceedings, should ever fancy that we regard our class-instruction as an end instead of a means, or as a means to certain material advantages of the particular student, rather than to the moral elevation of himself and of the class to which he belongs.[45]

By the end of the century, though, the London Working Men's College was encouraging its students to sit for outside examinations – in science and art for the Board of Education at South Kensington, in languages and art for the Society of Arts, and in a range of commercial subjects for the London Chamber of Commerce. Some classes were also offered to help prepare students for the London Matriculation Examinations.[46]

Mention of female students in examination passes at the London college, however, is sparse. In 1907, for example, all the candidates for science and art examinations were men. The only female students listed were the four who successfully passed their music examinations – Miss D. Kleem, Miss A. Quar, Miss B. Francis and Miss S. Hughes.[47] These women were probably members of a mixed-sex music class.

A number of other colleges, such as those at Halifax, Sheffield, Salford and Leicester, allowed their students to enter for the Society of Arts examinations much earlier than the main London college. Few female candidates are recorded in these colleges. At Halifax, where the competitive examinations were seen as 'the very life of our College' and 'a great inducement to exertion in learning',[48] such comments relate only to the men. In 1861, for example, three male students at the college all passed the society's examinations – Henry Balme, aged 21, a wool-sorter; William Brear, aged 17, a warehouseman; and John Dyson, aged 19, a clerk.[49] No women's names appear. Women could, however, be given 'prizes' for good work in needlework, shirt-making, knitting stockings, darning stockings and regularity of attendance, as the following reveals:

YOUNG WOMEN'S INSTITUTE, HALIFAX WORKING MEN'S COLLEGE, 1860

Prizes given by Mrs. Akroyd for Needlework, etc – 1st Division: For Needlework in general, H. Spencer, E. Hudson, (additional) J. Smith, for Best Shirt made in School, M. Devonport; for Stocking Knitting, F. Simms; for Stocking Darning, M. A. Sandwell. 2nd Division: for Needlework in general, G. E. Walton, E. Oates, M. H. Spencer, E. Leach; for Stocking Knitting, M. A. Varley.

For Regularity of Attendance, H. Spencer, A. Spencer, S. A. Hartley, M. Holden, E. Lacy, H. Priestley, N. Carle.

3rd Division: H. Hinchcliffe, C. Walton, M. Duckworth.[50]

Such awards undoubtedly lacked the rigour of external examinations and also restricted scholastic excellence for female students to practical skills and good attendance. Such practical skills were associated with femininity and with women's work within the home.

At the colleges at Sheffield, Salford and Leicester, a similar pattern emerges in that the students entering for examinations of the Society of Arts were overwhelmingly male. Occasionally we find a few women candidates but these are more likely to be listed in annual college examinations than those of an external outside body. At Salford in 1861, for example, Elizabeth Collins of the female writing class was awarded a certificate for being the most distinguished student in her group, while Virginia Tiplady received an 'honourable mention' as second in order of merit.[51]

Overall then, those working men's college that admitted women appear to have offered two main kinds of curriculum that were shaped by assumptions about the social class background of the students and by middle-class ideals about femininity. However, the ladylike curriculum for women of the labour aristocracy lower-middle class and the more limited, basic curriculum for women in the less affluent sections of the working classes were not the only curricula available to women students within the working men's college movement. The separate women's colleges and the unique co-educational college offered some alternative choices.

The separate colleges

The separate colleges marked a distinctive stage in the working men's college movement in that two alternative curricular patterns were offered to women students – one emphasizing the pursuit of knowledge for its own sake, the other emphasizing much more the moral and vocational aspects of education. The key variables shaping these two curricular forms appear to have been the aims and ideals of the founders of the colleges and the social class background of the students.

Although women's education within the working men's colleges did not follow the pattern of the liberal, humane curriculum that was often possible for men, such an emphasis was found in the Working Women's College, established by Elizabeth Malleson in October 1864. The aim of the college, as we saw in the last chapter, was to provide 'the widest and most liberal education for women then attainable, without limiting it to any special employment or destiny that might follow upon their student life'; in addition, all that was necessary for 'good intellectual effort' was the 'pleasure of learning'.[52] Not surprisingly, the curriculum to be offered was to be knowledge for its own sake and not for any practical end. The ideal of femininity that pervaded this college was, unusually, that of the 'good scholar'.

The students at the Working Women's College came from a variety of occupations within the working and lower-middle class. Some, as we saw in the last chapter, were teachers, dressmakers, domestic servants, shopgirls, and milliners, while others were employed in various handicrafts. Unlike the main London College, which offered no preparatory classes to women, the Working Women's College included such provision alongside the advanced classes[53] – all in the evenings. The curriculum included not just reading, writing, arithmetic, English literature, history and drawing – but also subjects usually offered to men, such as geometry, algebra and physiology.[54] Physiology, for example, gave women the opportunity to enter the male world of science, as the following description offered by Arthur J. Munby, of a class he observed taught by Elizabeth Garrett Anderson, shows:

Wednesday, 3 January 1866 ... to the Conversazione of the Working Men's College. Miss Garrett the female doctor was there: I was introduced to her whilst she was busy tying up the toes of a live frog, whose foot was to be inspected under the microscope. It was amusing to see how the women around watched the process; partly horror stricken at her cruelty to the poor beast, partly admiring her surgical skill.[55]

But it is perhaps in the Latin class, begun in the autumn of 1865 by Munby himself, that the pursuit of knowledge for its own sake, without any vocational or domestic usefulness, is epitomized. Here the 'good scholar', who wished to study this language, perhaps out of intellectual curiosity or simply for the pleasure of learning, might be found. Munby describes his first meeting with his seven Latin students in the following terms:

There were seven pupils, all girls of 20 or so; respectably & plainly drest; probably shopgirls & the like. Most had left their bonnets & shawls downstairs. They sat facing me, & answered questions & took notes; behaving with quiet frankness; not giggling, not yet too grave. Not one (they said) knew anything of Latin: so I discoursed of the why & wherefore, & they seemed interested & fairly intelligent.[56]

In October the following year '3 new girls' joined the class, including 'a tall goodlooking young married woman' who had just three mistakes in her Latin exercises after a week's introduction to the subject.[57] January 1867 brought another two new students, one of whom simply wanted to understand the meaning of the Latin inscription she painted:

At 8 to my Latin class at the Working Women's College: first evening of new term. Two new girls, one of whom knew nothing of Latin, but *begged* to join because she is employed at Powell's glassworks in painting inscriptions on churchwindow glass, & she wants to know what they mean: the inscriptions being mostly in Latin.[58]

Sometimes a new student was 'not a staid commonplace girl like the rest' but 'an elegant fashionable young person, of pretty face and serenely selfpossest manners' who exclaimed 'Oh how nice!' when Munby explained a point. One wonders if this woman was one of the three remaining students who persevered with Virgil's *Aeneid* until 12 March 1873, when declining numbers forced the Latin class to close.[59] We have no way of knowing whether the drop in student numbers was due to difficulty of the subject, lacking of teaching skills on Munby's part or a host of other factors related to the personal lives of the young women.

In keeping with the emphasis upon knowledge for its own sake, Elizabeth Malleson and her supporters at the college were strongly against prizes of any kind or preparing students for examinations. Although the students often used the knowledge gained in college classes to enter for outside examinations, the teaching was 'never shaped' by such considerations.[60] Indeed, the informal learning through various forms of social interaction between staff and students, such as discussion, teas, soirees and conversaziones, was regarded as just as important as the formal learning in the classroom. The coffee room, open each evening from seven to ten and supplied with periodicals and newspapers, was one place where such activities might flourish. In addition, there were 'lady superintendents' who welcomed the students, discussed their needs, offered advice about classes and generally acted as counsellors.[61] Such support, together with an academic curriculum within a single-sex environment, may have created a sense of community and female bonding. In such a separate female world, women students may have gained confidence and freedom to express themselves. However, as we saw in Chapter 7, the Working Women's College existed for just ten years, since in 1874 the majority of the council helped the college to become the co-educational College for Men and Women, while the minority worked to establish the rival women-only institution, the College for Working Women.

At the College for Men and Women, the 'ardent personality' of its founder, Elizabeth Malleson, 'impressed itself upon each and all'; consequently the college continued the tradition of emphasizing the pursuit of knowledge for its own sake, unrelated to any vocational purpose. One of the teachers spoke of the 'delightful air' this aim created in the college and how students were learning 'because they liked it and not because they were going to sell their knowledge and grudged the labour'.[62]

The emphasis upon the informal mixing of staff and students through events such as discussions and debates was continued also, to foster a spirit of 'mutual help and fellowship'.[63] The coffee room, a 'merry place' between nine and 11 each evening, was the focal point for such interaction.[64]

Since the classes were co-educational, the curriculum was not differentiated by sex. And what is particularly significant is that this curriculum embraced the widest range of subjects to which women had access in any of the colleges within the working men's college movement. In 1878 both male and female students could sign up for classes in Anglo Saxon, arithmetic, algebra, botany, divinity, English language, English literature, French language, French literature, geometry, German language, German literature, history, logic, music, physiology and the laws of health, political economy and zoology.[65]

However, a common curriculum for men and women did not necessarily mean an equal distribution of the sexes in all subject areas. In particular, it appeared that the sex of the teacher could be one variable influencing student choice of subject. Maria Grey, when speaking at a meeting held in 1875 of the council and friends of this college, pointed out that she had only one complaint to make – 'when a male teacher gave place to a lady the male students showed a tendency to drop off, as if they were still possessed by the antiquated idea of the inferiority of women as teachers'.[66] For men to be taught by women was to challenge the expected form of gender control in nineteenth-century society. Female teachers were mainly teachers of children and young women.[67]

The ideal of the 'good scholar', which was developed by the Working Women's College and supported by the College for Men and Women, underwent a slight modification as the college developed. In 1876 the Froebel Society sponsored classes in kindergarten occupations at the college. Some 30 to 40 people attended, mainly assistant teachers and mothers.[68] Two years later some students were prepared for outside examinations – those of the Cambridge Higher Local Examinations. Thus during the autumn of 1878 and the following winter, courses of lessons were given in some of the required subjects, provided 12 students could be found for each class.[69]

Where the pressure for the latter move came from we do not know, but it is quite possible that it was from the students themselves rather than Mrs Malleson. Some of the women students may have wished to enter higher education, especially at London University which, in 1878, became the first university to admit women to degree examinations on equal terms with men. Although women students at Cambridge were formally admitted to university degree examinations in 1881, they could not be awarded a degree; similar conditions were found at Oxford where, from 1884, the university examinations were gradually becoming open to women.[70]

The preparatory classes for the Cambridge Higher Local Examinations brought into the college many well-qualified female teachers who had academic credentials from various higher educational institutions. By 1879

Miss Lewis, from London University, was teaching arithmetic, and Miss Borchardt and Miss Arthur, both from Girton, were taking classes in geometry and algebra, and logic, respectively; Miss Jane Harrison, who took her tripos in classical studies at Newnham in 1879, taught Greek, Latin, French and German.[71]

By 1901, when the College for Men and Women closed, many students had passed through its doors. Despite the fact that the college had been founded after the passing of the 1870 Education Act, some of these students had been illiterate and were introduced, as the following shows, not only to reading and writing but also to a wide range of knowledge:

When I first joined the college, it was only with the hope of learning to read and write. ... Thanks to the kindness and ability of the teachers, I passed rapidly through the preparatory classes and, emboldened by the encouragement I received, ventured to take up college classes. I have attended classes in English history, grammar and literature, arithmetic, physiology, French, Egyptian and Greek history, and most of these subjects have been made, by the teachers' mode of tuition, quite as pleasant as profitable.[72]

In contrast to the College for Men and Women, students at the rival institution, the College for Working Women, may have found from the date of its foundation in 1874 less emphasis upon knowledge for its own sake and more emphasis upon the moral and vocational aspects of education. As we saw in the last chapter, the majority of students at the College for Working Women were young, single women in occupations such as dressmaking, shop work, schoolteaching and domestic service. Miss Frances Martin, the main founder of the college, claimed that such students could study 'any subject' they wished, provided it was approved by the committee and a voluntary teacher could be found..[73] One forms the impression from the available sources, though, that this was not so. The selection of subjects appears very much to have been made by those 'above' based on the perceived needs of the students, rather than arising from demands from 'below'.

Like many middle-class philanthropists before her, Frances Martin saw the education of these young working-class women as a means of remedying previous defective education rather than aiding social mobility. In particular, she stressed not scholarly ability but enrichment of personality through good behaviour, self-sacrifice, habits of prudence and forethought, engaging in healthy and rational entertainment, forming friendships with women of similar views and reading wholesome fiction:

if they learn anything from a teacher, they learn much more than he professes to teach. They learn that life is, and ought to be, something more than mere living, less for one's self, and more for others; they learn to sympathise with deeds of thoughtful love, to understand the meaning of self-sacrifice, to know that, although wealth and station seem to separate the rich and the poor, yet God has made of one blood all the dwellers upon the earth. ... The College ... seeks to promote culture, to teach habits of prudence and forethought; it gives thoughtful women an opportunity of meeting each other and forming valuable friendships, and it offers healthy and rational entertainment as a recreation to the older, and a means of guiding and forming the tastes of its younger members. . . . Wholesome fiction is freely supplied.[74]

The transmission of knowledge within this college was seen as less important than socialization into appropriate forms of behaviour. Miss Martin also hoped that the college would save young working-class girls from the 'temptations' of the city of London, which brought so many young, lonely women 'to ruin'.[75] Others spoke too about the college helping to preserve young women from 'the dangers of the London streets'.[76] The task of 'saving' young working-class women from drifting into prostitution was something that had never been openly emphasized in any of the colleges considered so far.

The ideal of femininity that appears to have been upheld for the female students at this college was that of the 'good workwoman'. It was implicit in all that Frances Martin said that the students were not to become middle-class 'ladies' but were firmly to remain working-class 'women' who were morally 'sound' and also conscientious about their paid jobs. And this ideal was frequently expounded by other middle-class supporters of the college. Professor Morley, at a college opening address in 1885, reminded his audience that, though in the past it was believed that education 'spoilt young people for their work', now employers of women were grateful to those employees who 'endeavoured to fit themselves more completely for their daily duties'.[77]

The curriculum offered by the college covered both basic and more advanced knowledge. Thus in 1877 there were elementary classes in reading and writing, as well as more advanced classes in arithmetic, book-keeping, drawing, English, French, geometry, German, history, Latin, literature, precis and business letter-writing, physiology, singing and writing.[78] Some of these subjects, such as book-keeping, arithmetic, and precis and letter-writing, could have a direct vocational value for those women employed as dressmakers, or shop assistants or in domestic service, as well as relevance for any housekeeping duties within the home.

On the other hand, languages such as French, German and Latin would probably have less vocational relevance unless the students wished to teach in private establishments. But such subjects were part of the 'liberal' tradition within the working men's college movement, and could enrich minds and extend knowledge. Hannah Cullwick, for example, the domestic servant who was secretly married to Arthur J. Munby, joined the French class at the college. Such knowledge would have been of no use to her in her daily tasks of scrubbing and cleaning, though she might have believed that it would help her to become the 'lady' her middle-class husband deserved. Thus on 21 October 1874, Munby records in his diary that Hannah was

in high spirits at the thought of going tonight to the Working Women's College, to join the French class. 'You'll see I shall learn French quite well!' she said; 'and I shall behave quite respectful too, and as a servant should'. And what shall you put yourself in the book, dear? 'I shall put "Hannah Cullwick, Servant, aged 41"; and the master will say "Dear me, I wonder you can do French so well, after being 30 years in service!"[79]

Hannah tried the English literature class too. And once again, Munby records the delight she experienced when, on Friday 22 October 1875, she attended the first meeting:

Home 10.30 to H., who had been to the Working Women's College, and had for the first time attended the English Literature class. She was in high spirits, and had much to tell me about the Puritans and Charles II; and told it all in her own childlike rustic way, and with all the eagerness of a schoolgirl.[80]

Even allowing for Munby's patronizing tone, there is no doubt that for working-class women such as Hannah, being a student at this college *could* be exciting and enlightening. The aims and ideals espoused by Frances Martin and her supporters do not always describe student experience.

As in many other cases where the education of women was separate from, rather than integrated with, the education of men, various skills traditionally associated with women and with domesticity were added to the curriculum. In 1879 it was proposed to open classes in 'artizan and other cookery'.[81] Frances Martin believed that a cookery school was 'much needed' in the neighbourhood.[82] By 1880 other gender-specific subjects, such as needlework, were taught at the College for Working Women. The St John Ambulance had also run courses on sick nursing and aid to the injured.[83]

Some middle-class commentators saw these new developments in the curriculum as part of an exercise in teaching the female students 'thrift'.[84] But it is perhaps the existence of a Penny Bank of the college which underlines the importance attached to learning this habit. As Frances Martin reminded her listeners:

when the lesson is ended, there is the Penny Bank, which the teacher tells you about, urging you to remember that a rainy day will come, and you should save a penny whenever you can spare it.[85]

How many of the students heeded her advice over the years, we do not know. But during 1878, 107 of them deposited £118 17s 3d, which with the £276 7s 1d already there made a grand total of £395 4s 4d.[86] The *Journal of the Women's Education Union* commented very favourably upon this, stating that the bank was very useful in 'encouraging provident habits'; when work is slack, it continued, many of the students were grateful for having a small sum of money to fall back upon.[87]

By 1880 the demand for elementary classes at the College for Working Women had declined (see figure 8.1), and the hope was expressed that every female student under the age of 20 would be able to read and write.[88] By this time too, the college had established links with the Society of Arts and actively encouraged its students to sit, free of charge, the society's examinations.[89] In February 1878, for example, 17 students sat the society's examinations in elementary subjects, ten obtaining certificates. The following month, 22 women sat the commercial examinations, which included subjects such as book-keeping, 13 gaining certificates; such numbers did not substantially change during the next academic year.[90] It would appear that women students within the working men's college movement had greater access to Society of Arts examinations in a single-sex setting, such as this college, where such a policy was endorsed, than in the mixed-sex colleges at Halifax, Sheffield, Salford and Leicester. Such a form of public assessment may have boosted the confidence of many a student as well as enhanced job prospects.

Although the demand for elementary classes in the College for Working Women had steadily declined, the college continued to survive well into the twentieth century. In the 1940s the Frances Martin College, as it was now known, was still offering classes in subjects such as shorthand, typewriting and languages and claiming that it could offer something distinct to its female students – 'the shelter of women's friendship and understanding'.[91] In 1958 the college lost its premises and the female students were 'charitably' taken under the roof of the London Working Men's College, though they were there 'only in fact and not in principle and are supposed to be quite separate'.[92] As noted earlier, it was not until 1966 that these

College for Working Women,

(Founded in 1874 in Memory of F. D. MAURICE.)

7, Fitzroy Street, London, W.

34th SESSION.

Chairman, REV. J. LLEWELYN DAVIES, M.A., D.D.

Treasurers, GEORGE A. MACMILLAN, Esq., D.Litt., and FRANCIS MORRIS, Esq.

Hon. Secretary, MISS FRANCES MARTIN.

Lady Superintendent, MISS ARNOLD.

OPEN EVERY EVENING, from 6.30 to 10 p.m.

Classes in **French, German, Book-keeping, Drawing, Dress-cutting, Singing, Arithmetic, Gardening, History, Geography, Elocution, Literature, Musical Drill, &c.** Ambulance Classes, James Canthie, Esq., F.R.C.S. First Aid, Sick Nursing and Hygiene.—Holiday Guild, Benefit Club, Free Lending Library.

FEES, from 1s. 3d.   PRIZES AND SCHOLARSHIPS

PROSPECTUS ON APPLICATION.

Membership Fee   1s. each Term

Figure 8.1 Advertisement for the College for Working Women, 1908 (from *Working Men's College Journal*, July 1908).

two separate worlds of male and female education were merged on the site of the male college.

The lecture programme

Now that we have discussed curricular provision in classes within the mixed-sex working men's colleges, the women's colleges and the co-educational college, some examination of the content of lecture programmes is necessary. As in the case of the mechanics' institutes, lecture provision within the working men's colleges was an important aspect of the educational provision. Chadwick, when offering a 'few practical suggestions' for the efficient management of working men's colleges, recommended, among other things, that weekly, fortnightly or monthly lectures should be delivered by teachers and friends of the college during the winter months on a Saturday evening, or some other day, so as not to interfere with any of the classes.[93] Many of the 'male' colleges offered evening lectures along these lines and it would appear that in many instances women were admitted.

At the London Working Men's College, it seems that admittance of women to the lectures was at the discretion of the lecturer. Thus on 23 September 1859, Litchfield 'admitted ladies' to his talk about his travels in Switzerland, Turin, Milan, Padua and Venice; on previous occasions, John Ruskin had also done so.[94] Yet the fact that the admittance of women might depend upon the consent of the lecturer underlined, yet again, the marginal status of women within the colleges. And Litchfield's reference in his lecture to the women in his audience, complimenting them on 'the delightful contrast they presented in face, to their Continental sisters, in voice to their American ones', makes it clear that the very presence of females at such an event could evoke comments about their personal appearance that singled them out for attention.[95]

In 1861, the year following the discontinuation of the women's classes at the London college, a new series of general lectures was launched which, it was hoped, would give students the opportunity to hear about the great subjects bearing on the present life of the world.[96] Since women were no longer a part of the student body, they could not attend in that capacity, though *some* may have accompanied their menfolk. This was probably the case also at the working men's colleges at Cambridge, Manchester, Wolverhampton and Cheltenham, where the classes were only for men. At Wolverhampton, for example, the hope was expressed that the working classes would attend in large number 'with their wives and families'.[97] Similarly at Leicester Working Men's College, before women's classes were established in 1880, women only had access to the Saturday evening lectures as 'wives and friends of male members'.[98] Such a policy, as we have seen, was common in the mechanics' institutes; and it was found again in the working men's colleges.

The lectures at the majority of working men's colleges tended towards literary, social and general interest themes rather than scientific issues – though the latter were not entirely ignored. At Cambridge in 1859, lectures on ancient Jerusalem, the Alps, the works of Leonardo da Vinci, the history of Cambridge and chemistry or geography were arranged.[99] At Manchester during 1858-60, lectures were given on surgical aid in case of accident, the balance between animal and vegetable life, the ballad poetry of England, Crabbe and his poetry, self-culture, the electric telegraph, the study of history, Iphigenia – the religion of Greek drama, and the history of the useful arts in connection with general civilization.[100] At Leicester during the winter of 1862-3, the Saturday evening lectures included talks on 'America', 'Co-operation', 'Trades Unions', 'Tennyson', 'English Lyrics', 'An Hour at the Wash Tub', 'Chemistry of the Atmosphere', 'Cleansing Properties of Soap', and 'Metals and Mining'; sometimes these highly popular evening would be interspersed with Penny Readings from Dickens and Shakespeare and, in later years, with concerts.[101]

Women at the South London College from 1868 to 1880 might listen to Saturday evening talks on the co-education of men and women, geometry and its practical application, the life of Dr Johnson, the aims of moral and mental culture, the construction of the Rosse telescope, chemical astronomy, the human hand and the study of poetry and art; by 1881, free lectures were also offered on Tuesday evenings.[102] At Cheltenham during the 1885-6 session, the lecture themes included ice and its work in earth shaping, the age of reptiles, church lands, Chaucer, sculpture and its gods, and the charm of life in art.[103] And at the Saturday evening lectures at the London Working Men's College in the 1890s, which women frequently attended, a range of talks on travel, art, and social and political themes were offered. In October 1891 Mr R. D. Roberts, secretary of the Cambridge University Extension Syndicate, spoke (with the aid of a magic lantern) on 'the life history of a river'; other topics included the prevention of strikes, Elizabethan London, Pickwick, the educational system of China and excavation in Egypt.[104] The lecture in 1894 on Velasquez and Rembrandt was especially attended by art students, 'a great many ladies among them'.[105]

In contrast, the lecture programme at the working men's colleges at Sheffield and Halifax were much less varied and often linked to the mechanics' institutes. The 20 women who were members of Sheffield Working Men's College in 1856 might hear Mr Barnett Blake, agent and lecturer in the Yorkshire Union of Mechanics' Institutes, speak on 'the advantages of education'; the Yorkshire Union also lent the college manuscript lectures, including one on the 'Education of the Working Classes, Male and Female', which was read to the members of the discussion class.[106] Other lectures that women might attend over the 1857-8 session were on 'The Life and Poetry of Ebenezer Elliott', 'The Life and Poetry of Robert Burns', 'Self-made Men' and 'Education, Economy and Ebriety'.[107]

The Halifax college appears to have offered an even more restricted lecture programme than that at Sheffield, since the college authorities believed lectures to be a 'fallacious form of instruction'.[108] During the late 1850s, for example, yearly lectures were offered; thus in 1857 Dr Burnett, the Vicar of Bradford, spoke on 'Enthomology', in 1858 Dr Hook, the Vicar of Leeds, lectured on 'The Character of Queen Elizabeth' and in 1859 the Rev A. Barry, Headmaster of Leeds School, took 'Self Education' as his theme.[109] Women listening to the Rev Barry stressing the need for a balanced education that gave due attention to the body, mind and heart might question whether this accurately reflected their own experiences. As we saw earlier, the women's classes at Halifax were in the three Rs, sewing, cookery and some basic general knowledge.

Women at Halifax and elsewhere in the provinces would rarely hear a woman lecture at a working men's college. The college at Cheltenham was unusual in this respect. In 1885 Miss Higgins gave a talk on Charles Kingsley as a Christian Socialist, while the following year Miss Robertson's theme was 'Fair trade and free trade'.[110] The well-known principal of the Cheltenham Ladies College, Miss Dorothea Beale, was a speaker here too, on 'Self support and self government from the point of view, not of the individual, but of the College'.[111] Women speakers were apparently to be found mainly at the London Working Men's College, from the 1890s. And women students may have been particularly attracted to these talks given by members of their own sex.

The first woman to give a Saturday evening lecture at the main London college was the classical scholar and British Museum lecturer Jane Harrison, who in February 1891 drew a large crowd when she spoke on 'The Parthenon Marbles – in special relation to recent investigations'; in the same year Miss Colenso gave a 'very popular' lecture on Zululand and Mrs T. H. Green spoke on trade in a medieval town.[112] Over the next 17 years, female lecturers included Miss Hughes on ancient Athens, Miss Rowe on simple wood carving,[113] Clara Collett on old and new novels, Mary Kingsley on her travels in West Africa,[114] Mrs Verrall on the goddesses of Athens, Miss Smith on aspects of Siamese life,[115] Miss Spurgeon on John Ruskin and Mrs Julian Marshall on the study of harmony.[116]

To what extent any of these women lecturers spoke about woman's place in society is impossible to know. But their very presence indicated at least that women could have a public voice as authorities on selected subjects. And there were some female speakers at the London college during the 1890s who were actively involved in the women's movement, including the expansion of higher education for women. Miss Penrose, the Principal of Bedford College, well known for the lectures she gave on classical archaeology at the British Museum, spoke at the London Working Men's College in 1897. She had been the first woman to be placed in the First Class in 'Literae Humaniores' at Oxford University and had studied archeology abroad as well as helped her father, an eminent architect, in aspects of his work.[117] What exactly Miss Penrose told her audience at the London College is not recorded. But this woman, who was eventually to become principal of Somerville College, Oxford, and was to be very influential in the battle for the right of women to take a degree on the same terms as men, was not likely to mince her words. Although she has been described as lacking 'both ease and charm' and possessing 'a stern, repellent quality', she also had an 'impartial sense of justice'.[118]

Millicent Garrett Fawcett, who, as we saw in the last chapter, was a firm supporter of the single-sex College for Working Women and one of the leaders, during the 1880s, of the women's suffrage movement, spoke at the London Working Men's College in 1890 and in 1895 on 'the value of economic study' and on 'Ideals of womanhood, old and new', respectively.[119] It is the latter talk in particular that would have opened discussion on woman's position in society by challenging many of those precepts about the female sex that were articulated by the middle classes for much of the nineteenth century.

Millicent Garrett Fawcett began by reminding her audience that the question of the general position of women was one of the most urgent and interesting of the age. In particular, she argued, the growth of the women's movement implied a change in the ideal type of womanhood and in the ideal relations between men and women. The old ideas emphasized that a woman should experience 'complete absorption in her husband'[120] and have characteristics such as softness, grace and submission. But now, Mrs Fawcett insisted:

A woman is ... to be valued as a human being: her value does not depend on her relationship to other people, but on what she is herself, and what she does in the world. And is not this the right way of looking at men and woman too? All the old platitudes, such as that women are wax and men are iron, that man is the sturdy oak and woman the graceful ivy which he supports, are false both practically and theoretically.[121]

Despite insisting upon the right of women to be considered as human beings, Mrs Fawcett did not avoid the issue of women as mothers and as homemakers. But this was not woman's sphere alone; the influence of the father and husband was felt in 'every scene and act of the domestic drama'. But, she insisted, the relations between men and women within the family should involve no dispute about superiority and inferiority; instead, men and women should be 'fellow-servants', developing in one another and in themselves all that was beautiful and good. Women's influence should not be located within the family alone, however; women should not be barred from those spheres of activity, such as politics, which had been almost wholly appropriated by men:

Why should the virtues of the female character and the sanctity of the home be damaged by women taking an interest in national concerns? Women played a very important part in the anti-slavery agitation, and a great part also in the movement which led to the emancipation and unification of Italy. Female character and the home were thrown into the cauldron of politics then, and all that was pure metal in them came out refined and brightened, while the dross was burned away. . . .[122]

The large audience, about half of whom were women, apparently greeted the lecture with 'much cheering'.[123] The content of this talk, which was rare in the history of the London Working Men's College, shows how even such a male-centred institution could offer space for discussion on the 'woman question' and invite female lecturers who spoke on feminist issues.

The main London college was also one of the few working men's colleges to link up with university extension schemes which offered part-time higher education to adults. The origins of university extension are usually traced back to the autumn of 1867, when various associations of middle-class women particularly concerned with standards in school-teaching asked James Stuart, a Fellow of Trinity College, Cambridge, to deliver a course of lectures in Leeds, Liverpool, Manchester and Sheffield.[124] A link between university extension and the working men's college movement was inevitable: after all, four of the founders of the London Working Men's College were Trinity men and the emphasis in the working men's college movement upon the pursuit of liberal, humanistic studies within a collegiate structure foreshadowed university involvement in the education of adults.[125]

In 1876, the London Society for the Extension of University Teaching was established and Thomas Hughes, who was by now principal of the London Working Men's College, was a member of the committee; he arranged for his college and the College for Men and Women jointly to sponsor a series of extension lectures on elementary mechanics which were open to men and women alike.[126] It is not clear how many women, especially working-class women, attended these lectures. Generally, the university extension movement made no attempt to reach working-class women and passed them by.[127] This series of lectures was also not a success, perhaps because the fees were too high for most working-class people, and the link with the extension movement was temporarily abandoned.[128]

The attempt by the Leicester Working Men's College to link up with the university extension movement was a failure also. But in this case, women were barred from participating. The series of lectures during 1873–4 on 'Political Economy' was 'limited to men'.[129] It is ironic that women were excluded from this course, since the demands of some women's groups for improvements in their higher education had been a key impetus in the university extension movement!

Lecture provision in the separate colleges

Of the three separate colleges it was the first women-only college, the Working Women's College, Queen Square, established in 1864, that offered the broadest lecture programme free, on Saturday evenings, on subjects of 'special interest' as the opportunity occurred.[130] What is impressive is not only the number of lectures but also the wide range of distinguished male and female speakers, including some well-known feminists.

The list of male lecturers included the Rev F. D. Maurice, Thomas

Hughes, Professor Cairnes, Professor David Masson, Sir John Seeley, Frederic Harrison, Professor Huxley, Sir Sydney Colvin, Mr Edmund Gosse, Sir John Lubbock, Robert Louis Stevenson, Mark Pattison, Henry Irving, Professor Henry Sidgwick, Arthur J. Munby and Mr Ralston.[131] Although we do not have the topics and texts of these talks, some of the speakers may have debated woman's place in nineteenth-century society, thinking such debates would be of special interest in a women-only college; after all, the 1860s were a time when the woman question was being keenly discussed as the organized women's movement began to form. Frederic Harrison, for example, a follower of the positivist Auguste Comte, held a traditional view of women, supporting those partriarchal and familial ideologies discussed in Chapter 3. The true function of women, he claimed, was to educate not only the children but also men, so that society could attain a 'high civilisation', and women were to do this not by writing books or preaching sermons about such things, but by 'the magic of the voice, look, word, and all the incommunicable graces of woman's tenderness'.[132] Professor Henry Sidgwick, on the other hand, may have raised rather different issues if he spoke on a 'woman' theme, since in 1869 he suggested that lectures for women should be organized at Cambridge University and was generally supportive to women's education there.[133]

One thing we do know, Arthur J. Munby spoke at the college on Saturday, 9 May 1867, on 'the beauty of manual labour and the weakness of being ashamed of it'. Munby, a great admirer of physically strong working-class women, was not at this time married to Hannah Cullwick. He described the Saturday meeting as follows:

We met in the coffeeroom (Queen Anne's Parlour) and sat about in groups: three or four ladies, 20 or 30 of the girls, and myself, the only man present. I opened the talk with a short speech about the nobleness & noble effects of robust and hardhanded labour, for women as well as for men; and read an apropos passage from the Bothie: and then they, or rather the ladies & one or two only of the students, commented & questioned: the net result being, of course, that these lower middle class London girls showed themselves quite unable to realize the charm of rustic women & rustic work, or even to see that of service and its work & dress, though they professed not to be above working. But I put it very feebly and ill; partly because they are not the right sort of girls, being but weakly stitchers and strummers; & partly for that I could not say out frankly all I knew....[134]

Although the female students were reluctant to question Munby after his talk, this may not have been the case when Munby's friend Mr Ralson spoke on 'Our fairy tales, their meaning and origin' on Saturday, 7 February 1874. The crowded room was 'lighted up by an apt humour which the women present (for nearly all were women) enjoyed heartily'.[135] Similar numbers may have come to hear the talks by well-known women, such as Dr Elizabeth Blackwell, Jane Harrison and Frances Power Cobbe.

Elizabeth Blackwell spoke at the college in 1870 on 'How to Keep a Household in Health'. She was the world's first trained and registered female doctor, having graduated in the USA in 1849, and had therefore a public importance as a woman who had successfully entered the male world of medicine. However, while seeing herself as particularly suited to follow a 'male' career, Dr Blackwell believed that for most women motherhood, not paid or professional work, was the highest calling.[136]

The female students at the Working Women's College therefore did not hear a feminist message about women's rights, but about how 'suitable marriage, a regulated family, sober habits, and moral life'[137] were the essential foundations of a sound constitution for children and for a healthy household. Furthermore, fresh air, variety of food, cleanliness, exercise and cheerfulness helped to keep a household in health. In particular, Dr Blackwell emphasized the mother's part in these matters, especially in the rearing of sons:

I hold it to be the imperative duty of every parent, and particularly of the mother, whether rich or poor, to make herself the intelligent guardian of her children's health .... Most emphatically is it the duty of a mother to watch wisely over her son; and I can assert for the encouragement of mothers, that the most ennobling and restraining influence that can be bought to bear upon a young man, is that of a mother who is also a wife and friend to her son.[138]

This stress upon domesticity for women was, as we saw earlier, a common theme in the education of working-class women. Dr Blackwell gave scant attention in her talk to women's paid work. But if an occupation was unhealthy and overcrowded, then she advised women to emigrate.[139] There was no suggestion that such female workers should try to improve their work conditions, join trade unions and fight for higher wages.

In contrast, while we do not have the text for Frances Power Cobbe's talk at the Working Women's College, it is probable that this well-known figure in feminist circles (though never one of its leaders),[140] described by Munby as being 'round and fat as a Turkish sultana, with yellow hair, and face mature & pulpy, but keen & shrewd & pleasantly humorous',[141] discussed the woman question with a primarily female audience. Although rather conventional in some of her ideas, Miss Cobbe wrote many articles that supported women's issues, e.g. married women's property laws, single women, the fitness of women for the ministry, female suffrage, husbands' violence towards their wives, the education of women. And lecturers such as Miss Cobbe and Dr Blackwell showed the students at the college that a woman could be successful in the 'public' world of men *and* be single. This was a very different message about woman's place to that conveyed by those influential middle-class familial ideologies that identified women with the private sphere of the home, marriage and children.

When the Queen Street college became the College for Men and Women, the Saturday evening weekly lectures continued. Some of the speakers at the 'old' institution, e.g. Thomas Hughes, Frederic Harrison and Frances Power Cobbe, continued to give lectures at the 'new' college. Once again we find a sprinkling of women lecturers, including some active in the women's movement.

Elizabeth Malleson and Maria Grey, for example, both gave talks on the advantages of co-education. Elizabeth Malleson, as honorary secretary of the college and main inspiration for its foundation, perhaps felt it necessary to address the issue on the college's opening night. Women had no objection to learning with men, she reiterated; and mixed education could only bring increased understanding between male and female students.[142] Maria Grey staunchly supported such 'progressive' views, since she believed that, both on intellectual and moral grounds, mixed education was best.[143] Maria Grey's sister, Emily Sherriff, also actively involved in the National Union for the Improvement of the Education of Women of All Classes, spoke at this co-educational college on 20 March 1875 on 'the enjoyment of life'.[144] Emily Sherriff believed in a broad, liberal education which included gardening, sports, nature walks, art, music and reading for pleasure.[145] In her book *Intellectual Education, and Its Influence on the Character and Happiness of Women*, published in 1858, she pointed out:

It is not ... against pleasure that I write, but against living for pleasure; – against that systematic frivolity, that laborious idleness, that solemn consecration of existence to amusement, which girls do not seek, but which is thrust upon them.[146]

She was also aware however, that many women, through 'want of definite occupation' and through fear of poverty, saw marriage as 'their only resource'.[147] Such ideas may have informed her talk to the students.

The lectures given by men at the College for Men and Women tended to focus upon a different range of themes. In 1876 Professor Sheldon Amos gave a course of lectures on the science of politics, while the following year Professor Seeley's subject was 'Evolution and the geological evidences which bear upon the origin of the existing races of plants and animals'.[148] Themes of general and literary interest were covered too, when Mr Micklethwaite spoke on 'Westminster Abbey' and Mr Pike Thompson held a session of readings from the poet Robert Browning.[149] But some of the male lecturers also raised special issues pertaining to women.

In 1872 Joshua Fitch, one of Her Majesty's Inspectors of Schools, spoke at the college. His interest in women's education may have been kindled through his friendship with John Llewelyn Davies, brother of Emily Davies; at the 1864 meeting of the Social Science Association, Fitch read Miss Davies's paper about the deplorable state of education for middle-class girls.[150] The theme of Fitch's talk in 1872 was the relationship between studying and a 'toilsome' or working life. After extolling the advantages for the student of studying languages, he proceeded in the final part of his talk to concentrate upon the 'real wrongs' that had been directed against women:

It is the commonest of commonplaces ... to say, as kindly people often do, that fondness for books or for abstract studies is incompatible with the domestic claims on a woman, with the nurture of children, the supervision of servants, or the management of a house. Yet I never hear it said of a man who evinces a love for mathematics, for archaeology, for poetry, or for any intellectual pursuit remote from the business of his life, that it makes him a worse lawyer or doctor, or that, though it may happen to sharpen his wits for his profession, it renders him less genial or companionable in the sanctuary of home.[151]

The truth is, he continued, that men would rebel against any attempt on the part of women or of society to prescribe what they should study. And for Fitch, women had an equal right to rebel against those unwritten traditions which declared her unsuited for certain enquiries and studies. But this was not all. Changes had also to take place in employment for women, the legal position of women and the education of women, if these wrongs were to be righted. The inadequate provision for educating middle-class women was especially fiercely attacked:

It is little short of a national disgrace, that while public provision of a costly kind has been made all over the country for the higher instruction of boys and men, the entire secondary education of their sisters has been relegated to what is called private enterprise. . . . It has never been presumed that average young men could be induced to study merely for the disinterested love of learning: other and less ethereal motives have been supplied to urge them to exertion. In connection with the Universities, the amount of this pecuniary encouragement is already so large, valuable exhibitions are so numerous and can be obtained with such ease, that they operate, not unfrequently, rather as a premium on mediocrity than as a stimulus to intellectual exertion. And it is quite obvious that, on principles both of equity and of public policy, provision of the same kind should be made for women, to supply them with new motives for study, to help them onwards in their intellectual pursuits, and to offer to the worthiest that recognition and reward which, both to man and woman, is the legitimate guerdon of successful and well-directed toil.[152]

Such words may have inspired some of the female students in Fitch's audience to aim higher than the education offered at the College for Men and Women. Others may have felt unable to contemplate such things. But what Fitch's talk would have conveyed to his listeners was the extent of inequalities between the sexes in England in the 1870s.

The rival institution to the College for Men and Women, the College for Working Women, Fitzroy Street, did not have a regular weekly lecture slot. Instead, Saturday nights were set aside for 'social entertainment', which included concerts, readings, recitations and dramatic performances – as well as lectures;[153] before these occasions, which were highly popular, teachers, friends and students met for tea in the coffee room.

The themes of the lectures appear to have been less varied than those at the co-educational college. George Bartley and Joshua Fitch drew the attention of the female students to the importance and duty of thrift and economy, while Professor Morley urged them to join the special classes for the Society of Arts examinations.[154] Eight years later, in 1885, Professor Morley again reminded the women that employers of the 1880s welcomed those who tried to educate themselves for their work.[155] Lectures given by women appear to have been rare, though in 1880 Miss Concordia Lofving of Stockholm gave a 'theoretical and practical course of lectures, comprising instruction in scientific physical education, to a limited number of educational ladies, who wish to qualify themselves as teachers on this subject'.[156] In 1878 Miss Lofving had been appointed by the London School Board as Superintendent of Physical Education in Girls' Schools. As Fletcher and McCrone point out, this was an important 'progressive' appointment, since up to this time working-class girls had been taught mainly 'desk drill' rather than the exercises, organized by an army drill sergeant, that the boys engaged in.[157] It is likely that Concordia Lofving's lectures at the Working Women's College were connected with her school board appointment.

At the college's 1907 summer festival, key speakers stressed themes that would undoubtedly appeal to Miss Martin, who was present at the proceedings. Thus the Rev Llewelyn Davies, chair of the college council, pointed out that the institution was founded on the 'lofty principles of universal knowledge'; Mrs Nathaniel Cohen compared the educational opportunities then available for women with those of 60 years previously, while Mr Lucas reminded his audience that the college enabled the working women to acquire not just special knowledge and companionship but the chance, through personal guidance, to live up to a high standard.[158] It is not known whether the women students themselves interpreted their college education in these terms.

Overall then, the lecture programme of all the various colleges within the working men's college movement, though not as extensive as those within the mechanics' institute movement, still offered women students access to areas of knowledge that frequently differed from the content of the classes. In particular, the lectures could open spaces for discussion of women's issues.

Conclusion

As in the case of the mechanics' institutes, the majority of working men's colleges offering classes to women organized separate rather than mixed education. This had profound implications for women, since separate education meant a separate curriculum from that studied by men. Although the social class differentiation between women students appears to have been less pronounced than in the mechanics' institutes, nevertheless we do find two main forms of female curriculum that are shaped by ideal of the middle-class 'lady' and the working class 'good wife and mother'. Thus for women of the labour aristocracy/lower middle class, a daytime curriculum was offered in general knowledge and some 'ladylike' accomplishments, such as singing and drawing. For working women, however, and especially those in working-class occupations, evening classes were organized in the three Rs, plain sewing and some elementary knowledge. In many ways, this curriculum was similar to that offered to working-class women in the mechanics' institutes and was not radically different from that studied by working-class girls in day schools.

The three separate colleges, however, offered an education to women that was different from the previously described pattern. The single-sex Working Women's College emphasized the acquisition of knowledge for its own sake and upholding the ideal of the 'good scholar', included classes not just in the three Rs but also in English literature, history, geometry, algebra, physiology and Latin. The co-educational College for Men and Women continued this tradition and offered women the widest choice of curriculum that could be found in any college within the movement.

The other separate college, the single-sex College for Working Women, appears to have been more concerned with moral and vocational education and supported a concept of the 'good workwoman'. Thus, in addition to the three Rs, there were more advanced classes in arithmetic, book-keeping, drawing, English, French, geometry, German, history, Latin, literature, business letter-writing, physiology, singing and writing. However, other subjects thought 'specially' necessary for women, such as cookery, needlework and sick nursing, were offered also.

The lecture programmes however, might offer to women the opportunity to listen to a range of literary, social and general themes, including radical ideas about the women's movement. And the latter opportunity was especially found in the Working Women's College and the College for Men and Women. Such debates were not their prerogative, however, since even such a male-centred institution as the London Working Men's College included women speakers on women's issues.

Part IV

CONCLUSION

9

CONCLUSION

Present-day historians of the mechanics' institute and working men's college movements in nineteenth-century England have focused their attention upon the activities of working-class men. However, the evidence presented here reveals that working-class women had also been students, often in large numbers, in the institutes and colleges. The reason why such working-class female education has been 'forgotten' can perhaps be found in the nature of histories of the nineteenth century, which traditionally have concentrated upon class relations and employment patterns. In addition, historians have tended to associate elementary education in the nineteenth century with elementary schools and with young children. These twentieth-century perspectives on the past therefore have given less recognition than is due to the basic education that mature men and women of the 'lower' orders received in formal institutions offering a part-time education. Even the growth of interest among feminist historians in women's education in the nineteenth century has not focused on the experiences of working-class women but upon that minority of middle-class women who, from the 1870s, fought to enter the high-prestige male preserves of the universities. The rescue from oblivion of that much larger number of working-class women who struggled to enter low-status institutions, such as the mechanics' institutes and working men's colleges, is long overdue.

Since this research has been written from a feminist perspective, making working-class women visible in these adult education movements has been an important goal. Another central concern of feminists – examining the power relationships between men and women – has also been a key theme; thus I have identified power relations between the sexes as manifested in the control and participation by men and women in two major adult education movements of the nineteenth century. This theme adds another dimension that differs from traditional male-centred histories of this period. The latter have tended to examine the class context of the mechanics' institutes and working men's colleges and, in particular, the conflict between the largely middle-class providers and the working-class clientele that the institutes and colleges hoped to attract. However, once the power relations between men and women become a key issue, the analysis shifts its focus.

This research has shown how mechanics' institutes and working men's colleges were not merely shaped by class cultures but also, more often than not, controlled by men and shaped in their interests; women had to struggle to enter such places and, once admitted, their presence still caused considerable controversy. Such findings do not deny that for women students the class context was critical; after all, both the mechanics' institute and working men's college movements were largely initiated by the middle classes for the working classes. However, the research presented here demonstrates the importance of *integrating* a class and gender analysis rather than giving priority to the former (as many socialist-feminist historians tend to do) or concentrating exclusively upon the latter (as radical-feminist historians stress).

What is also apparent in this research is the extent to which various ideologies concerning the relationship between the sexes and especially woman's place in society affected the educational movements studied. In particular, middle-class patriarchal and family ideologies concerning a woman's place framed the dominant ideological constructions of womanhood. Key aspects of this concept of womanhood were that ideally women should be located within the private sphere of the home, as full-time wives and mothers, and as being 'inferior', 'relative' and 'subordinate' to men – as well as economically and emotionally 'dependent' upon men. Such views were constantly reiterated by founders and key figures within the mechanics' institutes and working men's colleges, irrespective of their social class background. The repercussions could be found in the assumptions made about women students, the identification of their specific needs, the moulding of the curricula offered to fit such a student clientele, and the limited access women acquired to institute and college facilities.

Yet, as we have seen, the image about womanhood held by the providers of adult education bore little resemblance to the daily reality of life for working-class women. One of the questions asked in the introduction to Part III of this book was – how far did the providers of adult education understand the lives of their potential clientele? The answer seems to be – very little. As shown in Chapter 2, single and married working-class women were forced, out of economic necessity, to earn a living in addition to the unpaid duties that were expected within the home (which was not the 'cosy' environment idealized by the adult education providers). Throughout the nineteenth century, the range of occupations in which working-class women were concentrated were lowly paid jobs that involved long hours of toil and held few prospects of improvement. Single working-class women were likely to be found in domestic service, millinery, dressmaking, slop work, factory work and schoolteaching. Married working-class women, especially those with young dependents, were concentrated mainly in agricultural work and in home-based employment that was unskilled, casual and overstocked (such as sewing, taking in lodgers and taking in washing). To save the few pennies for an adult class, and to find the time and energy for part-time study, would have required much determination and hardship.

Arguably, within the mechanics' institute movement vocationally useful courses could have been designed for working-class women as well as for their menfolk, since such course might have helped them to change or improve their employment prospects. However, as we have seen, such provision for working-class women was rare. Within the working men's college movement, working women could have been offered that liberal, humane curriculum open to men, a curriculum which might have helped them to extend their knowledge, enrich their personality and achieve self-confidence. However, once again, such an option was only occasionally presented. Both vocationally and intellectually, therefore, these adult education movements offered to working-class women a limited range of choices that tended to confirm or give support to their occupational status and social position rather than directly help to shift it. The social role of working-class women as mothers was seen as more significant than their economic role as wage earners.

Women had not only to struggle to gain access to these male-orientated institutes and colleges, but also to fight against the notion that they did not need an education for their own right – only an education in order to make them 'better' wives and mothers. Since there were no comparable adult education movements designed specifically for working-class women, women struggled to 'fit' into the already established mechanics' institute and working men's college movements. Even the few women-only institutes and colleges were designed and founded within movements aimed at working-class men, i.e. they took the model of organization, principles, and goals from existing organizations rather than providing a radical, alternative movement. This is not unexpected; as Ramelson[1] notes, the demand for women's rights in 'every field of human endeavour' is unlikely to be met *before* men of the same social class have gained theirs.

If women students struggled against the dominant concept of education for 'womanhood', they would also have had to make sense of the tensions found in the ideologies of these adult education movements. Various ideological forces and, in particular, feminist ideas (expressed by visiting speakers or in library books and periodicals) infiltrated some of the institutes and colleges, making these educational institutions sites of ideological debates. The messages received by women students were often therefore not simple definitions of woman's 'domestic' role in society but contained the ideological contradictions faced by women in the Victorian era. The struggle for women's rights affected the institutes and colleges, revealing conflicting ideals about women and complex arguments about the nature of sex differences, the 'natural' order of society, the family and women's work.

Such ideas seem to have been introduced particularly through the lecture programmes rather than class provision. As we have seen, some of the women lecturers in the institutes and colleges were active in the women's movement; these women speakers, familiar with both the world of adult education and the struggle for women's rights, represented attempts to radicalize the women students who came to hear them. Similarly, debates about women in other political movements, such as socialism and Christian Socialism, were part of the context of the mechanics' institute and working men's college movements. The education that women received, then, seems to have been shaped not just by the transmission of basic educational skills and knowledge but by radical elements in the wider society outside the educational context. The mechanics' institute and working men's college movements clearly were not insulated from the political ferment of nineteenth-century society – rather they were part of it.

Nevertheless, despite such complexity, there was considerable and rather crude differentiation in the education offered to working-class men and women, especially in the class provision. Working-class female students did not have access to the same curricula as their menfolk. Working-class men were assumed to be located within the public sphere of paid work outside the home and were offered a curriculum that might be vocationally useful. Despite their labours in various trades, it was assumed that working-class women, on the other hand, should remain within the private sphere of the home, ideally as full-time wives and mothers. For such a role a curriculum based on the teaching of the three Rs, plain sewing and some elementary knowledge was thought adequate. Not only was such a curriculum unimaginative and only generally useful for working-class women workers, but such subjects were also not a sophisticated preparation for the many tasks women faced in nurturing and educating children, in maintaining the moral discipline of the family and in caring for the male workforce. In regard to another key issue raised in the Introduction to Part III, namely whether the education offered to working-class women was more suitable to their daily lives than that offered to working-class girls, the answer would seem to be that this was seldom so. Indeed, paradoxically it seems that although the female curriculum was designed for adults the narrow range of subjects was not very different from that offered to working-class girls in day elementary schools. The institutes and colleges might therefore have been used by working-class women as alternative institutions to schools, providing a second chance to learn or improve the skills learnt in childhood and perhaps forgotten when older.

Such a 'second chance' education, however, like all literacy programmes, contained radical elements in that students could have sought more advanced education and perhaps even entered jobs offering a limited degree of social mobility. As we saw in Chapter 8, a former student of the

College for Men and Women, who initially joined the college in order to learn to read and write, eventually became a member of college classes in English history, grammar and literature, arithmetic, physiology, French, and Egyptian and Greek history.[2] Whether college attendance enabled this student to enter new forms of employment, we do not know. But this was the case for some women students. A former member of the Huddersfield Female Educational Institute, who became a student at Homerton Teacher Training School, thanked the secretary of the institute, in 1859, for all that she had learnt there, including sewing, which was a compulsory part of the training for women teachers in elementary schools:

I am glad that I was ever a member of the Female Educational Institute; what I learnt there will be useful to me through life – every dress I have brought with me I made myself in the Institute, thanks to the Sewing Class, which I hope will continue to prosper.[3]

A past student of the women's classes at Northowram Mechanics' Institute was appointed in December 1860 as schoolmistress of a National school near Bristol.[4] And there are undoubtedly other examples, lost in history, of other female students who went on to more advanced education and perhaps 'improved' themselves in their job prospects.

But for the majority of women students, the experience of an institute or college education may have related much more to personal and social benefits. As we saw in Chapter 8, Elizabeth Rossiter, a student at the London Working Men's College in 1859, claimed that the day classes for women 'made me understand the true nature of a wife's position in her family'.[5] Another student at the College for Men and Women gratefully acknowledged, 'You have taught us to live happier, better and more useful lives'.[6] At the Huddersfield Female Institute, an address on 'Preparation for Life', written by the vice president, Joseph Batley, and read by the president on Monday evening, 8 February 1858, was so 'exceedingly well received by the pupils'[7] that some of the women wrote to thank the writer. Ellen Crabtree expressed her 'obligation' to Mr Batley and other gentlemen who took an active part in the education of the women students, trusting that 'by good conduct and attention to our Teacher we may prove that we are not ungrateful for the privileges we enjoy both in the Class Room and in the Library'. Martha Robinson hoped that Mr Batley's wishes would be realized in that the women students 'shall all become active and useful in our day & generation'. Elizabeth Russell, in a letter also signed by 80 of her sister students, voiced some familiar sentiments:

The fact of our attending the Institution shows that we are not insensible to the importance of acquiring useful knowledge and should we ever be called upon to occupy the responsible positions you mention we hope it will be seen that we have not neglected to prepare ourselves for performing our duties with credit to ourselves and advantage to the world.[8]

Examples such as these illustrate how problematic it is for the researcher to interpret the meaning of education for those working-class women who became students within the mechanics' institutes and various colleges. At one level, it seems that these institutions offered working-class women a conservative education that appeared to function primarily as a form of social control; as Delamont and Duffin argue, the stress on domestic skills for women not only limits the horizons of students but also produces a pool of unskilled labour whose talents are not developed.[9] Yet for those women who actually made the effort to attend an education class on a voluntary basis after long hours of paid work, as, for example, factory hands, milliners, domestic servants, dressmakers or home workers of various kinds, such an educational experience could have been liberating. For some it might have represented a form of 'fighting back' against the poverty of daily life, against the views of society about women's subordinate place, against the prejudices of husbands, lovers, brothers, fathers and sons; and for others it may also have lead to a 'better' job, perhaps as an elementary schoolteacher.

Yet despite such personal efforts, working-class female students within the institutes and colleges were defined and treated as second-class citizens in comparison with the male membership. Gender differentiation was institutionalized in the different status accorded to male and females and in the access granted to each sex to institute and college facilities. For example, when women first entered the mechanics' institutes in the 1830s, it was common to admit them only to the lectures and library; entrance to newsrooms and reading rooms was also usually not permitted, though gradually during the 1860s such restrictions were lifted. Similarly, when women were first admitted to the working men's colleges in the 1850s, they were usually given limited access to certain facilities and no right to vote or hold office.

The women-only institutes and colleges brought into focus a range of debates about the advantages and disadvantage of single-sex education versus co-education, especially in the working men's college movement within the London region, where the separate women-only colleges and the new co-educational college were founded by women. The women-only institutes and colleges offered working-class women the right, under certain conditions, to vote for the election of officers and to hold office themselves. In addition, such single-sex institutions offered women, especially from the middle class, the opportunity to hold key influential positions in a way that was not possible within 'male' mixed-sex institutions. The debates focusing around the issue of single-sex education versus co-education illustrated some of the complexities involved when trying to educate working-class women in movements aimed primarily at working-class men.

It was assumed by the providers of the institutes and colleges that the prime clientele of working-class men would be engaged in paid work during the daytime, and thus evening classes were offered with apparently no discussion about whether day classes should also be organized. However, once women were allowed entry to such male institutions the organization of their educational provision became complicated. Many proponents of adult education for women assumed that some female students would be 'free' during the daytime, probably because they were thought to be wives, mothers or unmarried daughters at home. The debates around this provision, especially about whether 'working-class' and 'working' women would be able to attend in the daytime, did not arise in the case of working-class men. As we have seen, it was probably women in the more affluent sections of the working classes and lower-middle classes who became daytime students; women in other sections of the working class and 'working' women were more likely to attend only in the evenings.

The timing of the classes for women, plus their cost, were also related to ideas about the function of education for women. And it is here that the class differences between women become especially evident. It was not just working-class women who became students in the institutes and colleges – middle-class women also attended. The assumed social class background of the students affected the content of the curriculum, especially in so far as it was shaped by ideals of femininity thought appropriate for women in the different social strata. The ideals of a middle-class 'lady' and a working-class 'good wife and mother' were clearly important aspects of educational planning. Thus women of the labour aristocracy and lower-middle classes were offered a daytime curriculum in general knowledge and some 'ladylike' accomplishments, while working-class women were offered evening classes in the three Rs, plain sewing and some elementary knowledge. These different forms of female curriculum helped to maintain the social differences between women.

By the end of the nineteenth century, the mechanics' institute and working men's college movements were in decline. The social and educational conditions of 1900 were very different to those of half a century earlier, and especially to those found in the 1820s, when the first mechanics' institutes were established. A. V. Dicey, Principal of the London Working Men's College, looking back from 1904 to 1854, when the college was founded, summed up the changes in this way:

Education has spread far and wide. The Universities have been nationalised, they are no longer the property of a sector or of a class; they are certainly accessible to men whom poverty would, fifty years ago, have forbidden to study at Oxford or Cambridge. Schemes for University extension which were once dreams have become realities, and have brought the best University teachers into contact with the whole of the middle classes. Elementary education for the people has become a national concern. It is hardly conceivable that an artisan of superior intelligence should now scarcely know how to read or write. The State provides much technical training both for children and adults. ...

The spread of education ... and its supply at the expense of the State, is an outward and visible sign of a revolution in public opinion.

In 1854 reformers laid unlimited stress upon the virtue of self help. They hardly perceived that in a society where men did not start with equal advantages, self help ... was not enough. ...

In 1904 the tendency of opinion is to lay immense, some may think excessive, emphasis upon the duty of society to help its individual members.[10]

Such changes had influenced the individual institutes and colleges and helped to determine their overall status and impact.

We saw in Chapter 6 that, as the state became increasingly involved in the provision of elementary day schooling after the 1870 Education Act, the demand for the teaching of the three Rs in the mechanics' institutes declined. Although at this time the movement was still vigorous, with new institutes being founded as late as 1875, many institutes had disappeared between 1850 and 1875.[11] During the last quarter of the nineteenth century, the revival of the adult school movement may also have met the growing demand for adult literacy more adequately than the mechanics' institutes. Such schools, operating on a humbler level than the institutes, had a long tradition of teaching basic education to working-class men and women.[12] By 1899 there were 350 schools with 45,000 members,[13] the Quaker section of the movement under the Adult Schools of the Friends' First-day School Association had enrolled the majority (28,017) of these scholars – 18,970 men, 7,839 women and 1,208 juniors.[14]

Those mechanics' institutes surviving into the last quarter of the nineteenth century became increasingly drawn into other educational movements and developments. In the 1860s the London Mechanics' Institution (renamed the Birkbeck Literary and Scientific Institution in 1866) became drawn into the external degree system established in 1858 by London University. Degree work became an increasingly important part of the institute's activities and on 20 October 1920 Birkbeck College, as it was now called, officially became a constituent college of London University.[15] In the 1870s some of the institutes, such as those at Crewe and Nottingham, played an important part in the development of university extension.[16] Other institutes, especially in the north of England, became increasingly involved in technical education, in collaboration with or in opposition to the local authorities,[17] who were empowered, after the Technical Instruction Act of 1889, to support technical instruction from the rates. Mechanics' institutes were eventually forced to transfer technical instruction to local authorities; in some cases, as at Leeds, Huddersfield, Birmingham, Manchester, Bolton, Crewe, Hyde, Keighley, Preston and Thornton, the institutes were converted into maintained technical colleges.[18] In some institutes, too, such as those at Leeds and Liverpool, the design departments became separate art colleges.[19]

During the latter decades of the nineteenth century many institutes were drawn into a public library service. The Public Libraries Act of 1850 and subsequent legislation enabled local authorities to set up free libraries supported by the rates. In a number of cases, as with the institutes at Leicester, Whitehaven in Cumberland, Devonport in Devon, Bridport in Dorset, Gateshead and South Shields in Durham, Basingstoke in Hampshire, Hitchin in Hertfordshire, Fleetwood and Haslingden in Lancashire, Newport in Monmouthshire, Blyth, Newcastle and Tyne-mouth in Northumberland, Evesham in Worcestershire, and Castleford, Skipton and Thornton in Yorkshire, the institute itself became a public library or its library formed the basis for such a venture.[20] In some instances, a public museum originated from the museum in a mechanics' institute.[21] In the minority of instances where a day school was a part of an institute, as at Liverpool and Leeds, the school could develop into a secondary school which came under the control of the Local Education Authorities established by the 1902 Education Act.[22] Other institutes that survived into the first decade of the twentieth century existed primarily as social clubs.[23]

In contrast to the 'legacy of useful public institutions'[24] that the mechanics' institute movement left behind, the working men's college movement which, it is said, had never 'stirred the masses' nor taken 'firm root in the country',[25] had a 'very modest measure of success'.[26] As noted earlier, the number of colleges and students in this movement had never reached the scale achieved by the mechanics' institute movement. By the end of the nineteenth century, many of the working men's colleges had perished. Some, such as those at Halifax, Salford, Boston and Ipswich, had survived during the 1880s mainly as centres for vocational instruction – despite the liberal ethos of the movement; but as local authority technical education advanced from 1889, they seem to have declined.[27] The South London Working Men's College opened the first free library and reading room in South London in 1878, which by 1884 had been converted into a 'Free Library, Reading Room, and Art Gallery'.[28] The unique co-educational College for Men and Women closed its doors in 1901, while the College for Working Women survived well into the twentieth century until it merged with the London Working Men's College in 1966.

For many historians, the contribution of the working men's colleges to the history of adult education is not in terms of a legacy of institutions but in regard to the important analytical distinction between liberal and technical adult education. As Kelly notes, before the working men's college movement, adult education – whether elementary as in adult schools or more advanced as in mechanics' institutes – was quite generalized in character; however, once the movement made a distinction between education for life rather than paid work, it was a distinction that was never lost sight of, and arguably played a vital part in the subsequent development and organization of adult education.[29] In 1908 Sir Michael Sadler summed up the influence of the working men's college movement in the following way:

The great work which Maurice and his friends accomplished was the setting up of a new and more liberal ideal of adult education for men and women engaged during the daytime in the duties of the workshop, the office or the home. This new ideal had had a far-reaching influence both on University opinion and on educational effort in its different forms throughout the country. The thoughts to which the founders of the Working Men's College in London gave expression both in their writings and in their practical work as teachers were the outcome of a new social movement. ... The same current of thought and feeling affected the work of the Young Men's Christian Associations and of many of the Mechanics' Institutes. It appeared later in the University extension movement. ... It has been continuous in its influence ... that no system of evening classes can fully meet the needs of the community unless it includes the provision of social institutes, in which the idea of brotherhood and fellow service permeates educational and recreative work alike.[30]

Yet despite these positive claims made by historians (also noted in the Introduction) about the importance of the mechanics' institutes and working men's colleges for the history of adult education, little consideration has been given to their impact on women. Even at the turn of the nineteenth century, female students still had not achieved equivalent membership status with male students in those institutes and colleges that survived. The struggle to gain admittance to these male-orientated institutions and to obtain an education had not given equal rights to women students.

The mechanics' institute movement and the working men's college movement failed to challenge and undermine the gender differentiation between men and women and the social class differentiation between women – despite the efforts of reformers and the various debates about 'equality' for women. Therefore, towards the end of the nineteenth century, such organizing principles continued and were further institutionalized in new forms of adult education provision. This was especially the case where the main aims of education were vocational, as in the new technical colleges and non-advanced further education institutions that began to emerge by the end of the nineteenth century.

Blunden, for example, suggests that, in Gloucestershire and Wiltshire after 1890, vocational education was closely linked to local industries. However, sex segregation was maintained in this training, since it was mainly provided for male, rather than female, workers. In Swindon, for example, where 80 per cent of the economically active men in 1908 were employed by the Great Western Railway, the local authority provided engineering courses which the employees were encouraged to attend. In the textile and clothing industries (where women made up a large proportion of the workforce) the vocational courses offered were largely for those in positions of formal authority, where women were not found (i.e. in posts as managers and foremen). Although vocational training for women was not entirely ignored, it was less widespread than that for men and limited to a narrower range of occupations, such as office and domestic work. Evening courses that might lead to office employment were especially sought by many young working-class and lower middle-class women keen to 'get on' in the world. A typical example was Ruth Slate, born in 1884 in Manor Park, East London. Her father was a commercial clerk whose employment was not always stable, and consequently the daughter left school at the age of 13 to take a job as a packer for an export druggist firm; by 1902 she had progressed to the post of clerk in the saleroom of a firm of grocers. A keen participant in adult education, Ruth joined a shorthand class soon after taking up her new post, 'hoping to get on quickly so as to get another place and more money, for we are very pinched at home.'[31]

In Stroud, where there was a shortage of female domestic workers, the middle-classes sought to establish a School of Domestic Economy which would supply a pool of trained women.[32] Here again we can see the strength of the 'domestic' ideal of working-class womanhood which, as this research has shown, was so prevalent in working-class female education in the nineteenth century. Indeed, Blunden suggests that a domestic element could even be found in vocational courses for women where it was not strictly relevant to the job. Thus such an aspect was included in various commercial training schemes for women in the 1920s, despite the fact that it was not a 'vital requirement' in most secretarial posts.[33] Similarly, the evening schools with a 'domestic' bias, run by the London County Council in the first decade of the twentieth century, were for young women only – in this particular case, mainly factory women.[34]

The social class differences between women, so evident in the mechanics' institutes and working men's colleges, were also subsequently to be found in a number of other forms of adult education. For example, around the beginning of the twentieth century, fears were expressed that if the British population were not to increase fast enough to fill 'the empty spaces of the empire', then others would; as a result, claims Davin, a powerful ideology of motherhood emerged, firmly rooted in nineteenth-century assumptions about women, domesticity and individualism.[35] Although this ideology transcended social class, it was particularly directed at working-class mothers, since the infant mortality rate among the working class was high. In order to train working-class women to become 'good' mothers,[36] a number of voluntary societies, usually with the support of the Ministry of Health, set up various centres. Such 'Schools for Mothers' and 'Babies Welcomes', as they were often called, were part of a wider infant and child welfare movement, and usually arranged classes and talks for mothers on the care of young children as well as for the mother herself.[37]

The first School for Mothers was founded in St Pancras in 1907; by 1917 some 321 voluntary societies known to the Local Government Board were running 446 infant welfare centres (as they became more commonly known by the First World War), while a further 396 centres were run by local authorities.[38] The curriculum offered to these working-class mothers involved, yet again, a range of 'useful' subjects that, it was believed, would instill that 'absence of method' which was the cause of 'domestic shortcomings'.[39] Thus at the St Pancras school mothers were taughts how to bath a baby and how to make a cradle (for one shilling) out of a banana crate, complete with draperies, a mattress and pillow (stuffed with shavings).[40] The sewing class, run by a 'lady', mainly centred around the knitting of woollen vests and hoods for babies, and sometimes 'ladies' came to sing or recite to the students as they worked. Afternoon classes in cookery as well as evening lectures on hygiene (which fathers could also attend), were also arranged.[41] The prizes that were offered were not books but mainly 'useful' articles, e.g. cooking utensils for a cookery prize, made-up garments or materials for a sewing or knitting prize and fire-guards for a health-care prize.[42]

In contrast to this education in practical childcare skills thought appropriate for working-class women were those classes in handicrafts, music, drama and civics offered to women, mainly from the middle classes, who were members of the National Union of Townswomen's Guilds. The origins of this women's organization were directly linked with the women's suffrage movement. In 1918, when women of 30 were given the vote, the National Union of Women's Suffrage Societies changed its name to the National Union of Societies for Equal Citizenship (NUSEC). Then in 1928, when the right of women over the age of 21 to vote was won, Millicent Fawcett, the non-militant suffragette leader who (as we saw earlier) had been a keen supporter of the College for Working Women and a lecturer at the London Working Men's College,[43] urged the NUSEC to turn its attention to educating women for their new responsibilities as voting citizens.[44]

It was agreed to launch a new movement for townswomen similar to the women's institute movement which flourished in rural areas.[45] Eventually the NUSEC separated its roles into two distinct organizations – the National Council for Equal Citizenship and the National Union of Townswomen's Guild.

Margery Corbett Ashby, one of the founders of the first guild, at Haywards Heath, Sussex, on 25 January 1929, claimed that the aim of the new organizations was to give 'the ordinary woman at home' in the towns 'not only training in and enjoyment of arts and crafts but also training in the responsibility of citizenship'.[46] By 1932, 146 guilds had been founded.[47] An analysis, in 1933, of the programmes of 120 of these guilds revealed that lectures on handicrafts – such as rugmaking, dressmaking, toymaking, embroidery and glovemaking – were the most popular, followed by lectures on homecraft and gardening, then civics, with health subjects at the bottom of the list.[48]

Such developments in the twentieth century reveal the legacy of nineteenth-century adult education. The significance of the mechanics' institute and working men's college movements for the twentieth century is that they helped shape patterns of provision that reinforced patriarchal and familial ideologies as well as the divisions between the social classes and between men and women. This pattern of provision was evident inside these adult education movements in the different educations offered to working-class and middle-class students and in the typically male and female educational routes.

What this research has shown is that the nineteenth century has left a tradition whereby working-class women became part-time students, generally in the evenings. Ironically, in the twentieth century, women form the majority of students in adult education – though we are still left with similar social class differences between women in regard to the form of provision and the kind of courses studied.[49] The debate about coeducation versus single-sex education, especially evident in the working men's college movement, is still ongoing and reasserting itself.[50] The issue of whether women can be 'fitted into' a male educational paradigm is still valid.[51] Women–only 'access courses' and 'second-chance courses', which aim especially to attract working-class women, are still an arena for political controversy.[52] It would be fair to say that women's experiences in the mechanics' institute and working men's college movements of the nineteenth century were significant aspects of educational history which have left a legacy for the present.

NOTES

Abbreviations

HFEI	Huddersfield Female Educational Institute
HWJ	History Workshop Journal
JWEU	Journal of the Women's Education Union
MMI	Manchester Mechanics' Institution
PP	Parliamentary Papers
RYUMI	Report of the Yorkshire Union of Mechanics' Institutes
TNAPSS	Transactions of the National Association for the Promotion of Social Science
TWMCJ	The Working Men's College Journal
TWMCM	The Working Men's College Magazine

Introduction

1 See, for example, Bremner, *Education of Girls and Women*; Zimmern, *The Renaissance of Girls' Education in England*; Stephen, *Emily Davies and Girton College*; Tuke, *A History of Bedford College for Women*; Percival, *The English Miss To-day and Yesterday*; Tylecote, *The Education of Women at Manchester University*; Brittain, *The Women at Oxford*; Kamm, *Hope Deferred*; Pedersen, *The Reform of Women's Secondary and Higher Education*; Turner, *Equality for Some*; McWilliams-Tullberg, *Women at Cambridge*; McWilliams-Tullberg, 'Women and degrees at Cambridge University'; Delamont, 'The contradictions in ladies' education', and 'The domestic ideology and women's education'; Pedersen, 'The reform of women's secondary and higher education'; Bryant, *The Unexpected Revolution*; Burstyn, *Victorian Education and the Ideal of Womanhood*; Vicinus, '"One life to stand beside me"'; Hunt (ed.), *Lessons for Life*. For an overview of the education of both middle-class and working-class women, see Purvis, 'Towards a history of women's education in nineteeth-century Britain'.

2 The main publications here are Purvis, 'Working-class women and adult education in nineteenth-century Britain'; Purvis, '"Women's life is essentially domestic, public life being confined to men" (Comte)'.

3 Delamont, 'The contradictions in ladies' education', and 'The domestic ideology and women's education'; Dyhouse, *Girls Growing Up in Late Victorian and Edwardian England.*

4 Tylecote, *The Mechanics' Institutes of Lancashire and Yorkshire Before 1851*, p. 293.

5 Harrison, *Learning and Living*, pp. 58, 228. Other accounts of the mechanics' institutes tend also to give little or no space to the activities of women – see, for example, Steer, *The Chichester Literary and Philosophical Society and Mechanics' Institute*; Royle, 'Mechanics' institutes and the working classes 1840–1860'; Shapin and Barnes, 'Science, nature and control'; Roderick and Stephens, 'Approaches to technical education in nineteenth-century England'; Inkster, 'The social context of an educational movement'.

6 Harrison, *A History of the Working Men's College.*

7 See, for example, Davies (ed.), *The Working Men's College*; Atkins (ed.), *The Vaughan Working Men's College*; Allaway, *Vaughan College Leicester 1862–1962.*

8 Oakley, *Gender and Society*, p. 158, argues that 'sex' refers to the biological difference between males and females while 'gender' refers to the psychological and cultural aspects that distinguish masculinity and femininity. Masculinity and femininity are thus socially constructed categories.

9 Defined in Chapter 1; see section 'Feminist challenges'.

Chapter 1 Hidden from History

1 Johnson, 'Culture and the historians', p. 41.

2 Ibid. See also, for example, Johnson, 'Thompson, Genovese and socialist-humanist history'; Johnson, 'Three problematics'; Samuel, 'The British Marxist historians'; the exchange between Hall, Johnson and Thompson in Samuel (ed.), *People's History and Socialist Theory*; McLennan, *Marxism and the Methodologies of History*; Sutton, 'Radical liberalism, Fabianism and social history'; Kaye, *The British Marxist Historians.*

3 'Liberal' and 'Marxist' histories are defined later in this chapter. The editorial in *HWJ*, 13 (spring 1982) states that socialist history means not merely the history of socialist movements or labour movements, but 'the reinterpretation of all dominant social and cultural institutions in terms of a class perspective.' Within this broad definition one may place both 'Marxist' histories and 'non-Marxist' socialist histories, such as those of R. H. Tawney.

4 Gray, *Liberalism*, p. x, identifies the following elements in liberal political thought: 'It is *individualist*, in that it asserts the moral primacy of the person against the claims of any social collectivity; *egalitarian*, inasmuch as it confers on all men the same moral status and denies the relevance to legal or political order of differences in moral worth among human beings; *universalist*, affirming the moral unity of the human species and according a secondary importance to specific historic associations and cultural forms; and *meliorist* in its affirmation of the corrigibility and improvability of all social institutions and political arrangements. It is this conception of man and society which gives liberalism a definite identity which transcends its vast internal variety and complexity'.

5 Matthews, 'Barbara Bodichon', p. 118.

6 Miles, *The Women's History of the World*, p. xii.

7 Thomson, *England in the Nineteenth Century*, p. 187.

8 Butterfield, *The Whig Interpretation of History*, p. 11.
9 Marwick, *The Nature of History*, p. 45.
10 See, for example, F. Engels, letter to J. Bloch (21 September 1890), in his *Selected Correspondence*, p. 475.
11 Thompson, *The Making of the English Working Class*, pp. 9–10.
12 Centre for Comtemporary Cultural Studies Education Group, *Unpopular Education*, p. 32.
13 Kaye, *The British Marxist Historians*, pp. 5–6.
14 Thompson, *The Making*.
15 Hobsbawm, *Labouring Men*; Hobsbawm, 'Man and woman in socialist iconography', p. 121.
16 Alexander, Davin and Hostettler, 'Labouring women', p. 175.
17 Hobsbawm, *The Age of Empire 1875–1914*, pp. 197–8.
18 Ibid., p. 197. For a discussion of the way the ideology of domesticity for women served both the interests of industry and of empire in Britain at the beginning of the twentieth century, see Davin, 'Imperialism and motherhood'.
19 Rule, *The Labouring Classes in Early Industrial England*.
20 Ibid., p. 393.
21 See Horn, *The Victorian Country Child*; Horn, *Education in Rural England*; Sanderson, *Education, Economic Change and Society in England*; Stephens, *Education, Literacy and Society*.
22 See, for example, Birchenough, *History of Elementary Education in England and Wales*; Curtis, *History of Education in Great Britain*; Sellman, *Devon Village Schools in the Nineteenth Century*; Sturt, *The Education of the People*; Wardle, *English Popular Education*; Johnson, *Derbyshire Village Schools in the Nineteenth Century*; Hurt, *Education in Evolution*; Honey, *Tom Brown's Universe*; Roderick, *Education and Industry in the Nineteenth Century*; Hurt, *Elementary Schooling and the Working Classes*; Roach, *A History of Secondary Education in England*; Marsden, *Unequal Educational Provision in England and Wales*.
23 Rothblatt, *The Revolution of the Dons*.
24 Reeder, 'Predicaments of city children', pp. 89, 90.
25 Hurt, *Elementary Schooling*, p. 136, my emphasis.
26 It is very difficult to quantify the amount of space given to the schooling of working-class girls in Stephens, *Education, Literacy and Society*, and Horn, *The Victorian Country Child*, since references to working-class girls are scattered throughout these books and are part of a wider discussion about working-class children. At a generous estimate, possibly 38 out of the 268 pages in Stephens and four of the 52 pages in the three chapters about schooling in Horn relate specifically to girls.
27 Johnson, 'Educational policy and social control in early Victorian England'; Johnson, 'Notes on the schooling of the English working class 1780–1850'. Silver and Simon, see note 28.
28 H. Silver, *The Concept of Popular Education*, p. xi; Simon, *The Two Nations and the Educational Structure*, p. 13.
29 Roderick and Stephens, *Post School Education*.
30 Harrison, *Learning and Living*.
31 Kelly, *A History of Adult Education in Great Britain*, pp. 80, 187.
32 Norris, 'Women's history', p. 7; Lewis, 'Women lost and found', p. 58; Purvis, 'A feminist perspective on the history of women's education', p. 1.
33 See, for example, Rowbotham, *Woman's Consciousness, Man's World*, especially Chapter 2. For definitions of social/Marxist feminism, see note 42.
34 Rowbotham, *Hidden from History*.

35 See, for example, Carroll, *Liberating Women's History*; Bridenthal and Koonz (eds.), *Becoming Visible*; Davies (ed), *Rewriting Nursing History*; Beddoe, *Discovering Women's History*; Crawford, *Exploring Women's Past*; Ferguson, Quilligan and Vickers (eds), *Rewriting the Renaissance*; Legget, *Local Heroines*.

36 Norris, 'Women's history', p. 7.

37 Fox-Genovese, 'Placing women's history in history', p. 9; Editorial, 'Women's history and men's history'.

38 This remark was made at a meeting of the Historical Association in January 1986; *The Guardian* (14 January 1986).

39 Richards, *The Sceptical Feminist*, p. 1; Oakley, *Subject Women*, p. 335; Spender, *Women of Ideas*, p. 7; Stanley and Wise, *Breaking Out*, pp. 51–2; Smith, 'Racism and Women's Studies', p. 49; Jaggar, *Feminist Politics and Human Nature*, p. 5.

40 Banks, *Faces of Feminism*.

41 The issue is further complicated by the fact that the terms applied to the main divisions are often used in different ways by different people – see, for example, the discussion on this issue offered in Acker, 'Sociology, gender and education', pp. 67–80.

42 I draw here particularly on Jagger, *Feminist Politics and Human Nature*, and Eisenstein, *Contemporary Feminist Thought*. Generally *Marxist feminism* sees the oppression of women as stemming from social class divisions within society and from the private ownership of property. However, it is the social class inequalities that are seen as the major kind of inequalities which must be abolished, and the interests of women must be considered alongside the broader aims of eliminating a class society. Once a classless, communist society is established, the subordination of women will end. For the Marxist feminist, the issue of women's liberation is part of a much broader struggle. *Radical feminism* sees the power relationships between the sexes, rather than the class divisions within a society, as the key to understanding women's subordinate position. Since the social, political and economic dominance of men over women is seen as the source of women's oppression, the concept of 'patriarchy' (see notes 74 and 76) is central for explaining women's subordination. Women's liberation will only occur when patriarchal control is swept away. *Socialist feminism* incorporates aspects of both Marxist feminism and radical feminism in that it is argued that the subordinate position of women within society may be attributed to the nature of capitalist society and to the control that men exercise over women. Preconditions for women's liberation include the building of a socialist society in which patriarchal control does not exist. *Liberal feminism*, in contrast to the three approaches described so far, advocates gradual and piecemeal reform rather than any radical transformation. The emphasis is upon equal rights for men and women and, in particular, for each individual woman to choose her own social role with the same degree of freedom enjoyed by men. A liberal feminist might press therefore for eliminating those legal, cultural and social constraints that prevent women from sharing equal opportunities with men. *Cultural feminism* emphasizes that women's liberation will be achieved mainly through the development and establishment of a separate woman's culture rather than through explicit political and economic policies which will radically transform society.

   Such groupings within feminism have been increasingly criticized by black feminists in Britain but especially in the USA. In particular, such groupings are accused of concentrating upon issues that are of most relevance to white, Western, middle-class women. *Black feminism* emphasizes that social class, race, gender and sexuality must be incorporated into any analysis of women's lives and points to the cultural and class bias in the analyses offered by many white feminists. For example, white feminists frequently argue that the contemporary family is the source of oppression for women. However, as Carby argues in 'White women listen!', p. 214, while black feminists would not wish to deny that the family can be a source of oppression, they also wish to examine how the black family has functioned as a prime source of resistance to oppression. Furthermore, ideologies of black female sexuality do not stem primarily from the black family: the gender of black women is constructed in a different way to that of white women since it is also subject to racism. For further discussion on black feminism, see Hull, Scott and Smith; Hooks, *Ain't I A Woman; Feminist Review*; and Bryan, Dadzie and Scafe, *The Heart of the Race*.

43 For example, Roberts, *A Woman's Place*, p. 1, states, 'Although this is a book about women it is not an obviously feminist history, although I believe it to be a contribution to that literature. I began and indeed ended, my research as a feminist'.

44 See the contribution by Davin in 'What is women's history?', pp. 47–8.

45 Davin, 'Women and history', p. 216.

46 Lerner, 'Placing women in history: a 1975 perspective', in Carroll (ed.), p. 365.

47 Matthews, *Good and Mad Women*, p. 18. For further discussion of some of these points and of the challenges generally that feminist history pose, see Purvis, 'Reflections upon doing historical documentary research from a feminist perspective'; Purvis, 'Breaking the chains'.

48 Spender, *Women of Ideas*, p. 9.

49 Spender, *Mothers of the Novel*.

50 Kelly-Gadol, 'The social relations of the sexes', p. 810.

51 Degler, *Is There a History of Women?*, p. 4.

52 Quoted in Matthews, 'Barbara Bodichon', p. 120.

53 Perkin, *The Origins of Modern English Society*, p. 149.

54 Davin, 'Women and history', p. 216.

55 Ross, 'Survival networks', pp. 4–5. See also Ross, 'Labour and love'.

56 See, for example, Summers, 'A home from home'; Prochaska, *Women and Philanthropy in Nineteenth-Century England*; John, *By the Sweat of their Brow*; Widdowson, *Going Up into the Next Class*; Lown, 'Not so much a factory, more a form of patriarchy'; Turnbull, '"So extremely like parliament"'; Vicinus, *Independent Women*; Westover, '"To fill the kids' tummies"'; Bornat, '"What about that lass of yours being in the union?"'; Osterud, 'Gender divisions and the organisation of work in the Leicester hosiery industry'; Hunt, 'Opportunities lost and gained'; Morris, 'The characteristics of sweating'; Higgs, 'Domestic service and household production'; M. Zimmeck, 'Jobs for the girls'; Burke, 'The decline of the independent Bal Maiden'; Bornat, 'Lost leaders'; Dyhouse, 'Miss Buss and Miss Beale'; Billington and Billington, '"A burning zeal for righteousness"'; Hollis, 'Women in council'; Hollis, *Ladies Elect*; Summers, *Angels and Citizens*.

57 D.Thompson, 'Women and nineteenth-century radical politics'; Liddington and Norris, *One Hand Tied Behind Us*; Malmgreen, *Neither Bread nor Roses*; Taylor, *Eve and the New Jerusalem*.

58 Carr, *What is History?*, p. 132.

59 Kelly-Gadol, 'Did women have a Renaissance?'; Lewis, *Women in England 1870–1950*, p. 222; Dyhouse, *Girls Growing Up*, p. 2; Prentice, 'The education of 19th century British women', p. 219.

60 See, for example, the critiques offered by West, 'Women, sex and class'; Delphy, 'Women in stratification studies'; Murgatroyd, 'Gender and occupational

stratification'; Stanworth, 'Women and class analysis'; Walby, 'Gender, class and stratification'; Delphy and Leonard, 'Class analysis, gender analysis, and the family'; Stacey, 'Gender and stratification'.

61 Marx, *Manifesto of the Communist Party*.

62 Ludlow and Jones, *Progress of the Working Class*, p. 3.

63 Jones, *Outcast London*; Alexander, 'Women's work in nineteenth-century London', p. 59.

64 Defining the middle class is a complex task. Banks, in *Prosperity and Parenthood*, p. 51, estimates that in mid-Victorian England a middle-class family would have an income of between £150 and £1500 per annum. Davidoff and Hall, in *Family Fortunes*, pp. 23–4, argue that from £200 to £300 per annum secured a place within the middle class for an average family and distinguish between higher and lower strata within the middle class generally. The main focus of their work is upon the gendered nature of class formation and the way sexual differences always influenced class belonging.

65 Alexander, 'Women's work', pp. 64–5; Taylor, *Eve and the New Jerusalem*, pp. 77–9.

66 Widdowson, *Going Up into the Next Class*, p. 57.

67 Horn, *Education in Rural England*, p. 220.

68 The dividing line between a 'woman' and a 'girl' in the nineteenth century is somewhat arbitrary. Following Walvin, *A Child's World*, p. 13, I shall take 14 years as the upper age limit for a Victorian child, though by that time many children (especially in the working classes) had lost 'any characteristics of childhood'.

69 See, for example, Tilly and Scott, *Women, Work and Family*; Jordanova, 'The history of the family'; Davidoff and Westover, '"From Queen Victoria to the Jazz Age"'; Boxer and Quataert, *Connecting Spheres*.

70 Kelly, 'The doubled vision of feminist theory', p. 221, author's emphasis.

71 Quoted in D. Copelman, '"A new comradeship between men and women"', p. 183.

72 Alexander, 'Women's work'; Burstyn, *Victorian Education*.

73 Dyhouse, *Girls Growing Up*, p. 26.

74 For discussion of 'patriarchy', see Millett, *Sexual Politics*; Delphy, *Close to Home*; Walby, *Patriarchy at Work*; Nielsen, 'Maps of patriarchy'.

75 Taylor, *Eve and the New Jerusalem*, p. 38; Showalter, *The Female Malady*.

76 See Beechey, 'On patriarchy'.

77 See, for example, S. Rowbotham, 'The trouble with "patriarchy"'; Eisenstein, 'Some notes on the relations of capitalist patriarchy'.

78 London Feminist History Group, *The Sexual Dynamics*, p. 1.

79 S. Alexander, 'Women, class and sexual differences in the 1830s and 1840s', p. 128.

80 See note 42.

81 Hartmann, 'The unhappy marriage of Marxism and feminism'.

82 Ross, 'Women's history in the USA', in Samuel (ed.), p. 182; Newton, Ryan and Walkowitz (eds.), *Sex and Class in Women's History*, p. 2. For examples of radical-feminist approaches by American writers to women's history, see Smith-Rosenberg, *Disorderly Conduct* and the Introduction to Marcus (ed.), *Suffrage and the Pankhursts*.

83 See notes 16, 18, 33, 34, 44, 57, 63.

84 E. Sarah, 'Female performers on a male stage', p. 137.

85 Ibid., pp. 137–8.

86 Sarah, 'Christabel Pankhurst, in Spender (ed.), *Feminist Theorists*, p. 272.

87 Title page to S. Jeffreys, *The Spinster and her Enemies*.

88 Gordon, Buhle and Dye, 'The problem of women's history', in Carroll (ed.), pp. 83–4.
89 Widdowson, *Going Up into the Next Class*; Liddington and Norris, *One Hand Tied Behind Us*.
90 Kelly-Gadol, 'The social relation of the sexes', p. 809.
91 Johanson, '"Herstory" as history, in Carroll. (ed.)

Chapter 2 The Double Shift of Work and Home

1 Tilly and Scott, *Women, Work and Family*, p. 5; Pleck, 'Two worlds in one'; Davidoff and Westover, '"From Queen Victoria to the Jazz Age"', p. 1, and Roberts, *Women's Work 1840–1940*, p. 12.
2 Tilly and Scott, *Women, Work and Family*, p. 63.
3 E. Higgs, 'Women, occupations and work in the nineteenth century', p. 60; Alexander, 'Women's work', pp. 64–6 and Roberts, *Women's Work*, pp. 18–19.
4 See Hakim, 'Census reports as documentary evidence'.
5 *Census of Great Britain 1851*, Summary Tables, England and Wales, Occupations of the People, Ages – Females, Table XXV, p. ccxxvi.
6 Davidoff and Hall, *Family Fortunes*. For a feminist critique of the 'separation' thesis, see Rose, '"Gender at work"'.
7 Lewis, *Women in England*, p. 145.
8 Banks, *Becoming a Feminist*, p. 41.
9 See Smelser, *Social Change in the Industrial Revolution*; Lazonick, 'The subjection of labour to capital'.
10 Pinchbeck, *Women Workers and the Industrial Revolution 1750–1850*, pp. 123–4.
11 M. Barrett and M. McIntosh, 'The "family wage"', pp. 53–6.
12 There are those who argue that such changes brought many improvements to the lives of married working-class women. Pinchbeck, in *Women Workers*, p. 307, states that the industrial revolution improved the domestic conditions of the married women, since, once the home was no longer a workshop, many women were able 'to devote their energies to the business of home making and the care of their children'. Humphries, in 'Class struggle and the persistence of the working-class family', suggests that the campaign for a family wage among certain sections of the working class, together with the withdrawal of some working-class people (such as women and children) from the labour market, could raise the real wages of the employed and generally improve working-class standards of living. Others, however, disagree with these views. For example, Oakley, in *Housewife*, emphasizes that the identification of married women with the role of housewife, as a consequence of industrialization, brought both a physical and a psychological restriction to women's lives that was oppressive and non-liberating. Barrett and McIntosh, in 'The "family wage"', take a similar line. The debate about the changes industrialization brought for working-class single women is also contentious. Pinchbeck argues that industrialization opened up a wider range of job opportunities for single women, especially in state-regulated factory work. Perkin, in *The Origins*, p. 158, claims that factory women 'led the way' in liberating women from the burden of continuous child-bearing. Other writers are less optimistic in their assessments. For example, Richards, in 'Women in the British economy since about 1700', p. 347, emphasizes that by the middle of the nineteenth century there was a 'surplus army' of

employable women who had gained little from the diversification of the labour market. Hartmann, in 'Capitalism, patriarchy and job segregation by sex', p. 217, argues that the labour market that developed with industrial capitalism strengthened the dominant position of men and reinforced job segregation between males and females; women's jobs were lower paid, considered less skilled and often involved less exercise of authority.

13 Horn, *The Rise and Fall of the Victorian Servant*, Chapter 4; McBride, *The Domestic Revolution*, Chapter 3.

14 Mrs Wrigley, 'A plate-layer's wife', p. 58; Mayhew, *London Labour and the London Poor*, vol. 1, p. 412.

15 Stanley (ed.), *The Diaries of Hannah Cullwick, Victorian Maidservant*, p. 105.

16 Ibid., p. 105, Hannah records, 'Had my tea & ask'd leave to go to the play'; Horn, *The Rise and Fall of the Victorian Servant*, pp. 113–24.

17 Thompson, *Lark Rise to Candleford*, p. 174.

18 Horn, *The Rise and Fall of the Victorian Servant*, p. 96; Salmon, 'Domestic service and democracy', p. 409.

19 L. Davidoff, 'Mastered for life', p. 409.

20 Quoted in Thomas and Grimmett, *Women in Protest 1800–1850*, p. 24; Banks, *Prosperity and Parenthood*, p. 82, and Horn, *The Rise and Fall of the Victorian Servant*, pp. 131, 125.

21 Thompson, *Lark Rise*, pp. 174–5.

22 Horn, *The Rise and Fall of the Victorian Servant*, p. 106; McBride, *The Domestic Revolution*, p. 85; Mrs Layton, 'Memories of seventy years', in Llewelyn Davies (ed.), *Life*, p. 29.

23 *Report of the British and Foreign School Society*, 1822, pp. 43–4.

24 *Reports of Special Assistant Commissioners on the Employment of Women and Children in Agriculture*, p. 213; A Suffering Mistress, 'On the side of the mistresses', p. 465.

25 McBride, *The Domestic Revolution*, pp. 83–5.

26 Thompson and Yeo (eds), *The Unknown Mayhew*, p. 518: Mayhew offered the following distinction between dressmaking and millinery: 'The dressmaker's work is confined to the making of ladies' dresses, including every kind of outwardly-worn gown or robe. The milliner's work is confined to making caps, bonnets, scarfs, and all outward attire worn by ladies other than the gown; the bonnets, however, which tax the skill of the milliners, are what are best known as "made bonnets" – such as are constructed of velvet, satin, silk, muslin, or any other textile fabric ....When the business is sufficiently large, one or more millinery hands are commonly kept solely to bonnet-making .... The milliner is accounted a more skilled labourer than the dressmaker'. For a definition of slop work, see note 31.

27 'Milliners' apprentices', pp. 308–9.

28 'The point of the needle', p. 36.

29 'Milliners' apprentices', p. 311, 'The point of the needle', p. 36.

30 'Ellen M', a mantle maker, in a letter dated 24 May 1858, published in the *Manchester Guardian*, reprinted in *The Englishwoman's Journal*' (July 1858), p. 359, tells how the establishment in which she and other women were employed in Manchester expected employees to work overtime and that if they refused, 'We should be discharged'. The wages of 8s a week worked out at 2d per hour. Nearly all the women employees were 'hurrying to a premature grave'.

31 Neff, *Victorian Working Women*, p. 129.

32 T. Hughes, *A Lecture on the Slop-System*, pp. 4–5, 8.

33 Thompson and Yeo (eds), p. 519.

34 [Shaw,] *An Affectionate Pleading for England's Oppressed Female Workers*, p. 14.

35 *Slop Shops, and Slop Workers*, pp. 9–10.

36 [Shaw,] *An Affectionate Pleading*, p. 18.

37 Walkowitz, *Prostitution and Victorian Society*, p. 15; Tilly and Scott, *Women, Work and Family*, p. 117.

38 Hughes, *A Lecture on the Slop-System*, p. 12.

39 Neff, *Victorian Working Women*, p. 113; Boucherett, Blackburn and some others, *The Conditions of Working Women and the Factory Acts*, p. 40.

40 D. Bythell, *The Sweated Trades*, p. 66; J. Morris, *Women Workers and the Sweated Trades*.

41 Pinchbeck, *Women Workers*, p. 193.

42 Ibid., p. 192.

43 Liddington and Norris, *One Hand Tied Behind Us*, pp. 95–6.

44 Quoted in Boucherett and Blackburn, *The Conditions of Working Women*, p.4.

45 Ibid., pp. 13, 12, 7.

46 Hewitt, *Wives and Mothers in Victorian Industry*, p. 17.

47 Pinchbeck, *Women Workers*, pp. 184–5, 190.

48 Aveling and Aveling, *The Factory Hell*, p. 42: 'Whatever reports, of whatever year, are taken, it is the same sad and hideous story. Evasions of the Acts, recklessness as to the health and life of the workers, diseases and accidents .... Things are scarcely any better today with the actual workers than they were fifty years ago'.

49 J. Ginswick (ed.), *Labour and the Poor in England and Wales*, p. 16.

50 Chew, *The Life and Writings of a Working Woman*, p. 76.

51 A. Foley, *A Bolton Childhood*, p. 51.

52 Hutchins, *Women in Modern Industry*, pp. 58–9.

53 Collier, *The Girl in Industry*, pp. 10–11.

54 Hutchins and Harrison, *A History of Factory Legislation*, p. 77. See also Silver, 'Ideology and the factory child'; and Brown, 'The Gregs and their school at Styal'. Joyce, in *Work, Society and Politics*, p. 172, notes: 'Factory schools, entirely paid for by the employer and often run on the premises, were never widespread, but employers continued to finance and manage schools long beyond the 1870 Education Act'.

55 Quoted in Johnson, *Derbyshire Village School in the Nineteenth Century*, pp. 113–14.

56 M. Merryweather, *Experience of Factory Life*, pp. 21–5.

57 R. Roberts, *A Ragged Schooling*, pp. 12–13.

58 Foley, *A Bolton Childhood*, p. 8.

59 Stearns, 'Working-class women in Britain, 1890–1914', p. 110; Liddington and Norris, *One Hand Tied Behind Us*, pp. 112–13.

60 Holcombe, *Victorian Ladies at Work*, p. 34.

61 Ibid., p. 35; Purvis, 'Women and teaching in the nineteenth century', p. 364.

62 *Minutes of the Committee of Council on Education for 1846*, p. 2.

63 Horn, *Education in Rural England*, p. 101.

64 Ibid., p. 222; Holcombe, *Victorian Ladies*, p. 36.

65 Letters of Miss Rose Knowles kept at Northamptonshire Record Office, reference number YZ.5541. P. Horn, 'The problems of a village head-mistress in the 1880s', is based on these letters and I am indebted to this article.

66 Thompson, *Lark Rise*, p. 212.

67 Grant, *Farthing Bundles*, p. 35.

68 Widdowson, *Going Up into the Next Class*, p. 36.

69 Horn, *Education in Rural England*, pp. 209–15.

70 Ibid., p. 217.

71 Pinchbeck, *Women Workers*, pp. 67, 110; Snell, *Annals of the Labouring Poor*,

Chapter 6.

72 *Reports of Special Assistant Commissioners on the Employment of Women and Children in Agriculture*, p. 70.
73 Ibid., p. 68.
74 Ibid., p. 66.
75 Ibid., p. 66.
76 Ibid., p. 70.
77 Ibid., p. 68.
78 Ibid., pp. 86, 89, 90.
79 Ibid., p. 119.
80 Ibid., p. 25.
81 Ibid., pp. 109, 275. See also Kelly, *A History of Adult Education*, p. 148.
82 Hudson, *The History of Adult Education*, pp. 9–10; Martin, *The Adult School Movement*, p. 55.
83 Cadbury, Matheson and Shawn, *Women's Work and Wages*, p. 149; see also Pennington and Westover, *A Hidden Workforce*.
84 Razzell and Wainwright (eds), *The Victorian Working Class*, p. 125.
85 Malcolmson, in *English Laundresses*, p. 127, notes that hand laundry reached its peak in 1881 and thereafter lost its ground to mechanized processes.
86 *Reports of Special Assistant Commissioners on the Employment of Women and Children in Agriculture*, p. 109; Kathleen Woodward remembers her mother, who had to support her half invalid husband and children on her wash-tub earnings, saying this: K. Woodward, *Jipping Street*, p. 12.
87 Mayhew, *London Labour and the London Poor*, p. 172.
88 Layton, 'Memories of seventy years', in Llewelyn Davies (ed.), *Life*, p. 37.
89 L. Davidoff, 'The separation of home and work?', pp. 83–4.
90 Elizabeth, *The Works of Charlotte Elizabeth*, p. 500.
91 *Reports of Special Assistant Commissioners on the Employment of Women and Children in Agriculture*, p. 348, 295–6.
92 Hughes, *A Lecture on the Slop-System*, p. 8.
93 Shaw, *An Affectionate Pleading*, p. 15.
94 Hughes, *A Lecture on the Slop System*, p. 9.
95 It was not until the early twentieth century that the first attempt was made to regulate wages for women in such lowly paid jobs as tailoring, dressmaking, skirt-making, chain-making, cardboard-box making and lace-making: see Neff, *Victorian Working Women*, p. 146.
96 Cadbury, Matheson and Shawn, *Women's Work*, pp. 158, 161.
97 Taylor, in *Eve and the New Jerusalem*, p. 32, notes that, during the first half of the nineteenth century, 'It was as fathers and husbands that men oppressed women; it was as daughters, wives and mothers that women experienced their most direct subjection. Sexual subordination was basically a family affair'. Malcolmson, in *English Laundresses*, p. 39, suggests, 'The authority of the working-class male was based primarily on his role as the principal breadwinner'.
98 *The Pioneer*, 22 March 1834, p. 262.
99 *The Englishwoman's Review* (15 October 1877), p. 466.
100 Oren, 'The welfare of women in labouring families', p. 227.
101 *The Pioneer*, 29 March 1934, p. 274.
102 Quoted in Taylor, *Eve and the New Jerusalem*, p. 269.
103 *The Pioneer*, 12 April 1834, p. 295.
104 Pole, *A History of the Origins and Progress of Adult Schools*, p. 29.
105 Quoted in Taylor, *Eve and the New Jerusalem*, p. 232.

106 *The Pioneer*, 8 February 1834, p. 191.
107 Layton, 'Memories of seventy years' in Llewelyn Davies (ed.), *Life*, pp. 48-9.
108 Ibid., p. 49.
109 Nash, 'Co-operator and citizen', p. 76.

Chapter 3 Ideologies about Women's Place

1 Hall, 'The early formation of Victorian domestic ideology', in Burman (ed.), *Fit Work for Women*, p. 15; Davidoff and Hall, *Family Fortunes*, especially Chapter 3; Nead, *Myths of Sexuality*.
2 See Williams, *The Long Revolution*, Part 2, Chapter 1.
3 For discussion about male dominance over women in the nineteenth century see, for example, Strachey, *The Cause*, Chapter 1; Banks and Banks, *Feminism and Family Planning in Victorian England*, Chapter 2; Basch, *Relative Creatures*, Chapter 1; Eisenstein, *The Radical Future of Liberal Feminism*, especially Chapters, 2, 5; Hall, 'Gender divisions and class formation in the Birmingham middle class, 1780-1850'; Gorham, *The Victorian Girl and the Feminine Ideal*, Chapter 1.
4 Ellis, *The Daughters of England*, p. 3.
5 Walker, *Women Physiologically Considered as to Mind, Morals, Matrimonial Slavery, Infidelity and Divorce*, p. 13.
6 Darwin, *On the Origin of Species*; Darwin, *The Descent of Man*, pp. 557, 563-4.
7 Burstyn, *Victorian Education*, p. 78.
8 Maudsley, 'Sex in mind and in education', p. 468.
9 Spencer, *Education: intellectual, moral and physical*, p. 174.
10 Stephen, *Liberty, Equality, Fraternity*, p. 228.
11 Ellis, *The Women of England*, p. 149; Ruskin, *Sesame and Lilies*, p. 124; Yonge, *Womankind*, p. 39.
12 Leitner, 'Comment on Emma Wallington', p. 563; Moore, Address to the British Medical Association, p. 315.
13 'Treatment of women', p. 225.
14 In particular, the Married Women's Property Act of 1882 gave married women the same property rights enjoyed by men and single women. L. Holcombe, in *Wives and Property*, pp. 202-3, notes that the Act spelt out precisely what, in the absence of a marriage settlement, was to be treated as a married woman's separate property. 'Women who married after the act came into effect on 1st January 1883 were to have all property, of whatever kind and from whatever source, which they possessed or were entitled to at the time of marriage and which they acquired or became entitled to after marriage. Women married before 1883 were to have all property which they acquired or became entitled to after the act came into effect, as well ... as the property they already held under the provisions of the act of 1870.' Holcombe claims that the reform of the married women's property law is 'one of the greatest achievements, if not the greatest, of the Victorian women's movement' (p. 217); however, she also asserts that the 1882 Act did not bring 'equality' for married women (p. 234). This point is developed by J. Brophy and C. Smart, 'From disregard to disrepute: the position of women in family law', *Feminist Review*, 9 (autumn 1981), p. 5: 'By the end of the nineteenth century ... , legislation gave women rights to property which were formally equal to those of a man or a single woman, but she had far fewer rights in general. For example she had no right to leave her husband without his permission and if she did he could physically restrain her. She had no rights to maintenance if she could not prove that her husband had committed a matrimonial offence. Although she could "pledge

her husband's credit" this was of little value to poor women and became increasingly unpopular with creditors. Her right to divorce (which was not extended in practice to working-class women) was also more restricted than her husband's as he could divorce her on a single act of adultery whilst she had to establish adultery combined with another matrimonial offence. It is therefore quite inaccurate to talk of an equalisation of rights between husbands and wives at this time although the principle of married women's rights had begun to enter into law.'

15 Parkes, *Essays on Women's Work*, p. 74.
16 See note 14.
17 Murray, *My First Hundred Years*, p. 79; 'Caius and Caia', p. 56; 'Queen bees or working bees?', p. 576.
18 Ellis, *The Daughters of England*, p. 315; 'Rights and wrongs of women', p. 159.
19 Sandford, *Woman, in her Social and Domestic Character*, p. 13.
20 Ibid., p. 157.
21 'The probable retrogression of women', p. 11.
22 Webb, *My Apprenticeship*, pp. 350–1.
23 *Minute Book of the Chichester Literary Society and Mechanics' Institute*, Annual Meeting Report (4 October 1876).
24 Burgon, *To Educate Young Women Like Young Men*, p. 17.
25 Grey, 'Men and women', p. 673.
26 Davidoff and Hall, *Family Fortunes*, Chapter 3.
27 Gisborne, *An Enquiry into the Duties of the Female Sex*, p. 2.
28 Comte, *A General View of Positivism* p. 226; Harrison, *Realities and Ideals*, p. 75.
29 Ruskin, *Sesame and Lilies*, pp. 147–8.
30 Walker, *Women Physiologically Considered*, p. 43; Greg, 'Why are women redundant?' p. 339.
31 *RYUMI* (Leeds, Edward Baines and Sons, 1852), p. 67.
32 Smiles, *Character*, p. 299.
33 'The English Woman's Journal', p. 370.
34 Brown, *Young Men and Maidens*, quoted in Banks and Banks, *Feminism and Family Planning*, p. 59.
35 Davidoff and Hall, *Family Fortunes*, p. 182.
36 Ellis, *The Wives of England*, p. 95; A Widowed Wife, *A Whisper to a Newly Married Pair*, p. 79.
37 Oxiensis, 'The education of women', p. 547.
38 Quoted in Basch, *Relative Creatures*, p. 6. See also Christ, 'Victorian masculinity and the angel in the house'.
39 Lewis, *Woman's Mission*, pp. 132–3.
40 Banks, *Faces of Feminism*, p. 91.
41 Engels, *The Origin of the Family*.
42 See, for example, De Beauvoir, *The Second Sex*, pp. 85–7; Hall and Himmelweit, *Development of Family and Work in Capitalist Society*, pp. 44–5.
43 Taylor, *Eve and the New Jerusalem*, p. 193.
44 See, for example, Hall and Himmelweit, *Development of Family and Work*, p. 45.
45 See, for example, the discussion offered in Foucault, *Discipline and Punishment*.
46 A Retired Governess ... , *A Legacy of Affection, Advice and Instruction*, p. 145; Burgon, *To Educate Young Women*, p. 29; 'Her strength is in her weakness', p. 100.
47 See Taylor, *Eve and the New Jerusalem*.
48 Wollstonecraft, *Vindication of the Rights of Woman*, pp. 108–9.
49 Thompson, *Appeal of One Half the Human Race*, pp. 79, 66, 196, 199; Reid, *A Plea*

for Woman, p. 175.

50 Rossi (ed.), *Essays on Sex Equality*, attributes *The Subjection of Women* (see note 51) to both J. S. Mill and H. Taylor; Eisenstein, *The Radical Future*, Chapter 6; Banks, *The Biographical Dictionary of British Feminists*, pp. 208–10.

51 Mill, *The Subjection of Women*, p. 1.

52 *English Woman's Journal* (1 August 1858), p. 364.

53 Repr. in Cobbe, *The Duties of Women*, pp. 31–2.

54 Woodward, *Men, Women and Progress*, p. 151.

55 See the useful discussion in Banks, *Faces and Feminism*, Chapter 6. D. Thompson, 'Women, work and politics in nineteenth-century England; in Rendall (ed.), p. 80, discussing the 'masculinisation' of the public sector and the 'feminisation' of the private sphere, suggests that the 'strange ideology of the moral superiority of women' (which rested partly on the concept of the home as a haven of purity), far from raising the status of women in any but the most marginal areas, must, for those who subscribed to it, have 'lowered' her authority, since women who worked outside home and family were in a sense 'automatically degraded' by that very fact.

56 Thorburn, *Female Education from a Physiological Point of View*, p. 10.

57 Smiles, *Character*, p. 57.

58 Arnot, 'Male hegemony, social class and women's education', p. 66.

59 Eisenstein, *The Radical Future*, p. 129.

60 See, for example, Davidoff, *The Best Circles*; Jalland, *Women, Marriage and Politics 1860–1914.*, Chapter 1.

61 Grey, *On the Education of Women*, p. 19.

62 Davies, Speech at a Conference held at Liverpool, p. 26; Davidoff, in *The Best Circles*, p. 50, notes that by the middle of the nineteenth century the rules of chaperonage were very strict.

63 Quoted in Woodham-Smith, *Florence Nightingale 1820–1910*, p. 35, to describe the boredom and uselessness that many young middle-class women, such as Florence Nightingale, felt about their existence at home. Miss Nightingale's father was an 'English country gentleman' (p. 6).

64 A Mother, 'Defects in the moral training of girls', p. 86.

65 *The New Moral World* (12 January 1839), p. 178; *Englishwoman's Journal* (1 October 1858), p. 81; Ruskin, *Sesame and Lilies*, p. 168.

66 Bryant, *The Unexpected Revolution*, pp. 35–40; J. Rendall, *The Origins of Modern Feminism*, Chapter 5.

67 *The Englishwoman's Review* (15 November 1880), p. 52: presumably such 'young ladies' had well-spoken voices.

68 Peel, *Life's Enchanted Cup*, p. 62. See also the discussion of the 'modern girl' in Gorham, *The Victorian Girl*, pp. 56–8.

69 Ellis, *The Wives of England*, p. 261.

70 Parkes, *Essays*, p. 74; Grey, *Idols of Society*, p. 7.

71 Ellis, *Education of the Heart*, pp. 14–15.

72 Banks and Banks, *Feminism and Family Planning*, p. 58.

73 A Widowed Wife, *A Whisper*, p. 118; Sandford, *Women*, p. 2.

74 *Woman's Worth, or Hints to Raise the Female Character*, p. 120.

75 Banks and Banks, *Feminism and Family Planning*, p. 65.

76 Beeton, *The Book of Household Management*, p. 1.

77 Carpenter, *Love's Coming-of-Age*, pp. 43–4.

78 Vicinus, 'Introduction: the perfect Victorian lady', p. ix.

79 Banks and Banks, *Feminism and Family Planning*, p. 65.

80 Vicinus, 'Introduction: the perfect Victorian lady', p. ix; Vicinus, *Independent*

Women; D. Rubinstein, *Before the Suffragettes*, pp. 17–19.

81 *Punch*, (14 July 1894), p. 22, quoted in Rubinstein, ibid., p. 17.

82 Cobbe, 'The little health of ladies', pp. 280–1.

83 Grey, *Idols of Society*, p. 7.

84 Gaskell, *Mary Barton*; Gaskell, *Ruth*.

85 Basch, *Relative Creatures*, pp. 184, 247.

86 D. Hudson, *Munby, Man of Two Worlds*, p. 371; for a fascinating account of the relationship between Munby and Hannah, see Davidoff, 'Class and gender in Victorian England'.

87 Taylor, in *The Present of a Mistress to a Young Servant*, p. 124, warned 'a dressy servant is a disgrace to a house, and renders her employers ridiculous, as well as herself .... Dressy girls are not aware, how vulgar they appear, and how very far from *genteel* (if this is their aim).' Horn, in *The Rise and Fall of the Victorian Servant*, p. 113, notes that female servants were usually expected to find their own clothes – lilac, blue or pink cotton working-dresses with white aprons and caps for the mornings, and in the afternoons, at least for housemaids and parlourmaids, a formal black dress, worn with frilled apron and cap. Jewellery was not permitted.

88 Austin, *Two letters on Girls' Schools and on the Training of Working Women*, p. 26.

89 Gaskell, *Artisans and Machinery*, p. 127; reported in a speech by Lord Ashley to the House of Commons, 15 March 1844, (Hansard 1844, vol. LXXIII, col. 1095).

90 Ibid., col. 1096.

91 Neff, *Victorian Working Women*, pp. 57–8; Stephens, *Education, Literaracy and Society*, p. 264.

92 Engels, *The Condition of the Working Class in England in 1844*, p. 113.

93 Greg, 'Why are women redundant?', pp. 373–4.

94 Engels, *The Condition*, p. 147.

95 Ingestre, *Social Evils*, p. 12; PP (1840) XXIV, p. 75.

96 Greg, 'Why are women redundant?', p. 373; J. Hole, *The Homes of the Working Classes*, p. 116.

97 Calder, 'Cookery in elementary schools', p. 134.

98 Austin, *Two Letters*, p. 25.

99 Sigsworth and Wyke, in 'A study of Victorian prostitution and venereal disease', p. 87, note that all the available evidence suggests that a supply of prostitutes was drawn from the working classes while the demand upon which contemporary opinion concentrated came from the wealthier classes of society. Thus prostitution not only satisfied the sexual appetites of the middle-class male, but also performed the important social function of preserving the 'virgins' of the wealthier classes and shielding their married women from the grosser passions of their husbands, though at a considerable risk of infection with venereal diseases. For a discussion of the way middle-class women became involved in rescue work with prostitutes and fallen women and thus helped to maintain the distinction between 'pure' and 'impure' women, see J. L'Esperance, 'Women's mission to woman'. Ehrenreich and English, in *Complaints and Disorders*, pp. 19–67, suggest that women of the upper classes in the nineteenth century were seen as 'sick' while women of the working classes were seen as 'sickening'.

100 Hudson, *Munby*, p. 171; Anderson, 'Sex in mind and education', p. 585.

101 Blackwell, *How to Keep a Household in Health*, pp. 5–6; Milne, *Industrial and Social Position of Women in the Middle and Lower Ranks*, p. 156.

102 See note 82.

103 Ford, *Women's Wages*, p. 4. The phrase 'the drudge' appears to have been particularly applied to general domestic servants; see, for example, Hudson, *Munby*, p. 124, where Munby refers to Hannah as 'a mere kitchen drudge', and 'Maids-of-all-work and Blue Books', p. 281, where maids-of-all-work or general maids are referred to as 'our poor little household drudges'.

104 A. Davin, '"Mind that you do as you are told"', p. 90.

105 PP (1843) XVI, pp. 25–6.

106 Brewer, 'Workhouse visiting', pp. 298–300.

107 Hewitt, *Wives and Mothers*, p. 77.

108 *Annals of the Poor*, p. 1.

109 Ibid., p. 16.

110 *Household Proverbs for Women*, pp. 5–6.

111 Ibid., p. 15.

112 Ibid., pp. 8–9.

113 Ibid., p. 9.

114 Booth, *On the Female Education of the Industrial Classes*, p. 12.

115 Ibid., p. 12.

Chapter 4   Schooling and Working-class Girls

1 See, for example, Birchenough, *History of Elementary Education*; Sturt, *The Education of the People*; Wardle, *English Popular Education*; Johnson, *Derbyshire Village Schools*; Hurt, *Education in Evolution*; Hurt, *Elementary Schooling*; Gardner, *The Lost Elementary Schools of Victorian England*.

2 The few accounts include Purvis, 'The double burden of class and gender'; Purvis, 'The experience of schooling for working-class boys and girls in nineteenth century England'; and M. Gomersal, 'Ideals and realities'. Other accounts about the schooling of working-class girls in the nineteenth century have focused mainly on the post-1870 situation – see, for example, Dyhouse, 'Social Darwinistic ideas'; Dyhouse, 'Good wives and little mothers'; Dyhouse, 'Towards a "feminine" curriculum for English schoolgirls'; Davin, '"Mind that you do as you are told"'; Dyhouse, *Girls Growing Up*; Purvis, 'Domestic subjects since 1870'; Turnbull, 'Learning her womanly work'.

3 Delamont, 'The contradictions in ladies' education'; Purvis, 'Class and gender in the schooling of working-class girls', p. 98.

4 See Delamont, 'The contradictions in ladies' education' and 'The domestic ideology and women's education'; Bryant, *The Unexpected Revolution*, pp. 30–3; Pedersen, 'The reform of women's secondary and higher education', p. 193; David, *The State, The Family and Education*, p. 22; Dyhouse, *Girls Growing Up*, Chapter 2; Gorham, *The Victorian Girl*, pp. 20–4.

5 Dyhouse, ibid., p. 40.

6 Purvis, 'Towards a history', p. 51.

7 Bryant, *The Unexpected Revolution*, p. 40.

8 Delamont, 'The domestic ideology and women's education', p. 164; Turnbull, 'Learning her womanly work', p. 83; Purvis, 'The double burden'; Digby and Searby, *Children, School and Society in Nineteenth-Century England*, p. 46; Beddoe, *Discovering Women's History*, p. 52; Gomersal, 'Ideals and realities'.

9 Laqueur, 'Working-class demand and the growth of English elementary education, 1750–1850', p. 199.

10 R. Johnson, 'Elementary education', p. 8.

11 Dawes, *Mechanics' Institutes and Popular Education*, pp. 17–18.

12 Kay-Shuttleworth, *Four Periods of Public Education*, p. 102.
13 R. Aldrich, 'Educating our mistresses', p. 96. For plait and lace schools, see Kitteringham, *Country Girls in 19th Century England*, pp. 60-8, and Horn, *The Victorian Country Child*, pp. 97-108. For factory schools, see Chapter 2, note 54.
14 Gardner, *The Lost Elementary Schools*, p. 46.
15 Quoted in ibid., p. 48.
16 *Census of Great Britain 1851, Education* (England and Wales), p. xxxvi.
17 Ibid., p. xxxvii.
18 Ibid., p. xxxvii.
19 Pole, *A History of the Origins and Progress of Adult Schools*, p. 66.
20 Quoted in McCann, 'Popular education, socialisation and social control', p. 4.
21 Bruce, *Anna Swanwick*, pp. 43-4.
22 Aldrich, 'Educating our mistresses', p. 96.
23 Quoted in Gardner, *The Lost Elementary Schools*, p. 50.
24 *Census of Great Britain 1851, Education*, p. xxix.
25 Rubinstein, *School Attendance in London*, p. 56; Merson, *Once There Was*, p. 41.
26 Lawson, *Letters to the Young on Progress in Pudsey During the Last Sixty Years*, p. 65.
27 Anderson, *Family Structure in Nineteenth-Century Lancashire*, p. 76. See also Davin, 'Child labour, the working-class family, and domestic ideology in 19th century Britain'.
28 Mayhew, *London Labour and the London Poor*, vol. 2, p. 314.
29 PP (1867) XXII, p. 114.
30 Layton, 'Memories of seventy years', p. 4. Merryweather, *Experience of Factory Life*, p. 13; Madoc-Jones, in 'Patterns of attendance and their social significance', p. 47, found that 'Helping at home and child minding' was the reason given for 10 per cent of girls leaving school but only 1 per cent of the boys. The most common reason given for boys leaving (57 per cent) was 'Work' and for girls (35.5 per cent) 'Unspecified'. Madoc-Jones suggests that the category 'Unspecified' probably included many heading for work or helping at home.
31 Pinchbeck, *Women Workers*, p. 108.
32 Quoted in Johnson, *Derbyshire Village Schools*, p. 193.
33 Mitchell (ed.), *The Hard Way Up*, pp. 42-3.
34 E. Roberts, 'Learning and living', p. 16.
35 Tilly and Scott, *Women, Work and Family*, p. 31.
36 Field, 'Private schools in Portsmouth and Southampton, 1850-1870', p. 11.
37 Gardner, *The Lost Elementary Schools*, p. 64; Laqueur, 'Working-class demand', p. 197.
38 Purvis, 'Women and teaching', p. 365; Gardner, *The Lost Elementary Schools*, p. 128.
39 Barnard, *A History of English Education from 1760*, p. 2; Sutherland, *Elementary Education in the Nineteenth Century*, p. 12.
40 PP (1867-8) XVII, pp. 390, 294.
41 Gardner, *The Lost Elementary Schools*, p. 22; Laqueur, 'Working-class demand', p. 197.
42 McCann, 'Popular education', p. 29.
43 Lacqueur, 'Working-class demand', p. 199.
44 Gardner, *The Lost Elementary Schools*, p. 211.
45 Ibid., p. 20.
46 T. Cooper, *The Life of Thomas Cooper*, p. 7; *Minutes of the Committee of Council of Education (1841-42).* p. 260.
47 M. Smith, *The Autobiography of Mary Smith*, pp. 24-5.

48 Gardner, *The Lost Elementary Schools*, p. 113.

49 Kitteringham, in *Country Girls*, p. 60; Stephens, *Education, Literacy and Society*, p. 176, notes that in Bedfordshire in the 1840s it was difficult to establish girls' National schools since parents had a preference for lace and plait schools. At this time there were no girls' National schools in Luton, Dunstable or Leighton Buzzard.

50 Horn, *The Victorian Country Child*, p. 97.

51 Hurt, *Elementary Schooling*, p. 4.

52 Jones, *The Charity School Movement*, p. 144; Lacqueur, *Religion and Respectability*, p. 4.

53 Ibid., p. 143.

54 Laqueur, *Religion and Respectability*, pp. 33, 189, 239, 189. For a critique of Lacqueur's claim that by the early nineteenth century Sunday schools were expressions of working-class culture, see M. Dick, 'The myth of the working-class Sunday school', and 'Religion and the origins of mass schooling'.

55 Laqueur, 'Working-class demand', p. 201.

56 Quoted by Horn in *Education in Rural England*, p. 32.

57 Laqueur, *Religion and Respectability*, pp. 99–100.

58 Lacqueur, *Religion and Respectability*, Chapter 5; McCann, in 'Popular education, socialisation and social control', pp. 10–11, notes that at Spitalfields Wesleyan Methodist Sunday School writing was considered a privilege of which about one in five of the children were allowed to partake. Frith, in 'Socialisation and rational schooling: elementary education in Leeds before 1870', in McCann (ed.) p. 82, notes that the flourishing state of the Sunday schools administered by the New Connexion and Protestant Methodists in Leeds in 1833 was attributed to the fact that they taught writing while other Sunday schools in the city did not.

59 Laqueur, *Religion and Respectability*, p. 250.

60 Ure, *The Philosophy of Manufactures*, p. 411.

61 Farningham, *A Working Woman's Life*, p. 44.

62 Laqueur, *Religion and Respectability*, pp. 117–8.

63 Quoted in E. P. Thompson, *The Making*, p. 415.

64 Quoted in John, *By the Sweat of their Brow*, p. 41.

65 Lacqueur, *Religion and Respectability*, p. 123.

66 Lawson and Silver, *A Social History of Education in England*, p. 181; Birchenough, *History of Elementary Education*, p. 15; Simon, in 'Was there a charity school movement?' is critical of the tendency of Jones, in *The Charity School Movement*, to put together all forms of free education for the poor under the term 'charity' school. Simon suggests that the 'charity school movement' involved three different types of school – the parish school with a few free places for the poor, the charity school specifically designed to relieve the problem of urban poverty, and the catechetical school with strong Anglican overtones.

67 See, for example, *The Reports of the Society for Bettering the Condition and Increasing the Comforts of the Poor* (London, W. Bulmer and Co., 1800), vol. II, pp. 9–10: 'It is the endeavour of the society ... to search for and disseminate "useful and practical knowledge with regard to the poor"'; Jones, *The Charity School Movement*, Chapter 1.

68 *The Reports of the Society for Bettering the Condition and Increasing the Comforts of the Poor*, 1800, p. 308.

69 W. Davis, *Hints to Philanthropists*, p. 152.

70 Cappe, *Account of Two Charity Schools for the Education of Girls*, p. 17.

71 Firth, 'Socialisation and rational schooling', p. 69.

72 *The Fifth Report of the Society for Bettering the Condition and Increasing the Comforts of the Poor*, 3rd edn (London, W. Bulmer, 1798), p. 275.
73 Gordon, *Demands for the Education of Girls, 1790–1865*, p. 111.
74 PP (1850) XLIII, vol. III, p. 8.
75 Ibid., pp. 10–11.
76 Davis, *Hints*, p. 27.
77 Ibid., p. 26.
78 Ibid., p. 11.
79 Ibid., p. 11.
80 Ibid., p. 16.
81 See note 51.
82 *Eleventh Annual Report of the National Society for Promoting the Education of the Poor in the Principles of the Established Church* (London, 1822), List of Committee and Officers of the Society.
83 *First Annual Report of the National Society for Promoting the Education of the Poor in the Principles of the Established Church*, (London, 1812), p. 18.
84 *Annual Report of the National Society* (London, 1841), quoted in Gomersal, 'Ideals and realities' p. 43, and *National Society Monthly Papers* (1862) quoted in Johnson, *The Education of Girls in Derby and Derbyshire 1800–1930*, p. 77.
85 Birchenough, *History of Elementary Education*, pp. 51–2.
86 Johnson, *Derbyshire Village Schools*, p. 33.
87 *First Annual Report of the National Society, 1812*, p. 36.
88 Merson, *Once There Was*, p. 9.
89 *First Annual Report of the National Society, 1812*, p. 36.
90 Gadd, *Victorian Logs*, p. 128.
91 *First Annual Report of the National Society, 1812*, p. 36.
92 Burgess, 'Educational history of the National Society', p. 56; Table 4.1 of this chapter.
93 *Second Annual Report of the National Society for Promoting the Education of the Poor in the Principles of the Established Church*, (London, 1814), p. 194.
94 PP (1845) XXXV, pp. 78–9.
95 PP (1867) XXII, Appendix I, p. 234.
96 Ibid., p. 178.
97 Ibid., p. 65; Merson, *Once There Was*, p. 7.
98 PP (1870) XXII, Appendix I on elementary schools, pp. 153–4.
99 Quoted in Gomersal, 'Ideals and realities', p. 44.
100 PP (1870) XXII, Appendix I, pp. 28–9, 67.
101 Quoted in Dawes, *Effective Primary Instruction*, p. 79.
102 PP (1867) XXII, Appendix I, pp. 233, 86.
103 Arnold, *Reports on Elementary Schools 1852–1882*, p. 17.
104 *Second Annual Report of the National Society, 1814*, p. 195.
105 Horn, *Education in Rural England*, pp. 42–3.
106 Ibid., p. 43.
107 Gomersal, 'Ideals and realities', p. 45.
108 *Reports of Special Assistant Commissioners on the Employment of Women and Children in Agriculture*, p. 203.
109 Horn, *Education in Rural England*, p. 35.
110 Gordon, *Demands for the Education of Girls*, p. 107. See also Binns, *A Century of Education*, p. 78.
111 *Report of the British and Foreign School Society*, (London, Bensley and Son, 1819), p. 101. See also the 1846 report of HMI Joseph Fletcher, repr. in Digby and Searby (eds), pp. 77–9.

112 *Fifty-Ninth Report of the British and Foreign School Society* (London, J. and W. Rider, 1864), p. vii.

113 *Report of the British and Foreign School Society to the General Meeting, May 1816* (London, R. and A. Taylor, 1816), p. 29; *17th Report of the British and Foreign School Society* (London, R. and A. Taylor, 1822), p. 84.

114 *Report of the British and Foreign School Society, 1819*, p. 55; *Fifty-Ninth Report of the British and Foreign Society* (1864), p. 54.

115 *17th Report of the British and Foreign School Society, 1822*, p. 76; *Twenty-Eighth Report of the British and Foreign School Society* (London, S. Bagester Jun., 1833), p. 8.

116 *Report of the British and Foreign School Society* (London, R. and A. Taylor, 1818), p. 38.

117 *Report of the British and Foreign School Society* (London, R. and A. Taylor, 1820), p. 29.

118 *20th Report of the British and Foreign School Society* (London, R. and A. Taylor, 1825), p. 58.

119 *Report of the British and Foreign School Society* (London, R. and A. Taylor, 1824), p. 76.

120 *22nd Report of the British and Foreign School Society* (London, J. B. G. Vogel, 1827), p. 57.

121 Sturt, *The Education of the People*, pp. 30–7.

122 PP (1845) XXXV, p. 69.

123 Ibid., p. 69. Purvis, in 'The experience of schooling', p. 103, cites examples where monitors played with pupils and accepted bribes.

124 Goldstrom, 'The content of education and the socialisation of the working-class child 1830–1860', in McCann (ed.), pp. 100–3.

125 Birchenough, *History of Elementary Education*, p. 255.

126 Ibid., p. 256.

127 Purvis, 'The double burden', p. 110; Ball, in 'Practical subjects in mid-Victorian elementary schools', p. 115, notes practical work was always less generally popular for boys than for girls; Digby and Searby, p. 34, point out that in the 1840s and 1850s girls might be excluded from geography or more advanced mathematics in elementary schools because of the socially perceived need for them to be instructed in plain needlework; Stephens, in *Education, Literacy and Society*, p. 18, notes that by the mid-nineteenth century the school curriculum for girls was less directed to writing than that for boys. One survey of pupils in 1857, for example, found that 62 per cent of boys but only 56 per cent of girls were learning to write, although the proportions learning to read were about the same.

128 *The Normal Schools of the British and Foreign Society (Female Department)* ([printed by the Society], 1854), p., 17.

129 Horn, *The Victorian Country Child*, p. 41.

130 Birchenough, *History of Elementary Education*, pp. 301–2.

131 Horn, *Education in Rural England*, p. 126.

132 Horn, *The Victorian Country Child*, p. 42.

133 Lawson and Silver, *A Social History of Education in England*, pp. 321–2: education was made compulsory in 1880 up to the age of 13 with exemptions from the age of ten (raised to 11 in 1893 and 12 in 1899); the 1891 Act enabled elementary schools to admit children free and claim a fee grant in compensation.

Chapter 5 Women and the Mechanics' Institute Movement

1 J. Hole, *An Essay on the History and Management of Literary, Scientific and Mechanics' Institutions*, p. 5. Kelly, in *A History of Adult Education*, pp. 118–19, traces the events leading directly to the movement to free classes for mechanics offered from 1799 to 1804 by Dr George Birbeck, Professor of Natural Philosophy at Anderson's Institution, Glasgow.

2 Tylecote, *The Mechanics' Institutes*, p. 57.

3 Baines, *The Life of Edward Baines*, p. 126; Harrison, *Learning and Living*, p. 60.

4 Green, *History of the Nottingham Mechanics' Institution*, p. 1; Tylecote, *The Mechanics' Institutes*, pp. 129–30; Slight, *A Chronicle History of Portsmouth*, p. 12.

5 Smith, *Conflict and Compromise*, pp. 81, 139.

6 Tylecote, *The Mechanics' Institute*, p. 225.

7 Duppa, *A Manual for Mechanics' Institutions*, p. 12.

8 Hole, *An Essay*, p. 35.

9 Tylecote, *The Mechanics' Institutes*, pp. 114–15.

10 W. T., 'To the members and managers of the mechanics' institutions in Britain and Ireland', *The Co-operative Magazine* (January–February 1826), p. 46.

11 Taylor, *Eve and the New Jerusalem*, p. 233.

12 Detrosier, *An Address Delivered at the New Mechanics' Institution*, pp. 11–13.

13 Wise, *Speech Delivered at the Opening of the New Mechanics' Institution*, pp. 40–1.

14 Searle, 'Huddersfield', p. 239.

15 Harrison, *Learning and Living*, pp. 119–20.

16 Hole, *An Essay*, p. 36.

17 Duppa, *A Manual*, p. 143.

18 Kelly, *George Birkbeck, Pioneer of Adult Education*, pp. 208, 259.

19 Ibid., p. 230.

20 A letter to the editor of the *Mechanic's Magazine* (12 June 1830), pp. 250–1.

21 Kelly, *George Birkbeck*, p. 86; Kelly, *A History of Adult Education*, p. 117.

22 For discussion of 'skilled', see Phillips and Taylor, 'Sex and skill', p. 79, where they note that skill definitions are saturated with sexual bias: 'The work of women is often deemed inferior simply because it is women who do it.'

23 Rowbotham, *Hidden from History*, p. 12.

24 Tynan, 'Lewes Mechanics' Institution', p. 15.

25 Taylor, *Eve and the New Jerusalem*, p. 233.

26 *RYUMI* (Leeds, Edward Baines and Sons, 1850), p. 24.

27 Ibid., p. 37.

28 Kelly, *George Birkbeck*, p. 126.

29 Quoted by David Johnston in his address to the 'Annual soiree of the Huddersfield Female Educational Institute', *The Huddersfield Examiner* 29 October 1864.

30 Ibid.

31 Hole, *An Essay*, p. 39.

32 Tylecote, *The Mechanics' Institutes*, p. 264. The female institute at Keighley was called the Keighley Female Improvement Society; however, it was affiliated to the Yorkshire Union of Mechanics' Institutes and regarded as an institute.

33 'Education amongst the working women of Huddersfield and Bradford', p. 185.

34 See, for example, reports of committee meetings for 8 April 1857 and 23 May 1864 in HFEI, *Minute Book*.

35 Dyhouse, *Girls Growing Up*, pp. 64–5.

36 *RYUMI* (Leeds, Edward Baines, 1862), p. 83; HFEI, *Minute Book*, Annual Meeting 8 April 1857; *RYUMI* (1860), p. 71.

37 *RYUMI* (1860), p. 71; *RYUMI* (1862), p. 84.

38 Pedersen, 'The reform of women's secondary and higher education', p. 62.

39 *JWEU* (15 December 1878), advertisement for the National Union.

40 Hertz, 'Mechanics' institutes for working women'.

41 Kelly, *George Birkbeck*, p. 258.

42 Ibid., p. 207.

43 Ibid., p. 212.

44 Ibid., footnote, p. 207: it is suggested that the majority of the literary and scientific institutions were not middle class in character, though a few in London were apparently so.

45 Ibid., p. 259: Kelly estimates that there were 698 mechanics' and literary and scientific institutes in existence in 1851.

46 For example, Hudson, in *The History of Adult Education*, p. vi, suggests that there were 102,050 members of literary and mechanics' institutions in England in 1851, nearly double the number I arrive at.

47 Tylecote, in *The Mechanics' Institutes*, p. 265, estimates that there were about 1,200 women members in Yorkshire Institutes in 1849 and about half that number in Lancashire.

48 *Census of Great Britain 1851, Education* (England and Wales), pp. 215–58.

49 Tylecote, *The Mechanics' Institutes*, p. 83.

50 This division by size of membership is found in Kelly, *George Birkbeck*, p. 264.

51 *Census 1851, Education*, p. 243, 249, 227.

52 Kelly, *George Birkbeck*, p. 264.

53 *Census 1851, Education*, pp. 224, 246, 230.

54 *RYUMI* (1850), Tabular View.

55 See Chapter 5.

56 See, for example, Hudson, *The History of Adult Education*, p. 131.

57 O'Brien, *Women's Liberation in Labour History*, p. 4.

58 As we shall later see, working-class women were to be found mainly in the small institutes in the north. For the failure to attract large numbers of working-class men, especially in southern England, see Ludlow and Jones, *Progress of the Working Class*, p. 174; Kelly, *A History of Adult Education*, p. 126; Roderick and Stephens, *Post-School Education*, p. 176.

59 Tylecote, *The Mechanics' Institutes*, p. 265.

60 *MMI, Annual Report* (Manchester, Cave and Sever, 1846), p. ix.

61 Ibid., p. 42.

62 MMI, *Annual Report* (1863), p. 13; *Annual Report* (1864), p. 12; *Annual Report* (1866), p. 14.

63 MMI, *Annual Report* (1866), p. 12.

64 Tylecote, *The Mechanics' Institutes*, p. 265.

65 *RYUMI* (Leeds, Edward Baines and Sons, 1846), p. 50.

66 Tylecote, *The Mechanics' Institutes*, p. 75.

67 *RYUMI* (Leeds, Edward Baines and Sons, 1861), p. 97; *RYUMI* (Leeds, Edward Baines and Sons, 1857), p. 91.

68 *RYUMI* (1859), p. 101.

69 Kelly, *A History of Adult Education*, p. 198. Much more research needs to be undertaken about the southern mechanics' institutes.

70 Basingstoke Mechanics' Institution, *Sixteenth Annual Report* (1857), p. 2.

71 Alton Mechanics' Institute, *Minute Book*, reports of meeting 13 September 1886 and 9 October 1888.

72 Ibid., reports of meetings held 19 October 1891 and 5 May 1892.
73 *RYUMI* (1846), p. 48; *RYUMI* (1847), p. 14.
74 *RYUMI* (1850), p. 24, Tabular View.
75 *RYUMI* (Leeds, Edward Baines and Sons, 1862), p. 102; HFEI, *Book of Pupil Entries*, entries for 1866.
76 *RYUMI* (Leeds, Edward Baines and Sons, 1858), p. 96.
77 *RYUMI* (1859), p. 92; Hemming, *Adult Education in Huddersfield*, p. 157.
78 *The Huddersfield Examiner*, 29 October 1864.
79 'Education amongst the working women of Huddersfield and Bradford', p. 184.
80 Hertz, 'Mechanics' institutes for working women', p. 352.
81 Ibid., p. 353.
82 *RYUMI* (1862), p. 83.
83 Ibid., p. 124.
84 *RYUMI* (1859), Tabular View.
85 *RYUMI* (1862), p. 84.
86 Ibid., p. 84.
87 *RYUMI* (1857), p. 25.
88 *RYUMI* (Leeds, Edward Baines and Sons, 1852), Tabular View.
89 *Census 1851, Education*, p. 227.
90 Kelly, *George Birkbeck*, p. 126; Tynan, 'Lewes Mechanics' Institution', p. 15; MMI, *Annual Report* (Manchester, William Simpson, 1838), p. 69.
91 *Rules and Regulations of the Andover Mechanics' Institution for the Diffusion of Useful Knowledge*, p. 9; *RYUMI* (1846), p. 35.
92 *RYUMI* (1847), pp. 62–3.
93 See notes 90 and 99.
94 Duppa, *A Manual*, p. 143, my emphasis.
95 *RYUMI* (1860), p. 87.
96 Kelly, *George Birkbeck*, pp. 238–9.
97 *The Poor Man's Guardian* 14 September 1833, p. 293; *The Regenerator*, 2 November 1839, p. 19.
98 MMI, *Annual Report* (1838), p. 34.
99 MMI, *Annual Report* (1862), p. 13. Traice, *Hand-Book of Mechanics' Institutions*, p. 106; Powell, *A History of the County of Essex*, p. 317.
100 *RYUMI* (1857), p. 70.
101 Harrison, *Learning and Living*, p. 31.
102 See Rendall, "A moral engine?".
103 MMI, *Annual Report* (Manchester, A. Ireland and Co., 1861), pp. 11–12, 23.
104 *RYUMI* (1861), p. 76.
105 MMI, *Annual Report 1828 with the Rules and Regulations of the Institution* (Manchester, R. Robinson, 1828), pp. 24–5.
106 Tylecote, *The Mechanics' Institutes*, p. 137.
107 MMI, *Annual Report* (1862), pp. 10, 15.
108 Blackburn, *Women's Suffrage*, p. 20; Stephen, *Emily Davies*, pp. 41–2, 50–1; Herstein, *A Mid-Victorian Feminist*, pp. 78–80; Lacey, 'Introduction', in *Barbara Leigh Smith and the Langham Place Group*.
109 Kelly, *George Birkbeck*, p. 219; Thomas, in 'The mechanics' institutes of the Home Counties', p. 70, notes that at Luton, where straw-hat manufacturers constituted one-third of the committee of the institute in 1846, women were not allowed to vote.
110 *Rules, By-Laws and Regulations of the Worksop Reading Society and Mechanics' Institute*, p. 19; *Rules of the Worksop Reading Society and Mechanics' Institute* (Worksop, Francis

Sissons, 1831), p. 7.

111 Kelly, *George Birkbeck*, p. 219.

112 Ibid., pp. 246–7; Duppa, *A Manual*, p. 143.

113 *RYUMI* (Leeds, Edward Baines and Sons, 1848), p. 43; *RYUMI* (1846), p. 37.

114 Kelly, *George Birkbeck*, p. 126; a similar situation prevailed at Wakefield Mechanics' Institute: *RYUMI* (Leeds, Edward Baines, 1847), p. 72, notes that at Wakefield a rule had 'lately passed, allowing members to send their sons under 14, and any females of their family, to any class, without other charge than the class fee.'

115 Dyer, 'Nineteenth-century community centres', p. 19.

116 Hole, *An Essay*, pp. 39–40.

117 *RYUMI* (1848), p. 60.

118 HFEI, *Minute Book*, Annual Meeting 23 May 1864.

119 *Rules of the Bradford Female Educational Institute*, p. 3.

120 Ibid., pp. 2–3.

121 Godwin, 'The Bradford Mechanics' Institute', p. 340.

122 *Rules of the Bradford Female Educational Institute*, p. 2.

123 Hertz, 'Mechanics' institutes for working women', p. 352.

124 *RYUMI* (1861), p. 102; Hughes, *The History of the Township of Meltham, near Huddersfield*, p. 231.

125 Traice, *Hand-Book*, p. 36.

126 MMI, *Annual Report* (1846), p. 21; *RYUMI* (1857), p. 91; Hill, *National Education*, p. 201.

127 MMI, *Annual Report* (Manchester, Harrison and Crosfield, 1835), p. 30, and *Annual Report* (1838), p. 2; *RYUMI* (1860), p. 82.

128 Traice, *Hand-Book*.

129 Silverstone, 'Accountancy', p. 20.

130 MMI, *Annual Report* (1862), pp. 14–15.

131 *The Manchester Examiner and Times* (1 March 1878), p. 4.

132 Pankhurst, *The Suffragette Movement*, pp. 12, 34–52; entries for Richard Pankhurst and Lydia Becker in Banks, *The Biographical Dictionary of British Feminists*; Romero, *E. Sylvia Pankhurst*, p. 39. Lydia Becker also edited the *Women's Suffrage Journal* until her death, by suicide, in 1890.

133 *The Manchester Examiner and Times* (1 March 1878), p. 4.

134 Pankhurst, *The Suffragette Movement*, p. 15.

135 Blackburn, *Women's Suffrage*, pp. 139–88; Pankhurst, *The Suffragette Movement*, p. 15.

136 Blackburn, *Women's Suffrage*, p. 145; for an analysis of the relationship between political and educational rights for women in the nineteenth century, see Aldrich, 'Educating our mistresses'.

137 Liddington and Norris, *One Hand Tied Behind Us*, pp. 26, 75.

Chapter 6   An Institute Education

1 Duppa, *A Manual*, p. 143.

2 Tylecote, *The Mechanics' Institutes*; p. 264.

3 *RYUMI* (1857), p. 121.

4 *RYUMI* (1848), p. 63.

5 MMI, *Annual Report* (1863), p. 13.

6 Dyer, 'Nineteenth century community centres', p. 17; *RYUMI* (1857), p. 117.

7 *RYUMI* (1857), p. 117.

8 *RYUMI* (Leeds, Edward Baines and Sons, 1852), p. 76; *RYUMI* (1850), p. 24.

9 *RYUMI* (1857), p. 93, Tabular View.

10 *RYUMI* (1861), p. 97; MMI *Annual Report* (1846), p. 43.

11 Burns, *Short History of Birbeck*, p. 35.

12 Smiles, 'A work that prospered', p. 387.

13 *Report of the Manchester District Association of Literary and Scientific Associations*, pp. 17–18.

14 *RYUMI* (1850), pp. 72, 48.

15 Merryweather, *Experience of Factory Life*, pp. 39–40.

16 Granger, *Nottingham Mechanics' Institution*, p. 25; *RYUMI* (1857), p. 80; *Plymouth Mechanics' Institute Prospectus Second Half of Session, 1895–96* (Plymouth, W. F. Westcott, at the Frankfort Press, n.d.).

17 Kamm, *Hope Deferred*, p. 175; Purvis, 'Towards a history', pp. 54–5.

18 Purvis, 'Working-class women and adult education', p. 197.

19 Sir Benjamin Heywood in his address at the opening of the new building of the Manchester Mechanics' Institution, quoted in Rev Dr Hook, 'On institutions for adult education', in Ingestre (ed.), p. 27.

20 Banks, *"Onward"*, p. 23.

21 Ibid., p. 24.

22 Hertz, 'Mechanics' institutes for working women', pp. 348–9.

23 Coates, *Report of the State of Literary, Scientific and Mechanics' Institutions in England*, p. 41.

24 See, for example, Wollstonecraft, *Vindication*, p. 287.

25 'The suppressed sex', p. 446.

26 Hole, *An Essay*, p. 39.

27 *RYUMI* (1848), p. 63.

28 Hole, *An Essay*, p. 39.

29 MMI, *Annual Report* (1862), p. 34.

30 MMI, *Annual Report* (1868), p. 11; *Annual Report* (Manchester, Johnson and Rawson, 1871), p. 11.

31 MMI, *Annual Report* (Manchester, A. Ireland and Co., 1881), p. 24.

32 Ibid., p. 25.

33 MMI, *Annual Report* (1863), p. 12.

34 MMI, *Annual Report* (1881), pp. 25, 49.

35 MMI, *Annual Report* (1863), p. 12.

36 MMI, *Annual Report* (1846), p. ix. See Chapter 5, note 60.

37 MMI, *Annual Report* (Manchester, Johnson, Rawson and Co., 1851), p. 7; MMI, *Annual Report* (1846), p. 41.

38 Davidoff, *The Best Circles*, p. 46.

39 Ibid., pp. 49–50.

40 MMI, *Annual Report* (1861), p. 12.

41 Digby, 'New schools for the middle-class girl', p. 5.

42 MMI, *Annual Report* (1861), p. 12.

43 MMI, *Annual Report* (1862), p. 23; *Annual Report* (1869), p. 11.

44 MMI, *Annual Report* (Manchester, Cave and Sever, 1847), p. 44; MMI, *Annual Report* (1846), p. 42.

45 Bryant, *The Unexpected Revolution*, p. 32.

46 Widdowson, *Going Up into the Next Class*, pp. 21–2.

47 Kaye, *A History of Queen's College*, pp. 38, 49.

48 Peterson, 'The Victorian governess: status incongruence in family and society', pp. 9–16.

49 Percival, *The English Miss*, p. 99; Davidoff, L'Esperance and Newby, 'Landscape

with figures', pp. 166–7.

50 MMI, *Annual Report* (1871), p. 9. A school for boys had been opened in 1834 and one for girls a year later; the fees were 4s per quarter for the sons and daughters or sisters and brothers of members of the Institution, and 5s per quarter for all other scholars (see *Annual Report* (1835), p. 31). The schools prospered for some years but then faced difficulties and were discontinued during 1838–9. When classes began in 1846 for young ladies and the 'Commercial and Scientific Day School for Boys' was established in the 1860s, the directors were aiming at a much older clientele than the pupils in the earlier schools.
51 MMI, *Annual Report* (1871), p. 9.
52 Ibid., p. 10.
53 MMI, *Annual Report* (1865), p. 11.
54 Levine, *Victorian Feminism 1850–1900*, p. 35.
55 Stephen, *Emily Davies*, pp. 100–1.
56 PP (1867–8), XXVIII, part I, *Schools Inquiry Commission*, vol. I, 548–9.
57 MMI, *Annual Report* (1869), p. 10.
58 MMI, *Annual Report* (1881), pp. 21–2; *Annual Report* (Manchester, A. Ireland and Co., 1882), p. 22.
59 *Annual Report* (1882), p. 22.
60 For discussion of these issues, see *Union of Lancashire and Cheshire Institutes, 1839–1939, A Hundred Years of Educational Service* (Manchester, 1939), pp. 15–16; Harrison, *Learning and Living*, pp. 213–15; Garner, 'The Society of Arts and the mechanics' institutes'.
61 MMI, *Annual Report* (1882), p. 22.
62 MMI, *Annual Report* (1881), p. 22.
63 Ibid., pp. 20–1.
64 Purvis, 'Domestic subjects from 1870', p. 156.
65 Quoted in Lawson and Silver, *A Social History of Education*, p. 338.
66 Burstall, *The Story of the Manchester High School for Girls 1871–1911*, pp. 35, 24.
67 Ibid., p. 41.
68 MMI, *Annual Report* (1882), p. 18.
69 MMI, *Annual Report* (1881), pp. 5, 21.
70 Blackburn, *Women's Suffrage*, pp. 71–2.
71 Ibid., p. 20; Fawcett, *Women's Suffrage*, p. 22.
72 Delamont, 'The contradictions in ladies' education', p. 141.
73 *RYUMI* (1857), p. 25.
74 *RYUMI* (1859), p. 21 – my emphasis on *man's*.
75 *RYUMI* (1846), pp. 36, 10–11.
76 *RYUMI* (1847), pp. 72–3, 13.
77 *RYUMI* (1848), p. 86.
78 *RYUMI* (1846), p. 36.
79 *RYUMI* (1848), p. 60.
80 Ibid., pp. 50–1.
81 *RYUMI* (1850), p. 70; *RYUMI* (1852), p. 76.
82 *RYUMI* (1861), pp. 78, 103.
83 *RYUMI* (1862), p. 83.
84 Hertz, 'Mechanics' institutes for working women', p. 353.
85 Shepherd (ed.), *Speeches Literary and Social by Charles Dickens*, pp. 163–4.
86 *RYUMI* (1859), p. 93.
87 *RYUMI* (1862), p. 83.
88 Smiles, 'A work that prospered', p. 392.

89 *Union of Lancashire and Cheshire Institutes, 1839–1939, A Hundred Years*, pp. 15–16; MMI, *Annual Report* (1882), p. 27.
90 Green, *History of the Nottingham Mechanics' Institution*, p. 45.
91 Liddington and Norris, *One Hand Tied Behind Us*, p. 102.
92 *RYUMI* (1857), p. 93.
93 *RYUMI* (1861), p. 113.
94 *RYUMI* (1857), p. 102.
95 Best, in *Mid-Victorian Britain 1851–75*, pp. 223–4, notes that within the Victorian family hours weekly, even daily, were devoted to needlework by mothers and daughters with 'any pretensions to gentility: ornamental, strictly *useless* needlework, for the most part; the *useful* stuff, the men's shirts and women's dresses and underwear, was done by working women.'
96 Dyhouse, *Girls Growing Up*, p. 89.
97 *RYUMI* (1846), p. 11; *RYUMI* (1861), p. 104; *RYUMI* (1857), p. 107.
98 Gaskell, *Artisans and Machinery*, p. 175.
99 S. S. [Samuel Smiles], 'The women of the working classes', p. 422.
100 Hertz, 'Mechanics' institutes for working women', p. 349.
101 *RYUMI* (1862), p. 83.
102 *RYUMI* (1860), pp. 16–17.
103 Hewitt, *Wives and Mothers*, pp. 80–1.
104 Dyhouse, *Girls Growing Up*, p. 89.
105 Quoted in Turnbull, 'Learning her womanly work', p. 88.
106 *RYUMI* (1861), pp. 78–9, 113.
107 This appears to have been particularly so at the Huddersfield Female Institute – see table 6.1 of this chapter.
108 MMI, *Annual Report* (1881), pp. 27–8.
109 Hyde, *How to Win Our Workers*, p. 42.
110 Harrison, *Learning and Living*, pp. 213, 212.
111 *RYUMI* (1857), p. 91.
112 *RYUMI* (1860), p. 58; Turbull, in 'Learning her womanly work', pp. 92–3 notes that the Society of Arts organized a number of domestic economy congresses, the first held in Birmingham in 1877 when 600 people attended. These congresses included discussions on nutrition, thrift, needlework, housing and sanitation.
113 MMI, *Annual Report* (1881), p. 29.
114 MMI, *Annual Report* (1871), p. 26.
115 *Union of Lancashire and Cheshire Institutes*, p. 141; MMI, *Annual Report* (1871), p. 25.
116 MMI, *Annual Report* (1866), pp. 23–4.
117 MMI, *Annual Report* (1867), p. 23.
118 MMI, *Annual Report* (1868), p. 23.
119 *RYUMI* (1862), p. 57.
120 *RYUMI* (1859), pp. 93–4, *RYUMI* (1860), p. 71.
121 *RYUMI* (1860), pp. 71, 93.
122 *Huddersfield Chronicle* (3 May 1879).
123 Ibid.
124 Quoted in Hemming, 'Adult Education in Huddersfield', p. 158.
125 MMI, *Annual Report* (1882), p. 63.
126 MMI, *Annual Report*(1882), p. 27.
127 Kelly, *George Birkbeck*, p. 249.
128 The problems experienced by Wilsden Mechanics' Institute, Yorkshire, during 1849–50 (when 144 men and 56 women were recorded as members) were not uncommon – 'The number of lectures has only been two; the audiences were

very small at both the lectures. The inhabitants had been so often deceived by persons lecturing, whose object was only to make money, that it is with difficulty that an audience can be convened together, unless the subject be of a very interesting character' – *RYUMI* (1850), p. 73.

129 Tylecote, *The Mechanics' Institutes*, p. 264; Kelly, *George Birkbeck*, p. 247.

130 Quoted in I. Inkster, 'Science and the mechanics' institute, 1820–1850: the case of Sheffield', *Annals of Science*, 32 (1975), p. 460.

131 Tynan, 'Lewes Mechanics' Institution', p. 22.

132 *RYUMI* (1846), pp. 64, 18.

133 *RYUMI* (1857), p. 85; *RYUMI* (1858), p. 95; *RYUMI* (1859), p. 93, *RYUMI* (1860), p. 93. Mr Batley's address was read by the president of the institute.

134 MMI, *Annual Report* (1838), p. 69.

135 Kelly, *George Birkbeck*, p. 227.

136 A key middle-class exponent of the virtues of self-help among the working classes was Samuel Smiles in his *Self Help; with Illustrations of Character and Conduct* (London, John Murray 1860); Smiles lectured on 'Self Help in Man' at Leeds Mechanics' Institute in 1852 (*RYUMI* (1852), p. 67). Other lectures often referred to such a theme. Harrison, in *Learning and Living*, p. 55, notes that in the Victorian era, adult education 'was soon recognised as one of the most desirable forms of self-help in which the working classes should be encouraged. Like thrift and saving, it combined excellent opportunities for developing strength of character through self-denial with sound economic and social benefits to the community at large.'

137 M. D. Stephens and G. W. Roderick, 'British artisan scientific and technical education in the early nineteenth century', p. 93.

138 Coates, *Report of the State of Literary, Scientific and Mechanics' Institutions*, p. 59.

139 Tylecote, *The Mechanics' Institutes*, p. 264.

140 Coates, *Report of the State of Literary, Scientific and Mechanics' Institutions*, pp. 60–1.

141 Ibid., pp. 60–1.

142 Tylecote, *The Mechanics' Institutes*, p. 265.

143 Taylor, *Eve and the New Jerusalem*, pp. 147–50, 190.

144 Quoted in ibid., p. 133.

145 Ibid., p. 134.

146 Ibid., p. 123.

147 *RYUMI* (1846), p. 68; *RYUMI* (1847), p. 78.

148 *RYUMI* (1848), p. 87, *RYUMI* (1850), p. 75.

149 *The Englishwoman's Review* (15 July 1873), p. 322.

150 In 1847, for example, she spoke at the Bradford and Leeds institutes (*RYUMI* (1847), pp. 26, 56), and in 1848 at Bradford, Bramley, Halifax, Holmfirth, Leeds, Ripon and Sheffield (*RYUMI* (1848), pp. 32, 34, 45, 48, 65, 74, 77). Her 1857 programme included lectures at Bradford, Scarborough, Selby and Stanningley and also a talk on 'Thoughts on Female Education' at Huddersfield Female Educational Institute (*RYUMI* (1857), pp. 68, 110, 111, 117, 85). In 1859 she lectured at Wakefield (*RYUMI* (1859), p. 117) and her lecture tour included the institutes at Barnsley, Bingley and Pontefract (*RYUMI* (1862), pp. 79, 82, 124). Mrs Balfour appears to have given fewer lectures in mechanics' institutes in southern England, though she did speak at Basingstoke in 1856 and gave another two lectures there in 1859 (Basingstoke Mechanics' Institution, *15th Annual Report* (Basingstoke, Robert Cottle, 1856), p. 4; *18th Annual Report* (Basingstoke, Chandler, 1859), p. 4. The fees Clara Balfour charged for her lectures varied. For example, when she spoke on 'The Influence of Women upon Society' and 'The Female Sovereigns of Europe' in

1847 at the institute at Leicester, she charged £10.10/- for the two talks; the events were evidently popular since the takings amounted to £13 19s 6d (F. B. Lott, *The Story of the Leicester Mechanics' Institute 1833-1871*. (Leicester, W. Thornley and Son, (1935), p. 14). Twelve years later, the fees she charged the Yorkshire Union of Mechanics' Institutes were substantially lower than the Leicester fees – £4 4s for one lecture, £7 7s for two, and £3 3s each for a series (*RYUMI* (1859), p. 55).

151 Balfour, *Women and the Temperance Reformation*, p. 256.
152 Balfour, *Women Worth Emulating*, pp. 57–8.
153 B. and P. Russell, *The Amberley Papers*, p. 330.
154 Ibid., p. 332.
155 Ibid., pp. 336–7.
156 Ibid., p. 331.
157 Banks, *The Biographical Dictionary of British Feminists*, p. 131.
158 Basingstoke Mechanics' Institution, *Thirty-Sixth Annual Report* (Basingstoke, C. J. Jacob, 1877), p. 44; *Minute Book of the Chichester Literary Society and Mechanics' Institute*, Annual Meeting Report October 1877, List of Lecturers and Entertainers for *1877–8*.
159 Quoted in Banks and Banks, *Feminism and Family Planning*, p. 90.
160 R. T. Van Arsdel, 'Mrs. Florence Fenwick-Miller and *The Woman's Signal, 1895–1899'*, p. 108.
161 Mrs Noyes and Mrs Ware were listed to speak on these subjects in the list of lecturers for mechanics' institutes given in Coates, *Report of the State of Literary, Scientific and Mechanics' Institutions*, pp. 110–11; Mrs de Lancy spoke at Keighley and Mrs Bonwell at Ossett (*RYUMI* (1850), p. 49; *RYUMI* (1862), p. 123).
162 Basingstoke Mechanics' Institute and Club, *Fifty-Eighth Annual Report* (Basingstoke, Jacob, 1899), p. 1; Frank, *A Voyager Out*, p. 24.
163 *RYUMI* (1857), p. 91; H. McCormac, *On The Best Means of Improving the Moral and Physical Condition of the Working Classes*, pp. 12–13.
164 Booth, *On the Female Education of the Industrial Classes*, p. 13.
165 Ibid., pp. 14–15.
166 Banks, *The Biographical Dictionary of British Feminists*, p. 229.
167 Quoted in Strachey, *The Cause*, p. 121.
168 Quoted in Hole, *An Essay*, p. 30.
169 Green, *History of the Nottingham Mechanics' Institution*, p. 16; MMI, *Annual Report* (1851), p. 11; Basingstoke Mechanics' Institution, *15th Annual Report* (Basingstoke, Robert Cottle, 1856), p. 4.
170 Shepherd (ed.), pp. 114, 136.
171 Powell (ed.), pp. 316–17.
172 Chichester Literary Society and Mechanics' Institute, *Minute Book*, List of *Lecturers and Entertainers for 1886–7*.
173 *RYUMI* (1857), p. 91.

Chapter 7   Women and the Working Men's College Movement

1 Ludlow and Jones, *Progress of the Working Class*, p. 174.
2 See, for example, Kelly, *A History of Adult Education*, pp. 183–4; Harrison, *A History of the Working Men's College*, pp. 5–7. Dobbs, in *Education and Social Movements 1700–1850*, p. 184 links the development of the working men's college movement not only to Chartism but also to the Sheffield People's College founded in 1842 by the Rev R. S. Bayley. Kelly, ibid., p. 183, also

acknowledges that the Sheffield College 'inspired' the foundation of the London Working Men's College; the People's College, offering classes to men and women for 9d per week, included not just elementary subjects in the curriculum but also laid great stress on the humane studies – literature and composition, history, logic, Greek, Latin and modern languages. In this respect, Kelly continues, 'the College did pioneer work comparable with that done by the Dissenting academies of the eighteenth century in the field of secondary education, for although these subjects were not new in working-class adult education they had never before been given the dominant place' (p. 182).

3 For excellent accounts of women's involvement in Chartism, see Thompson, 'Women and nineteenth-century radical politics'; Jones, 'Women and Chartism'; D. Thompson, *The Chartists*, Chapter 7.

4 Hodgen, *Workers' Education in England and the United States*, pp. 71, 72–3.

5 Harrison, *A History of the Working Men's College*, pp. 6–7.

6 [F. D. Maurice], *Tracts on Christian Socialism*, no. 1: *Dialogue Between Somebody (A Person of Respectability) and Nobody (The Writer)* (London, George Bell, n.d.), p. 1, states, 'I seriously believe that Christianity is the only foundation of Socialism, and that a true socialism is the necessary result of a sound Christianity.' See also Raven, *Christian Socialism* and Backstrom, *Christian Socialism and Co-operation in Victorian England*. Norman, in *The Victorian Christian Socialists*, p. 2, suggests that although contemporaries in the nineteenth century came to speak of a Christian Socialist 'movement' or tradition, there was nothing so coherent or durable.

7 Norman, ibid., p. 9.

8 The Rev F. D. Maurice, speaking at a general meeting of the Manchester, Ancoats and Salford working men's colleges on 5 January 1859 emphasized how the stormy events of 1848 brought to the attention of the men who were to found the London Working Men's College the importance of co-operation between social classes. 'We believe that what we saw was as handwriting upon the wall, clearly sent us by God himself: testifying that if either rank, or wealth, or knowledge is not held as a trust for men, if any one of these things is regarded as a possession of our own, it must perish. We believed and felt that unless the classes in this country, which had received any degree of knowledge more than their fellows, were willing to share it among their fellows, to regard it as precious because it bound them to their fellows, England would fall first under an anarchy, then under a despotism, in which life would die, death would live, in which all classes would be crushed, in which nothing would be so crushed as speech and thought. That was the lesson which we gathered from the events of that year; therefore, for our own sakes, to preserve any little we might have of professional knowledge or of common knowledge, we sought for some method of binding outselves to the working classes of the country.' *Supplement to TWMCM* (February 1859), p. 30.

9 Moore Smith, *The Story of the People's College, Sheffield, 1842–1878* (Sheffield, J. W. Northend, 1912), p. 121; see also note 2 of this chapter.

10 Moore Smith, ibid., p. 71; D. Chadwick, 'On working men's colleges', *TNAPSS* (1859), p. 324; Sadler, *Continuation Schools in England and Elsewhere*, pp. 44–5; 'A Scotch working men's college', p. 93; 'Birkenhead Working Men's College', p. 167; 'Mrs David J. Vaughan', p. 118; Kelly, *Outside the Walls*, p. 7. Sometimes one finds a discrepancy in the primary sources as to the date of foundation of a college; when this has occurred, I have taken the most commonly cited date.

11 Ludlow and Jones, *Progress of the Working Class*, p. 175; *RYUMI* (1859), p. 14; Kelly, *A History of Adult Education*, pp. 187–8; *Cheltenham Working Men's College Magazine*, 1, 1. (October 1884).

12 Kelly, *A History of Adult Education*, p. 187.

13 Kelly, *Outside the Walls*, p. 7. In 1861 the Manchester Working Men's College merged into the evening classes of Owens College, the trustees of which agreed to reduce their fees to a level within the reach of working-class students.

14 Deciding who is, and who is not, a founder of the London Working Men's College is not entirely a straightforward matter. At one debate on this, on the 50-year jubilee of the college, in 1904, John Westlake decided that 'those who took part in the meetings in 1854, previous to the actual opening, provided that they also took part as teachers, not necessarily in the first term' could be called 'founders' – quoted in Harrison, *A History of the Working Men's College*, p. 32. Harrison himself adopts this definition and describes the eight men listed here.

15 Sadler, *Continuation Schools*, pp. 44–5; *TWMCM* (l March 1859), p. 59.

16 Chadwick, 'On working men's colleges', p. 328.

17 Atkins, 'The story of the College', in Atkins (ed.), p. 43.

18 Harrison, *Learning and Living*, p. 88.

19 Chadwick, in 'On working men's colleges', p. 329, notes that the college at Wolverhampton owed its origins to the efforts of 'a few earnest working men'; even so, the Earl of Dartmouth was its president. Although the college at Boston was also founded by working men, its principal was a clergyman, the Rev G. B. Blenkin, M A: *TWMCM* (1 May 1860), p. 83; Bibby, 'The South London Working Men's College', p. 211.

20 Dobbs, *Educational and Social Movements*, pp. 183–4.

21 See, for example, Maurice, *Learning and Working* and also Maurice's introductory lecture on the studies of the (London) Working Men's College', *TWMCM* (1 January 1859). Eagleton, in *Literary Theory*, p. 27, stresses in particular the importance played upon the teaching of 'English' by pioneers such as F. D. Maurice and Charles Kingsley, who emphasized solidarity between social classes, the cultivation of 'larger Sympathies', the instillation of national pride and the transmission of 'moral' values. 'English' as an academic subject was first institutionalized not in the universities but in the mechanics' institutes, working men's colleges and the university extension programmes. It was the poor man's Classics, claims Eagleton, a way of providing a cheapish 'liberal' education for those beyond the charmed circles of public school and Oxbridge.

22 Furnivall, 'History of the London Working Men's College', p. 166, my emphasis.

23 *TWMCM* (1 February 1859), p. 17.

24 See note 3.

25 Quoted in D. Thompson, 'Women and nineteenth-century radical politics', p. 127.

26 *TWMCM* (1 February 1861), p. 26.

27 Norman, *The Victorian Christian Socialists*, p. 19.

28 Whiteing, *My Harvest*, p. 41.

29 Davies, 'F. D. Maurice', in Davies (ed.), p. 9.

30 Kaye, *A History of Queen's College*, pp. 12–19.

31 Maurice, *Learning and Working*, p. 38.

32 R. B. Litchfield, 'The Social Science Association and the employment of

women', p. 146.

33 Extract from T. H. Huxley, *The School Boards*, pp. 197–8.
34 [Communicated by the Senior Tutor], 'History of the Halifax Working Men's College', p. 103.
35 'Halifax – Annual Report', p. 103.
36 Quoted in Furnivall, 'History of the London Working Men's College', p. 146.
37 Rev F. D. Maurice, 'Plan of a female college for the help of the rich and the poor', p. 2.
38 Ibid., p. 2.
39 Quoted in ibid., p. 2.
40 Ibid., p. 3.
41 Ibid., pp. 3–4.
42 Ibid., p. 10.
43 J. Roebuck, 'The education of women in "working men's" colleges', p. 182.
44 Ibid., p. 181.
45 *TWMCJ* (August – September 1911), p. 144.
46 Cowan, 'Mechanics' institutes and science and art classes in Salford in the nineteenth century', p. 203.
47 H. Solly, 'Reasons for a working men's college', p. 110.
48 Atkins, 'The story of the College', p. 53.
49 Ibid., pp. 60–1.
50 Leicester Working Men's College, Union Street, *Minute Book*, entry for meeting 3 May 1880.
51 [Communicated by the Senior Tutor], 'History of the Halifax Working Men's College', p. 160.
52 Letter signed 'A member of the WMC', *TWMCM* (1 September 1861), p. 134.
53 Ibid., p. 134.
54 [Communicated by the Senior Tutor], 'History of the Halifax Working Men's College', p. 161.
55 Roebuck, 'The education of women in "working men's" colleges', p. 184.
56 [Communicated by the Senior Tutor], 'History of the Halifax Working Men's College', p. 161.
57 Letter signed, 'A student of the Working Men's College, London', *TWMCM* (1 August 1860), p. 133; Roebuck, 'The education of women in "working men's" colleges', p. 184.
58 *TWMCM* (1 October 1859), p. 118; *TWMCJ* (December 1900), p. 313.
59 Jacob, 'Mrs Tansley', p. 356.
60 Harrison, *A History of the Working Men's College*, p. 107.
61 Banks, *The Biographical Dictionary of British Feminists*, entry on Elizabeth Malleson, p. 119; Banks notes Mallenson deserves to be better known for her contribution to the education of working-class women.
62 Malleson, *Elizabeth Malleson 1828–1916*, p. 116, 73.
63 Ibid., p. 57.
64 Hudson, *Munby*, p. 177.
65 Malleson, *Elizabeth Malleson*, p. 64.
66 Ibid., p. 61.
67 Ibid., p. 60.
68 *TWMCJ* (February 1903), p. 46.
69 *TWMCJ* (March 1903), p. 63.
70 Malleson, *Address upon the Opening of the College to Men as well as Women*, pp. 7–8.
71 *The Englishwoman's Review* (January 1876), p. 20.
72 Malleson, *Address*, p. 4.

73 Malleson, *Elizabeth Malleson*, p. 68.

74 *JWEU* (15 December 1874), p. 184. Maria Grey's support for co-education is also expressed in her article 'Men and women: a sequel', *Fortnightly Review*, new series, 29 (1881), pp. 776–93.

75 Harris, 'Frances Martin College', p. 225; Harrison, *A History of the Working Men's College*, p. 109; *The Story of the Frances Martin College* (London, Frances Martin College, 1947) [leaflet].

76 G. Weiner, 'Harriet Martineau: a reassessment' in Spender (ed.), *Feminist Theorists*, p. 62; Banks, *The Biographical Dictionary of British Feminists*, entry on Harriet Martineau, p. 125.

77 Manton, *Elizabeth Garrett Anderson*, esp. Chapters 3 and 5; Banks, *The Biographical Dictionary of British Feminists*, entry on Millicent Garrett Fawcett, p. 80.

78 Ridley, *Frances Mary Buss and Her Work for Education*, p. 51; PP (1867–8), XXVIII, part I, *Schools Inquiry Commission*, V, p. 682.

79 Tuke, *A History of Bedford College*, p. 308.

80 Martin, 'A college for working women', p. 488.

81 Ibid., p. 488.

82 Ludlow and Jones, *Progress of the Working Class*, p. 175; Allaway, *Vaughan College*, p. 16; Harrison, *A History of the Working Men's College*, p. 126.

83 Bell, *Octavia Hill*, p. 41; Roebuck, 'The education of women in "working men's" colleges', p. 182.

84 'Fourth annual report of the London Working Men's College', Supplement to *TWMCM* (1 April 1859), p. 78.

85 Malleson, *Elizabeth Malleson*, p. 63.

86 *The Englishwoman's Review* (15 November 1880), p. 513.

87 *The Englishwoman's Review* (15 November 1886), p. 504.

88 Kelly, *A History*, p. 188.

89 Leicester Working Men's College, Union Street, *Minute Book*, entry for 2 May 1881.

90 *TWMCM* (1 June 1861), p. 78.

91 Cowan, 'Mechanics' institutes and science and art classes in Salford', p. 203.

92 Tabular Views in *RYUMI* (1857), (1858), (1859).

93 *RYUMI* (1858), p. 83.

94 *RYUMI* (1862), p. 95.

95 *TWMCM* (1 February 1859), pp. 41–2.

96 See note 13.

97 *RYUMI* (1859), Tabular View and p. 84.

98 See notes 85 and 86.

99 Supplement to *TWMCM* (1 April 1859), p. 80.

100 *TWMCM* (1 June 1861), p. 78.

101 Harrison, in *A History of the Working Men's College*, pp. 49–50, notes that during the first term of the London Working Men's College, four-fifths of the students lived in the areas immediately around the college – Holborn, Clerkenwell, Gray's Inn Road, Bloomsbury, Camden Town and Somers Town. North London was still an area of small handicraftsmen, and it was these men who constituted 'the aristocracy of labour, better paid, educated, and organised than the mass of unskilled workers' who became the first students.

102 Ludlow and Jones, *Progress of the Working Class*, p. 177.

103 'Afternoon classes for women', *TWMCM* (1 July 1859), p. 118.

104 Ibid., p. 118. I have assumed that the teacher who wrote this article was a woman, since it was usual practice for women to teach women at the London

Working Men's College.

105 Quoted in A Student's Wife, 'Will college night classes be of use to women?', p. 2.
106 Ibid., p. 3.
107 *TWMCM* (1 March 1860), p. 55.
108 Letter signed 'A Student's Wife', *TWMCM* (1 April 1860), pp. 65–6.
109 *TWMCM* (1 October 1859), p. 151.
110 *The Englishwoman's Review* (April 1868), p. 469.
111 Bibby, 'The South London Working Men's College', p. 214.
112 Malleson, *Elizabeth Malleson*, pp. 61, 63.
113 Hudson, *Munby*, p. 215.
114 'College for working women', pp. 38–9.
115 Martin, 'A college for working women', p. 487.
116 *JWEU* (15 June 1879), p. 94.
117 Martin, 'A college for working women', p. 484.
118 Ibid., p. 483.
119 Allaway, *Vaughan College Leicester*, p. 28.
120 One penny per meeting or twopence weekly was the fee charged for the men's classes when the college first opened in 1862, and the penny fee seems to have been the normal rate for each meeting up to the turn of the nineteenth century – see Atkins, 'The story of the College', p. 47; Allaway *Vaughan College Leicester*, p. 29.
121 Leicester Working Men's College, Union Street, *Minute Book*, entry for Annual Meeting 10 April 1890.
122 Atkins, 'The story of the College', p. 94. Since a shilling entrance fee had already been charged in some of the women's classes with, claims Atkins, 'satisfactory results', the social origins of the women students was probably already mixed by 1899. Such a fee, points out Atkins, together with the free services of voluntary teachers, had enabled the Women's Department to become self-supporting.
123 *RYUMI* (1857), Tabular View.
124 *RYUMI* (1860), p. 86; *RYUMI* (1858), p. 83.
125 Martin, 'A college for working women', p. 488.
126 Ibid., p. 486.
127 *RYUMI* (1859), Tabular View.
128 Bibby, 'The South London Working Men's College', pp. 213–14.
129 *TWMCM* (1 May 1861), p. 75; *TWMCM* (1 September 1859), p. 151.
130 See note 112; *JWEU* (15 June 1879), p. 94.
131 *JWEU* (15 February 1875), p. 19.
132 *TWMCM* (1 October 1859), p. 159; Atkins, 'The story of the College', p. 81.
133 *TWMCM* (1 May 1861), p. 75.
134 *TWMCM* (1 October 1859), p. 151.
135 *RYUMI* (1862), p. 95.
136 Charlesworth, 'Social work', in Atkins (ed.), pp. 128–9.
137 Allaway, *Vaughan College Leicester*, pp. 49–50.
138 Reminiscence of Miss Florence Pole, quoted in ibid., p. 126, footnote 1.
139 *TWMCJ* (October 1907), p. 171.
140 [T. Hughes], *Early Memories for the Children*, pp. 64–5.
141 J. Roebuck, 'Reminiscences of an old student', in Davies (ed.), p. 72.
142 Litchfield, 'The social economy of a working men's college', p. 788.
143 *RYUMI* (1862), p. 94.
144 For accounts of these clubs, see J. Roebuck, 'Reminiscences of an old student',

and Marks, 'The College clubs', in Davies (ed.).
145 'Furnival Cycling Club', p. 331.
146 *TWMCJ* (September 1890), p. 128. On 14 January 1893, the Economic Club held a discussion on 'The emancipation of women' – *TWMCJ* (January 1893), p. 167.
147 Marks, 'The College clubs', p. 229.
148 Ludlow and Jones, *Progress of the Working Class*, p. 176.
149 Chadwick, 'On working men's colleges', pp. 332–4.
150 Quoted in Furnivall, 'History of the London Working Men's College', p. 165.
151 Harrison, *A History of the Working Men's College*, p. 92.
152 Ibid., pp. 92, 98.
153 F. J. Furnivall, '"Heads versus Heels": the defendant's answer', p. 21.
154 Litchfield, 'Work and play: or, heads and heels', pp. 4–5. Octavia Hill, a teacher of the women's classes at the London Working Men's College, had attended one of the dances (probably in August 1859) and had 'a glorious evening'. She also joined in one of the Sunday excursions, of which Maurice greatly disapproved – see Maurice (ed.), *Life of Octavia Hill as Told in Her Letters*, p. 156. Allaway, in *Vaughan College Leicester*, p. 48, notes that the Committee of Management at the Leicester College were worried about what attitude to adopt toward whist drives, dances and dramatic performances during the years 1908–10. For many years afterwards, dancing and play-acting could only be enjoyed outside the college, though card-playing was permitted.
155 'Conferences on the amusement question', pp. 24–5.
156 Ibid., p. 23.
157 Maurice (ed.), *Life of Octavia Hill*, p. 73.
158 Harrison, *A History of the Working Men's College*, p. 92.
159 Chadwick, 'On working men's colleges', p. 330.
160 *RYUMI* (1859), p. 83.
161 Allaway, *Vaughan College Leicester*, p. 45.
162 Evans, 'Mrs Vaughan 1833–1911', in Atkins (ed.), p. 32.
163 Bibby, 'The South London Working Men's College', p. 219.
164 Tuke, *A History of Bedford College*, pp. 59–60.
165 Kamm, *John Stuart Mill in Love*, pp. 148–9, 216–7; Hollis, *Ladies Elect*, pp. 90–110.
166 Bibby, 'The South London Working Men's College', p. 219.
167 Malleson, *Elizabeth Malleson*, p. 58.
168 Ibid., p. 60.
169 College for Men and Women, *Report of the Council*, p. 7.
170 Ibid., p. 7.
171 See Chapter 5.
172 Malleson, *Elizabeth Malleson*, p. 66.
173 Ibid., p. 71.
174 Stephen, *Emily Davies*, p. 228; Clough, *A Memoir of Anne Jemima Clough*, p. 166.
175 *The Englishwoman's Review*, (January 1876), p. 21.
176 Ibid., p. 21.
177 'In memoriam', *Contemporary Review* (1916), p. 783.
178 *TWMCJ* (August–September 1907), p. 164.

Chapter 8   A College Education

1 'Mixed education', *JWEU* (15 July 1878), p. 121. However, women were not admitted to the Faculty of Medicine at London University at this time.

2 Furnivall, 'History of the London Working Men's College', p. 147.

3 Ibid., p. 148.

4 *TWMCM* (1 August 1859), p. 135.

5 Malleson, *Elizabeth Malleson*, p. 64.

6 For example, Miss Wood, the Secretary of the College for Men and Women, arranged a trip to Keston for Saturday, 15 June 1901, and invited any of the male members from the London Working Men's College to 'join the ladies'. 57 people took part in the excursion, which included a train ride to Hayes Common Station, a walk to Keston (where they had tea), and another walk to 'Wilberforce seat' in Holmwood Park. The party returned home after 10 p.m. Some four weeks earlier, on Saturday 18 May, members of the Furnivall Sculling Club 'entertained' a party from the College for Men and Women by taking them to Kew by boat and then returning to the club for tea, 'prepared by the girls' – *TWMCJ* (July 1901), pp. 115, 125.

7 *TWMCJ* (August–September 1911), p. 144.

8 Malleson, *Elizabeth Malleson*, p. 64.

9 Harrison, *A History of the Working Men's College*, p. 109.

10 Jacob, 'The College education', in Llewelyn Davies (ed.), p. 258.

11 Personal communication to me from David Muspratt, Archivist of the London Working Men's College.

12 *TWMCM* (1 December 1860), p. 193.

13 *RYUMI* (1861), p. 80; Atkins, 'The story of the College', p. 112.

14 Ibid., p. 112.

15 See Chapter 7, note 31.

16 Walkowitz, *Prostitution and Victorian Society*, Chapter 4.

17 Phillips, *Divided Loyalties*, p. 39.

18 Quoted in Roebuck, 'The education of women in "working men's" colleges', p. 182; Leicester Working Men's College, Union Street, *Minute Book*, Report of meeting held on 29 April 1870.

19 *TWMCM* (1 October 1859), p. 161; Roebuck, 'The education of women in "working men's" colleges', p. 183.

20 'Afternoon classes for women', *TWMCM* (1 July 1859), p. 118.

21 Supplement to *TWMCM* (1 April 1859), p. 80.

22 'Afternoon classes for women', *TWMCM* (1 August 1859), p. 125 – the writer of this article called the provision offered to women rather meagre (p. 123); *TWMCM* (1 March 1860), p. 38.

23 Maurice (ed.), *Life of Octavia Hill*, p. 80, notes that Octavia Hill taught drawing to the women students at the London Working Men's College and on one occasion, when the teacher of the botany class did not appear, also taught botany – about which she felt she 'knew nothing ... but a great deal about flowers; and as there happened to be a bunch of flowers in the room, I talked to the women about them, and I do not think the time was wasted.' See also O. H. [Octavia Hill], 'Hints on a few principles of instruction of working women, suggested by a teacher', *TWMCM* (1 October 1859), p. 162, for mention of the singing class.

24 *TWMCM* (1 March 1860), p. 37.

25 Elizabeth Rossiter, 'A student's wife's notion of college and classes', *TWMCM* (1 October 1859), p. 154.

26 Bibby, 'The South London Working Men's College', p. 214; *The Englishwoman's Review* (April 1868), p. 469.

27 Supplement to *TWMCM* (1 April 1859), p. 7.

28 Harrison, *Learning and Living*, p. 88, footnote 3.

29 *RYUMI* (1858), p. 83.

30 *RYUMI* (1859), p. 84.

31 Ibid., p. 84.

32 [Communicated by the Senior Tutor], 'History of the Halifax Working Men's College', p. 160.

33 *RYUMI* (1858), p. 83.

34 *RYUMI* (1859), p. 113.

35 *RYUMI* (1858), p. 117.

36 Allaway, *Vaughan College*, p. 28.

37 Evans, 'Mrs Vaughan 1833–1911'.

38 Leicester Working Men's College, Union Street, *Minute Book*, entries for 17 September 1862, 14 March 1867, 6 April 1869.

39 Atkins, 'The story of the College', p. 60.

40 Ibid., p. 44.

41 Bibby, 'The South London Working Men's College, pp. 214, 212.

42 Harrison, *A History of the Working Men's College*, p. 121; Jacob, 'The College education', p. 276.

43 Hudson, *Munby*, pp. 49–50.

44 Supplement to *TWMCM* (1 April 1859), p. 76.

45 Quoted by Harrison, *A History of the Working Men's College*, p. 60.

46 Jacob, 'The College education', p. 277.

47 *TWMCJ* (October 1907), p. 117.

48 *RYUMI* (1858), p. 82; *TWMCM* (1 October 1859), p. 159.

49 *RYUMI* (1861), p. 31.

50 *TWMCM* (1 May 1860), p. 82.

51 *TWMCM* (1 December 1861), p. 187.

52 See Chapter 7, notes 79 and 66.

53 Malleson, *Elizabeth Malleson*, p. 59.

54 Ibid., p. 61; C. P. Lucas, 'George Tansley', in Davies (ed.), p. 142.

55 Hudson, *Munby*, p. 216.

56 Ibid., p. 211.

57 Ibid., p. 229.

58 Ibid., p. 236.

59 Ibid., pp. 277, 319, 323.

60 Malleson, *Elizabeth Malleson*, p. 61.

61 Ibid., pp. 59–60.

62 Ibid., p. 68.

63 *The Englishwoman's Review* (15 July 1876), p. 306.

64 Quoted in Malleson, *Elizabeth Malleson*, p. 70.

65 *JWEU* (15 November 1878), p. 186.

66 *JWEU* (15 November 1875), p. 169.

67 Purvis, 'Women and teaching'.

68 Ellsworth, *Liberators of the Female Mind*, p. 242.

69 *The Englishwoman's Review* (15 July 1878), p. 309.

70 Mrs H. Sidgwick, 'The higher education of women', p. 203.

71 *The Englishwoman's Review* (15 September 1879), p. 407.

72 Quoted in Malleson, *Elizabeth Malleson*, pp. 67–8. It is interesting to note that this college and its predecessor, the Working Women's College, in contrast to the London Working Men's College, had an open-door policy that demanded no entry qualifications. As we saw in Chapter 7, note 22, the London Working Men's College did not admit illiterate working men, though an Adult School was established in 1855 to prepare such a clientele for college entrance; in addition, from 1856 preparatory classes were offered to act as a bridge between the School and College classes (see Harrison, *A History of the Working Men's College*, pp. 52, 71).

73 Martin, 'A college for working women', p. 484.

74 Ibid., p. 485.

75 Ibid., p. 487.

76 'College for working women', *JWEU* (15 June 1879), p. 95.

77 *The Englishwoman's Review* (14 November 1885), p. 525.

78 *JWEU* (15 May 1877), p. 80.

79 Hudson, *Munby*, pp. 374–5.

80 Ibid., p. 380.

81 'College for working women', *JWEU* (15 June 1879), p. 95.

82 Martin, 'A college for working women', p. 487.

83 *The Englishwoman's Review* (15 November 1880), p. 514.

84 Ibid., p. 514.

85 Martin, 'A college for working women', p. 484.

86 'College for working women', *JWEU* (15 June 1879), p. 94.

87 Ibid., p. 94.

88 *The Englishwoman's Review* (15 November 1880), p. 514.

89 Martin, 'A college for working women', p. 485.

90 'College for working women', *JWEU* (15 June 1879), pp. 94–5; *The Englishwoman's Review* (15 November 1879), pp. 501–2.

91 Harris, 'Frances Martin College', p. 226.

92 'College still retains spirit of self-help', *The Guardian*, (12 August 1965).

93 Chadwick, 'On working men's colleges', p. 335.

94 *TWMCM* (1 October 1859), p. 166.

95 Ibid., p. 166.

96 *TWMCM* (1 November 1861), p. 173.

97 *TWMCM* (1 June 1859), p. 104.

98 J. Charlesworth, 'Social Work' in Atkins (ed.), p. 131.

99 *TWMCM* (1 March 1859), p. 57.

100 *TWMCM* (1 August 1860), p. 123.

101 Charlesworth, 'Social Work', pp. 130–1.

102 Bibby, 'The South London Working Men's College', pp. 213–16, 219.

103 *Cheltenham Working Men's College Magazine* (later called *The Philistine*), 1, 5 (February 1885), p. 91; 1, 6 (March 1885), p. 113; *The Philistine* (n.d. [probably December 1885]), p. 69; *The Philistine* (February 1886), p. 101.

104 *TWMCJ* (December 1891), p. 338; *TWMCJ* (March 1893), p. 205; *TWMCJ* (May 1893), p. 238; *TWMCJ* (March 1898), p. 39; *TWMCJ* (June–July 1898), p. 75; *TWMCJ* (December 1898), p. 127.

105 *TWMCJ* (December 1894), p. 136.

106 *RYUMI* (1857), p. 113.

107 Ibid., p. 113; *RYUMI* (1858), p. 117.

108 *RYUMI* (1858), p. 82.

109 Ibid., p. 82, *TWMCM* (1 March 1859), p. 61.

110 *Cheltenham Working Men's College Magazine*, 1, 4 (January 1885), p. 72; *The Philistine*

(January 1886), p. 96.

111 Raikes, *Dorothea Beale of Cheltenham*, pp. 297–8.

112 *TWMCJ* (February 1891), p. 204; *TWMCJ* (November 1891), p. 324. Jane Harrison was among the first generation of British women academics. She was a student at Newnham, Cambridge, passing the classical tripos in 1879. From 1880 to 1879 she studied and worked in London, her publications during these years reflecting the influence of her training at the British Museum. In 1898, she returned to Newnham as a research fellow and then became a lecturer there. For an account of her life, see S. J. Peacock, *Jane Ellen Harrison: the mask and the self* (New Haven and London: Yale University Press, 1988).

113 *TWMCJ* (December 1893), p. 300; *TWMCJ* (October 1894), p. 105.

114 *TWMCJ* (March 1896), p. 43; Harrison, *A History of the Working Men's College*, p. 139.

115 *TWMCJ* (December 1898), p. 135.

116 *TWMCJ* (November 1907), p. 195; *TWMCJ* (March 1908), p. 286.

117 *TWMCJ* (February 1897), p. 125; Tuke, *A History of Bedford College for Women*, p. 141.

118 Brittain, *The Women at Oxford*, p. 121.

119 *TWMCJ* (December 1890), p. 169; Saturday Night Lecture, 'Ideals of womanhood – old and new', *TWMCJ* (April 1895), pp. 208–10.

120 Ibid., 'Ideals of womanhood', p. 209.

121 Ibid., p. 210.

122 Ibid., p. 209.

123 Ibid., p. 210.

124 Jepson, *The Beginnings of English University Adult Education – Policy and Problems*, pp. 38–9.

125 Ibid., p. 52; Harrison, *A History of the Working Men's College*, pp. 21, 56.

126 Harrison, *A History of the Working Men's College*, p. 105.

127 S. Rowbotham, 'Travellers in a strange country', p. 71; Purvis, 'Working-class women and adult education', p. 206.

128 Harrison, *A History of the Working Men's College*, pp. 105–6.

129 Allaway, *Vaughan College Leicester*, p. 11.

130 Malleson, *Elizabeth Malleson*, p. 59.

131 Ibid., pp. 62–3.

132 F. Harrison, 'The emancipation of women', p. 445.

133 Clough, *A Memoir of Anne Jemima Clough*, p. 147.

134 Hudson, *Munby*, p. 237.

135 Ibid., p. 360.

136 Forster, *Significant Sisters*, p. 551. Forster further notes (p. 57) that Elizabeth Blackwell dreaded above all else any suggestion that women were *not* different from men or that they ought to make themselves the same. It was in this she separated herself from the women's rights movement. She told women to treasure their female nature, to believe it existed, to make more and not less of it, to realise that 'rights' in themselves were nothing.

137 Blackwell, *How to Keep a Household in Health*, p. 10.

138 Ibid., pp. 20–1.

139 Ibid., pp. 21–2.

140 Banks, *The Biographical Dictionary of British Feminists*, p. 54.

141 Hudson, *Munby*, p. 226.

142 Malleson, *Address*, pp. 7, 10.

143 Ellsworth, *Liberators of the Female Mind*, p. 142. Maria Grey spoke on mixed

education on at least two separate occasions at the College for Men and Women – on its opening night in 1874 (see Chapter 7, note 74) and in 1877 (*The Englishwoman's Review* (15 October 1877), p. 463).

144 Advertisement in *JWEU* (15 January 1876) stating this lecture now to be published (by W. Ridgway) 'at the request of the members of the College'.

145 Ellsworth, *Liberators of the Female Mind*, p. 161.

146 Shirreff, *Intellectual Education*, p. 403.

147 Ibid., p. 413.

148 *The Englishwoman's Review* (14 October 1876), p. 46; *JWEU* (15 November 1877), p. 175.

149 *TWMCJ* (November 1894), p. 124.

150 Banks, *The Biographical Dictionary of British Feminists*, entry on Joshua Fitch, p. 81; E. Davies, 'Secondary instruction as relating to girls'.

151 J. G. Fitch, *An Address Delivered to the Students at the Opening of the College Session*, p. 16.

152 Ibid., p. 22.

153 Martin, 'A college for working women', p. 486.

154 Quoted in ibid., p. 485; *The Englishwoman's Review* (15 November 1877), pp. 499–500.

155 *The Englishwoman's Review* (14 November 1885), p. 545.

156 *The Englishwoman's Review* (15 November 1880), p. 522.

157 Fletcher, *Women First*, p. 19; McCrone, *Sport and the Physical Emancipation of English Women 1870–1914*, p. 104.

158 *TWMCJ* (August–September 1907), p. 164.

Chapter 9   Conclusion

1 Ramelson, *The Petticoat Rebellion*, p. 32.

2 See Chapter 8, note 72.

3 *RYUMI* (1859), p. 93.

4 *RYUMI* (1861), p. 104. The benefits that middle-class women might experience through membership of a local mechanics' institute, working men's college or working women's college must not be forgotten either. For example, Charlotte, Anne and Emily Brontë, whose father was a curate in the Yorkshire Village of Haworth, would walk the four miles from their home to the mechanics' institute at Keighley to borrow books from the library – Mills, *Technical Education*, p. 17. One wonders to what extent this library service helped the Brontë sisters to write their novels.

5 See Chapter 8, note 25.

6 Malleson, *Elizabeth Malleson*, p. 69.

7 *RYUMI* (1858), p. 95.

8 HFEI, *Minute Book*, entry for committee meeting 17 March 1858.

9 Delamont and Duffin, 'Introduction', in Delamont and Duffin (eds.) p. 19.

10 Dicey, 'The College as it is now', in Davies (ed) pp. 244–5.

11 Kelly, *George Birkbeck*, p. 271.

12 Kelly, *A History of Adult Education*, pp. 260, 200.

13 Ibid., p. 260.

14 Rowntree and Binns, *A History of the Adult School Movement*, p. 42. In some areas, women were admitted to these schools after their menfolk. In a letter to me dated 12 December 1979, Miss E. M. Willmott, Subject Adviser for Local Studies for the City of Bradford Metropolitan Council, quoting from *The*

Bradford Friends Adult School Jubilee 1875–1925, notes that women were not admitted to these adult schools until 1886.

15 Kelly, *George Birkbeck*, pp. 203–4.
16 Kelly, *A History of Adult Education*, p. 199; Welch, *The Peripatetic University*, pp. 50–3.
17 Kelly, *George Birkbeck*, p. 274.
18 Ibid., p. 274.
19 Ibid., p. 274.
20 Ibid., p. 275. The information about the Devonport Mechanics' Institute comes from Blight, 'Devonport Mechanics' Institute held Great Exhibition in miniature', *Western Morning News* (6 January 1953).
21 Blight, 'Devonport Mechanics' Institute'; Kelly, *A History of Adult Education*, p. 199.
22 Kelly, *George Birkbeck*, pp. 275–6.
23 Kelly, *A History of Adult Education*, p. 199.
24 Ibid., p. 200.
25 Dobbs, 'Historical survey', pp. 44–50.
26 Kelly, *A History of Adult Education*, p. 188.
27 Ibid., pp. 187–8.
28 Bibby, 'The South London Working Men's College', p. 218.
29 Kelly, *A History of Adult Education*, pp. 188–9.
30 Sadler, *Continuation Schools in England and Elsewhere*, pp. 45–6.
31 Blunden, 'Vocational education for women's work in England and Wales', in Acker, Megarry, Nisbet and Hoyle (eds), p. 158; T. Thompson, *Dear Girl*, p. 111: Ruth's close friend Eva Slawson, born in 1882, the illegitimate child of a baker's daughter, was brought up by her grandparents. She too left school at 13 and, like Ruth, was a keen participant in adult education. Thus once her grandparents were 'better-off', she attended classes in shorthand and typing and changed her job from domestic servant to typist.
32 Blunden, p. 158.
33 Ibid., p. 159.
34 Devereux, *Adult Education in Inner London 1870–1980*, p. 64.
35 Davin, 'Imperialism and motherhood', pp. 10, 13.
36 Ibid., p. 13.
37 Lewis, *The Politics of Motherhood*, p. 96; Dwork, *War is Good for Babies and Other Young Children*, pp. 147–54.
38 Lewis, *The Politics of Motherhood*, p. 96.
39 Bunting, Bunting, Barnes and Gardiner, *A School for Mothers*, p. 62.
40 Ibid., pp. 59, 48.
41 Ibid., pp. 58, 59–60.
42 Ibid., p. 63.
43 See Chapter 7, notes 75 and 77, and Chapter 8, note 121.
44 Kelly, *A History of Adult Education*, p. 304.
45 Ibid., pp. 302–3, notes that the institutes were concerned with a range of public issues – such as housing, water supplies, sanitation, diet, education, child welfare – as well as drama, music, domestic crafts and teaching women how to speak in public, frame resolutions, and chair a meeting. Jenkins, in *The History of the Women's Institute Movement of England and Wales*, p. 61, notes that in 1927, 12 years after the first institute was established in Britain, there were 3,997 institutes with 250,000 members.
46 Stott, *Organisation Women*, p. 10. Harrison, in *Prudent Revolutionaires*, p. 185, claims that Margery Corbett Ashby epitomized 'twentieth-century feminist diplomacy'.

47 Ibid., p. 20.

48 Ibid., p. 24.

49 J. Thompson, in *Learning Liberation*, p. 64, notes that women outnumber men by about there to one in adult education today and that students in classes run by local education authorities tend to be lower-middle class as distinct from the more solidly middle-class background of students in university extra-mural and Worker' Educational Association classes.

50 See, for example, Arnot, 'A cloud over co-education', and Deem (ed.), *Co-education Reconsidered*.

51 See especially Spender, 'Education: the patriarchial paradigm and the response to feminism', Spender and Sarah (eds), *Learning to Lose*, and Taking Liberties Collective, *Learning the Hard Way*.

52 See especially *Women, Class and Adult Education* and Thompson, *Learning Liberation*, Chapter 10.

BIBLIOGRAPHY

Acker, S., 'Sociology, gender and education', in *World Yearbook of Education 1984: women and education*, ed. S. Acker, J. Megarry, S. Nisbet and E. Hoyle (London: Kogan Page, 1984).

'Afternoon classes for women', *The Working Men's College Magazine* (1 July 1859).

'Afternoon classes for women', *The Working Men's College Magazine* (1 August 1859).

Aldrich, R., 'Educating our mistresses', *History of Education*, 12, 2 (1983).

Alexander, S., 'Women, class and sexual differences in the 1830s and 1840s: some reflections on the writing of a feminist history', *History Workshop Journal*, 17 (spring 1984).

——, 'Women's work in nineteenth-century London: a study of the years 1820–50', in *The Rights and Wrongs of Women*, ed. J. Mitchell and A. Oakley (Harmondsworth: Penguin, 1976).

Alexander, S., Davin, A. and Hostettler, E., 'Labouring women: a reply to Eric Hobsbawm', *History Workshop Journal*, 8 (autumn 1979).

Allaway, A. J., *Vaughan College Leicester 1862–1962* (Amsterdam: Leicester University Press, 1962).

Alton Mechanics' Institute, *Minute Book*.

Anderson, E. Garrett, 'Sex in mind and education: a reply', *Fortnightly Review* (May 1874).

Anderson, M., *Family Structure in Nineteenth-Century Lancashire* (Cambridge: Cambridge University Press, 1971).

Annals of the Poor [lacking cover and name of publisher; probably the Religious Tract Society, n.d. (?1845)].

'Annual soiree of the Huddersfield Female Educational Institute', *The Huddersfield Examiner* (29 October 1864).

Arnold, M., *Reports on Elementary Schools 1852–1882*, ed. the Right Hon. Sir Francis Sandford (London: Macmillan, 1889).

Arnot, M., 'A cloud over co-education: an analysis of the forms of transmission of class and gender relations', in *Gender, Class and Education*, ed. S. Walker and L. Barton (London: Croom Helm, 1983).

——, 'Male hegemony, social class and women's education', *Journal of Education*, 164, 1 (winter 1982).

Atkins, Rev E., 'The story of the College', in *The Vaughan Working Men's College, Leicester 1862-1912*, ed. Rev E. Atkins (London and Leicester: Adams Bros. and Shardlow Ltd., 1912).

Atkins, Rev E. (ed.), *The Vaughan Working Men's College, Leicester 1862-1912* (London and Leicester: Adams Bros. and Shardlow Ltd., 1912).

Austin, Mrs, *Two Letters on Girls' Schools and on the Training of Working Women* (London: Chapman and Hall, 1857).

Aveling, E. and Aveling, E. Marx, *The Factory Hell* (London: Socialist League Office, 1885).

Backstrom, P. N., *Christian Socialism and Co-operation in Victorian England* (London: Croom Helm, 1974).

Baines, E., *The Life of Edward Baines, by his Son* (London: Longman, Brown, Green and Longmans, 1851).

Balfour, C. L., *Women and the Temperance Reformation* (1849), quoted in J. Rendall, *The Origins of Modern Feminism: women in Britain, France and the United States, 1780-1860* (London: Macmillan, 1985).

Balfour, C. L., *Women Worth Emulating* (London: Sunday School Union, n.d. [first pubd 1877]).

Ball, N. 'Practical subjects in mid-Victorian elementary schools', *History of Education*, 8, 2 (1979).

Banks, G. Lennaeus, *'Onward': an Inaugural Address delivered to the Directors and Members of the Institute, and to the Inhabitants of the Town, in the Victorian Room, Low Harrogate, on Tuesday Evening, November 14th, 1848, on the Occasion of Re-establishing the Harrogate and Literary Institute* (London: R. Groombridge and Sons, 1858).

Banks, J. A., *Prosperity and Parenthood: a study of family planning among the Victorian middle classes* (London: Routledge and Kegan Paul, 1954).

Banks, J. A. and Banks, O., *Feminism and Family Planning in Victorian England* (Liverpool: Liverpool University Press, 1964).

Banks, O., *Becoming a Feminist: the social origins of 'first wave' feminism* (Brighton: Wheatsheaf Books, 1986).

——, *The Biographical Dictionary of British Feminists*, vol. 1: *1800-1930* (Brighton: Harvester Press, 1985).

——, *Faces of Feminism* (Oxford: Martin Robinson, 1981).

Barnard, H. C., *A History of English Education from 1760*, sixth impression, with amendments (London: University of London Press, 1969 [first pubd 1947]).

Barrett, M. and McIntosh, M., 'The "family wage": some problems for socialists and feminists', *Capital and Class*, 11 (summer 1980).

Basch, F., *Relative Creatures: Victorian women in society and the novel 1837-67* (London: Allen Lane, 1974).

Basingstoke Mechanics' Institution, *Reports* (1856, 1857, 1859, 1877, 1899).

Beddoe, D., *Discovering Women's History: a practical manual* (London: Pandora Press, 1983).

Beechey, V., 'On patriarchy', *Feminist Review*, 3 (1979).

Beeton, Mrs. I., *The Book of Household Management* (London: S. O. Beeton, 1861).

Bell, E. Moberly, *Octavia Hill: a biography* (London: Constable and Co., 1942).

Best, G., *Mid-Victorian Britain 1851-75* (London: Weidenfeld and Nicolson, 1971).

Bibby, C., 'The South London Working Men's College, a forgotten venture', *Adult Education*, 28 (1955-6).

Billington, L., and Billington, R., '"A burning zeal for righteousness": women in the British Anti-Slavery Movement, 1820-1869', in *Equal or Different: women's politics 1800-1914*, ed. J. Rendall (Oxford: Basil Blackwell, 1987).

Binns, H., *A Century of Education: being the centenary history of the British and Foreign School*

Society 1808–1908 (London: J. M. Dent, 1906).

Birchenough, C., *History of Elementary Education in England and Wales from 1800 to the Present Day* (London: University Tutorial Press, 1914).

'Birkenhead Working Men's College', *The Working Men's College Magazine* (1 November 1861).

Blackburn, H., *Women's Suffrage: a record of the women's suffrage movement in the British Isles with biographical sketches of Miss Becker* (Oxford: Williams and Norgate, 1902).

Blackwell, Dr E., *How to Keep a Household in Health: an address delivered before the Working Women's College* (London: Victoria Press, 1870).

Blight, F. S., 'Devonport Mechanics' Institute held Great Exhibition in miniature', *Western Morning News* (1 January 1953).

Blunden, G., 'Vocational education for women's work in England and Wales', in *World Yearbook of Education 1984: women and education*, ed. S. Acker, J. Megarry, S. Nisbet and E. Hoyle (London: Kogan Page, 1984).

Booth, Rev Dr J., *On the Female Education of the Industrial Classes: being the substance of a lecture delivered on the 20th November 1855, at the Mechanics' Institution, Wandsworth* (London: Bell and Daldy, 1855).

Bornat, J., 'Lost leaders: women, trade unionism and the case of the General Union of Textile Workers, 1875–1914', in *Unequal Opportunities: women's employment in England 1800–1918*, ed. A. V. John (Oxford: Basil Blackwell, 1986).

——, '"What about that lass of yours being in the union?": textile workers and their union in Yorkshire, 1888–1922', in *Our Work, Our Lives, Our Words: women's history and women's work*, ed. L. Davidoff and B. Westover (London: Macmillan, 1986).

Boucherett, J., Blackburn, H. and some others, *The Conditions of Working Women and the Factory Acts* (London: Elliot Stock, 1896).

Boxer, M. J. and Quataert, J. H., *Connecting Spheres: women in the western world, 1500 to the present* (Oxford: Oxford University Press, 1987).

Bremner, C. S., *Education of Girls and Women in Great Britain* (London: Swan Sonnenschein and Co., 1897).

Brewer, Rev J. S., 'Workhouse visiting', in *Lectures to Ladies on Practical Subjects*, ed. F. D. Maurice, 3rd rev. edn (Cambridge: Macmillan, 1857 [first pubd 1856]).

Bridenthal, R. and Koonz, C. (eds.), *Becoming Visible: Women in European history* (Boston: Houghton Mifflin, 1977).

British and Foreign School Society, *Reports* (London: 1816, 1818, 1819, 1820, 1822, 1824, 1825, 1827, 1833, 1864).

Brittain, V., *The Women at Oxford: a fragment of history* (London: George Harrap, 1960).

Brophy, J. and Smart, C., 'From disregard to disrepute: the position of women in family law', *Feminist Review*, 9 (autumn 1981).

Brown, C., 'The Gregs and their school at Styal', *History of Education Society Bulletin*, 26 (autumn 1980).

Brown, J. R., *Young Men and Maidens: a pastoral for the times* (London, 1871), quoted in J. A. Banks and O. Banks, *Feminism and Family Planning in Victorian England* (Liverpool: Liverpool University Press, 1964).

Bruce, M. L., *Anna Swanwick: a memoir and recollections 1813–1899* (London: T. Fisher Unwin, 1903).

Bryan, B., Dadzie, S. and Scafe, S., *The Heart of the Race: black women's lives in Britain* (London: Virago, 1985).

Bryant, M., *The London Experience of Secondary Education* (London: Athlone Press, 1987).

——, *The Unexpected Revolution: a study in the education of women and girls in the nineteenth century* (London: University of London Institute of Education, 1980).

Bunting, E. M., Bunting, D. E. L., Barnes, A. E. and Gardiner, B., *A School for Mothers* (London: Horace Marshall and Son, 1907).

Burgess, H. J. 'Educational history of the National Society', quoted in P. Silver and H. Silver, *The Education of the Poor: the history of a National School 1824-1974* (London: Routledge and Kegan Paul, 1974).

Burgon, J. W., *To Educate Young Women Like Young Men, and with Young Men, - A thing Inexpedient and Immodest: a sermon preached before the University of Oxford, in the Chapel of New College, on Trinity Sunday, June 8th 1884* (London: Parker and Co., 1884).

Burke, G., 'The decline of the independent Bal Maiden: the impact of change in the Cornish mining industry', in *Unequal Opportunities: women's employment in England 1800-1918*, ed. A. V. John (Oxford: Basil Blackwell, 1986).

Burns, C. D., *Short History of Birkbeck* (1924), quoted in E. Kaye, *A History of Queen's College, London 1848-1972* (London: Chatto and Windus, 1972).

Burstall, S. A., *The Story of the Manchester High School for Girls 1871-1911* (Manchester: The University Press, 1911).

Burstyn, J., *Victorian Education and the Ideal of Womanhood* (London: Croom Helm, 1980).

Butterfield, H., *The Whig Interpretation of History* (London: G. Bell and Sons, 1931).

Bythell, D., *The Sweated Trades: outwork in nineteenth-century Britain* (London: Batsford, 1978).

Cadbury, E., Matheson, M. C. and Shawn, G., *Women's Work and Wages* (London, T. Fisher and Unwin, 1906).

'Caius and Caia', *The Saturday Review* (18 July 1857).

Calder, F. L., 'Cookery in elementary schools', in *Some National and Board School Reforms*, ed. Lord Brabazon (London: Longmans, Green and Co., 1887).

Cappe, C., *Account of Two Charity Schools for the Education of Girls: and of a Female Friendly Society* (York: William Blanchard, 1800).

Carby, H., 'White women listen! Black feminism and the boundaries of sisterhood', in Centre for Contemporary Cultural Studies, *The Empire Strikes Back: race and racism in 70s Britain* (London: Hutchinson, 1982).

Carpenter, E., *Love's Coming-of-Age*, 2nd edn (London: Methuen and Co., 1915 [first pubd 1896]).

Carr, E. H., *What is History* (Harmondsworth: Penguin, 1964 [first pubd 1961]).

Carroll, B. A., *Liberating Women's History: theoretical and critical essays* (Urbana: University of Illinois Press, 1976).

Census of Great Britain, 1851 and *1891*.

Centre for Contemporary Cultural Studies, *The Empire Strikes Back: race and racism in 70s Britain* (London: Hutchinson, 1982).

Centre for Contemporary Cultural Studies Education Group, *Unpopular Education: schooling and social democracy in England since 1944* (London, Hutchinson, 1981).

Chadwick, D., 'On working men's colleges', *Transactions of the National Association for the Promotion of Social Science* (1859).

Charlesworth, J., 'Social work', in *The Vaughan Working Men's College, Leicester, 1862-1912*, ed. Rev E. Atkins (London and Leicester: Adams Bros. and Shardlow Ltd., 1912).

Chew, A. N., *The Life and Writings of a Working Woman (remembered and collected by Doris Nield Chew)* (London: Virago, 1982).

Chichester Literary Society and Mechanics' Institute, *Minute Book*.

Christ, C., 'Victorian masculinity and the angel in the house', in *A Widening Sphere: changing roles of Victorian women*, ed. M. Vicinus (Bloomington: Indiana University Press, 1977).

Clough, B. A., *A Memoir of Anne Jemima Clough* (London: Edward Arnold, 1897).

Coates, T., *Report of the State of Literary, Scientific and Mechanics' Institutiions in England, with a list of such Institutions and a list of Lecturers* (London: Society for the Diffusion of Useful Knowledge, 1841).

Cobbe, F. Power, *The Duties of Women: a course of lectures* (London: William and Norgate, 1881).

——, 'The little health of ladies', *Contemporary Review* (January 1878).

College for Men and Women, *Report of the Council* (London: Kenny and Co., 1874).

'College for working women', *The Englishwoman's Review* (15 January 1884).

Collier, D. J. *The Girl in Industry* (London: G. Bell and Sons, 1918).

[Communicated by the Senior Tutor], 'History of the Halifax Working Men's College', *The Working Men's College Magazine* (1 October 1859).

Comte, A., *A General View of Positivism*, trans. from the French edn of 1848 by J. H. Bridges (London: Trubner and Co., 1865).

'Conferences on the amusement question', *The Working Men's College Magazine* (1 February 1861).

Cooper, T., *The Life of Thomas Cooper* (London: Hodder and Stoughton, 1872).

Copelman, D., '"A new comradeship between men and women": family, marriage and London's women teachers, 1870–1914', in *Labour and Love: women's experiences of home and family 1850–1940*, ed. J. Lewis (Oxford: Basil Blackwell, 1986).

Cowan, I. R., 'Mechanics' institutes and science and art classes in Salford in the nineteenth century', *The Vocational Aspect of Education*, 20 (1968).

Crawford, P., *Exploring Women's Past* (London: Allen and Unwin, 1984) [first pubd 1983 by Sisters Publishing Ltd.].

Curtis, S. J., *History of Education in Great Britain* (London: University Tutorial Press, 1948).

Darwin, C., *The Descent of Man*, 2nd edn (London: John Murray, 1894 [first pubd 1871 in 2 volumes]).

——, *On the Origin of Species by Means of Natural Selection, or The Preservation of Favoured Races in the Struggle for Life* (London: John Murray, 1859).

David, M., *The State, the Family and Education* (London: Routledge and Kegan Paul, 1980).

Davidoff, L., *The Best Circles: society, etiquette and the season* (London: Croom Helm, 1973).

——, 'Class and gender in Victorian England: the diaries of Arthur J. Munby and Hannah Cullwick', *Feminist Studies*, 5, 1 (spring 1979).

——, 'Mastered for life: servant and wife in Victorian and Edwardian England', *Journal of Social History* (summer 1974).

——, 'The separation of home and work? Landladies and lodgers in nineteenth- and twentieth-century England', in *Fit Work for Women*, ed. S. Burman (London: Croom Helm, 1979).

Davidoff, L. and Hall, C., *Family Fortunes: men and women of the English middle class 1780–1850* (London: Hutchinson, 1987).

Davidoff, L., L'Esperance, J. and Newby, H., 'Landscape with figures: home and community in English society', in *The Rights and Wrongs of Women*, ed. J. Mitchell and A. Oakley (Harmondsworth: Penguin, 1976).

Davidoff, L. and Westover, B., '"From Queen Victoria to the Jazz Age"': women's world in England, 1880–1939', in *Our Work, Our Lives, Our Words: women's history and women's work*, ed. L. Davidoff and B. Westover (London: Macmillan, 1986).

Davies, C. (ed.), *Rewriting Nursing History* (London: Croom Helm, 1980).

Davies, E., 'Secondary instruction as relating to girls', read at the Annual Meeting of the Social Science Association, 1864, reprinted in *Thoughts on Some Questions Relating to Women, 1860–1908* (Cambridge: Bowes and Bowes, 1910).

Davies, E., Speech at a Conference held at Liverpool on 20th January 1874 on Higher Education in Connection with the Universities, *Journal of The Women's Education Union* (15 February 1874).

Davies, Rev J. Llewelyn, 'F. D. Maurice', in *The Working Men's College 1854–1904*, ed. Rev J. Llewelyn Davies (London: Macmillan, 1904).

Davies, Rev J. Llewelyn (ed.), *The Working Men's College 1854–1904* (London: Macmillan, 1904).

Davin, A., 'Child labour, the working-class family, and domestic ideology in 19th century Britain', *Development and Change*, 13, 4 (October 1982).

——, 'Imperialism and motherhood', *History Workshop Journal*, 5 (spring 1978).

——, '"Mind that you do as you are told": reading books for Board School girls', *Feminist Review*, 3 (1979).

——, 'What is women's history?', *History Today* (June 1985).

——, 'Women and history', in *The Body Politic: women's liberation in Britain 1969–1972*, ed. M. Wandor (London: Stage 1, 1972).

Davis, W., *Hints to Philanthropists* (Bath: Wood, Cunningham and Smith, 1821).

Dawes, R., *Effective Primary Instruction* (London: Groombridge and Sons, 1857).

Dawes, R., *Mechanics' Institutes and Popular Education. An Address Delivered at the Annual Soiree of the Huddersfield Institute, December 13th, 1855* (London: Groombridge and Sons, 1856).

De Beauvoir, S., *The Second Sex* (Harmondsworth: Penguin, 1972 [first pubd 1949]).

Deem, R. (ed.), *Co-Education Reconsidered* (Milton Keynes: Open University Press, 1984).

Degler, K., *Is There a History of Women? An inaugural lecture delivered before the University of Oxford on 14 March 1974* (Oxford: Clarendon Press, 1975).

Delamont, S., 'The contradictions in ladies' education', and 'The domestic ideology and women's education', in *The Nineteenth-Century Woman: her cultural and physical world*, ed. S. Delamont and L. Duffin (London: Croom Helm, 1978).

Delamont, S. and Duffin, L., 'Introduction' to *The Nineteenth-Century Woman: her cultural and physical world*, ed. S. Delamont and L. Duffin (London: Croom Helm, 1978).

Delphy, C., *Close to Home* (London: Hutchinson, 1984).

——, 'Women in stratification studies', in *Doing Feminist Research*, ed. H. Roberts (London: Routledge and Kegan Paul, 1981).

Delphy, C. and Leonard, D., 'Class analysis, gender analysis, and the family', in *Gender and Stratification*, ed. R. Crompton and M. Mann (Oxford: Polity Press, 1986).

Detrosier, R., *An Address Delivered at the New Mechanics' Institution* (Manchester: T. Forrest, 1829).

Devereux, W., *Adult Education in Inner London 1870–1980* (London: Shepheard-Walwyn, in collaboration with Inner London Education Authority, 1982).

Dicey, A. V., 'The College as it is now', in *The Working Men's College 1854–1904*, ed. Rev J. Llewelyn Davies (London: Macmillan and Co., 1904).

Dick, M., 'The myth of the working-class Sunday school', *History of Education*, 9, 1 (1980).

——, 'Religion and the origins of mass schooling', in *The Churches and Education*, ed. V. A. McClelland (Leicester: History of Education Society, 1984).

Digby, A., 'New schools for the middle-class girl', in *Educating the Victorian Middle Class*, ed. P. Searby (Leicester: History of Education Society, 1982).

Digby, A. and Searby, P., *Children, School and Society in Nineteenth-Century England* (London: Macmillan, 1981).

Dobbs, A. E., *Education and Social Movements 1700–1850* (London: Longmans, Green and Co., 1919).

——, 'Historical survey', in *Cambridge Essays on Adult Education*, ed. R. St John Parry (Cambridge: Cambridge University Press, 1920).

Duppa, B. F., *A Manual for Mechanics' Institutions* (London: Longman, Orme, Brown, Green and Longmans, 1839).

Dwork, D., *War is Good for Babies and Other Young Children: a history of the infant and child welfare movement in England 1898–1918* (London: Tavistock, 1987).

Dyer, L. J., 'Nineteenth-century community centres, 1: Thornton Mechanics' Institute', *Adult Education*, 21 (1948–9).

Dyhouse, C., *Girls Growing Up in Late Victorian and Edwardian England* (London: Routledge and Kegan Paul, 1981).

——, 'Good wives and little mothers: social anxieties and the schoolgirl's curriculum, 1890–1920', *Oxford Review of Education*, 3, 1 (1977).

——, 'Miss Buss and Miss Beale: gender and authority in the history of education', in *Lessons for Life: the schooling of girls and women 1850–1950*, ed. F. Hunt (Oxford: Basil Blackwell, 1987).

——, 'Social Darwinistic ideas and the development of women's education in England, 1880–1920', *History of Education*, 5, 1 (1976).

——, 'Towards a "feminine" curriculum for English schoolgirls: the demands of ideology, 1870–1963', *Women's Studies International Quarterly*, 1, 4 (1978).

Eagleton, T., *Literary Theory: an introduction* (Oxford: Basil Blackwell, 1983).

'Editorial', *History Workshop Journal*, 13 (spring 1982).

'Editorial: women's history and men's history', *History Workshop Journal*, 19 (spring 1985).

'Education amongst the working women of Huddersfield and Bradford', *The Englishwoman's Review* (April 1869).

Ehrenreich, B. and English, D., *Complaints and Disorders: the sexual politics of sickness* (London: Writers and Readers Publishing Cooperative, 1973).

Eisenstein, H., *Contemporary Feminist Thought* (London: Unwin, 1984).

Eisenstein, Z., *The Radical Future of Liberal Feminism* (New York: Longman, 1981).

——, 'Some notes on the relations of capitalist patriarchy', in *Capitalist Patriarchy and the Case for Socialist Feminism*, ed. Z. R. Eisenstein (New York: Monthly Review Press, 1979).

Elizabeth, C., *The Works of Charlotte Elizabeth*, vol. II (New York: M. W. Dodd, 1846).

'Ellen M.', a mantle maker, letter pubd in the *Manchester Guardian*, reprinted in *The Englishwoman's Journal* (July 1858).

Ellis, Mrs, *The Daughters of England: their position in society, character and responsibilities* (London: Fisher, Son and Co., 1842).

——, *Education of the Heart: women's best work* (London: Hodder and Stoughton, 1869).

——, *The Wives of England: their relative duties, domestic influence, and social obligations* (London: Fisher, Son and Co., 1843).

——, *The Women of England: their social duties and domestic habits* (London: Fisher, Son and Co., 1839).

Ellsworth, E. W., *Liberators of the Female Mind, the Shirreff Sisters, Educational Reform, and the Women's Movement* (Westport, CT: Greenwood Press, 1979).

Elton, G., Comment reported in *The Guardian* (14 January 1986).

Engels, F., *The Condition of the Working Class in England in 1844*, trans. by F. K. Wischnewetzky (London: Allen and Unwin, 1920 [first pubd 1892]).

——, 'Letter to J. Bloch, 21 September 1890', in F. Engels, *Selected Correspondence*, quoted in M. MacDonald, *The Curriculum and Cultural Reproduction, II* (Milton Keynes, Open University Press, 1977) [Unit 19 of OU Course E202 *Schooling and Society*].

——, *The Origin of the Family, Private Property and the State* (Harmondsworth: Penguin, 1985 [first pubd 1884]).

'The English Woman's Journal', *The Saturday Review* (10 April 1858).

Evans, A., 'Mrs Vaughan', in *The Vaughan Working Men's College, Leicester, 1862–1912*, ed. Rev E. Atkins (London and Leicester: Adams Bros. and Shardlow Ltd., 1912).

Farningham, M., *A Working Woman's Life* (London: James Clarke, 1907).

Fawcett, M. Garrett, *Women's Suffrage: a short history of a great movement* (London: T. C. and E. C. Jack, 1912).

Feminist Review, 17 (1986), *Many Voices, One Chant, Black Feminist Perspectives* [special issue].

Ferguson, M. W., Quilligan, M. and Vickers, N. J. (eds.)., *Rewriting the Renaissance: the discourses of sexual difference in early modern Europe* (Chicago: University of Chicago Press, 1986).

Field, J. L., 'Private schools in Portsmouth and Southampton, 1850–1870', *Journal of Educational Administration and History* (July 1978).

Fitch, J. G., *An Address Delivered to the Students at the Opening of the College Session, October 1872*

(London: Victoria Press, 1873).

Fletcher, S., *Women first: the female tradition in English physical education 1880–1890* (London: Athlone Press, 1984).

Foley, A., *A Bolton Childhood* (Manchester: Manchester University Extra-Mural Department and the North Western District of the Workers' Educational Association, 1973).

Ford, I., *Women's Wages, and the Conditions Under Which They are Earned* (London: William Reeves, 1893).

Forster, M., *Significant Sisters: the grassroots of active feminism 1839–1939* (London: Secker and Warburg, 1984).

Foucault, M., *Discipline and Punishment: the birth of the prison* (London: Allen Lane, 1979).

'Fourth annual report of the London Working Men's College', Supplement to *The Working Men's College Magazine* (1 April 1859).

Fox-Genovese, E., 'Placing women's history in history', *New Left Review*, 133 (1983).

Frank, C., *A Voyager Out: the life of Mary Kingsley* (London: Hamish Hamilton, 1987 [first pub. 1986]).

Frith, S., 'Socialisation and rational schooling: elementary education in Leeds before 1870', in *Popular Education and Socialization in the Nineteenth Century*, ed. P. McCann (London: Methuen, 1977).

Furnivall, F. J., '"Heads versus heels": the defendant's answer', *The Working Men's College Magazine* (1 February 1861).

——, 'History of the London Working Men's College', *The Working Men's College Magazine* (1 November 1860).

'Furnivall Cycling Club', *The Working Men's College Journal* (June 1902).

Gadd, E. W., *Victorian Logs* (Studley: Brewin Books, 1979).

Gardner, P., *The Lost Elementary Schools of Victorian England* (London: Croom Helm, 1984).

Garner, A. D., 'The Society of Arts and the mechanics' institutes: the co-ordination of endeavour towards scientific and technical education, 1851–54', *History of Education*, 14, 4 (1985).

Gaskell, E., *Mary Barton: a tale of Manchester life* (London: Chapman and Hall, 1848).

Gaskell, E., *Ruth* (London: Chapman and Hall, 1853).

Gaskell, P., *Artisans and Machinery* (London: John Parker, 1836).

Ginswick, J. (ed.), *Labour and the Poor in England and Wales 1849–1851* vol. 1 (London: Frank Cass, 1983).

Gisborne, T., *An Enquiry into the Duties of the Female Sex*, 3rd edn (London, T. Cadell Jun. and W. Davies, 1789).

Godwin, J. V., 'The Bradford Mechanics' Institute', *Transactions of the National Association for the Promotion of Social Science* (1859).

Goldstrom, J. M., 'The content of education and the socialisation of the working-class child 1830–1860' in *Popular Education and Socialization in the Nineteenth Century*, ed. P. McCann (London: Methuen, 1977).

Gomersal, M., 'Ideals and realities: the education of working-class girls, 1800–1870', *History of Education*, 17, 1 (1988).

Gordon, A. D., Buhle, M. J. and Dye, N. S., 'The problem of women's history', in *Liberating Women's History: theoretical and critical essays*, ed. B. Carroll (Urbana: University of Illinois Press, 1976).

Gordon, S. C., *Demands for the Education of Girls, 1790–1865* (MA Thesis, University of London, 1950).

Gorham, D., *The Victorian Girl and the Feminine Ideal* (London: Croom Helm, 1982).

Granger, J., *Nottingham Mechanics' Institution: a retrospect* (Nottingham: W. Burrows, 1912).

Grant, C. E., *Farthing Bundles* (London: C. E. Grant, 1929).

Gray, J., *Liberalism* (Milton Keynes: Open University Press, 1986).

Green, J. A. H., *History of the Nottingham Mechanics' Institution, 1837–1887* (Nottingham: Stevenson, Bailey and Smith, 1887).

Greg, W. R., 'Why are women redundant?' (1862), reprinted in W. R. Greg, *Literary and Social Judgments* (London: Trubner and Co., 1868).

Grey, M. G., 'Men and women', *Fortnightly Review*, 32 (1 November 1879).

——, 'Men and women: a sequel', *Fortnightly Review*, new series, 29 (1881).

Grey, Mrs W., *Idols of Society: or, Gentility and Femininity* (London: William Ridgway, 1874).

——, *On the Education of Women: a paper read at the meeting of the Society of Arts, May 31st, 1871* (London: William Ridgway, 1871).

Hakim, C., 'Census reports as documentary evidence: the census commentaries 1801–1951', *Sociological Review*, 28, 3 (1980).

'Halifax – Annual Report', *The Working Men's College Magazine* (1 June 1859).

Hall, C., 'The early formation of Victorian domestic ideology', in *Fit Work for Women*, ed. S. Burman (London: Croom Helm, 1979).

——, 'Gender divisions and class formation in the Birmingham middle class, 1780–1850', in *People's History and Socialist Theory*, ed. R. Samuel (London: Routledge and Kegan Paul, 1981).

Hall, C. and Himmelweit, S., *Development of Family and Work in Capitalist Society*, Unit 8 of OU Course U221, *The Changing Experience of Women* (Milton Keynes: Open University Press, 1983).

Hall, S., 'In defence of theory', in *People's History and Socialist Theory*, ed. R. Samuel (London: Routledge and Kegan Paul, 1981).

Harris, R. M., 'Frances Martin College', *Further Education*, 1 (1947–8).

Harrison, B., *Prudent Revolutionaries: portraits of British feminists between the wars* (Oxford: Oxford University Press, 1987).

Harrison, F., 'The emancipation of women', *Fortnightly Review*, new series (1 October 1891).

——, *Realities and Ideals: social, political, literary and artistic* (London: Macmillan and Co., 1908).

Harrison, J. F. C., *A History of the Working Men's College 1856–1954* (London: Routledge and Kegan Paul, 1954).

——, *Learning and Living, 1790–1960: a study of the history of the English adult education movement* (London: Routledge and Kegan Paul, 1961).

Hartmann, H., 'Capitalism, patriarchy and job segregation by sex', in *Capitalist Patriarchy and the Case for Socialist Feminism*, ed. Z. Eisenstein (New York: Monthly Review, 1979).

——, 'The unhappy marriage of Marxism and feminism: towards a more progressive union', in *Women and Revolution: the unhappy marriage of Marxism and feminism: a debate on class and patriarchy*, ed. L. Sargent (London: Pluto Press, 1981).

Heyhew, H., *London Labour and the London Poor*, vols. 1 and 2 (London: George Woodfall, 1851).

Hemming, J. P., *Adult Education in Huddersfield* (MEd thesis, University of Manchester, 1966).

Herstein, S. A., *A Mid-Victorian Feminist, Barbara Leigh Smith Bodichon* (New York: Yale University Press, 1985).

'Her strength is in her weakness', *The Englishwoman's Review* (January 1869).

Hertz, F., 'Mechanics' institutes for working women, with special reference to the manufacturing districts of Yorkshire', *Transactions of the National Association for the Promotion of Social Science* (1859).

Hewitt, M., *Wives and Mothers in Victorian Industry* (London: Rockliff, 1958).

Higgs, E., 'Domestic service and household production' in *Unequal Opportunities: women's employment in England 1800–1918*, ed. A. V. John (Oxford: Basil Blackwell, 1986).

——, 'Women, occupations and work in the nineteenth century', *History Workshop*

Journal, 23 (spring 1987).

Hill, F., *National Education: its present state and prospects*, vol. II (London: Charles Knight, 1836).

O. H. [Hill, O.], 'Hints on a few principles of instruction of working women, suggested by a teacher', *The Working Men's College Magazine* (1 October 1859).

Hobsbawm, E. J., *The Age of Empire 1875–1914* (London: Weidenfeld and Nicolson, 1987).

——, *Labouring Men: studies in the history of labour* (London: Weidenfeld and Nicolson, 1964).

——, 'Man and woman in socialist iconography', *History Workshop Journal*, 6 (autumn 1978).

Hodgen, M. T., *Workers' Education in England and the United States* (London: Kegan Paul, 1925).

Holcombe, L., *Victorian Ladies at Work: middle-class working women in England and Wales 1850–1914* (Newton Abbot: David Charles, 1973).

——, *Wives and Property: reform of the married women's property law in 19th-century England* (Oxford: Martin Robertson and Co., 1983).

Hole, J., *An Essay on the History and Management of Literary, Scientific and Mechanics' Institutions* (London: Longman, Brown, Green and Longmans, 1853).

——, *The Homes of the Working Classes with Suggestions for Their Improvement* (London: Longman, Green and Co., 1866).

Hollis, P., *Ladies Elect: women in English local government 1865–1914* (Oxford: Oxford University Press, 1987).

——, 'Women in council: separate spheres, public space', in *Equal or Different: women's politics 1800–1914*, ed. J. Rendall (Oxford: Basil Blackwell, 1987).

Honey, J. S. de S., *Tom Brown's Universe: the development of the Victorian public school* (London: Millington, 1977).

Hook, Rev Dr, 'On institutions for adult education', in *Social Evils: their causes and their cure*, ed. Viscount Ingestre (London: William Parker, 1853).

Hooks, B., *Ain't I a Woman: black women and feminism* (Boston: South End Press, 1982).

Horn, P., *Education in Rural England 1800–1914* (New York: St Martin's Press, 1978).

——, 'The problems of a village head-mistress in the 1880s', *History of Education Society Bulletin*, 26 (autumn 1980).

——, *The Rise and Fall of the Victorian Servant* (Dublin: Gill and Macmillan, 1975).

——, *The Victorian Country Child* (Kinston: Roundwood Press, 1974).

Household Proverbs for Women (London: John Shaw, n.d. [c. 1860]).

Huddersfield Female Educational Institute, *Book of Pupil Entries*.

Huddersfield Female Educational Institute, *Minute Book*.

Hudson, D., *Munby, Man of Two Worlds: the life and diaries of Arthur J. Munby 1828–1910* (London: John Murray, 1972).

Hudson, J. W., *The History of Adult Education* (London: Longman, Brown, Green and Longmans, 1851).

Hughes, Rev J., *The History of the Township of Meltham, near Huddersfield*, ed. with additions by C. H. (London: John Russell Smith, 1866).

Hughes, T., *A Lecture on the Slop-System, Especially as it Bears Upon the Females Engaged In It* (Exeter: W. and H. Pollard, 1852).

[Hughes, T.,] *Early Memories for the Children* (London: Thomas Burleigh, 1899).

Hull, G. T., Scott, P. B. and Smith, B., *All the Women are White, All the Blacks are Men, But Some of us are Brave: black women's studies* (New York: Feminist Press, 1982).

Humphries, J., 'Class struggle and the persistence of the working-class family', *Cambridge Journal of Economics*, 1 (1977).

Hunt, F., 'Opportunities lost and gained: mechanisation and women's work in the London bookbinding and printing trades', in *Unequal Opportunities: women's employment in*

England 1800–1918, ed. A. V. John (Oxford: Basil Blackwell, 1986).

Hunt, F. (ed.), *Lessons for Life: the schooling of girls and women 1850–1950* (Oxford: Basil Blackwell, 1987).

Hurt, J. S., *Education in Evolution* (London: Rupert Hart-Davis, 1971).

——, *Elementary Schooling and the Working Classes 1860–1918* (London: Routledge and Kegan Paul, 1979).

Hutchins, B. L., *Women in Modern Industry* (London: G. Bell and Sons, 1915).

Hutchins, B. L. and Harrison, A., *A History of Factory Legislation*, 2nd rev. edn (London: P. S. King and Son, 1911).

Huxley, T. H., *The School Boards: what they can do and what they may do* (1870), extract reprinted in C. Bibby (ed.), *The Essence of T. H. Huxley: selections from his writings edited with several brief interpretative essays* (London: Macmillan, 1967).

Hyde, Mrs, *How to Win our Workers: a short account of the Leeds Sewing School for Factory Girls* (London: Macmillan and Co., 1862).

Ingestre, Viscount (ed.), *Social Evils: their causes and their cure* (London: William Parker, 1853).

Inkster, I., 'The social context of an educational movement: a revisionist approach to the English mechanics' institutes, 1820–1850', *Oxford Review of Education*, 2, 3 (1976).

'In memoriam', *Contemporary Review* (January 1876).

Jacob, L., 'The college education', in *The Working Men's College 1854–1904*, ed. Rev J. Llewelyn Davies (London: Macmillan, 1904).

——, 'Mrs Tansley', *The Working Men's College Journal* (June 1905).

Jaggar, A. M., *Feminist Politics and Human Nature* (Brighton: Harvester Press, 1983).

Jalland, P., *Women, Marriage and Politics 1860–1914* (Oxford: Clarendon Press, 1986).

Jeffreys, S., *The Spinster and her Enemies: feminism and sexuality 1880–1930* (London: Pandora Press, 1985).

Jenkins, I., *The History of the Women's Institute Movement of England and Wales* (Oxford: Oxford University Press, 1953).

Jepson, N. A., *The Beginnings of English University Adult Education – Policy and Problems: a critical study of the early Cambridge and Oxford University extension movements between 1873 and 1907, with special reference to Yorkshire* (London: Michael Joseph, 1973).

Johanson, S. R., '"Herstory" as history: a new field or another fad', in *Liberating Women's History: theoretical and critical essays*, ed. B. Carroll (Urbana: University of Illinois Press, 1976).

John, A. V., *By the Sweat of their Brow: women workers at Victorian coal mines* (London: Croom Helm, 1980).

Johnson, H. M., *The Education of Girls in Derby and Derbyshire 1800–1930* (MEd Thesis, University of Nottingham, 1966).

Johnson, M., *Derbyshire Village Schools in the Nineteenth Century* (Newton Abbot: David and Charles, 1970).

Johnson, R., 'Against absolutism', in *People's History and Socialist Theory*, ed. R. Samuel (London: Routledge and Kegan Paul, 1981).

——, 'Culture and the historians', and 'Three problematics: elements of a theory of working-class culture', in *Working-Class Culture: studies in history and theory*, ed. J. Clarke, C. Critcher and R. Johnson (London: Hutchinson, 1979).

——, 'Educational policy and social control in early Victorian England', *Past and Present*, 49 (November 1970).

——, 'Elementary education: the education of the poorer classes', in *Education in Britain*, ed. G. Sutherland (Irish University Press, 1977).

——, 'Notes on the schooling of the English working class 1780–1850', in *Schooling and Capitalism* ed. R. Dale, G. Esland and M. MacDonald (London: Routledge and Kegan Paul, 1976).

——, 'Thompson, Genovese and socialist-humanist history', *History Workshop Journal*, 6 (autumn 1978).

Jones, D., 'Women and Chartism', *History*, 68 (February 1983).

Jones, G. Steadman, *Outcast London: a study of the relationship between classes in Victorian society* (Oxford: Oxford University Press, 1971).

Jones, M. G., *The Charity School Movement: a study of eighteenth-century puritanism in action* (London: Frank Cass, 1964).

Jordanova, L. J., 'The history of the family', in Cambridge Women's Studies Group, *Women in Society* (London: Virago, 1981).

Joyce, P., *Work, Society and Politics: the culture of the factory in later Victorian England* (Brighton: Harvester Press, 1980).

Kamm, J., *Hope Deferred: girls' education in English history* (London: Methuen, 1965).

——, *John Stuart Mill in Love* (London: Gordon and Cremonesi, 1977).

Kay-Shuttleworth, J., *Four Periods of Public Education, as Reviewed in 1832, 1839, 1846, 1862* (London: Longmans, 1862).

Kaye, H. J., *The British Marxist Historians* (Oxford: Polity Press, 1984).

Kelly, J., 'The doubled vision of feminist theory: a postscript to the "Women and Power" Conference', *Feminist Studies*, 1 (spring 1979).

Kelly, T., *George Birkbeck, Pioneer of Adult Education* (Liverpool: Liverpool University Press, 1957).

——, *A History of Adult Education in Great Britain* (Liverpool: Liverpool University Press, 1962).

——, *Outside the Walls: sixty years of university extension at Manchester 1886–1946* (Manchester: Manchester University Press, 1950).

Kelly-Gadol, J., 'Did women have a Renaissance?', in *Becoming Visible: women in European history*, ed. R. Bridenthal and C. Koonz (Boston: Houghton Mifflin, 1977).

——, 'The social relations of the sexes: methodological implications of women's history', *Signs*, 1 (1976).

Kitteringham, J., *Country Girls in 19th Century England* (Oxford: History Workshop Pamphlet, n.d. [1973]).

Knowles, Miss R., Letters, kept at Northamptonshire Record Office, Ref. number YZ.5541.

Lacey, C. A., 'Introduction', in *Barbara Leigh Smith and the Langham Place Group*, ed. C. A. Lacey (New York and London: Routledge and Kegan Paul, 1987).

Laqueur, T., 'Working-class demand and the growth of English elementary education, 1750–1850', in *Schooling and Society: studies in the history of education*, ed. L. Stone (Baltimore: John Hopkins University Press, 1976).

Lacqueur T. W., *Religion and Respectability: Sunday schools and working-class culture 1780–1850* (New Haven: Yale University Press, 1976).

Lawson, J., *Letters to the Young on Progress in Pudsey During the Last Sixty Years* (Firle: Caliban Books, 1978 [first pubd 1887]).

Lawson, J. and Silver, H., *A Social History of Education in England* (London: Methuen, 1973).

Layton, Mrs, 'Memories of seventy years', in *Life As We Have Known It, by Co-operative Working Women*, ed. M. Llewelyn Davies (London: Virago, 1977 [first pubd 1931]).

Lazonick, W., 'The subjection of labour to capital: the rise of the capitalist system', *Review of Radical Political Economics*, 10 (spring 1978).

Legget, J., *Local Heroines: a women's history gazetteer to England, Scotland and Wales* (London: Pandora Press, 1988).

Leicester Working Men's College, Union Street, *Minute Book*.

Leitner, Professor, 'Comment on Emma Wallington: the physical and intellectual capacities of women equal to those of man', *Anthropologia*, 1 (1874).

Lerner, G., 'Placing women in history: a 1975 perspective', in *Liberating Women's History*, ed. B. Carroll (Urbana: University of Illinois Press, 1976).

L'Esperance, J., 'Women's mission to woman: explorations in the operation of the double standard and female solidarity in nineteenth-century England', *Social History* (November 1979).

Levine, P., *Victorian Feminism 1850–1900* (London: Hutchinson, 1987).

Lewis, J., *The Politics of Motherhood: child and maternal welfare in England, 1900–1939* (London: Croom Helm, 1980).

——, *Women in England 1870–1950* (Brighton: Wheatsheaf Books, 1984).

——, 'Women lost and found: the impact of feminism on history', in *Men's Studies Modified: the impact of feminism on the academic disciplines*, ed. D. Spender (Oxford: Pergamon Press, 1981).

Lewis, S., *Woman's Mission*, 8th edn (London: John W. Parker, 1840 [first pubd 1839]).

Liddington, J. and Norris, J., *One Hand Tied Behind Us: the rise of the women's suffrage movement* (London: Virago, 1978).

Litchfield, R. B., 'The social economy of a working men's college', *Transactions of the National Association for the Promotion of Social Science* (1862).

——, 'The Social Science Association and the employment of women', *The Working Men's College Magazine* (1 September 1861).

——, 'Work and play; or, Heads and heels', *The Working Men's College Magazine* (1 January 1861).

London Feminist History Group, *The Sexual Dynamics of History* (London: Pluto Press, 1983).

Lott, F. B. *The Story of the Leicester Mechanics' Institute 1833–1871* (Leicester: W. Thornley and Son, 1935).

Lown, J., 'Not so much a factory, more a form of patriarchy: gender and class during industrialisation', in *Gender, Class and Work*, ed. E. Gamarnikow, D. Morgan, J. Purvis and D. Taylorson (London: Heinemann, 1983).

Lucas, C. P., 'George Tansley', in *The Working Men's College 1854–1904* (London: Macmillan, 1904).

Ludlow, J. M. and Jones, L., *Progress of the Working Class 1832–1867* (London: Alexander Strahan, 1867).

McBride, T. M., *The Domestic Revolution: the modernisation of household service in England and France 1820–1920* (London: Croom Helm, 1976).

McCann, P., 'Popular education, socialisation and social control: Spitalfields 1812–1824' in *Popular Education and Socialization in the Nineteenth Century*, ed. P. McCann (London: Methuen, 1977).

McCormac, H., *On the Best Means of Improving the Moral and Physical Condition of the Working Classes: being an address delivered on the opening of the first monthly scientific meetings of the Belfast Mechanics' Institute* (London: Longman, Rees, Orme, Brown and Green, 1830).

McCrone, K., *Sport and the Physical Emancipation of English Women 1870–1914* (London: Routledge, 1988).

McLennan, G., *Marxism and the Methodologies of History* (London: Verso, 1981).

McWilliams-Tullberg, R., 'Women and degrees at Cambridge University, 1862–1887', in *A Widening Sphere: changing roles of Victorian women*, ed. M. Vicinus (Bloomington: Indiana University Press, 1977).

——, *Women at Cambridge: a men's university – though of a mixed type* (London: Victor Gollancz, 1975).

Madoc-Jones, B., 'Patterns of attendance and their social significance: Mitcham National School 1830–39', in *Popular Education and Socialization in the Nineteenth Century*, ed. P. McCann (London: Methuen, 1977).

'Maids-of-all-work and Blue Books', *Cornhill Magazine*, 30 (July–December 1874).

Malcolmson, P. E., *English Laundresses: a social history, 1850–1930* (Urbana and Chicago:

University of Illinois Press, 1986).

Malleson, E., *Elizabeth Malleson 1828–1916: autobiographical notes and letter, with a memoir by H. Malleson* (printed for private circulation, 1926).

Malleson, Mrs F. R., *Address upon the Opening of the College to Men as well as Women, delivered at St. George's Hall, Langham Place, October 1874*.

Malmgreen, G., *Neither Bread nor Roses: utopian feminists and the English working class, 1800–1850* (Brighton: 1978).

Manchester Mechanics' Institution, *Reports* (1828, 1835, 1838, 1846, 1861, 1862, 1863, 1864, 1866).

Manton, J., *Elizabeth Garrett Anderson* (London: Methuen, 1965).

Marcus, J., 'Introduction: re-reading the Pankhursts and women's suffrage', in *Suffrage and the Pankhursts*, ed. J. Marcus (London: Routledge and Kegan Paul, 1987).

Marks, R. H., 'The College clubs', in *The Working Men's College 1854–1904*, ed. Rev J. Llewelyn Davies (London: Macmillan and Co., 1904).

Marsden, W. E., *Unequal Educational Provision in England and Wales: the nineteenth-century roots* (London: Woburn Press, 1987).

Martin, F., 'A college for working women', *Macmillans Magazine* (1879).

Martin, G. Currie, *The Adult School Movement* (London: National Adult School Union, 1924).

Marwick, A., *The Nature of History* (London: Macmillan, 1970).

Marx, K., *Manifesto of the Communist Party* (Moscow, Foreign Languages Publishing House, n.d. [first pubd 1848]).

Matthews, J., 'Barbara Bodichon: integrity in diversity', in *Feminist Theorists: three centuries of women's intellectual traditions*, ed. D. Spender (London: Women's Press, 1983).

——, *Good and Mad Women: the historical construction of femininity in twentieth-century Australia* (London: Allen and Unwin, 1984).

Maudsley, H., 'Sex in mind and in education', *Fortnightly Review*, 15 (1874).

Maurice, C. E. (ed.), *Life of Octavia Hill as Told in Her Letters* (London: Macmillan and Co., 1913).

Maurice, F. D., *Learning and Working: six lectures delivered in Willis's Rooms, London, in June and July 1854* (Cambridge: Macmillan and Co., 1855).

Maurice, Rev F. D., 'Plan of a female college for the help of the rich and poor', in *Lectures to Ladies on Practical Subjects*, [ed. F. D. Maurice] 3rd edn (Cambridge: Macmillan, 1857 [first pubd 1856]).

[Maurice, F. D.,] *Tracts on Christian Socialism*, no. 1: *Dialogue Between Somebody (A Person of Respectability) and Nobody (The Writer)* (London: George Bell, n.d.)

Mayhew, H., *London Labour and the London Poor*, vols. 1 and 2 (London: George Woodfall, 1851).

A Member of the W M C, Letter in *The Working Men's College Magazine* (1 September 1861).

Merryweather, M., *Experience of Factory Life: being a record of fourteen years' work at Mr Courtauld's silk mill at Halstead, in Essex*, 3rd edn (London: Emily Faithfull, 1862).

Merson, E., *Once There Was ... the Village School* (Southampton: Paul Cave Publications, 1979).

Miles, R., *The Women's History of the World* (London: Michael Joseph, 1988).

Mill, J. S., *The Subjection of Women* (London: Longmans, Green, Reader and Dyer, 1869).

Millett, K., *Sexual Politics* (New York: Doubleday, 1969).

'Milliners' apprentices', *Fraser's Magazine*, 33 (1846).

Mills, C. T., *Technical Education: its development and aims* (London: Edward Arnold, 1925).

Milne, J. D., *Industrial and Social Position of Women in the Middle and Lower Ranks* (London: Chapman and Hall, 1857).

Minutes of the Committee of Council of Education (1841–42).

Minutes of the Committee of Council of Education for 1846.

Mitchell, G. (ed.), *The Hard Way Up: the autobiography of Hannah Mitchell, suffragette and rebel* (London: Faber and Faber, 1968).

'Mixed education', *Journal of the Women's Education Union* (15 July 1878).

Moore, Dr W., Address to the British Medical Association, Fifty-Fourth Annual Meeting, Brighton 1886, *The Lancet* (14 August 1886).

Morris, J., 'The characteristics of sweating: the late nineteenth-century London and Leeds tailoring trade', in *Unequal Opportunities: women's employment in England 1800–1918*, ed. A. V. John (Oxford: Basil Blackwell, 1986).

——, *Women Workers and the Sweated Trades: the origins of minimum wages legislation* (Aldershot: Gower, 1986).

A Mother, 'Defects in the moral training of girls', in *The Church and the World*, ed. Rev Shipley (London: Longmans, Green, Reader and Dyer, 1868).

'Mrs David J. Vaughan', *The Working Men's College Magazine* (1 June 1911).

Murgatroyd, L., 'Gender and occupational stratification', *Sociological Review*, 30, 4 (1982).

Murray, M., *My First Hundred Years* (London: William Kimber, 1963).

Nash, R., 'Co-operator and citizen', in *The Case for Women's Suffrage*, ed. B. Villiers (London: T. Fisher Unwin, 1907).

National Society for Promoting the Education of the Poor in the Principles of the Established Church, *Reports* (London: 1812, 1814, 1822, 1841).

Nead, L., *Myths of Sexuality: representations of women in Victorian Britain* (Oxford: Basil Blackwell, 1988).

Neff, W. F., *Victorian Working Women: an historical and literary study of women in British industries and professions 1832–1850* (London: Allen and Unwin, 1929).

Newton, J., Ryan, M. P. and Walkowitz, J. R. (eds.), *Sex and Class in Women's History* (London: Routledge and Kegan Paul, 1983).

Nielsen, S., 'Maps of patriarchy', *Trouble and Strife*, 6 (summer 1985).

Norman, E., *The Victorian Christian Socialists* (Cambridge: Cambridge University Press, 1987).

Norris, J., 'Women's history', in *North West Labour History Society Bulletin*, 7 (1980–81) [pubd in association with the Manchester Women's History Group].

Oakley, A., *Gender and Society* (London: Temple Smith, 1972).

——, *Housewife* (London: Allen Lane, 1974).

——, *Subject Women* (Oxford: Martin Robertson, 1981).

O'Brien, J., *Women's Liberation in Labour History: a case study from Nottingham* (Nottingham: Bertrand Russell Peace Foundation, n.d. [?1972]).

Oren, L., 'The welfare of women in labouring families: England, 1860–1950', in *Clio's Consciousness Raised: new perspectives on the history of women*, ed. M. Hartman and L. W. Banner (New York: Harper Colophon Books, 1974).

Osterud, N. G., 'Gender divisions and the organisation of work in the Leicester hosiery industry', in *Unequal Opportunities: women's employment in England 1800–1918*, ed. A. V. John (Oxford: Basil Blackwell, 1986).

Oxiensis, 'The education of women: a review of Frances Power Cobbe, *Essays on the Pursuits of Women*, London, Emily Faithfully, 1863', *Christian Observer* (July 1865).

Pankhurst, S., *The Suffragette Movement: an intimate account of persons and ideals* (London: Longmans, Green and Co., 1931).

Parkes, B. Rayner, *Essays on Women's Work* (London: Alexander Strahan, 1865).

Peacock, S. J., *Jane Ellen Harrison: the mask and the self* (New Haven, CT, and London: Yale University Press, 1988).

Pedersen, J. S., *The Reform of Women's Secondary and Higher Education: a study in elite groups* (Ph.D. diss, University of California, Berkeley, 1974).

——, 'The reform of women's secondary and higher education: institutional change and social values in mid and late Victorian England', *History of Education Quarterly* (spring 1979).

Peel, Mrs C. S., *Life's Enchanted Cup: an autobiography (1872–1933)* (London: The Bodley Head, 1933).

Pennington, S. and Westover, B., *A Hidden Workforce: homeworkers in England, 1850–1985* (London: Macmillan, 1989).

Percival, A. C., *The English Miss To-Day and Yesterday* (London: George Harrap, 1939).

Perkin, H., *The Origins of Modern English Society 1780–1880* (London: Routledge and Kegan Paul, 1969).

Peterson, M. J., 'The Victorian governess: status incongruence in family and society', in *Suffer and Be Still: women in the Victorian age*, ed. M. Vicinus (Bloomington and London: Indiana University Press, 1972).

Phillips, A., *Divided Loyalties: dilemmas of sex and class* (London: Virago, 1987).

Phillips, A. and Taylor, B., 'Sex and skill: notes towards a feminist economics', *Feminist Review*, 6 (1980).

Pinchbeck, I., *Women Workers and the Industrial Revolution 1750–1850* (London: Routledge and Sons, 1930).

Pleck, E., 'Two worlds in one: work and family', *Journal of Social History*, 10 (winter 1976).

Plymouth Mechanics' Institute Prospectus, 1894–5.

'The point of the needle', *All The Year Round* (5 September 1863).

Pole, T., *A History of the Origins and Progress of Adult Schools*, 2nd edn (Bristol: C. McDowall, 1816).

Powell, W. R., *A History of the County of Essex* (London: Oxford University Press, 1959).

PP (1840) XXIV, *Reports from Assistant Hand-Loom Weavers' Commissioners, Part IV*.

PP (1843) XVI.

PP (1845) XXXV, *Minutes of the Committee of Council of Education with Appendices*.

PP (1850) XLIII, *Minutes of the Committee of Council of Education (1848–50)*.

PP (1867) XXII, *Report of the Committee of Council of Education (1866–7)*.

PP (1867–8) XVII, Appendix part II (1868), *To the First Report of the Commissioners on the Employment of Children, Young Persons and Women in Agriculture*.

PP (1867–8) XXVIII, part I, *Schools Enquiry Commission*.

PP (1870) XXII, *Report of the Committee of Council of Education (1869–70)*.

Prentice, A., 'The education of 19th century British women: essay review', *History of Education Quarterly* (summer 1982).

'The probable retrogression of women', *The Saturday Review* (1 July 1871).

Prochaska, F. K., *Women and Philanthropy in Nineteenth-Century England* (Oxford: Clarendon Press, 1980).

Purvis, J., 'Breaking the chains', *The Times Higher Educational Supplement* (30 October 1987).

——, 'Domestic subjects since 1870', in *Social Histories of the Secondary Curriculum: subjects for study*, ed. I. F. Goodson (Lewes: Falmer Press, 1985).

——, 'The double burden of class and gender in the schooling of working-class girls in nineteenth-century England, 1800–1870', in *Schools, Teachers and Teaching*, ed. L. Barton and S. Walker (Lewes: Falmer Press, 1981).

——, 'The experience of schooling for working-class boys and girls in nineteenth-century England', in *Defining the Curriculum: histories and ethnographies*, ed. I. F. Goodson and S. J. Ball (Lewes: Falmer Press, 1984).

——, 'A feminist perspective on the history of women's education', in *The Education of Girls and Women*, ed. J. Purvis (Leicester: History of Education Society, 1985).

——, 'Reflections upon doing historical documentary research from a feminist perspective', in *Strategies of Educational Research: qualitative methods*, ed. R. Burgess (Lewes: Falmer Press, 1985).

——, 'Towards a history of women's education in nineteenth-century Britain: a sociological analysis', *Westminster Studies in Education*, 4 (1981).

——, 'Women and teaching in the nineteenth century', in *Education and the State*, vol. II: *Politics, Patriarchy and Practice*, ed. R. Dale, G. Esland, R. Ferguson and M. MacDonald (Lewes: Falmer Press, 1981).

——, '"Women's life is essentially domestic, public life being confined to men" (Comte): separate spheres and inequality in the education of working-class women, 1854–1900', *History of Education*, 10, 4 (1981).

——, 'Working-class women and adult education in nineteenth-century Britain', *History of Education*, 9, 3 (1980).

'Queen bees or working bees?', *The Saturday Review* (12 November 1859).

Raikes, E., *Dorothea Beale of Cheltenham* (London: Archibald Constable, 1908).

Ramelson, M., *The Petticoat Rebellion: a century of struggle for women's rights* (London: Lawrence and Wishart, 1976 [first pubd 1967]).

Raven, C., *Christian Socialism* (London: Macmillan and Co., 1920).

Razzell, P. E. and Wainwright, R. W. (eds.), *The Victorian Working Class: selections from letters to The Morning Chronicle* (London: Frank Cass, 1973).

Reeder, D., 'Predicaments of city children: late Victorian and Edwardian perspectives on education and urban society', in *Urban Education in the 19th Century*, ed. D. Reeder (London: Taylor and Francis, 1977).

Reid, M., *A Plea for Woman: being a vindication of the importance and extent of her natural sphere of action* (Edinburgh: William Tait, 1843).

Rendall, J., '"A moral engine?" Feminism, liberalism and the *English Woman's Journal*', in *Equal or Different: women's politics 1800–1914*, ed. J. Rendall (Oxford: Basil Blackwell, 1987).

Rendall, J., *The Origins of Modern Feminism: women in Britain, France and the United States, 1780–1860* (London: Macmillan, 1985).

Report of the British and Foreign School Society (London: R. and A. Taylor, 1822).

Report of the Manchester District Association of Literary and Scientific Associations; with observations upon the plan and management of mechanics' institutions, and suggestions for their improvement, adopted at the first annual meeting of the association, held in Manchester, October 1st, 1840. Also, the reports of the associated institutions made to the committee (Manchester: J. Gadsby, 1840).

Reports of Special Assistant Commissioners on the Employment of Women and Children in Agriculture (London: W. Clowes and Sons, 1843).

A Retired Governess to the Present Pupils of an Establishment for Female Education, which she conducted upwards of forty years, *A Legacy of Affection, Advice and Instruction* (London: Sir Richard Phillips and Co., 1827).

Richards, E., 'Women in the British economy since about 1700: an interpretation', *History*, 59 (1974).

Richards, J. R., *The Sceptical Feminist* (London: Routledge and Kegan Paul, 1980).

Ridley, A. E., *Frances Mary Buss and Her Work for Education* (London: Longmans, Green and Co., 1895).

'Rights and wrongs of women', *Household Words* (April 1854).

Roach, J., *A History of Secondary Education in England 1800–1870* (Harlow: Longman, 1987).

Roberts, E., 'Learning and living: socialisation outside school', *Oral History, Family History Issue*, 3, 2 (autumn 1975).

——, *A Woman's Place: an oral history of working-class women 1890–1940* (Oxford: Basil Blackwell, 1984).

——, *Women's Work 1840–1940* (London: Macmillan, 1988).

Roberts, R., *A Ragged Schooling* (Glasgow: Fontana, 1978 [first pubd 1976]).

Roderick, G. W., *Education and Industry in the Nineteenth Century* (London: Longman, 1978).

Roderick, G. W. and Stephens, M. D., 'Approaches to technical education in nineteenth-century England, part IV: The Liverpool Mechanics' Institution', *The Vocational Aspect of Education*, 25, 61 (1973).

——, *Post School Education* (London: Croom Helm, 1984).

Roebuck, J., 'The education of women in "working men's" colleges', *TWMCM* (1 December 1859).

——, 'Reminiscences of an old student', in *The Working Men's College 1854–1904*, ed. Rev J. Llewelyn Davies (London: Macmillan, 1904).

Romero, P. W., *E. Sylvia Pankhurst* (New Haven: Yale University Press, 1987).

Rose, S. O., '"Gender at work": sex, class and industrial capitalism', *History Workshop Journal*, 21 (spring 1986).

Ross, E., 'Labour and love: rediscovering London's working-class mothers, 1870–1918', in *Labour and Love: women's experience of home and family 1850–1940*, ed. J. Lewis (Oxford: Basil Blackwell, 1986).

——, 'Survival networks: women's neighbourhood sharing in London before World War I', *History Workshop Journal*, 15 (spring 1983).

——, 'Women's history in the USA', in *People's History and Socialist Theory*, ed. R. Samuel (London: Routledge and Kegan Paul, 1981).

Rossi, A. S. (ed.), *Essays on Sex Equality* (Chicago: University of Chicago Press, 1970).

Rossiter, E., 'A student's wife's notion of college and classes', *The Working Men's College Magazine* (1 October 1859).

Rothblatt, S., *The Revolution of the Dons: Cambridge and society in Victorian England* (London: Faber and Faber, 1968).

Rowbotham, S., *Hidden from History: 300 years of women's oppression and the fight against it* (London: Pluto Press, 1973).

——, 'Travellers in a strange country: working-class students, 1873–1910', *HWJ*, 12 (autumn 1981).

——, 'The trouble with "patriarchy"', *New Statesman*, (21–8 December 1979).

——, *Woman's Consciousness, Man's World* (Harmondsworth: Penguin, 1973).

Rowntree, J. W. and Binns, H. B., *A History of the Adult School Movement* (London: Headley Brothers, 1903).

Royle, E., 'Mechanics' institutes and the working classes 1840–1860', *Historical Journal*, 14 (1971).

Rubinstein, D., *Before the Suffragettes: women's emancipation in the 1890s* (Brighton: Harvester Press, 1986).

——, *School Attendance in London, 1870–1904: a social history* (New York: Augustus M. Kelley, 1969).

Rule, J., *The Labouring Classes in Early Industrial England 1750–1850* (Harlow: Longman, 1986).

Rules and Regulations of the Andover Mechanics' Institution for the Diffusion of Useful Knowledge (Andover: W. Deane, 1840).

Rules, By-Laws and Regulations of the Worksop Reading Society and Mechanics' Institute (Worksop: Robert White, 1857).

Rules of the Bradford Female Educational Institute (Bradford: George Harrison, 1860).

Rules of the Worksop Reading Society and Mechanics' Institute (Worksop: Francis Sissons, 1831).

Ruskin, J., *Sesame and Lilies* (London: Smith, Elder and Co., 1865).

Russell, B. and P., *The Amberley Papers: Bertrand Russell's family background*, vol. 2 (London: Allen and Unwin, 1937).

Sadler, M., *Continuation Schools in England and Elsewhere: their place in the education system of an industrial and commercial state*, 2nd edn (Manchester: Manchester University Press, 1908).

Salmon, E., 'Domestic service and democracy', *Fortnightly Review* (March 1888).

Samuel, R., 'The British Marxist historians', *New Left Review*, 120 (March–April, 1980).

Samuel, R. (ed.), *People's History and Socialist Theory* (London: Routledge and Kegan Paul, 1981).

Sanderson, M., *Education, Economic Change and Society in England 1780–1870* (London: Macmillan, 1983).

Sandford, Mrs J., *Woman, in her Social and Domestic Character* (London: Longman, Rees, Orme, Brown and Green, 1831).

Sarah, E., 'Christabel Pankhurst: reclaiming her power', in *Feminist Theorists: three centuries of women's intellectual traditions*, ed. D. Spender (London: Women's Press, 1983).

——, 'Female performers on a male stage: the First Women's Liberation Movement and the authority of men, 1890–1930', in *On the Problem of Men: two feminist conferences*, ed. S. Friedman and E. Sarah (London: Women's Press, 1982).

'A Scotch working men's college', *The Working Men's College Magazine* (1 July 1861).

Searle, J., 'Huddersfield: its physical, social, manufacturing, commercial and religious characteristics', *Tait's Edinburgh Magazine* (April 1849).

Sellman, R. S., *Devon Village Schools in the Nineteenth Century* (Newton Abbot: David and Charles, 1967).

Shapin, S. and Barnes, B., 'Science, nature and control: interpreting mechanics' institutes', *Social Studies of Science*, 7 (1977).

[Shaw, W.,] *An Affectionate Pleading for England's Oppressed Female Workers* (London: Swale and Wilson, 1850).

Shepherd, R. H. (ed.), *Speeches Literary and Social by Charles Dickens* (London: John Camden Hotten, 1870).

Shirreff, E., *Intellectual Education and its Influence on the Character and Happiness of Women* (London: John W. Parker and Son, 1858).

Showalter, E., *The Female Malady: women, madness and English culture, 1830–1980* (London: Virago, 1987 [first pubd 1985]).

Sidgwick, Mrs. H., 'The higher education of women', in *Education in the Nineteenth Century*, ed. R. D. Roberts (Cambridge: Cambridge University Press, 1901).

Sigsworth, E. M. and Wyke, T. J, 'A study of Victorian prostitution and venereal disease', in *Suffer and Be Still: women in the Victorian age*, ed. M. Vicinus (Bloomington and London: Indiana University Press, 1972).

Silver, H., *The Concept of Popular Education* (London: Methuen, 1977 [first pubd 1965]).

——, 'Ideology and the factory child: attitudes to half-time education', in *Popular Education and Socialization in the Nineteenth Century*, ed. P. McCann (London: Methuen, 1977).

Silver, P. and Silver, H., *The Education of the Poor: the history of a National School 1824–1974* (London: Routledge and Kegan Paul, 1974).

Silverstone, R., 'Accountancy', in *Careers of Professional Women*, ed. R. Silverstone and A. Ward (London: Croom Helm, 1980).

Simon, B., *The Two Nations and the Educational Structure 1780–1870* (London: Lawrence and Wishart, 1974 [first pubd 1960 under the title *Studies in the History of Education 1780–1870*]).

Simon, J., 'Was there a charity school movement? The Leicestershire evidence', in *Education in Leicestershire, 1540–1940*, ed. B. Simon (Leicester: Leicester University Press, 1968).

Slight, H., *A Chronicle History of Portsmouth*, 3rd edn (1838) [MS kept at Portsmouth City Library].

Slop Shops, and Slop Workers (London: John Olliver, 1850).

Smelser, N. J., *Social Change in the Industrial Revolution: an Application of Theory to the Lancashire Cotton Industry 1770–1840* (London: Routledge and Kegan Paul, 1959).

Smiles, S., *Character* (London: John Murray, 1884 [first pubd 1871]).

——, *Self Help: with illustrations of character and conduct* (London: John Murray, 1860).

——, 'A work that prospered', *Good Words* (1877), pp. 386–92.

S. S. [Samuel Smiles], 'The women of the working classes', *The Union* (1 January 1843).

Smith, B., 'Racism and women's studies' in *All the Women are White, All the Blacks are Men, But Some of Us are Brave: black women's studies*, ed. G. T. Hull, P. B. Scott, and B. Smith (New York: Feminist Press, 1982).

Smith, D., *Conflict and Compromise: class formation in English society 1830–1914* (London: Routledge and Kegan Paul, 1982).

Smith, G. C. Moore, *The Story of the People's College, Sheffield, 1842–1878* (Sheffield: J. W. Northend, 1912).

Smith, M., *The Autobiography of Mary Smith, Schoolmistress and Nonconformist* (Carlisle: Wordsworth Press, 1892).

Smith-Rosenberg, C., *Disorderly Conduct: visions of gender in Victorian America* (Oxford: Oxford University Press, 1985).

Snell, K. D. M., *Annals of the Labouring Poor: social change in agrarian England, 1600–1900* (Cambridge: Cambridge University Press, 1985).

Society for Bettering the Condition and Increasing the Comforts of the Poor, *Reports* (London: W. Bulmer and Co., 1798, 1800).

Solly, H., 'Reasons for a working men's college', *TWMCM* (1 July 1860).

Spencer, H., *Education: intellectual, moral and physical* (London: Watts and Co., 1929 [first pubd 1861]).

Spender, D., 'Education: the patriarchal paradigm and the response to feminism', in *Men's Studies Modified: the impact of feminism on the academic disciplines*, ed. D. Spender (Oxford: Pergamon Press, 1981).

——, *Mothers of the Novel* (London: Pandora Press, 1986).

——, *Women of Ideas and What Men Have Done to Them* (London: Routledge and Kegan Paul, 1982).

Spender, D. and Sarah, E. (eds.), *Learning to Lose: sexism and education* (London: Women's Press, 1980).

Stacey, M., 'Gender and stratification: one central issue or two?', in *Gender and Stratification*, ed. R. Crompton and M. Mann (Oxford: Polity Press, 1986).

Stanley, L. (ed.), *The Diaries of Hannah Cullwick, Victorian Maidservant* (London: Virago, 1984).

Stanley, L. and Wise, S., *Breaking Out: feminist consciousness and feminist research* (London: Routledge and Kegan Paul, 1983).

Stanworth, M., 'Women and class analysis: a reply to John Goldthorpe', *Sociology*, 18, 2 (May 1984).

Stearns, P. N., 'Working-class women in Britain, 1890–1914', in *Suffer and Be Still: women in the Victorian age*, ed. M. Vicinus (Bloomington: Indiana University Press, 1972).

Steer, F. W., *The Chichester Literary and Philosophical Society and Mechanics' Institute* (Chichester: Chichester City Council, 1962).

Stephen, B., *Emily Davies and Girton College* (London: Constable, 1927).

Stephen, J. F., *Liberty, Equality, Fraternity*, 2nd edn (London: Smith, Elder and Co., 1874).

Stephens, M. D. and Roderick, G. W., 'British artisan scientific and technical education in the early nineteenth century,' *Annals of Science*, 29, 1 (June 1972).

Stephens, W. B., *Education, Literacy and Society, 1830–70: the geography of diversity in provincial England* (Manchester: Manchester University Press, 1987).

The Story of the Frances Martin College (London: Frances Martin College, 1947).

Stott, M., *Organisation Women: the story of the National Union of Townswomen's Guilds* (London: Heinemann, 1978).

Strachey, R., *The Cause: a short history of the women's movement in Great Britain* (London: Virago, 1978 [first pubd 1928]).

A Student of the Working Men's College, Letter in *The Working Men's College Magazine* (1

August 1860).

A Student's Wife, Letter in *The Working Men's College Magazine* (1 April 1860).

A Student's Wife, 'Will college night classes be of use to women?', *The Working Men's College Magazine* (1 January 1860).

Sturt, M., *The Education of the People: a history of primary education in England and Wales in the nineteenth century* (London: Routledge and Kegan Paul, 1967).

A Suffering Mistress, 'On the side of the mistresses', *Cornhill Magazine*, 29 (January–June 1874).

Summers, A., *Angels and Citizens: British women as military nurses 1854–1914* (London: Routledge and Kegan Paul, 1988).

——, 'A home from home: women's philanthropic work in the nineteenth century', in *Fit Work for Women*, ed. S. Burman (London: Croom Helm, 1979).

'The suppressed sex', *The Westminster Review* (October 1856).

Sutherland, G., *Elementary Education in the Nineteenth Century* (London: Historical Association, 1971).

Sutton, D., 'Radical liberalism, Fabianism and social history', in Centre for Contemporary Cultural Studies, *Making Histories: studies in history-writing and politics* (London: Hutchinson, 1982).

Taking Liberties Collective, *Learning the Hard Way: women's oppression in men's education* (London: Macmillan, 1989).

Taylor, B., *Eve and the New Jerusalem: socialism and feminism in the nineteenth century* (London: Virago, 1983).

Taylor, Mrs, *The Present of a Mistress to a Young Servant, Consisting of Friendly Advice and Real Histories* (London: Taylor and Hessey, 1816).

Thomas, M. I. and Grimmett, J., *Women in Protest 1800–1850* (London: Croom Helm, 1982).

Thomas, R. A., 'The mechanics' institutes of the Home Counties, *c.* 1825–1870, part 1', *The Vocational Aspect of Education*, 31 (1979).

Thompson, D., *The Chartists* (London: Temple Smith, 1984).

——, 'Women and nineteenth-century radical politics: a lost dimension', in *The Rights and Wrongs of Women*, ed. J. Mitchell and A. Oakley (Harmondsworth: Penguin, 1976).

——, 'Women, work and politics in nineteenth-century England: the problem of authority', in *Equal or Different: women's politics 1800–1914*, ed. J. Rendall (Oxford: Basil Blackwell, 1987).

Thompson, E. P., *The Making of the English Working Class* (Harmondsworth: Penguin, 1972 [first pubd 1963]).

——, 'The politics of theory', in *People's History and Socialist Theory*, ed. R. Samuel (London: Routledge and Kegan Paul, 1981).

Thompson, E. P. and Yeo, E. (eds.), *The Unknown Mayhew: selections from The Morning Chronicle 1849–1850* (Harmondsworth: Penguin, 1973 [first pubd 1971]).

Thompson, F., *Lark Rise to Candleford* (London: Oxford University Press, 1954 [first pubd 1945]).

Thompson, J., *Learning Liberation: women's response to men's education* (London: Croom Helm, 1983).

Thompson, T. (ed.), *Dear Girl: the diaries and letters of two working women 1897–1917* (London: Women's Press, 1987).

Thompson, W., *Appeal of One Half the Human Race, Women, Against the Pretensions of the Other Half, Men, to Retain Them in Political, and Thence in Civil and Domestic, Slavery* (London: Longman, Hurst, Rees, Orme, Brown and Green, 1825).

W. T. [Thompson, W.], 'To the members and managers of the mechanics' institutions in Britain and Ireland', *The Co-operative Magazine* (January–February 1826).

Thomson, D., *England in the Nineteenth Century, 1815–1914* (Harmondsworth: Penguin,

1950).

Thorburn, J., *Female Education from a Physiological Point of View* (Manchester: Owens College, 1884).

Tilly, L. A. and Scott, J. W., *Women, Work and Family* (New York: Holt, Rinehart and Winston, 1978).

Traice, W. H. J., *Hand-Book of Mechanics' Institutions, with Priced Catalogue of Books suitable for Reading Rooms*, 2nd rev. edn (London: Longman, Green, Longman, Roberts and Green, 1863 [first pubd 1856]).

'Treatment of women', *Eliza Cook's Journal* (9 August 1851).

Turnbull, A., 'Learning her womanly work: the elementary school curriculum, 1870–1914', in *Lessons for Life: the schooling of girls and women, 1850–1950*, ed. F. Hunt (Oxford: Basil Blackwell, 1987).

——, '"So extremely like parliament": the work of the women members of the London School Board, 1870–1904', in London Feminist History Group, *The Sexual Dynamics of History: men's power, women's resistance* (London: Pluto Press, 1983).

Turner, B., *Equality for Some: the story of girls' education* (London: Ward Lock Educational, 1974).

Tylecote, M., *The Education of Women at Manchester University 1883–1933*, Publications of the University of Manchester, no. 277 (1941).

——, *The Mechanics' Institutes of Lancashire and Yorkshire Before 1851* (Manchester: Manchester University Press, 1957).

Tynan, A., 'Lewes Mechanics' Institution', *Rewley House Papers*, 3, 4 (1955–6).

Tuke, M. J., *A History of Bedford College for Women 1849–1937* (London: Oxford University Press, 1939).

Union of Lancashire and Cheshire Institutes, 1839–1939: a hundred years of educational service (Manchester, 1939).

Ure, A., *The Philosophy of Manufactures: or, An Exposition of the Scientific, Moral, and Commercial Economy of the Factory System of Great Britain* (London: Charles Knight, 1835).

Van Arsdel, R. T., 'Mrs Florence Fenwick-Miller and *The Woman's Signal, 1895–1899*', *Victorian Periodical Review* (fall 1982).

Vicinus, M., *Independent Women: work and community for single women 1850–1920* (London: Virago, 1985).

——, 'Introduction: the perfect Victorian lady', in *Suffer and Be Still: women in the Victorian age*, ed. M. Vicinus (Bloomington and London: Indiana University Press, 1972).

——, '"One life to stand beside me": emotional conflicts in first-generation college women in England', *Feminist Studies*, 8, 3 (fall 1982).

Walby, S., 'Gender, class and stratification', in *Gender and Stratification* ed. R. Crompton and M. Mann (Oxford: Polity Press, 1986).

——, *Patriarchy at Work* (Oxford: Polity Press, 1986).

Walker, A., *Women Physiologically Considered as to Mind, Morals, Matrimonial Slavery, Infidelity and Divorce*, 2nd edn (London: A. H. Baily, 1840).

Walkowitz, J. R., *Prostitution and Victorian Society: women, class and the state* (Cambridge: Cambridge University Press, 1980).

Walvin, J., *A Child's World: a social history of English childhood 1800–1914* (Harmondsworth: Penguin, 1978).

Wardle, D., *Education and Society in Nineteenth-Century Nottingham* (Cambridge: Cambridge University Press, 1971).

——, *English Popular Education 1780–1975*, 2nd edn (Cambridge: Cambridge University Press, 1976 [first pubd 1970]).

Webb, B., *My Apprenticeship* (Cambridge: Cambridge University Press, 1979 [first pubd 1929]).

Weiner, G., 'Harriet Martineau: a reassessment', in *Feminist Theorists: three centuries of women's intellectual traditions*, ed. D. Spender (London: Women's Press, 1983).

Welch, E., *The Peripatetic University: Cambridge Local Lectures 1873–1973* (Cambridge: Cambridge University Press, 1973).

West, J., 'Women, sex and class', in *Feminism and Materialism: women and modes of production*, ed. A. Kuhn and A. Wolpe (London: Routledge and Kegan Paul, 1978).

Westover, B., '"To fill the kids' tummies": the lives and work of Colchester tailoresses, 1880–1918', in *Our Work, Our Lives, Our Words: women's history and women's work*, ed. L. Davidoff and B. Westover (London: Macmillan, 1986).

Whiteing, R., *My Harvest* (London: Hodder and Stoughton, 1915).

A Widowed Wife, *A Whisper to a Newly Married Pair*, 7th edn (London: Houlston and Co., 1841).

Widdowson, F., *Going Up into the Next Class: women and elementary teacher training, 1840–1914* (London: Women's Research and Resources Centre Publications, 1980).

Williams, R., *The Long Revolution* (Harmondsworth: Penguin, 1965 [first pubd 1961]).

Wise, T., *Speech Delivered at the Opening of the New Mechanics' Institution, Mount-Street, Liverpool, on the 15th of September, 1837.*

Wollstonecraft, M., *Vindication of the Rights of Woman* (Harmondsworth: Penguin, 1975 [first pubd 1792]).

Woman's Worth, or Hints to Raise the Female Character, 2nd edn (London: Stevens and Co., 1844).

Women, Class and Adult Education, (Southampton: University of Southampton, Department of Adult Education, n.d.).

Woodham-Smith, C., *Florence Nightingale 1820–1910* (London: Constable, 1950).

Woodward, E., *Men, Women and Progress* (London: Dalau and Co., 1885).

Woodward, K., *Jipping Street* (London: Virago, 1983 [first pubd 1928]).

Wrigley, Mrs, 'A plate-layer's wife', in *Life As We Have Known It by Co-operative Working Women*, ed. M. Llewelyn Davies (London: Virago, 1977 [first pubd 1931]).

Yonge, C. M., *Womankind* (London: Mozley and Smith, 1876).

Yorkshire Union of Mechanics' Institutes, *Reports* (Leeds: Edward Baines and Sons, 1846, 1847, 1848, 1850, 1852, 1857, 1858, 1859, 1860, 1861, 1862).

Zimmeck, M., 'Jobs for the girls: the expansion of clerical work for women, 1850–1914', in *Unequal Opportunities: women's employment in England 1800–1918*, ed. A. V. John (Oxford: Basil Blackwell, 1986).

Zimmern, A., *The Renaissance of Girls' Education in England: a record of fifty years' progress* (London: A. D. Innes and Co., 1898).

INDEX

Index compiled by Meg Davies (Society of Indexers)

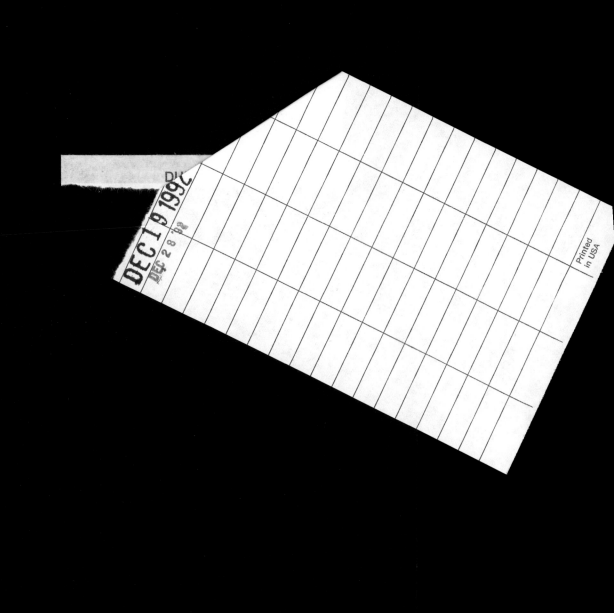

Printed
in USA